W9-DGZ-935

INTERNATIONAL LIBRARY OF
AFRO-AMERICAN LIFE AND HISTORY

Public Sale.

By virtue of a deed of trust executed to the subscriber by Mordecai Throckmorton, and Sarah M'Carty, his wife, to secure a certain sum of money therein mentioned, due to Warner Washington, (and by him transferred to Lawrence Lewise esq.) will be sold on the 15th day of **NOVEMBER** next, for ready money, to the highest bidder,

A TRACT OF LAND,

situate in the county of Loudoun, about one and a half miles from the Turnpike Road, at the foot of the Blue Ridge, containing 400 acres, being part of a larger tract, upon which the said Mordecai Throckmorton now resides. The land is considered as first rate, and well watered; more than 200 acres cleared, and under good enclosures. A more particular description is deemed unnecessary, as those disposed to purchase will view the premises of course. And also,

TWENTY NEGROES,

consisting of men, women, and children, together with their increase since the 26th of April, 1819.

The sale will take place on the premises, when as much of the property will be sold as will raise the sum of four thousand twenty-nine dollars and sixty cents. Attendance will be given by the trustee, and such a title made as is vested in him. **W. W. THROCKMORTON.**

August 10, 1821.

Library of Congress

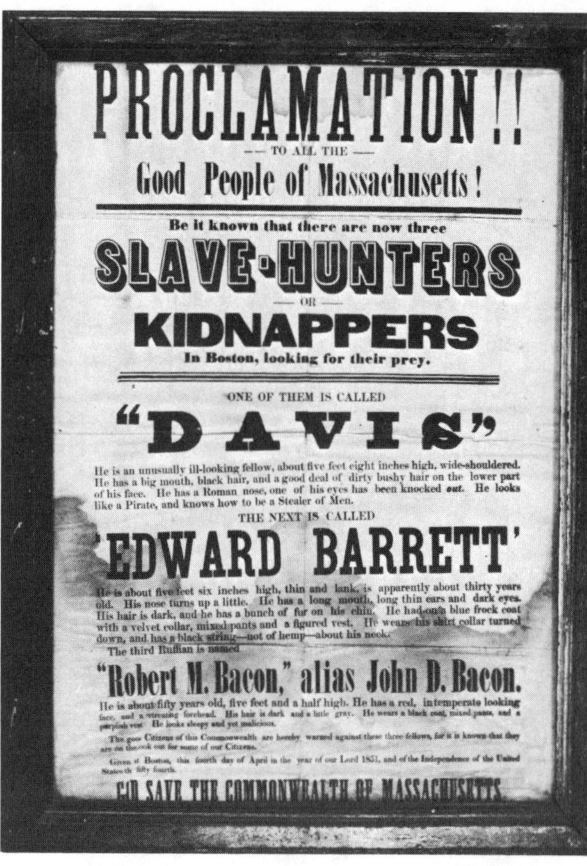

PROCLAMATION!!

— TO ALL THE —

Good People of Massachusetts!

Be it known that there are now three

SLAVE-HUNTERS

— OR —

KIDNAPPERS

In Boston, looking for their prey.

ONE OF THEM IS CALLED

"DAVIS"

He is an unusually ill-looking fellow, about five feet eight inches high, wide-shouldered. He has a big mouth, black hair, and a good deal of dirty bushy hair on the lower part of his face. He has a Roman nose, one of his eyes has been knocked *out.* He looks like a Pirate, and knows how to be a Stealer of Men.

THE NEXT IS CALLED

'EDWARD BARRETT'

He is about five feet six inches high, thin and lank, is apparently about thirty years old. His nose turns up a little. He has a long mouth, long thin ears and dark eyes. His hair is dark, and he has a bunch of fur on his chin. He had on a blue frock coat with a velvet collar, mixed pants and a figured vest. He wears his shirt collar turned down, and has a black string—not of hemp—about his neck.

The third Ruffian is named

"Robert M. Bacon," alias John D. Bacon.

He is about fifty years old, five feet and a half high. He has a red, intemperate looking face, and a retreating forehead. His hair is dark and a little gray. He wears a black coat, mixed pants, and a purplish vest. He looks sleepy and yet malicious.

The good Citizens of this Commonwealth are hereby warned against these three fellows, for it is known that they are on the look out for some of our Citizens.

Given at Boston, this fourth day of April in the year of our Lord 1851, and of the Independence of the United States the fifty fourth.

GOD SAVE THE COMMONWEALTH OF MASSACHUSETTS

Courtesy of Mother Bethel A.M.E. Church, Philadelphia.

Justus in *The Minneapolis Star*

Liederman in *The Long Island Daily Press*

I TOO AM AMERICA

Documents from 1619 to the Present

Compiled and Edited with an Introduction by
PATRICIA W. ROMERO

THE PUBLISHERS AGENCY, INC.
CORNWELLS HEIGHTS, PENNSYLVANIA
under the auspices of
THE ASSOCIATION FOR THE STUDY OF AFRO-AMERICAN LIFE AND HISTORY

A NON-PROFIT ORGANIZATION

LIBRARY OF CONGRESS CATALOG CARD NO. 68-56836

INTERNATIONAL STANDARD BOOK NUMBER 0-87781-206-3

PRINTED IN THE UNITED STATES OF AMERICA

REVISED EDITION

EXCLUSIVE WORLD-WIDE DISTRIBUTION BY

THE LIBRARY COMPANY, INC., WASHINGTON, D.C.

To

STEVE, ARTIE *and* JEFF

Preface

THE Association for the Study of Afro-American Life and History joins with Pubco Corporation in presenting this new series of volumes which treat in detail the cultural and historical backgrounds of black Americans. This Association, a pioneer in the area of Afro-American History, was founded on September 9, 1915, by Dr. Carter G. Woodson, who remained its director of research and publications until his death in 1950.

In 1916 Dr. Woodson began publishing the quarterly *Journal of Negro History*. In 1926 Negro History Week was launched, and since that time it has been held annually in February, encompassing the birth dates of Abraham Lincoln and Frederick Douglass. The *Negro History Bulletin* was first published in 1937 to serve both schools and families by making available to them little-known facts about black life and history.

During its sixty-one years of existence, the Association for the Study of Afro-American Life and History has supported many publications dealing with the contributions of Afro-Americans to the growth and development of this country. Its activities have contributed to the increasing interest in the dissemination of factual studies which are placing the Afro-American in true perspective in the mainstream of American history.

We gratefully acknowledge the contributions of previous scholars, which have aided us in the preparation of this *International Library of Afro-American Life and History*. Our grateful acknowledgment is also expressed to Charles W. Lockyer, president of Pubco Corporation, whose challenging approach has made possible this library.

Though each of the volumes in this set can stand as an autonomous unit, and although each author has brought his own interpretation to the area with which he is dealing, together these books form a comprehensive picture of the Afro-American experience in America. The three history volumes give a factual record of a people who were brought from Africa in chains and who today are struggling to cast off the last vestiges of these bonds. The anthologies covering music, art, the theatre and literature provide a detailed account of the black American's contributions to these fields—including those contributions which are largely forgotten today. Achievement in the sports world is covered in another volume. The volume on the Afro-American in medicine is a history of the black American's struggle for equality as a medical practitioner and as a patient. The selected black leaders in the biography book represent the contributions and achievements of many times their number. The documentary history sums up the above-mentioned material in the words of men and women who were themselves a part of black history.

CHARLES H. WESLEY

Washington, D.C.

Editor's Note

I AM extremely grateful to many people located in libraries and at schools in many areas of the country for their aid in obtaining the documents included in this volume. Particularly, I would like to thank Nancy Jensen and the staff of the Schomburg Collection, New York Public Library, and the staffs of the Moorland Room at Howard University Library, the New York Public Library Manuscript Division, the New York Historical Society, the Historical Society of Pennsylvania, the Library of Congress Manuscript Division, the Fisk University Race Relations Department and the Henry E. Huntington Library. Special thanks also go to Dr. Prince E. Wilson of Atlanta University; Professors Wilhelmena S. Robinson and David W. Hazel of Central State University; the Rev. Howard Asbury of Long Island, New York, and the late Professor Charles N. Young of Wilberforce, Ohio, for loaning me their materials for inclusion in this book.

The joint editorial work of Mary N. Eldridge and Emily Evershed was monumental, and I am grateful for their assistance. Allan Kullen helped immeasurably with his skill as a layout artist, and Wendy Schempp provided diligent and resourceful assistance.

The documents included in the volume are limited wherever possible to original materials. When it was impossible to obtain the originals, documents were taken from sources already printed and are so labeled.

P. W. R.

Acknowledgments

WE ARE grateful for permission to use the following material in this book.

BOOKS AND ARTICLES

"Du Bois on Washington: A Controversy," from *Dusk of Dawn* by W. E. B. Du Bois. Copyright © 1940, by W. E. B. Du Bois; copyright © 1968, by Shirley Graham Du Bois. Reprinted by permission of Harcourt, Brace & World, Inc.

"John Alexander's Military Experiences," from HM 28895 and HM 28913. Reprinted by permission of the Huntington Library, San Marino, California.

"James Weldon Johnson and the Anti-Lynching Bill," from *Along This Way*. Copyright © 1933 by Viking Press. Reprinted by permission of Viking Press.

"Walter White Investigates Lynchings," from "I Investigate Lynchings," *American Mercury,* January 1929. Reprinted by permission of *American Mercury*.

"A Black Man's Attitudes toward Red Russia," from *Black Man in Red Russia,* by Homer Smith. Copyright © 1964, by Johnson Publishing Company. Reprinted by permission of Johnson Publishing Company.

"Mary McLeod Bethune's 'Last Will and Testament' to Her People," from *Ebony,* August 1955. Reprinted by permission of *Ebony*.

"Daisy Bates and the Little Rock Children," from *The Long Shadow of Little Rock,* by Daisy Bates. Copyright © 1962, by Daisy Bates.

"There Is a Time for Anger," from *The Autobiography of Malcolm X,* by Malcolm X and Alex Haley. Copyright © 1964, by Malcolm X and Alex Haley.

"The Mississippi Summer Project of 1963," from *Letters from Mississippi,* edited by Elizabeth Sutherland. Copyright © 1965, by McGraw-Hill Company, Inc.

"A Negro Conservative Writes about the Contemporary Scene," from *Black and Conservative,* by George S. Schuyler. Copyright © 1966, by Arlington House Publishers. Reprinted by permission of Arlington House Publishers.

"Charles Evers on the Southern White Press," from *The Black American and the Press,* edited by Jack Lyle. Copyright © 1968, by the Regents of the University of California.

CARTOONS

Herblock, from the *Washington Post*.

Jay Jackson, from the *Chicago Defender*.

Justus, from the *Minneapolis Star*.

Liederman, from *The Long Island Daily Press*.

Mauldin, from the *NEA*.

Yardley, from the *Baltimore Sun*.

Table of Contents

Introduction

THE PURPOSE OF this volume is to relate the history of black people in America through the words of those who participated in or witnessed this great drama of human events. The documents have been chosen, primarily, because they reveal the dramatic aspects of the struggle for equality—the trials and tribulations, as well as the achievements and contributions.

If one were to single out an outstanding theme in the books, it would probably be the cyclical manner in which the history itself has occurred. The chronicle of the Afro-American in America is one of continual protest. Black militants did not suddenly emerge in the second half of the twentieth century; they have been here all along. Slaves protested for freedom, and free blacks spoke out in behalf of their enslaved brothers. The freedmen sought nothing less than their full rights, and the blacks of today protest for the implementation of the goals fought for so earnestly by their fathers and grandfathers.

Nothing better depicts a culture than the expression of the ideas of those within its influence. With this thought in mind, those documents were selected having a bearing on almost every aspect of American history, in order to illustrate the continual thread of consistent attitudes that existed through the years among the black community. Leaders arose from the masses who served not only their own people but often the entire nation. Life within black America almost paralleled that of white America, with individuals of both races experiencing the trauma that results from racial prejudice and discrimination.

This book provides the reader with an opportunity to become better acquainted with the past problems and disappointments, as well as the achievements, of Afro-Americans. It is primarily a social history, for it records the sentiments of a people who have sought during the past three hundred years to gain their social, economic and political rights and have met every known obstacle in their tireless efforts.

Much of the material in this volume has been edited to provide a larger scope of coverage. There are some documents printed here for the first time. Others, previously printed, have not been widely distributed to the general reading public. There are also documents that have been read more frequently but are included because of their relevance to the total historical pattern. In a few instances, it was decided to include the words of white Americans concerning the growth of the Afro-American protest movement. Owing to the existence now of several excellent volumes of public documents covering the subject of the Afro-American, most of the material in this book comes from non-public sources. The exceptions, of course, are the court cases and much of the material dealing with the black Congressmen.

In essence, this is a revealing testimony of a people's attempt to secure life, liberty and happiness in a society that, throughout its history, deterred them in their pursuit.

PATRICIA W. ROMERO

Worthington, Ohio

SECTION I

When Israel was in Egypt's land,
Let my people go;
Oppressed so hard they could not stand,
Let my people go.

Go down, Moses, 'way down in Egypt's land;
Tell ole Pharaoh,
Let my people go.

"Thus saith the Lord," bold Moses said,
Let my people go;
If not I'll smite your first-born dead,
Let my people go.

No more shall they in bondage toil,
Let my people go;
Let them come out with Egypt's spoil,
Let my people go.

The Lord told Moses what to do,
Let my people go;
To lead the children of Israel thro',
Let my people go.

When they had reached the other shore,
Let my people go;
They sang a song of triumph o'er,
Let my people go.

THE LAND OF LIBERTY.

New York Public Library

In the Land of Bondage

THE HISTORY OF the black man in America, as we know it, began with the first African captives who arrived at Jamestown in 1619. They came, originally, as indentured servants, filling the need for labor in the developing Virginia colony. Soon they were followed by more of their fellow Africans, all ostensibly brought here as servants, but most remaining under a modified form of slavery. The severe shortage of labor throughout the colonies as the early settlers struggled for survival in those formative years was met primarily with the importation of African slaves.

From 1619 to 1661, the black man enjoyed the possibility of gaining his freedom in the new land to which he had been brought. In the latter year, Virginia, followed in 1662 by Maryland, passed laws that legally recognized the slavery that already had begun in many areas. It was not long before the other colonies followed the example of Virginia and Maryland and passed legislation placing the black man in perpetual bondage.

It should be noted that not all Negroes were slaves at that time, nor at any time prior to the Civil War. Many were free men who engaged in much the same types of economic pursuits as their white counterparts. The free blacks at this time probably did not enjoy the full fruits of citizenship, but neither did the white man until he severed his connection with Great Britain through war.

While the Quakers were the first organized group to protest openly the harshness of slavery and the inhumanity of the slave trade, individual blacks themselves had spoken out against the practice from the beginning. The first recorded protest, made in 1788, was by a black man whom we know only as Othello.

Throughout the colonial period, the records show free blacks engaging in business enterprises, marrying and raising families, serving as artists and scientists and, most important, establishing a definite cultural identity, which has prevailed until today.

Two diverse attitudes seem to have developed in the colonies prior to the Revolution. On the one hand, men were moving ever closer to the philosophical doctrine of liberty and equality, while on the other hand, they were placing harsh and stringent laws into effect where the black man was concerned. As the protests against England became more pronounced and as men brought into the language such phrases as "all men are created equal" and "entitled to life, liberty, and the pursuit of happiness," Negroes took these verbal expressions to include them, too. Anxiously they sought to help free the nation from its foreign bondage and enlisted in the colonial militia—only to be rejected.

Later, after it became obvious to the colonial leaders that the British were wooing the black men through promises of freedom, the colonists amended their attitude and received these black volunteers into their army. Once in uniform, the blacks fought with merit and valor. No doubt it seemed to them that freedom would apply to them also at the war's end. Such was not the case, however, and many who had been promised their liberty if they fought were placed again in bondage. The words of the blacks themselves show this to be true.

After the Revolutionary War, when the points of liberty and equality were being discussed in the Constitutional Convention, the irony of the black man's position in America once more became pronounced. He received attention in this Convention, even if he did not receive his freedom; for the great minds of the united colonies saw fit to discuss him only in terms of how he should be counted in the census and how he should be apprehended if he chose to escape bondage. One concession was made, however, when the slave trade was discussed—a twenty-year supply of Africans was thought to be sufficient, and thus the trade was to be suspended at the end of that period.

As the nation approached its second war with England—to assert once and for all its freedom—Negroes again participated in the military operations. Freedom for the United States was reinforced, but freedom for the slave was once again ignored. The economy of the South was growing more dependent on slave labor, while that of the North was becoming increasingly industrialized. Immigrant labor from Europe helped fill the vacuum in the northern states, while the slave trade from Africa and the domestic slave trade with the border states kept the labor supply abundant for the Deep South.

The nation gradually became welded into a single unit; it expanded to the new frontiers of the West, carrying slavery with it and outlawing the "peculiar institution" in the northern territories. Before long, however, sectionalism began to develop between the North, West and South, with each area interested primarily in its own needs for economic development. The issue of the slave arose once more in the hallowed halls of Congress and in the sequestered chambers of the Supreme Court. The slave Dred Scott, who sued for his freedom in 1856 but was denied citizenship, represented the final bleak chapter in a long and harrowing struggle to bring about the recognition of the black man as worthy of and, indeed, contributory to his American citizenship.

The history of the Negro prior to the Civil War does not deal exclusively with slavery, even though the issue was central to every black man living in this country at the time. The first abolitionists were Negroes, men who worked long and fervently for their own freedom and for that of their contemporaries. Militants such as Paul Cuffee, who chose colonization as a harbor for an otherwise sinking ship of servitude, became legendary in Negro history. Henry Highland Garnet, an early abolitionist who refused to play second fiddle to the white abolitionists, left his mark on the future destiny of slavery, as did Frederick Douglass and many others.

The Underground Railroad, which aided in the escape of thousands of slaves from the Deep South, was from the first staffed with black agents. Former slaves dedicated to the cause of freedom for all returned to the South time and again after they themselves had sampled the cup of liberty.

Slaves who suffered retribution for every Gabriel Prosser, Denmark Vesey or Nat Turner insurrection did not capitulate to the white man's severity. Instead, they poisoned their masters, started numerous fires and even resorted to murder in final revenge for the circumstances under which they were forced to live.

Prosperous black businessmen in the northern states, who technically were free but were not allowed to participate freely as citizens in their respective localities, petitioned for their rights. They sought the opportunity to educate their children in the same manner and surroundings as the white children enjoyed. They looked to the Declaration of Independence and to the Constitution—both brilliant and timeless examples of the theory of civil liberty—for deserved protection, but they found the administrators of these documents lacking in the will to enforce them.

The slave trade, outlawed in 1808, persisted illegally until the Civil War. As more and more slaves fled to the North and freedom, a government controlled by southern interests placed greater restrictions on the hopes of the fugitives by passing harsher legislation aimed at forcing their return even from the free states to which they had escaped. Abolition daily became a more firmly entrenched institution in the North, while slavery had its roots buried deep in the very history of the South. Therefore, an alignment between West and South, coupled with the ever-expanding border of slavery, set the stage for the inevitable conflict of civil war.

Oh! Stand the Storm
It won't be long
We'll anchor by and by.

The First Negroes in Colonial America

In the American colonial period, Negroes first were brought to this country as indentured servants. John Rolfe, in a letter to the treasurer of the Virginia Company of London, reported the arrival of Negroes in Virginia in 1619.

About the latter end of August, a Dutch man of Warr of the burden of a 160 tunes [tons] arrived at *Point Comfort,* the commanders name Capt. Jope, his pilott for the West Indyes, one Mr. Marmaduke an Englishman. They met with the Trer in the West Indyes, and determyned to hold consort shipp hetherward, but in their passage lost one the other. He brought not anything but 20 and odd Negroes, which the Governor and Cape Marchant bought for victualle (whereof he was in great need as he ptended) at the best and easiest rates they could. . . .

John Smith, *The Generall History of Virginia, New England, and the Summer Isles* (London, 1624).

Negroes Arrive in Massachusetts

In 1638, Negroes were introduced into the colony of Massachusetts. The February 26, 1638 entry in the journal of John Winthrop gives the following information.

Mr. Pierce, in the Salem ship the *Desire,* returned from the West Indies after seven months. He had been at Providence, and bought some cotton, and tobacco, and negroes, etc., from thence, and salt from Tortugas; . . . Dry fish and strong liquors are the only commodities for those parts. He met there two men-of-war, set forth by the lords, etc., of Providence with letters of mart, who had taken divers prizes from the Spaniards and many negroes. . . . The ship *Desire* was a vessel of one hundred and twenty tons, built at Marblehead in 1636, one of the earliest built in the Colony.

George H. Moore, *Notes on the History of Slavery in Massachusetts* (New York, 1866).

The First Organized Protest against Slavery

The earliest known protest against slavery by an organization was a resolution drawn up in Germantown, Pennsylvania, in 1688, by a group of Quakers.

This is to the monthly meeting held at Richard Worrell's:

These are the reasons why we are against the traffic of men-body, as followeth: Is there any that would be done or handled at this manner? viz., to be sold or made a slave for all the time of his life? How fearful and faint-hearted are many at sea, when they see a strange vessel, being afraid it should be a Turk, and they should be taken, and sold for slaves into Turkey. Now, what is *this* better done, than Turks do? Yea, rather it is worse for them, which say they are Christians; for we hear that the most part of such negers are brought hither against their will and consent, and that many of them are stolen. Now, though they are black, we cannot conceive there is more liberty to have them slaves, as it is to have other white ones. There is a saying, that we should do to all men like as we will be done ourselves; making no difference of what generation, descent, or colour they are. And those who steal or rob men, and those who buy or purchase them, are they not all alike? Here is liberty of conscience, which is right and reasonable; here ought to be likewise liberty of the body, except of evil-doers, which is another case. But to bring men hither, or to rob and sell them against their will, we stand against. In Europe there are many oppressed for conscience-sake; and here there are those oppressed which are of a black colour. And we who know that men must not commit adultery—some do commit adultery *in* others, separating wives from their husbands, and giving them to others: and some sell the children of these poor creatures to other men. Ah! do consider well this thing, you who do it, if you would be done at this manner—and if it is done according to Christianity! You surpass Holland and Germany in this thing. This makes an ill report in all those countries of Europe, where they hear of [it], that the Quakers do here handel men as they handel there the cattle. And for that reason some have no mind or inclination to come hither. And who shall maintain this your cause, or plead for it? Truly, we cannot do so, except you shall inform us better hereof, viz.: that Christians have liberty to practice these things. Pray, what thing in the world can be done worse towards us, than if men should rob or steal us away, and sell us for slaves to strange countries; separating husbands from their wives and children. Being now this is not done in the manner we would be done at; therefore, we contradict, and are against this traffic of men-body. And we who profess that it is not lawful to steal, must, likewise, avoid to purchase such things as are stolen, but rather help to stop this robbing and stealing, if possible. And such men ought to be delivered out of the hands of the robbers, and set free as in Europe. Then is Pennsylvania to have a good report, instead, it hath now a bad one, for this sake, in other countries; Especially whereas the Europeans are desirous to know in what manner *the Quakers* do rule in *their* province; and most of them do look upon us with an envious eye. But if this is done well, what shall we say is done evil?

If once these slaves (which they say are so wicked and stubborn men,) should join themselves—fight for their freedom, and handel their masters and mistresses, as they did handel them before; will these masters and mistresses take the sword at hand and war against these poor slaves, like, as we are able to believe, some will not refuse to do? Or, have these poor negers not as much right to fight for their freedom, as you have to keep them slaves?

Now consider well this thing, if it is good or bad. And in case you find it to be good to handel these blacks in that manner, we desire and require you hereby lovingly, that you may inform us herein, which at this time never was done, viz., that Christians have such a liberty to do so. To the end we shall be satisfied on this point, and satisfy likewise our good friends and acquaintances in our native country, to whom it is a terror, or fearful thing, that men should be handelled so in Pennsylvania.

This is from our meeting at Germantown, held ye 18th of the 2d month, 1688, to be delivered to the monthly meeting at Richard Worrell's.

Garret Henderich,
Derick op de Graeff,
Francis Daniel Pastorius,
Abram op de Graeff.

P. G. Mode (ed.), *Source Book and Bibliographical Guide for American Church History* (Menashah, Wis., 1921).

Quakers Protest the Importation of Slaves

In 1698, ten years after the Quakers first spoke out against slavery, they issued this protest against the further importation of blacks.

from our monthly meeting at
philadelphia the 30th of 8th mo 98

dear friends
& brethren

It having been the sence of our yearly meeting that many negroes in these parts may prove preiudissial several wayes to us & our posteraty: it was Agreed that endevors should bee used to put A stop to the Importing of them; & in order theyrunto that those friends that have correspondences In ye west Indies should discurredg ye sending Any more hither; notwithstanding which; many negroes have been brought In this last summer; our meting taking it into consideration thought fit to signifie the same to you; desiring that friends off your Island in general might be Aquainted theyrwith; & its ye Request of our said meetings that no more negroes may bee sent to this River to friends or others & that as they see ocasion to Aquoint theyr Respective neighbours theyroff, that if possible A stop may bee put theyrto; so desiring your care herein wee conclude with very dear love

your dear friends & bretheren
signed by order & in behalfe
off our sd meeting by

Thomas Maisters	Samuel Carpenter
John Joanes	Thomas Ducket
Antony Morrise	James Fox
Wm Southebe	Humphrey Murey
	Nathan Stanberry

This a trew Coppy off ye paper sent
To the General Meeting off ffriends in
Barbadoes

[Endorsed on back in a later hand]
Coppy of a paper sent to Barbados to
discourage the sending Negroes hith^r

Philadelphia Yearly Meeting Minutes (MSS in the Friends' Record Room, Philadelphia), Book A II.

A Slave Petitions for Permission to Marry

In 1709, a slave petitioned the Court of General Sessions of Boston, Massachusetts, for permission to marry.

To the Hono^ble the Justices of her Maj^ties Court of General Sessions of the peace hold on at Boston on the first Tuesday of January Anno Domini 1709,
The Humble Petition of Jack a Negro—servant to Samuel Bill
SHEWETH

That a Marriage has been sometime since agreed upon between your Petitioner and Esther a Negro woman servant to Mr. Robert Gutteridge, to which your Petitioners Master and Mistress are Consenting. But the said Mr. Gutteridge refuses to give his Consent.

Your Petitioner also humbly craves leave to offer to your honours That in and by

. . . an Act of the General Court of this Province Exhibited An Act for the better preventing of a spurious and [illegible]. That no Master shall unreasonably deny Marriage to his Negro with one of the same Nation of which your Petitioner desires the Benefit.

Your Petitioner therefore humbly prays your honours that the sd Mr. Gutteridge may be ordered—to Appear before your honours, and that if he have no reasonable objection against it your Petitioner & sd Esther may be Marryed together.

And shall ever pray you.

Signed
Jack a Negro

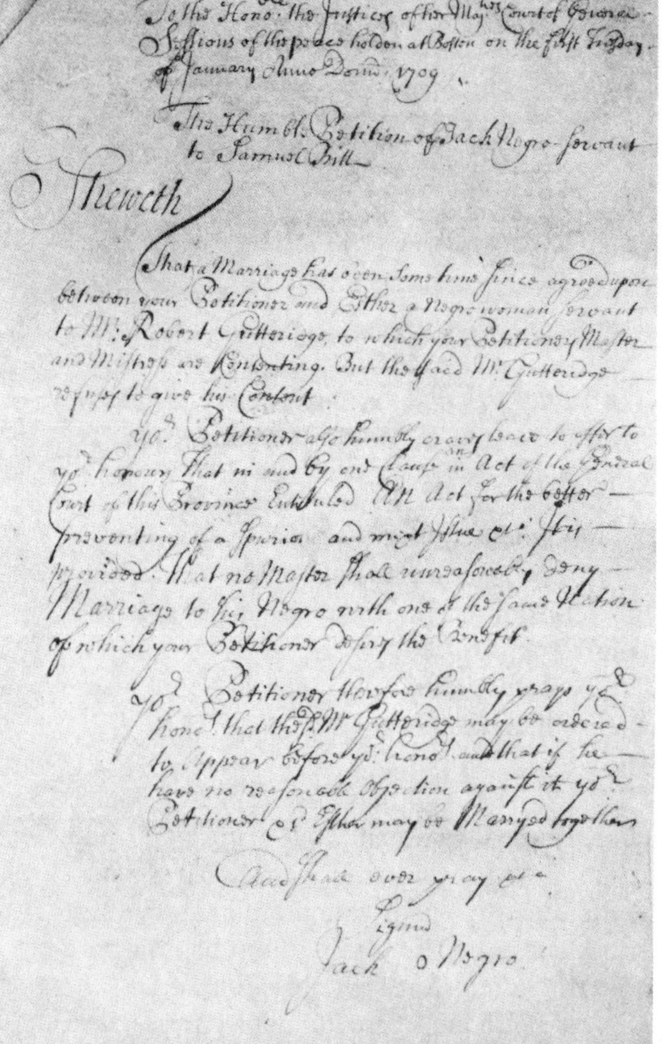

To the Hon.ble the Justices of her Maj.ties Court of General Sessions of the peace holden at Boston on the first Tuesday of January Anno Domini 1709

The Humble Petition of Jack Negro servant to Samuel Bill

Sheweth

That a Marriage has been some time since agreed upon between your Petitioner and Esther a Negro woman servant to Mr. Robert Gutteridge to which your Petitioners Master and Mistress are Consenting. But the said Mr. Gutteridge refuses to give his Consent.

Yo.r Petitioner also humbly craves leave to offer to yo.r honours That in and by one Clause in Act of the General Court of this Province Entituled An Act for the better preventing of a spurious and mixt Issue etc. It is provided That no Master shall unreasonably deny Marriage to his Negro with one of the same Nation of which your Petitioner desires the Benefit.

Yo.r Petitioner therefore humbly prays yo.r hono.rs that the s.d Mr Gutteridge may be ordered to Appear before yo.r hono.rs and that if he have no reasonable Objection against it yo.r Petitioner & Esther may be Marryed together

And shall ever pray etc.

Signed
Jack a Negro

New York Historical Society

Cotton Mather and Other Puritans Found the Society of Negroes

Cotton Mather and other Massachusetts Puritans made one of the earliest efforts to organize Afro-Americans when they founded the Society of Negroes in 1693. Although this particular society was established with the intention of keeping Negroes subservient to their masters, it was concerned also with providing the basic tenets of education and religious instruction.

RULES
For the Society of
NEGROES. 1693.

WE the Miſerable Children of *Adam*, and of *Noah*, thankfully Admiring and Accepting the Free-Grace of GOD, that Offers to Save us from our Miſeries, by the Lord Jeſus Chriſt, freely Reſolve, with His Help, to become the Servants of that Glorious LORD.

And that we may be Aſſiſted in the Service of our *Heavenly Maſter*, we now Join together in a SOCIETY, wherein the fallowing RULES are to be obſerved.

I. It ſhall be our Endeavour, to Meet in the *Evening* after the *Sabbath*; and *Pray* together by Turns, one to Begin, and another to Conclude the Meeting; And between the two *Prayers*, a *Pſalm* ſhall be Sung, and a *Sermon* Repeated.

II. Our coming to the Meeting, ſhall never be without the *Leave* of ſuch as have Power over us: And we will be Careful, that our Meeting may Begin and Conclude between the Hours of *Seven* and *Nine*; and that we may not be *unſeaſonably Abſent* from the Families whereto we pertain.

III. As we will, with the Help of God, at all Times avoid all *Wicked Company*, ſo we will Receive none into our Meeting, but ſuch as have ſenſibly *Reformed* their Lives from all manner of Wickedneſs. And therefore, None ſhall be Admitted, without the Knowledge and Conſent of the *Miniſter* of God in this Place; unto whom we will alſo carry every Perſon, that ſeeks for *Admiſſion* among us; to be by Him Examined, Inſtructed and Exhorted.

IV. We will, as often as may be, Obtain ſome Wiſe and Good Man, of the *Engliſh* in the Neighbourhood, and eſpecially the Officers of the Church, to look in upon us, and by their Preſence and Counſil, do what they think fitting for us.

V. If any of our Number, fall into the Sin of *Drunkenneſs*, or *Swearing*, or *Curſing*, or *Lying*, or *Stealing*, or notorious *Diſobedience* or *Unfaithfulneſs* unto their Maſters, we will *Admoniſh* him of his Miſcarriage, and Forbid his coming to the Meeting, for at leaſt *one Fortnight*; And except he then come with great Signs and Hopes of his *Repentance*, we will utterly Exclude him, with Blotting his *Name* out of our Liſt.

VI. If any of our Society Defile himſelf with *Fornication*, we will give him our *Admonition*; and ſo, debar him from the Meeting, at leaſt *half a Year*: Nor ſhall he Return to it, ever any more, without Exemplary Teſtimonies of his becoming a *New Creature*.

VII. We will, as we have Opportunity, ſet our ſelves to do all the Good we can, to the other *Negro-Servants* in the Town; And if any of them ſhould, at unfit Hours, be *Abroad*, much more, if any of them ſhould *Run away* from their Maſters, we will afford them *no Shelter*: But we will do what in us lies, that they may be diſcovered, and puniſhed. And if any *of us*, are found Faulty, in this Matter, they ſhall be no longer *of us*.

VIII. None of our Society ſhall be *Abſent* from our Meeting, without giving a *Reaſon* of the Abſence; And if it be found, that any have pretended unto their *Owners*, that they came unto the *Meeting*, when they were otherwiſe and elſewhere Employ'd, we will faithfully *Inform* their Owners, and alſo do what we can to Reclaim ſuch Perſon from all ſuch Evil Courſes for the Future.

IX. It ſhall be expected from every one in the Society, that he learn the *Catechiſm*; And therefore, it ſhall be one of our uſual Exerciſes, for one of us, to ask the *Queſtions*, and for all the reſt in their Order, to ſay the *Anſwers* in the *Catechiſm*; Either, The *New-Engliſh* Catechiſm, or the *Aſſemblies* Catechiſm, or the Catechiſm in the *Negro Chriſtianized*.

New York Public Library

An Early Slave Uprising in New York

The Society for the Propagation of the Gospel in Foreign Parts conducted a school in New York City for the purpose of imparting religious education to Negroes. In 1712, a slave insurrection nearly occurred in that city. The following report tells of the uprising and its effect on the schools.

In the mean Time, while the Society were thinking of farther Ways to advance this Work, a Calamity happened which mightily discouraged this Country from promoting the Instruction of their Slaves. In the Year 1712, a considerable Number of *Negroes* of the *Carmantee* and *Pappa* Nations, formed a Plot to destroy all the *English,* in order to obtain their Liberty; and kept their Conspiracy so secret, that there was no Suspicion of it, till it came to the very Execution. However, the Plot was, by God's Providence, happily defeated. The Plot was this: The *Negroes* sat Fire to a House in *York* City, on a Sunday Night, in *April,* about the going down of the Moon. The Fire alarmed the Town, who from all Parts ran to it; the Conspirators planted themselves in several Streets and Lanes leading to the Fire, and shot or stabbed the People as they were running to it. Some of the Wounded escaped, and acquainted the Government, and presently, by the Signal of firing a great Gun from the Fort, the Inhabitants were called under Arms, and prevented from running to the Fire. A Body of Men was soon raised, which easily scattered the *Negroes;* they had killed about eight Persons, and wounded 12 more. In their Flight some of them shot themselves, others their Wives, and then themselves; some absconded a few Days, and then killed themselves for Fear of being taken; but a great many were taken, and 18 of them suffered Death. This wicked Conspiracy was at first apprehended to be general among all the *Negroes,* and opened the Mouths of many, to speak against giving the *Negroes* Instruction. Mr. *Neau* durst hardly appear abroad for some Days, his School was blamed as the main Occasion of this barbarous Plot. But upon the Tryal of these Wretches, there were but two, of all his School, so much as charged with the Plot; and only one was a baptized Man, and in the Peoples Heat, upon slender Evidence, perhaps too hastily condemned; for soon after he was acknowledged to be innocent by the common Voice. The other was not baptized; it appeared plain that he was in the Conspiracy, but guiltless of his Master's Murder, Mr. *Hooghlands,* an eminent Merchant. Upon full Tryal, the guilty *Negroes* were found to be such as never came to Mr. *Neau's* School. . . .

The Society were fully satisfied with Mr. *Neau's* Behaviour, and continued to send him Numbers of Catechisms, and of small Tracts of Devotion and Instruction, to give among the Slaves and Servants at his Discretion. . . .

David Humphreys, *An Historical Account of the Incorporated Society for the Propagation of the Gospel in Foreign Parts: Containing Their Foundation, Proceedings, and the Success of Their Missionaries in the British Colonies, to the Year 1728* (London, 1730).

Slave Laws in the Colony of Virginia

In the early colonial period, harsh and stringent laws were enacted to subdue the slaves and thus lessen the possibility of insurrection. The English government insisted that these laws be read aloud in church twice a year. A typical list of regulations, which was used in the colony of Virginia, is included here.

Whereas the laws concerning Negroes and other slaves have not had the good effect by them intended for want of being duly executed . . . [it is hereby again stated that] it shall be unlawful for any Negro to arm himself with any club, staff, gun, sword, or any weapon of defense or offense, or to depart from his master's ground without a pass, to be granted only upon particular and necessary occasion . . . [or] to assemble at feasts or funerals . . . [and] no inhabitant shall suffer a strange Negro to remain upon his property above the space of four hours without examining him and his pass; . . . freemen will not repair to divine services or other assemblages unless armed to prevent surprise attacks of slaves . . . [and] any slave caught off his master's plantation without a pass after dark will be dismembered. . . .

Henry R. McIlwaine and W. L. Hall (eds.), *Executive Journals of the Council of Colonial Virginia* (5 vols; Richmond, Va., 1925–1945).

An Early New York Slave Law

A law was passed by the Common Council of the City of New York on April 22, 1731, to regulate the nocturnal activities of slaves.

BE *It Ordained by the Mayor, Recorder, Aldermen and Aſſiſtants of the City of* New-York, *convened in Common-Council, and it is hereby Ordained by the Authority of the ſame,* That from hence-forth no Negro, Mulatto or Indian Slave, above the Age of Fourteen Years, do preſume to be or appear in any of the Streets of this City, on the South-ſide of the Freſh-Water, in the Night time, above an hour after Sun-ſet; And that if any ſuch Negro, Mulatto or Indian Slave or Slaves, as aforeſaid, ſhall be found in any of the Streets of this City, or in any other Place, on the South ſide of the Freſh-Water, in the Night-time, above one hour after Sun-ſet, without a Lanthorn and lighted Candle in it, ſo as the light thereof may be plainly ſeen (and not in company with his, her or their Maſter or Miſtreſs, or ſome White Perſon or White Servant belonging to the Family whoſe Slave he or ſhe is, or in whoſe Service he or ſhe then are) That then and in ſuch caſe it ſhall and may be lawful for any of his Majeſty's Subjects within the ſaid City to apprehend ſuch Slave or Slaves, not having ſuch Lanthorn and Candle, and forth-with carry him, her or them before the Mayor or Recorder, or any one of the Aldermen of the ſaid City (if at a ſeaſonable hour) and if at an unſeaſonable hour, to the Watch-houſe, there to be confined until the next Morning) who are hereby authorized, upon Proof of the Offence, to commit ſuch Slave or Slaves to the common Goal, for ſuch his, her or their Contempt, and there to remain until the Maſter, Miſtreſs or Owner of every ſuch Slave or Slaves, ſhall pay to the Perſon or Perſons who apprehended and convicted every ſuch Slave or Slaves, the Sum of *Four Shillings* current Money of *New-York*, for his, her or their pains and Trouble therein, with Reaſonable Charges of Proſecution.

And be it further Ordained by the Authority aforeſaid, That every Slave or Slaves that ſhall be convicted of the Offence aforeſaid, before he, ſhe or they be diſcharged out of Cuſtody, ſhall be Whipped at the Publick Whipping-Poſt (not exceeding *Forty Lashes*) if deſired by the Maſter or Owner of ſuch Slave or Slaves.

Provided always, and it is the intent hereof; That if two or more Slaves (Not exceeding the Number of Three) be together in any lawful Employ or Labour for the Service of their *Maſter* or Miſtreſs (and not otherwiſe) and only one of them have and carry ſuch Lanthorn with a lighted Candle therein, the other Slaves in ſuch Company not carrying a Lanthorn and lighted Candle, ſhall not be conſtrued and intended to be within the meaning and Penalty of this Law, any thing in this Law contained to the contrary hereof in any wiſe notwithſtanding. *Dated at the City-Hall this Two and Twentieth Day of* April, *in the fourth year of His Majeſty's Reign,* Annoq; Domini 1731.

By Order of Common Council,

Will. Sharpas, *Cl.*

New York Public Library

A Ship's Captain Discusses the Economics of the Slave Trade

In 1737, the captain of a vessel that was used for transporting slaves from Africa to the colonies reported on his experiences.

Charlestown, May 25, 1737

Messrs. Sam C. Storke
& Company

Gentlemen:

I Bless God that I have the hapiness to lett you know of My Safe arrival from Guinia, with the Whole debt gave Me by the Directors with the mortality of one Slave, that belonging to myself and mate, the Others belonging to the Cargo being all well, & had they been according to Contract would have come to an exceeding good market, to 100 & upwards, at which Price we sold all those of any bigness. We have several that are but Children left, that will not fetch more than 70 pounds or 80 pounds or under, nor do People care to buy them, they are so very small, which I chose Rather to take . . . . As I lett the Company Know . . . and hope You'l Please to do the Same, by being paid children and Infants instead of boys and girls.

When I was in England, you seemed inclinable to adventure to Guinia and as to the legality of it I believe it will seem reasonable to allow, to bring children from a land of Ignorance and Barbarism to such a land as this must at least be warrantable action, and by what I can judge of the matters, were we not interested in it, it would be a commendable action.

Its my misfortune to go Round the World with so trivial a Cargo that not withstanding I go Safe there's little to be got.

I am satisfied (God Permitting) I could make one Voyage a year from here to Guinia and here again, wherein I could turn 1200 or 1400 pounds into 15,000 and more likely into 20,000 pounds currency (mortality of Slaves Excepted) and that with less Risque than to make a Voyage from here to London with a Loaded ship, in bringing only girles and boys wherein bringing is no risque . . . if we had had 1,000 of a suitable size from 4 to 5 feet could have sold them instantly, neither do I think there is any Markett in the King's Plantations, so good as this, nor pay so secure. . . .

Gentlemen

Your Most Oblig'd
and most Humble Servant

Robert Ball

New York Historical Society

"Sell Him for the Best Price You Can Get"

The following letter addressed to a Schenectady, New York, merchant concerns the sale of the writer's slaves. The contents of the letter indicate the ruthless business attitude that was assumed in selling human beings as if they were any common form of merchandise.

New York
April 29, 1738

Brother:

I have just received yours of the 24th inst. The butter is still on board. Butter is now almost unsalable. It has all been sold for 7 shillings and 6 shillings, but I shall do my best in order to sell this at a profit for you. Cousin Van Der Speigel does not want it. I sent you a letter by Cousin Ten Broeck, and am surprised to learn that you have not received it. I think it very strange that you do not even mention my blacks whom you have on sale for me. If the negress with the child is not sold, please do send her back by the first opportunity. However, if you can get 60 or even 58 pounds in cash for them or forty-eight pounds for her without the child, do so, but the sale must be for cash. Otherwise, you must send them back. As for the negro man sell him for the best price you can get, but do not sell the negress, otherwise than according to the directions above given. . . .

Your Affectionate Brother,

Duyckinck

To Mr. Henry V. Rensselaer, Merchant in Schenectady.

New York Historical Society

Advertisements for Fugitive Slaves

The following advertisements for fugitive slaves are from a period in our history when men, women and children were accorded the same status that today's newspaper advertisements give "lost and found" animals. It will be noted that many of the escaped slaves were literate and multilingual —evidence of education and, in some cases, preparation for flight to freedom.

Ran Away on Saturday Night Last from Moorhall in Chester County, a Mulatto Man Slave, aged about 22, has a likely whitish countenance, of a middle Stature; having on a chocolate colour'd Cloth coat, Linnen Waistcoat, Leather Breeches, grey Stockings, a Pess-burnt Wig, and a good Hat; has with him several white Shirts, and some Money: He speaks Swede and English well. Whoever secures the said Slave, so that his Master may have him again, shall be very handsomely Rewarded and all reasonable charges paid by

William Moore

The Pennsylvania Gazette (Philadelphia), July 31, 1740.

Run Away the 23rd of August from His Master Philip French of New Brunswick, in East-New-Jersey, a Negro Man *Claus,* of middle Stature yellowish complexion, about 44 Years of Age, Speaks Dutch and Good English.

Philip French

The Pennsylvania Gazette, September 24, 1741.

Run Away the 15th of May from John Williams, of Trenton Ferry, a Negro Man, named *James Bell,* about 30 Years of Age, middle stature, Speaks Very Good English and Very Fluent in His Talk; he formerly belonged to Slator Clay.

John Williams

The Pennsylvania Gazette, June 21, 1744.

Run-away the 2nd of July from Richard Colegate, of Kent County in Delaware, a Mulatto Man, named *James Wenyam,* of Middle Stature, about 37 Years of Age, has a red Beard a Scar on one Knee: Had on when he went away, a Kersey Jacket, a Pair of Plain Breeches, a Tow Shirt, and a Felt Hat. He swore when he went away to a Negro Man, whom he wanted to go with him, that he had often been in the back Woods with his Master, and That He Would Go to the French and Indians and Fight for Them. Whoever secures the said Mulatto Man, and gives Notice thereof to his Master, or to Abraham Gooding, Esq.; or to the High Sheriff of New Castle County, so that his Master may have him again, shall have Three Pounds Reward, and reasonable Charges, paid by

Richard Colegate

The Pennsylvania Gazette (Philadelphia), July 31, 1746.

Ran away from his Master *Eleazer Tyng, Esq.* at Dunstable, on the 26th May past, a Negro Man Servant Call'd *Robbin,* almost of the complexion of an Indian, short thick square shoulder'd Fellow, a very short neck, and thick legs, about 28 Years old, talks good English, can read and write, and plays on the Fiddle; he was born at Dunstable and It Is Thought He Has Been Entic'd to Enlist into the Service, or to go to Philadelphia: Had on when he went away, a strip'd cotton and Linnen blue and white Jacket, red Breeches with Brass Buttons, blue Yarn Stockings, a fine Shirt, and took another of a meaner Sort, a red Cap, a Beaver Hat with a mourning Weed in it, and sometimes wears a Wig. Whoever will apprehend said Negro and secure him, so that his Master may have him again, or bring him to the Ware-House of Messiers *Alford and Tyng,* in Boston, shall have a reward of *Ten Pounds,* and all reasonable Charges.

N.B. And all Masters of Vessels or others are hereby cautioned against harbouring, concealing or carrying off said Servant, on Penalty of the Law.

The New-York Gazette or Weekly Post-Boy, July 18, 1748.

Ran away from Hagerstown, Washington County, Maryland, in September last, a Negro wench named *Peggy,* but sometimes calls herself *Nancy,* about 26 years of age, talks on the Welsh accent, her complexion of a yellowish cast, the wool on her head is longer than negroes commonly have: Had on a blue petticoat of Duffil cloth, old shoes and stockings, her other clothes uncertain. It Is Supposed She Went off with a Portugese Fellow Who Served His Time with Mr. Jacob Funk: they probably may be in the neighborhood of Georgetown or Alexandria or gone towards camp, and that she will attempt to pass for a free woman, and wife to the Portugese fellow. Whoever takes her up and secures her in any gaol, so that the subscriber get her again, or delivers her to Daniel Hughes, Esq., in Hagerstown, shall have the above reward, and reasonable charges,

John Swan

The Maryland Journal and Baltimore Advertiser (Baltimore), October 19, 1779.

Absconded on or about the 1st instant, a Negro Fellow, named *Pero.* He is remarkably tall being nearly 6½ feet in height, his hands have been frost bitten, in consequence of which he has lost several of his finger nails. He speaks the French and English languages; Passes for a Doctor among People of His Color, and it is

Supposed Practices in That Capacity about Town. The above reward will be paid on his delivery at the Work-House, or the Subscriber

James George

N.B. All masters of vessels are forewarned from carrying him off the State as they will be prosecuted to the utmost rigor of the law.

The City Gazette and Daily Advertiser (Charleston, S. C.), June 22, 1797.

Run away in April last from *Richard Tilghman of Queen Anne County in Maryland* a Mulatto slave, Named *Richard Molson,* of Middle stature, about forty years old, and has had the Small Pox, *He Is in Company with a White Woman Named Mary, Who Is Supposed Now Goes for His Wife; and a White Man Named Garrett Choise, and Jane His Wife,* which said White People are servants to some Neighbors of the said Richard Tilghman. The said fugitives are Supposed to be gone to *Carolinas* or some other of his Majestys Plantations in America. Whoever shall apprehend the said Fugitives and cause them to be committed into safe custody, and give Notice thereof to their Owners shall be well rewarded. The White man has one of his fore fingers disabled.

Whoever shall carry them to the Sheriff of *Philadelphia* shall have Twenty Pounds current money paid him.

The Maryland Gazette (Annapolis), June 1, 1798.

Advertisements for Runaway Slaves Working as Privateersmen

These advertisements, describing runaway slaves prior to the American Revolution, refer to Negroes who served as privateersmen. They provide evidence of a skill that Negroes acquired and put to use for themselves when the opportunity arose.

Whereas Negro Jo (who formerly lived with Samuel Ogle, Esq; then Governor of Maryland, as his cook) about 13 Months ago run away from the Subscriber, who was then at Annapolis, and Has since Been out a Voyage in One of the Privateers Belonging to Philadelphia, and is returned there: These are to desire any Person to apprehend the said Negro, so that he may be had again, for which on their acquainting me therewith, they shall be rewarded with the Sum of Five Pounds, current Money: Or if the said Negro will return to me, at my House in St. Mary's County, he shall be kindly received, and escape all Punishment for his Offence.

Philip Key

The Pennsylvania Gazette (Philadelphia), November 7, 1745.

Run away from Samuel M'Call, jun. a Negro Man, named Tom, a very likely Fellow, about 22 or 23 Years of Age, about 5 Foot 10 Inches high, speaks good English, Has Been a Privateering; has several good Cloaths on, with Check Shirts, some new; formerly belonged to Dr. Shaw of Burlington. Whoever secures the said Negro in any County Gaol so that his Master may have him again, shall have a Pistole Reward and reasonable Charges paid by

Samuel M'Call

Philadelphia, July 3, 1746.

N.B. He is a sensible, active Fellow, and runs well.

The Pennsylvania Gazette, July 3, 1746.

A Manifest of Cargo from the Slave Trade

On the following page is a photograph of a manifest of cargo received as payment from a sale of slaves on the voyage of the Rhode Island *in 1748. This particular ship was owned by Philip Livingston and Sons, merchants in New York City. The voyage was made between the East Coast of Africa and New York City. It is interesting to note that the African slaves were considered as merchandise and were interspersed throughout the manifest with other items of cargo.*

Sloope Rhode Island Peter James Master ℘ Philip
Comminceing At Sevition Jan.ry 18 1748/9

		oz	ac	s	d
Jan.ry 18	By King Tom Custom for wood & warter		13		
Do. 19	By 31 lb of brass Pans @ 2½ ℘ . . # 12 : 2 By 2 Cuttases . . . . . . # 2 By 1 peice Nickene . . . . # 6 By 2 peices blew baft . . . . # 12 By 2 trading guns . . . . . # 8 By 2 muskets . . . . . . # 10 By 2 Buckener . . . . . . # 12 By 3 Cags Powder @ 3 ℘ . . . . # 9 By 5 Cags of Do @ 2½ ℘ . . . # 12 : 2 : 6 By 2 peices blew and white Caloco . . # 12 95 : 4 : 6	5	15	4	6
Do 20	By A Woman Slave No 1 @ # 60 By 6 peices blew & white Calocos @ 6 ℘ # 36 By 3 peices Read & white Do . . . . # 18 By 2 peices Cotten Nes @ 12 ℘ . . . . # 24 By 3 peices Patne Chinch @ 6 . . . . # 18 By 1 peice of blew baft . . . . . # 6 By 24 lb of beads @ 3 lb ℘ . . . . # 8 By 3 Kettels 28 lb @ 8 lb ℘ . . . . # 9 : 1 : 8 By 10 Iron bars . . . . . . # 10 By 2 Dozen hatts @ 8 ℘ . . . . # 16 By 38½ Cowres @ 2½ . . . . . # 15 : 1 : 8 By 6 trading guns @ 4 . . . . . # 24 By 13 Cuttases . . . . . . # 9 By 35 lb brass Pans @ 2½ ℘ . . . . # 12 : 1 : 8 By 1 Teeth 48 lb . . . . . . # 17 283	17	11		
Do: 20	By 6 Peices of blew & white Calocos . . # 36 By 1 Peice Patne Chinch . . . . . # 6 By 1 mesodepot . . . . . . # 8 By 1 meganepot . . . . . . # 8 By 75 lb Pewter basons @ 3 lb ℘ . . . # 25 By 16 hatts @ 8 ℘ Doz . . . . . # 10 : 3 : 4 By 20 lb of Screvelers at 6 ℘ . . . # 3 : 1 : 8 97	6	1		
Do: 21	By 2 Slaves one Boy one garl No: 2 : 3 @ # 84 By 2 Cags Powder @ 7 . . . . . # 14 By 6 Cuttass . . . . . . # 4 By 10 lb brass pans @ 2½ ℘ . . . . # 4 By 1 Buckener . . . . . . # 6 112	6	14		

New York Public Library

George Washington Sells His Slave Tom

Before the Revolutionary War, when he was a Virginia planter, George Washington both bought and sold slaves.

July 2, 1766:

Sir:

With this letter comes a Negro (Tom), which I beg the favour of you to sell, in any of the Islands you may go to, for whatever he will fetch, and bring me in return for him.

One hhd of best molasses
One ditto of best rum
One barrell of lymes if good and cheap
One pot of tamarinds containing about 10 lbs.
Two small ditto of mixed sweetmeats about 5 lbs. each.

And the residue, much or little, in good old spirits. That this fellow is both a rogue and a runaway (tho' he was by no means remarkable for the former, and never practiced the latter till of late) I shall not pretend to deny —But he is exceeding healthy, strong, and good at the hoe the whole neighbourhood can testifie and particularly M. Johnson and his son, who have both had him under them as foreman of the gang; which gives me reason to hope he may, with your good management, sell well, if kept clean and trim'd up a little when offered for sale.

I shall cherfully allow you the customary commissions on this affair, and must beg the favour of you (least he shoud attempt his escape) to keep him handcuffd till you get to sea—or in the bay—after which I doubt not but you may make him very useful to you.

I wish you a pleasant and prosperous passage, and a safe and speedy return, being Sir

Y[r] Very H[ble] Serv[t].
G[o] WASHINGTON

Worthington C. Ford (ed.), *The Writings of George Washington* (14 vols.; New York, 1889–1893).

A Slave Is Pardoned for Attempted Murder

The account below, written in 1770, tells of a slave who was convicted of attempting to kill his mistress but was pardoned on the condition that he leave the United States.

Province of New York, Js. Be it Remembered that on the

Twenty eighth Day of November in the Eleventh year of the Reign of our Sovereign Lord George the third by the Grace of God of Great Britain France and Ireland King Defender of the faith and so forth and in the year of our Lord One thousand seven hundred and seventy personally appeared before me Daniel Horsmanden Esquire Chief Justice of the Province of New York, Benjamin Douglas of the City of New York Taylor and acknowledged himself to be indebted unto our said Sovereign Lord the King—his Heirs and Successors in the sum of two hundred pounds Current Money of the Province of New York to be levied on his goods and Chattels—Lands and Tenements to the use of our said Lord the King his—Heirs and Successors if failure be made in the performance of the—Condition following.

WHEREAS in the Supreme Court of Judicature held for the Province of New York at the City Hall in the City of New York in the Term of July and August now last past a certain Negroe Man Slave commonly called and known by the Name of Falmouth the property of Robert Gibb of the City of New York Mariner was indicted Tryed and Convicted for attempting to kill Jane Gibb his Mistress. And whereas his Majesty by his letters—Patent under the Great Seal of the Province of New York bearing date the Twenty second Day of November aforesaid did Pardon Remise and Release the said Negroe man Falmouth of and from the Felony aforesaid and of and from all Felonies perpetrated by him at anytime before the date of the said Letters Patent and of and from all Judgments Executions Penalties Forfeitures and Imprisonments against him rendered or to be rendered or adjudged thereupon. Provided always, and the said Letters Patent were Nevertheless upon this Express Condition, that the said Negroe Man Slave Falmouth shall forthwith after his Discharge in virtue of the said Letters Patent be put on Board some Vessel and Transported or sent to one of the foreign West India Islands, and that he did not at anytime thereafter find within the said Province. Now the Condition of this Recognizance is such that if the said Negroe Man Slave Falmouth shall forthwith after his Discharge in virtue of the said recited Letters Patent be put on Board some Vessell and Transported or sent to one of the foreign West India Islands and there sold, then the aforegoing Recognizance to be void and of none Effect, otherwise to be and remain in full force and Virtue.

Taken and acknowledged the Day and Year first above written.
Before Me.

Dan Horsmanden

28th Nov. 1770 Benjamin Douglas to The King	Recognizances pursuant to the Condition of the Pardon of a Negro man Slave called Falmouth

New York Historical Society

A Physician's Report on a Master's Brutal Treatment of His Slave

An often-ignored facet of slavery deals with medical costs and treatment of slaves. In order to operate his plantation effectively, a "good" master had to assume the financial costs of providing at least the bare necessities of medical care. This report was made by a doctor who had treated a slave whose master had inflicted fatal wounds on him during a beating.

Ann Arundel County [Maryland]
April 19, 1773

This Day came Doctor John Archer before me, one of his Lordships Justices of the Peace for said County, and made oath, that Mr. James Lee Junior informed him that he had struck one of his Negros and had accidently cut him above one of his eyes and said, he tho't he should be obliged to send for him the [Doctor, who in this case is also the witness] Deponent; but Mr. Lee said he served it himself and the Negro was like to do well. Shortly after the Deponent saw Mr. Lee, who told him the Negro was costive and asked if it was necessary to give the Negro a purge or the like, he told him it was accordingly applied and got what was requisite, which Mr. Lee said had the desired effect and the Negro was better.

Some few days after, Mr. Lee came for the Deponent to visit his Negro, who he said was bad with a pain in the side, he then said Deponent went and examined the Negro called Jos. (who was wounded above the left eye) and found him very bad with a Plennitic Pain; but unable to give the anticedent symptoms common in that complaint, which he then alleged to proceed from inattention, he also asked the Negro (in presence of his Master) if he felt any pain or uneasiness in any other part who said he did not — The Negro died the next day about Noon.

About eight or ten days after the death of the Negro the Deponent being summoned by the Coroner of Balt. County to examine the body of Negro Jos. On examining the Plena, it was found inflamed in the part where he complained, but found no other cause of complaint in that part — The cranium being next examined and after removing the upper part thereof, there appeared a fracture and depression of that part of the Os Frontis which forms part of the socket of the eye, opposite to an external wound in the flesh which penetrated to the brain. The size of the fractured piece appeared to be about a quarter of an inch broad and about half an inch long.

The Deponent further deposeth that the fracture was sufficient to take the Negro's life, also that the Plena itself is a primary disease was sufficient and that inflammations of the meninges of the brain are often translated from thence to the Plena . . . from the appearance of the wound above the eye the Deponent is rather of the opinion that the inflammation was translated from the Meninges of the brain to the Plena, but would not determine positively as it can only be known positively by the Supreme Being.

Sworn before R. Eiselin

Mr. James Lee was very careful of the Negro in his sickness and did not to the knowledge of the Deponent let him want for anything that was directed.

New York Historical Society

Patrick Henry on Slavery

Patrick Henry, Virginia patriot, is best remembered for his ringing statement "I know not what course others may take, but as for me, give me Liberty or give me death." He is pictured here in a somewhat different role. While choosing liberty for himself and advocating it in a later day for Negroes, Henry apologetically wrote British abolitionist Granville Sharp of his opinions on the subject of slavery.

Hanover Jany. 18 1773

. . . .

Would any one believe that I am master of Slave[s], of my own purchase: I am drawn along by the general inconveniency of living without them, I will not, I cannot Justify it; however culpable my conduct, I will so far pay my duty as to own the Excellency and rectitude of her precepts, and to lament my want of confirmity to them

I believe a time will come, when an opportunity will be afforded, to abolish this lamentable evil; every thing we can do is to improve it, if it happens in our day, if not, let us transmit to our descendants, together with our Slaves, a pity for their unhappy Lot, and abhorrence for Slavery. If we cannot reduce this Reformation to practice, let us treat the unhappy victims with lenity; it is the furthest advance towards Justice. . . .

Patrick Henry

New York Historical Society

Phillis Wheatley's Correspondence with George Washington

When Washington was Commander-in-Chief of the Continental Army, he received the following letter and poem from Phillis Wheatley, Negro poetess. In his reply, which is included here, he invited her to visit him. This she did, at his camp near the Delaware River.

Providence
October 26, 1775

Sir:

I have taken the freedom to address your Excellency in the enclosed poem, and entreat your acceptance, though I am not insensible of its inaccuracies. Your being appointed by the Grand Continental Congress to be Generalissimo of the Armies of North America, together with the fame of your virtues, excite sensations not easy to suppress. Your generosity, therefore, I presume, will pardon the attempt. Wishing your Excellency all possible success in the great cause you are so generously engaged in, I am,

Your Excellency's most obedient
and humble servant,

Phillis Wheatley

Celestial choir! enthron'd in realms of light,
Columbia's scenes of glorious toils I write.
While freedom's cause her anxious breast
alarms,

She flashes dreadful in refulgent arms.
See mother earth her offspring's fate bemoan,
And nations gaze at scenes before unknown!
See the bright beams of heaven's revolving light
Involved in sorrows and the veil of night!
The goddess comes, she moves divinely fair,
Olive and laurel binds her golden hair:
Wherever shines this native of the skies,
Unnumber'd charms and recent graces rise.
Muse! bow propitious while my pen relates
How pour her armies through a thousand gates;
As when Eolus heaven's fair face deforms,
Enrapped in tempest and a night of storms;
Astonish'd ocean feels the wild uproar,
The refluent surges beat the sounding shore,
Or thick as leaves in Autumn's golden reign,
Such, and so many, moves the warrior's train.
In bright array they seek the work of war,
Where high unfurl'd the ensign waves in air.
Shall I to Washington their praise recite?
Enough thou know'st them in fields of fight,
Thèe, first in place and honours—we demand
The grace and glory of thy martial band.

Fam'd for thy valour, for thy virtues more,
Here every tongue thy guardian aid implore!
One century scarce performed its destin'd round.
When Gallic powers Columbia's furry found.
And so may you, whoever dares disgrace
The land of freedom's heaven-defended race!
Fix'd are the eyes of nations on the scales
For in their hopes Columbia's arm prevails,
Anon Britannia droops the pensive head
While round increase the rising hills of dead,
Oh! cruel blindness to Columbia's state!
Lament thy thirst of boundless power too late.
Proceed great chief with virtue on thy side,
Thy every action let the goddess guide.
A crown, a mansion, and a throne that shine,
With gold unfading, Washington be thine.

* * * * *

Cambridge
February 28, 1776

Miss Phillis:—

Your favor of the 26th of October did not reach my hands till the middle of December. Time enough, you will say, to have given an answer ere this. Granted. But a variety of important occurrences, continually interposing to distract the mind and withdraw the attention, I hope will apologize for the delay, and plead my excuse for the seeming, but not real neglect. I thank you most sincerely for your polite notice of me in the elegant lines you enclosed; and however undeserving I may be of such encomium and panegyric, the style and manner exhibit a striking proof of your poetical talents; in honor of which, and as a tribute justly due you, I would have published the poem, had I not been apprehensive that, while I only meant to give the world this new instance of your genius, I might have incurred the imputation of vanity. This, and nothing else, determined me not to give it a place in the public prints.

If you should ever come to Cambridge, or near headquarters, I shall be happy to see a person favored by the Muses, and to whom nature has been so liberal and beneficent in her dispensations.

I am, with great respect,
your obedient humble servant.

George Washington

Walter H. Mazyck, *George Washington and the Negro* (Washington, 1932).

A Slave's Will

The will of a slave, on the following page, was dictated to an unknown writer in 1773. It is unique in that few slaves had possessions which they could leave behind.

I CESAR Negro Man of Abijah Comstock of Norwalk in the County of Fairfield and Colony of Connecticut, Being of sound Mind and Memory And Calling To Mind my Mortallity, Knowing it is Appointed for all Men once to Die With the approbation of my Above s'd Master Do make and ordain this my Last Will and Testament. As follows, Viz.—

1st I give to my master Abijah Comstock my Great Bible, Confession of Faith, Mathew henry upon the Sacrament one old Trap of my Deceased Masters and woppit. Furthermore—

2nd I give to my Master's son David my small Bible & psalm Book, Willison's Explanation, Joseph Allen, Thomas Gouge, My new chest And young Bobben trap and half of my Money Except a reserve Hereafter made even the price of a silver Spoon Left at the Discrition of my Master to purchase &c.

3rd I give to my Masters son Enoch, Joseph Sewall, Dr. Watts Catechism, Thomas Shepperd Solomon Stodard and S Wright My clasp paper pocket Book My New Bever hat and Case And hayt trap And the other half of my Money Except the Value of one silver spoon.

David and Enoch. } *At Masters Decease my Great Bible to David And the rest to Enoch.*

If Either of my Masters above sd. sons Dye without heirs The survivors to take what I gave to the Deceased.

My silver spoon to Hannah
A silver spoon to Dinah
A silver spoon to Deborah } *My Master's Daughters*

To Thomas My Masters Eldest son The Dissenting Gentlemans Anss.

To Abigail Eells
To Moses Eells } *Ye Almost Christians and when Deced.*

To Hannah hanford—Four Books—Viz. Law & Grace, John Bunyon, Vincens Sudden and Certain Appearance to Judgment—Vincens Explanation upon the Catechism. John Fox, Time & End of time.

To Phineas hanford one trap called old Bobben.

To Samuel hanford one Book a Cordial to the fainting Saint.

My silver shoe Buckles & knee buckles & clasps which was above forgotten With my Tankard Quart pot and Bason To David with my sleeve Buttons and Gloves.

My old chest to Dwer and then to Dwer and Belinda all my caps and handkerchiefs, old shoe buckles to Dwer and knee buckles.

February ye 13th A. D. 1773. I appoint my Master Abijah Comstock to be Executor of this my last will and testament.

Daniel Lockwood.
Samuel Lockwood.

His
Cesar × Seal
Mark

New York Public Library

Lord Dunmore's Proclamation of 1776

By the time the revolt of the colonies had become a serious threat to the mother country, the policies of the British toward the Negro had altered. Earlier laws regulating the behavior of slaves were changed as efforts were made to unite Negroes in support of the British Army. In 1776, Lord Dunmore, Governor-General of Virginia, issued an emancipation proclamation which would guarantee freedom in return for military assistance.

By his Excellency the Right Honorable JOHN, *Earl of* DUNMORE, *his Majesty's Lieutenant and Governor-General of the Colony and Dominion of Virginia, and Vice-Admiral of the same,—*

A PROCLAMATION

As I have ever entertained hopes that an accommodation might have taken place between Great Britain and this Colony, without being compelled by my duty to this most disagreeable but now absolutely necessary step, rendered so by a body of armed men, unlawfully assembled, firing on his Majesty's tenders; and the formation of an army, and that army now on their march to attack his Majesty's troops, and destroy the well-disposed subjects of this Colony,—to defeat such treasonable purposes, and that all such traitors and their abettors may be brought to justice, and that the peace and good order of this Colony may be again restored, which the ordinary course of the civil law is unable to effect, I have thought fit to issue this my Proclamation; hereby declaring, that, until the aforesaid good purposes can be obtained, I do, in virtue of the power and authority to me given by his Majesty, determine to execute martial law, and cause the same to be executed, throughout this Colony. And, to the end that peace and good order may the sooner be restored, I do require every person capable of bearing arms to support his Majesty's standard, or be looked upon as traitors to his Majesty's Crown and Government, and thereby become liable to the penalty the law inflicts upon such offences,—such as forfeiture of life, confiscation of lands, &c., &c. And I do hereby further declare all indented servants, negroes, or others, (appertaining to rebels,) free, that are able and willing to bear arms, they joining his Majesty's troops, as soon as may be, for the more speedily reducing this Colony to a proper sense of their duty to his Majesty's crown and dignity. I do further order and require all his Majesty's liege subjects to retain their quit-rents, or any other taxes due, or that may become due, in their own custody, till such time as peace may be again restored to this at present most unhappy country, or demanded of them, for their former salutary purposes, by officers properly authorized to receive the same.

Given under my hand, on board the ship "William," off Norfolk, the seventh day of November, in the sixteenth year of his Majesty's reign.

DUNMORE.

God save the King!

J. T. Wilson, *Emancipation: Its Course and Progress* (Hampton, Va., 1882).

In Praise of Salem Poor

The following document commends Salem Poor, a Negro who took part in the Battle of Bunker Hill in 1775.

The Subscribers begg leave to Report to your Honble. House (Which Wee do in justice to the Caracter of so Brave a Man) that under Our Own observation, Wee declare that A Negro Man Called Salem Poor of Col Fryes Regiment. Capt. Ames. Company in the late Battle at Charleston, behaved like an Experienced Officer, as Well as an Excellent Soldier, to Set forth Particulars of his Conduct Would be Tedious, Wee Would Only begg leave to say in the Person of this sd. Negro Centers a Brave & gallant Soldier—The Reward due to so great and Distinguisht a Caracter, Wee submit to the Congress—

Cambridge Decr. 5th 1775

JONA. BREWER *Col*
THOMAS NIXON *Lt. Col*
WM. PRESCOTT *Colo.*
EPHM. COREY *Lieut*
JOSEPH BAKER *Lieut*
JOSHUA REED *Lieut*

To the Honorable General Court of the Massachusetts Bay.

JONAS RICHARDSON *Capt*
ELIPHELET BODWELL *Segt*
JOSIAH FOSTER *Leutn*
EBENR VARNUM *2d Lut*
WM HUDSON BALLARD *Cpt*
WILLIAM SMITH *Capn*
JOHN MARTEN *Surgt: of a Brec:*
LIEUT. RICHARD WELSH

In Council Decr. 21st. 1775
Read & Sent down
Perez Morton, *Dpy Secry*

Original in the Revolutionary Rolls Collection, Massachusetts State Archives, State House, Boston.

A Black Soldier's Participation in the American Revolution

This anonymous report from the Burlington, Vermont, Gazette *tells of a black soldier's participation in the Revolutionary War.*

The attention of many of our citizens has, doubtless, been arrested by the appearance of an old colored man, who might have been seen, sitting in front of his residence, in East Union street, respectfully raising his hat to those who might be passing by. His attenuated frame, his silvered head, his feeble movements, combine to prove that he is very aged; and yet, comparatively few are aware that he is among the survivors of the gallant army who fought for the liberties of our country, "in the days which tried men's souls."

On Monday last, we stopped to speak to him, and asked him how old he was. He asked the day of the month, and, upon being told that it was the 24th of May, replied, with trembling lips, "I am very old—I am a hundred years old to-day."

His name is Oliver Cromwell, and he says that he was born at the Black Horse, (now Columbus,) in this county, in the family of John Hutchin. He enlisted in a company commanded by Capt. Lowery, attached to the Second New Jersey Regiment, under the command of Col. Israel Shreve. He was at the battles of Trenton, Princeton, Brandywine, Monmouth, and Yorktown, at which latter place, he told us, he saw the last man killed. Although his faculties are failing, yet he relates many interesting reminiscences of the Revolution. He was with the army at the retreat of the Delaware, on the memorable crossing of the 25th of December, 1776, and relates the story of the battles on the succeeding days with enthusiasm. He gives the details of the march from Trenton to Princeton, and told us, with much humor, that they "knocked the British about lively" at the latter place.

The Loyalty and Devotion of Colored Americans in the American Revolution and War of 1812 (Boston, 1861).

An Unusual System of Induction

Colonists who were called to serve in the Continental Army could send instead one of their slaves, for whom they received a bounty.

I Say Received of Ezekiel Hawley of Salem the Sum of Seven pounds New York Currency as a Bounty for my Negros Going into the army for two month & half which is in part of his Bounty which fell to him By assesment by order of Convention. I Say Received By me

Solomon Closig

Salem August 26th yr 1777

New York Historical Society

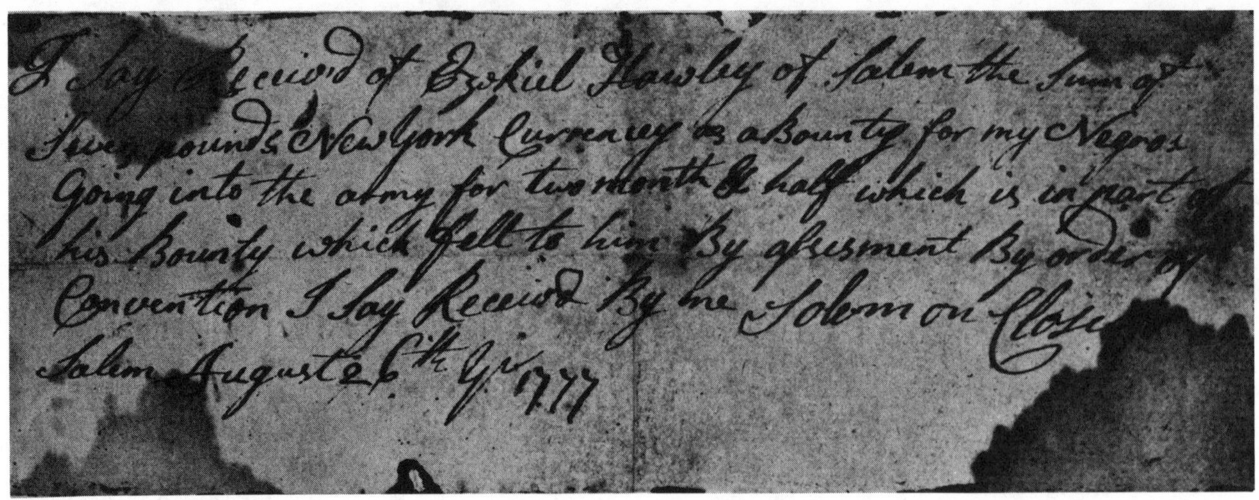

I Say Receiv'd of Ezekiel Hawley of Salem the Sum of Seven pounds New York Currency as a Bounty for my Negros Going into the army for two month & half which is in part of his Bounty which fell to him By assesment By order of Convention I Say Receiv'd By me Solomon Close
Salem August 26th Yr 1777

New York Historical Society

The actual handwritten document illustrating the unusual system of induction into the Revolutionary Army which is described on the previous page.

The Articles of this Vendue are as follows

1st The highest Bidder to be the Purchaser

2d Any Person or Persons, Purchasing the said Wench and Child Agreeable to Advertisement Shall have four Months Credit with given their Bond and Security if Required

3d Any Person or Persons Purchasing said Wench and Child and not Complying as above the said Wench and Child shall Be set up at Second Sale and if any Deficiency by said Second sale should Arise the first Purchaser shall make it good if any Overplush the first purchaser shall Reap no benefit

Brooklyn
April 23. 1790

William Elsworth Execur

New York Historical Society

The procedure for a slave sale.

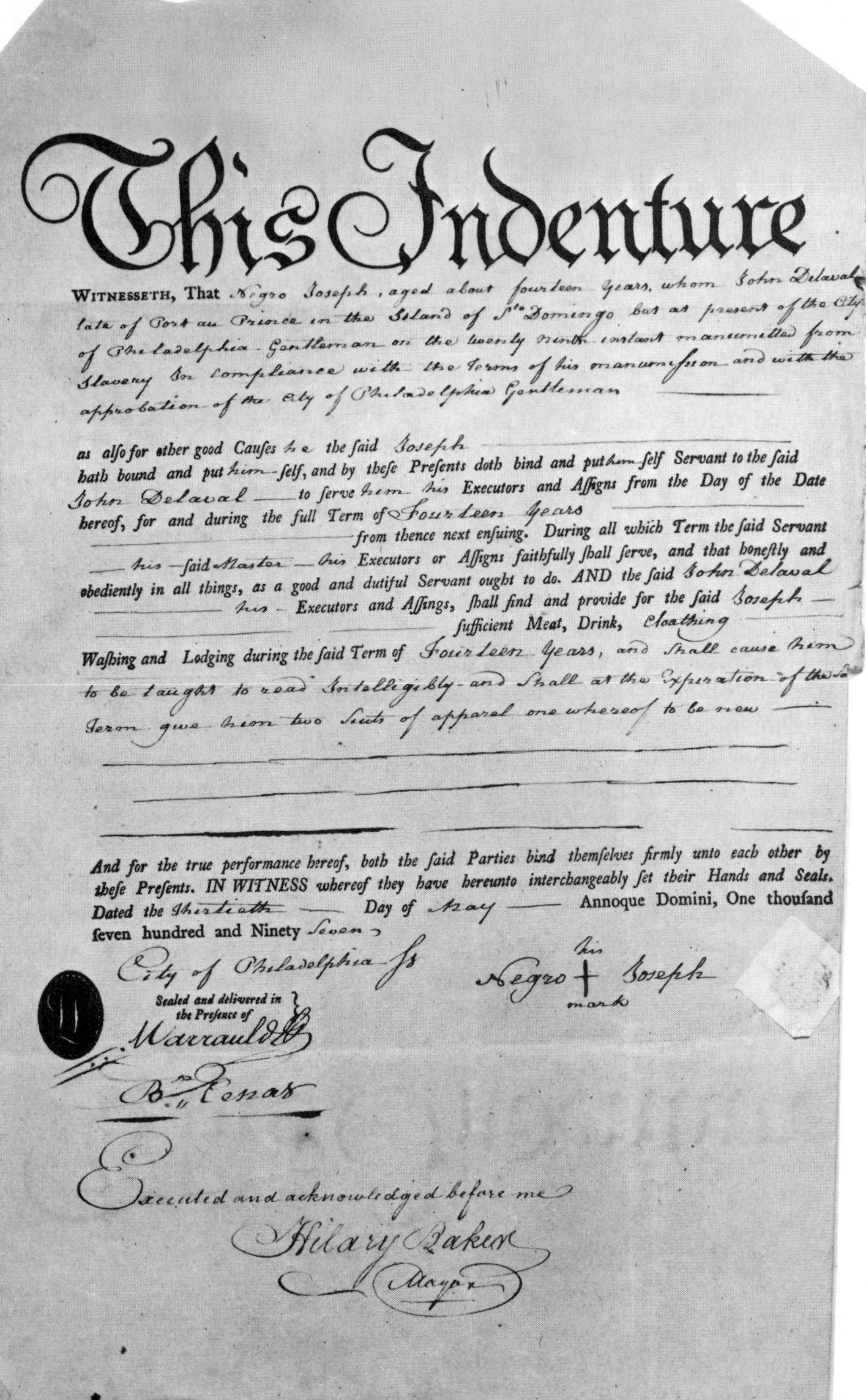

This Indenture

WITNESSETH, That Negro Joseph, aged about fourteen Years, whom John Delaval late of Port au Prince in the Island of St Domingo but at present of the City of Philadelphia Gentleman on the twenty ninth instant manumitted from Slavery In compliance with the Terms of his manumission and with the approbation of the City of Philadelphia Gentleman

as also for other good Causes he the said Joseph hath bound and put him-self, and by these Presents doth bind and put him-self Servant to the said John Delaval to serve him his Executors and Assigns from the Day of the Date hereof, for and during the full Term of Fourteen Years from thence next ensuing. During all which Term the said Servant his said Master his Executors or Assigns faithfully shall serve, and that honestly and obediently in all things, as a good and dutiful Servant ought to do. AND the said John Delaval his Executors and Assings, shall find and provide for the said Joseph sufficient Meat, Drink, Cloathing Washing and Lodging during the said Term of Fourteen Years, and shall cause him to be taught to read Intelligibly and shall at the Expiration of the said Term give him two Suits of apparel one whereof to be new

And for the true performance hereof, both the said Parties bind themselves firmly unto each other by these Presents. IN WITNESS whereof they have hereunto interchangeably set their Hands and Seals. Dated the Thirtieth Day of May Annoque Domini, One thousand seven hundred and Ninety Seven

City of Philadelphia ss

Negro his + mark Joseph

Sealed and delivered in the Presence of

Warrauld

B. Renar

Executed and acknowledged before me

Hilary Baker

Mayor

New York Historical Society

Negroes, as well as whites, served as indentured servants in eighteenth-century America. When the stipulated periods of indenture were over, they became free.

Freedom Proposed As a Reward for Military Service

During the Revolutionary War, many Negroes were promised freedom as a reward for serving in the Continental Army. Many volunteers, however, were returned to bondage after the war. Below is a petition from a Negro who had been thus betrayed.

To the Honorable General Assembly of the State of Connecticut to be holden in said State on the Second Thursday of May, Anno Domini, 1780.

The Petition of Joseph Mun a poor African Humbly sheweth that your unfortunate Petitioner while but a child was snatched by the hand of fraud and violence from his Native Land and all his dear connexions and brought into this Land and noting by the Constitution of the Great Parents of the Universe who hath made of one blood all nations of men for to dwell on the face of the earth he was in common with others entitled to Freedom and the Unalienable rights of Humanity yet in violation thereof he was sold a slave for life to Thomas Seymour, Esq. late of Hartford deceased with whom he lived sometime and then was sold to one Daniel Barber and so from one to another until he came into the hands of William Nicholls of Waterbury in this State who encouraged your Petitioner with his Freedom on condition of Faithful service for the term of three years, that at the expiration term said Nicholls refused to perform his said engagement, that your Petitioner being dissatisfied . . . proposed to his said Master to Enlist into the service, to which he consented, and your Petitioner did enlist and by the year 1776 . . . was stationed near New York under the command of General Wooster and had continued in Service almost ever since the War began, in the defense of the Rights & Liberties of this Country and in hope to lay foundations for organizing his own Freedom and is now enlisted in the Continental Army Colonel Wydys Regiment during this War and your Petitioner would beg Leave further to Represent that the said William Nicholls Entertaining the most unfriendly Sentiments to the Rights and Liberties of this Country hath gone over to and joined the Enemy and continues to hold . . . himself under their protection by which conduct he hath forfeited his whole Estate. That the said Nicholls with intent to elude the Law as your Petitioner conceives. Just as he was about to abscond and go off to the Enemy gave a Bill of Sale of your Petitioner to one Thomas Hecox, Junior, of said Waterbury by virtue whereof he (Hecox) Claims and Challenges your Petitioner into his Service and to hold him in bondage and slavery which your Petitioner Humbly Conceives upon Enquiry will be found to be Contrary to the Laws of Nature and Humanity. He therefore makes his Humble application to your Honors to whom he looks up as his only Refuge, and the protector of the Distressed, and most Humbly prays your Honors to take his Piteous and distressed Case into your wise and Compassionate Consideration and Order and devise that your Petitioner be made free from his Bondage, and Entitled to the privileges of Society in Common with mankind in General and he as in duty bound shall ever Pray. Dated at Farmington the Second Day of May Anno Dom. 1780

his
Joseph X Mun
Mark

Original in the State Archives, Connecticut State Library, Hartford. *Photostat courtesy of Dr. Lorenzo J. Greene, Lincoln University, Jefferson City, Mo.*

A Virginia Act To Emancipate Black Patriots

To eradicate practices which placed Negroes in jeopardy of being re-enslaved, the Virginia General Assembly in 1783 enacted legislation guaranteeing emancipation to those who had earned it through military service.

An Act directing the Emancipation of certain Slaves who have served as Soldiers in this State, and for the Emancipation of the Slave Aberdeen.

I. Whereas it hath been represented to the present General Assembly, that during the course of the war, many persons in this State had caused their slaves to enlist in certain regiments or corps raised within the same, having tendered such slaves to the officers appointed to recruit forces within the State, as substitutes for free persons whose lot or duty it was to serve in such regiments or corps, at the same time representing to such recruiting officers that the slaves so enlisted by their direction and concurrence, were freemen; and it appearing further to this Assembly, that on the expiration of the term of enlistment of such slaves, that the former owners have attempted again to force them to return to a state of servitude, contrary to the principles of justice, and to their own solemn promise;

II. And whereas it appears just and reasonable, that all persons enlisted as aforesaid, who have faithfully served agreeable to the terms of their enlistment, and have thereby of course contributed towards the establishment of American liberty and independence, should enjoy the blessings of freedom as a reward for their toils and labors;

Be it therefore enacted, That each and every slave, who by the appointment and direction of his owner, hath enlisted in any regiment or corps raised within this State, either on Continental or State establishment, and hath been received as a substitute for any free person whose duty or lot it was to serve in such regiment or corps, and hath served faithfully during the term of such enlistment or hath been discharged from such service by some officer duly authorized to grant such discharge, shall, from and after the passing of this act, be fully and completely emancipated, and shall be held and deemed free, in as full and ample a manner as if each and every of them were specially named in this act; and the Attorney-general for the Commonwealth is hereby required to commence an action, *in forma pauperis,* in behalf of any of the persons above described who shall, after the passing of this act, be detained in servitude by any person whatsoever; and if, upon such prosecution, it shall appear that the pauper is entitled to his freedom in consequence of this act, a jury shall be empanelled to assess the damages for his detention.

III. And whereas it has been represented to this General Assembly, that Aberdeen, a negro man slave, hath labored a number of years in the public service at the lead mines, and for his meritorious services is entitled to freedom; *Be it therefore enacted,* That the said slave Aberdeen shall be, and he is hereby emancipated and declared free in as full and ample a manner as if he had been born free.

William Waller Hening (ed.), *The Statutes at Large: Being a Collection of All the Laws of Virginia, from the First Session of the Legislature, in the Year 1619* (13 vols.; Richmond, Va., 1810–1823).

A Slave's Petition for Freedom

The ideas brought to the fore by the struggle of the colonists for independence inspired the slaves to take steps toward obtaining their own liberty. Below is the petition of a Negro slave requesting his freedom.

To the Honorable the General Assembly of the Governor and Company of the State of Connecticut Now Sitting at Hartford in said State—

The memorial of Pomp a Negro man Slave belonging to the Estate of Jeremiah Leaming late of Norwalk in the County of Fairfield in said State, . . . —Clerk now absconded and with the Enemy at open war with the United States of America and under their protection humbly shewith—

That on the 11th Day of July last past the said Jeremiah Leaming with his Family Voluntarily join'd the British Troops in said Norwalk and with them then went over to Long Island and New York and hath ever since their [*sic*] continued under their protection—

That your Honors. Memoralist being unwilling to go with his said master over to the Enemy made his Escape from him while the said Troops were in said Norwalk and is held and Considered as a part of the Estate of his said Master and forfeited to the said State of Connecticut—

That the said Jeremiah Leamings Estate hath been a Special County Court held at Fairfield with and for the County of Fairfield on the 4th Tuesday of September last past Declared and adjudged forfeit to said State and since Administration hath been granted thereon to Samuel Gruman of Sd. Norwalk who is now about to Inventory the same wherein your Honors Memoralist must be included and considered a part of his master['s] Estate as your Honors Memoralist is advised notwithstanding your Honors Memoralist at the Time of his Sd. Masters Joining the Enemy veryly tho't and believed by his remaining in said Norwalk and preventing by his Escape as aforesd. his masters taking him with him over to the Enemy he should have obtained his Freedom from Slavery and that your Honors Memoralist is about Thirty Years of Age and of a firm and healthy Constitution and able to well-provide for himself and a Wife and Child and that his Wife is a free woman and your Honors Memoralist is advised that he cannot be Emancipated without your Honors Consent as he is now become the property of the Sd. State altho the Selectmen of Sd. Norwalk Judge your Honors Memoralist a proper Subject of Freedom — Wherefore your Honors Memoralist humbly prays your Honors to take his Case into your wise Consideration and resolve that he be freed from his State of Slavery or in such other way grant him such relief in the premises as your Honors in your great Wisdom shall Judge proper and he as in Duty Bound shall Ever pray Dated at Norwalk the 20th Day of October A.D. 1779

his
Pomp X
mark

Original in the State Archives, Connecticut State Library, Hartford. *Photostat courtesy of Dr. Lorenzo J. Greene, Lincoln University, Jefferson City, Mo.*

An Indenture for Servitude

Below is a typical indenture for the transfer of the services of a Negro girl.

Know all men by these Presants that I, Eathel Barcheld Lyon of Brimfield has This day Rec. of John McClister of Enfield Ten pounds LMO [lawful money] in full for a Neagrow Girl Named Vianus way Nine Years of Age. And Said Girl is to Serve the Said John McClister or Sum Other of Majesties Leagal Subjects till the Terme of Eighteen Years and As much longer As the Law Directs Allso the Said Lyon does by these Presants Warrant and Clames of All and All manner of persons Shall and will Warrant and for Ever Defend As witness my hand Seal this 23 day of Jan 1778

Eathel Barcheld Lyon

Signed Sealed and delivered

In presants us said girl
Thos. Berry is free of any
alement or
Distemper

Shevebiak Ballard

Original in the State Archives, Connecticut State Library, Hartford. *Copy courtesy of Dr. Lorenzo J. Greene, Lincoln University, Jefferson City, Mo.*

"To Be Sold"

The following advertisements for the sale of Negroes and cattle appeared in newspapers in 1780.

To be SOLD or LETT, for a term of years, a strong, hearty, likely NEGRO GIRL.

The Continental Journal (Boston), October 19, 1780.

To be SOLD, a likely Negro Boy, about eighteen years of Age, fit for to serve a Gentleman, to tend horses or to work in the Country.

The Continental Journal, October 26, 1780.

To be SOLD, a likely Negro Boy, about thirteen years old, well calculated to wait on a Gentleman. Inquire of Printer.

To be SOLD, a likely young Cow and Calf. Inquire of Printer.

The Independent Chronicle (Boston), December 14, 1780.

A Negro Child, soon expected, of a good breed, may be owned by any Person inclining to take it, and Money with it.

The Continental Journal, December 21, 1780.

A Negro Woman Petitions for Divorce

In the following document a Negro woman seeks, through legal means, to break the bonds of matrimony.

To the Hon[ble] the Council & house
of Representatives
Genr[l] Court Assembled
March AD 1780

Humbly Sheweth Mercy Turner of Pembrook wife of Philip Turner of Scituate yeoman, that on the 14 Day of September 1777 She was unfortunately married to the sd Philip, & that She had at that Time a proper Affection & Regard for him, & Ever Since been ready & Desirous of Discharging Every part of her Duty to him as a wife, & has frequently in her own Person, & by her friends, Solicited him to take Care of Support & live with her as a wife & Discharge towards her the Duties of an husband but although there never has Subsisted any Quarrel between them he has Ever Since their marriage behaved with the utmost Coldness & Strangeness towards her, Leaving her Company and bed. Since the 32 first Days & nights of their marriage, & utterly Refusing to Cohabit with her, nay your Petitioner is Constrained to Declare that She has never yet been known by him as a wife, from What Cause She Cannot Determine & therefore Cannot apply to the Supreem Court of marriage & Divorce, to be by their Decree Separated from him but, as She Conceives this Conduct & behavour is utterly inconsistent with the marriage Covenant & has a Tendency to Produce very great Evils. She humbly prays your Honr, to Enquire into the Circumstances of the Case & by an Act of the Legislature Dissolve those bonds which now operate as an unreasonable Restraint which Counteract Instead of Support the Principles of Society, & that She may be Again Restored to her Liberty & as in Duty bound will Ever Pray.

Mercy Turner

In Council March 30 1780

Orderd that Mercy Turner, Notify her husband Philip Turner of Scituate by Serving him with a Copy of sd Petition & this order to Shew Cause if any he has on thursday next why the Prayer thereof Should not be Granted And the Bonds of marriage between them be Declared void by Law to be made for that Purpose.

New York Historical Society

Jupiter Hammon on Slavery

Many blacks were militant in their attempts to cast off the bonds of slavery. Others, however, like the Negro poet Jupiter Hammon, believed in submissive behavior. In 1787, Hammon addressed his people on their duties as slaves.

. . . When I was at Hartford in Connecticut, where I lived during the war, I published several pieces which were well received, not only by those of my own colour, but by a number of the white people, who thought they might do good among their servants. This is one consideration, among others, that emboldens me now to publish what I have written to you. Another is, I think you will be more likely to listen to what is said, when you know it comes from a negro, one of your own nation and colour, and therefore can have no interest in deceiving you, or in saying any thing to you, but what he really thinks is your interest, and duty to comply with. My age, I think, gives me some right to speak to you, and reason to expect you will hearken to my advice. I am now upwards of seventy years old, and cannot expect, though I am well, and able to do almost any kind of business, to live much longer. I have passed the common bounds set for man, and must soon go the way of all the earth. I have had more experience in the world than the most of you, and I have seen a great deal of the vanity and wickedness of it. I have great reason to be thankful that my lot has been so much better than most slaves have had. I suppose I have had more advantages and privileges than most of you, who are slaves, have ever known, and I believe more than many white people have enjoyed, for which I desire to bless God, and pray that he may bless those who have given them to me. I do not, my dear friends, say these things about myself, to make you think that I am wiser or better than others; but that you might hearken, without prejudice, to what I have to say to you on the following particulars.

1st. Respecting obedience to masters.—Now whether it is right, and lawful, in the sight of God, for them to make slaves of us or not. I am certain that while we are slaves, it is our duty to obey our masters, in all their lawful commands, and mind them unless we are bid to do that which we know to be sin, or forbidden in God's word. . . . If a servant strives to please his master and studies and takes pains to do it, I believe there are but few masters who would use such a servant cruelly. Good servants frequently make good masters. If your master is really hard, unreasonable and cruel, there is no way so likely for you to convince him of it, as always to obey his commands, and try to serve him, and take care of his interest, and try to promote it all in your power. If you are proud and stubborn and always finding fault, your master will think the fault lies wholly on your side; but if you are humble, and meek, and bear all things patiently, your master may think he is wrong; if he does not, his neighbours will be apt to see it, and will befriend you, and try to alter his conduct. If this does not do, you must cry to him, who has the hearts of all men in his hands, and turneth them as the rivers of waters are turned.

2d. The particular I would mention, is honesty and faithfulness.

You must suffer me now to deal plainly with you, my dear brethren, for I do not mean to flatter, or omit speaking the truth, whether it is for you, or against you. How many of you are there who allow yourselves in stealing from your masters. It is very wicked for you not to take care of your masters goods, but how much worse is it to pilfer and steal from them, whenever you think you shall not be found out. This you must know is very wicked and provoking to God. There are none of you so ignorant, but that you must know that this is wrong. Though you may try to excuse yourselves, by saying that your masters are unjust to you, and though you may try to quiet your consciences in this way, yet if you are honest in owning the truth, you must think it is as wicked, and on some accounts more wicked, to steal from your masters, than from others.

We cannot certainly, have any excuse either for taking any thing that belongs to our masters, without their leave, or for being unfaithful in their business. It is our duty to be faithful, *not with eye service as men pleasers*. We have no right to stay when we are sent on errands, any longer than to do the business we were sent upon. All the time spent idly, is spent wickedly, and is unfaithfulness to our masters. In these things I must say, that I think many of you are guilty. I know that many of you endeavour to excuse yourselves, and say, that you have nothing that you can call your own, and that you are under great temptations to be unfaithful and take from your masters. But this will not do, God will certainly punish you for stealing and for being unfaithful. All that we have to mind is our own duty. If God has put us in bad circumstances, that is not our fault, and he will not punish us for it. If any are wicked in keeping us so, we cannot help it, they must answer to God for it. Nothing will serve as an excuse to us for not doing our duty. The same God will judge both them and us. Pray then my dear friends, fear to offend in this way, but be faithful to God, to your masters, and to your own souls. . . .

New York Public Library

"God Is Their Only Friend"—Othello

More typical of the attitudes of slaves concerning their bondage are the words of a man known only as "Othello." Written in 1788, this is probably the first recorded protest of a Negro against the "practice of stealing or bartering for human flesh."

. . . When the united colonies revolted from Great Britain, they did it upon this principle, "that all men are by nature and of right ought to be free."—After a long, successful, and glorious struggle for liberty, during which they manifested the firmest attachment to the rights of mankind, can they so soon forget the principles that then governed their determinations? Can Americans, after the noble contempt they expressed for tyrants, meanly descend to take up the scourge? Blush, ye revolted colonies, for having apostatized from your own principles!

Slavery, in whatever point of light it is considered, is repugnant to the feelings of nature, and inconsistent with the original rights of man. It ought, therefore, to be stigmatized for being unnatural; and detested for being unjust. . . .

The importation of slaves into America ought to be a subject of the deepest regret to every benevolent and thinking mind.—And one of the greatest defects in the federal system is the liberty it allows on this head. . . .

The practice of stealing or bartering for human flesh is pregnant with the most glaring turpitude, and the blackest barbarity of disposition.—For can any one say that this is doing as he would be done by? . . . Who can bear the thought of his relatives being torn from him by a savage enemy; carried to distant regions of the habitable globe, never more to return; and treated there as the unhappy Africans are in this country? Who can support the reflection of his father—his mother—his sister—or his wife—perhaps his children—being barbarously snatched away by a foreign invader, without the prospect of ever beholding them again? Who can reflect upon their being afterwards publicly exposed to sale—obliged to labor with unwearied assiduity—and because all things are not possible to be performed by persons so unaccustomed to robust exercise, scourged with all the rage and anger of malignity until their unhappy carcasses are covered with ghastly wounds and frightful contusions? Who can reflect on these things when applying the case to himself without being chilled with horror at circumstances so extremely shocking? . . .

In Maryland, where slaves are treated with as much lenity as perhaps they are anywhere, . . . they live in wretched cots that scarcely secure them from the inclemency of the weather, sleep in the ashes or on straw, wear the coarsest clothing, and subsist on the most ordinary food that the country produces. In all things they are subject to their master's absolute command, and, of course, have no will of their own. Thus circumstanced, they are subject to great brutality, and are often treated with it. In particular instances they may be better provided for in this state, but this suffices for a general description. But in the Carolinas . . . the cruelties that have been wantonly exercised on those miserable creatures are without a precedent in any other part of the world. . . .

Might not the inhabitants of Africa, with still greater justice on their side than we have on ours, cross the Atlantic, seize our citizens, carry them into Africa, and make slaves of them, provided they were able to do it? But should this really be the case, every corner of the globe would reverberate with the sound of African oppression, so loud would be their complaint. . . .

To whom are the wretched sons of Africa to apply for redress if their cruel master treats them with unkindness? To whom will they resort for protection if he is base enough to refuse it to them? The law is not their friend —alas! too many statutes are enacted against them. The world is not their friend—the iniquity is too general and extensive. No one who hath slaves of his own will protect those of another, less [lest] the practice should be retorted. Thus when their masters abandon them, their situation is destitute and forlorn, and God is their only friend! . . .

Othello, "Negro Slavery," *American Museum,* IV (July–December 1788).

Benjamin Banneker's Letter to Thomas Jefferson

In 1791, Benjamin Banneker, who was a black astronomer and surveyor, sent an almanac he had compiled to Secretary of State Thomas Jefferson. Accompanying the almanac was a letter in which Banneker encouraged Jefferson to put into practice those concepts of equality cited in the Declaration of Independence. Jefferson, in his note thanking Banneker for the gift, gave more than a hint at his philosophy of these matters when he wrote: "Nobody wishes more than I do to see such proofs as you exhibit, that nature has given to our black brethren talents equal to those of the other colors of men, and that the appearance of want of them is owing merely to the degraded condition of their existence both in Africa and America." Below is an excerpt from Banneker's letter to Jefferson.

. . . I suppose it is a truth too well attested to you, to need a proof here, that we are a race of beings, who have long labored under the abuse and censure of the world; that we have long been looked upon with an eye of contempt; and that we have long been considered rather brutish than human, and scarcely capable of mental endowments. . . .

Sir, I have long been convinced, that if your love for yourselves, and for your inestimable laws, which preserved to you the rights of human nature, was founded on sincerity, you could not but be solicitous, that every individual, of whatever rank or distinction, might with you equally enjoy the blessings thereof; neither could you rest satisfied short of the most active effusion of your exertions, in order to their promotion from any state of degradation, to which the unjustifiable cruelty and barbarism of men may have reduced them. . . .

Benjamin Banneker, *Copy of a Letter from Benjamin Banneker to the Secretary of State, with his Answer* (Philadelphia, 1792).

Rules for Conducting a Slave Sale

The following notice was posted in Brooklyn, New York, in 1790. It lists the rules to be observed in conducting the sale of a Negro slave and her child.

The Articles of this Vendue are as follows—

1st The highest Bidder to be the purchaser

2[d] Any person or persons, purchasing the said Wench and Child Agreeable to

Advertisement, Shall have four months Credit with given their Bond and Security if Required—

3[d] Any person or persons purchasing said Wench and Child and not complying as above the said Wench and Child shall be set up at Second Sale and if any Deficiency by said Second sale should Arise the first purchaser shall make it good if any [Overpledge?] the first purchaser shall Reap no benefit

Brooklyn William Elsworth Executor
April 23[d], 1790

New York Historical Society

"To the People of Colour"

Richard Allen and Absalom Jones were free Negroes living in Philadelphia. In 1787, Allen left St. George's Methodist Episcopal Church and subsequently organized Bethel African Methodist Episcopal Church, the first of its kind in the country. Absalom Jones was the first Negro to become an Episcopal priest. Allen and Jones worked to aid the sufferers in Philadelphia during the calamity and disorder of the yellow fever epidemic of 1793. At that time, they issued their address "To the People of Colour."

Feeling an engagement of mind for your welfare, we address you with an affectionate sympathy, having been ourselves slaves, and as desirous of freedom as any of you; yet the hands of bondage were so strong, that no way appeared for our release, yet at times a hope arose in our hearts that a way would open for it, and when our minds were mercifully visited with the feeling of the love of God, then these hopes increased, and a confidence arose that he would make way for our enlargement, and as a patient waiting was necessary, we were sometimes favoured with it, at other times we were very impatient, then the prospect of liberty almost vanished away, and we were in darkness and perplexity.

We mention our experience to you, that your hearts may not sink at the discouraging prospects you may have, and that you may put your trust in God, who sees your condition, and as a merciful father pitieth his children, so doth God pity them that love him; and as your hearts are inclined to serve God, you will feel an affectionate regard towards your masters and mistresses, and the whole family where you live, this will be seen by them, and tend to promote your liberty, especially with such as have feeling masters, and if they are otherwise you will have the favour and love of God dwelling in your hearts, which you will value more than any thing else, which will be a consolation in the worst condition you can be in, and no master can deprive you of it; and as life is short and uncertain, and the chief end of our having a being in this world, is to be prepared for a better, we wish you to think of this more than any thing else: then will you have a view of that freedom which the sons of God enjoy; and if the troubles of your condition end with your lives, you will be admitted to the freedom which God hath prepared for those of all colours that love him; here the power of the most cruel master ends, and all sorrow and tears are wiped away.

To you who are favoured with freedom, let your conduct manifest your gratitude toward the compassionate masters who have set you free, and let no rancour or ill-will lodge in your breasts for any bad treatment you may have received from any; if you do, you transgress against God, who will not hold you guiltless, he would not suffer it even in his beloved people Israel, and can you think he will allow it unto us?

There is much gratitude due from our colour towards the white people, very many of them are instruments in the hand of God for our good, even such as have held us in captivity, are now pleading our cause with earnestness and zeal; and we are sorry to say, that too many think more of the evil, than of the good they have received, and instead of taking the advice of their friends, turn from it with indifference; much depends upon us for the help of our colour more than many are aware; if we are lazy and idle, the enemies of freedom plead it as a cause why we ought not to be free, and say we are better in a state of servitude, and that giving us our liberty would be an injury to us, and by such conduct we strengthen the bands of oppression, and keep many in bondage who are more worthy than ourselves; we intreat you to consider the obligations we lay under, to help forward the cause of freedom, we who know how bitter the cup is of which the slave hath to drink, O how ought we to feel for those who yet remain in bondage? Will even our friends excuse, will God pardon us, for the part we act in making strong the hands of the enemies of our colour.

New York Public Library

A Negro Who "Changed Color"

The medical report below contains an account of a free Negro, Henry Moss, who "changed color." It is possible that this is the first written account of the medical condition known as leukodermia.

Philadelphia 9th mo. 13th. 1796

This day Henry Moss, an African Descendant came to see me, and produced a Certificate of which the following is a Copy—

"I do hereby certify, that I have been well acquainted, with Henry Moss, who is the bearer hereof upwards of thirty years, the whole of which time he has supported an Honest character, in the late War he enlisted with me, in the Continental Army as a Soldier and behaved himself very well as such from the first of my acquaintance with him — 'Till within two or three years past, he was of as dark a complexion, as any African, & without any known cause, it has changed to what it is at present, he was free born, and served his time with Major John Brinttate of Charlotte County — Given under my Hand the 2nd September 1794.

Joseph Holt
Bedford County"

Henry Moss has all the Features, common to the African Race, tho not strongly marked, his Stature is about 5F 6 Inchs his age 42, his Hair is changing from the black wool of his countrymen to a soft curly Hair, easily drawn out to the length of several Inches; the Borders of his Face, from the Roots of his Hair on the sinciput, about an Inch in Breadth, extending round by his Ear on the right side is perfectly fair as any European, this stripe of white extends with some encrease of breadth under his Chin & upwards, on his left Cheek to within two Inches of his left Ear where his African Color, causes an interruption about 1 Inch broad but irregular in its approach from the left Corner of his mouth to the descending line of his left Ear where it descends by the left Ear side of his neck, of the breadth of about two Inches for the Depth of about 3 Inches but is irregularly indented, and insulated on the border like a map of Islands & Peninsulas, on the Chart of a Sea Coast — The whole of the back of his neck, Breast, Arms & Legs, so far as it was decent to expose them to a mixed company, were of a clear European Complexion, interspersed with small specks of the African Color, as Freckles on the Skin of a fair Woman appear in Summer, from the Eye Lids above both Eyes, the African complexion has entirely disappeared, for nearly One Inch in Latitude; under the right Eye there is a small white streak, & under the left Eye a broader one nearly half an Inch, but irregularly indented as above mentioned, around his Mouth is a streak of white, also irregularly indented, shaded by . . . another streak of the African Complexion reaching nearly to his Chin, under which he has a very fair European Complexion all around his neck, his arms & Legs are perfectly fair, the backs & palms of his Hands, are also perfectly fair, on the sides of his Hands from the Wrists to the end of his Thumbs & Fingers there are stripes of his former Color & on the outside of all his Thumbs & Fingers, there are indented spots of it, but generally between the Limbs & wherever Skin meets Skin & is covered by clothing the change is perfect from the Color of an African, to the Color of a fair European, the whole Area of African Color, I am persuaded if regularly measured would not amount to one square Foot — His Hair is undergoing a similar change, & whenever a white Spot can be discovered, it appears soft & long like that of an European, where the Skin remains of the African Color the Hair is crisped like wool — Upon pressing his Skin with my Finger the part pressed appeared white as in my own Skin & on removing the pressure of my Finger the Blood rushed in and shewed a suffusion of red. . . .

I examined the Borders of the black & white skin with a glass known in Ireland by the name of a Linen Teller . . . and it plainly appeared that the change was not external, by the pulling off of the Epidermis, but by the Dissolution of what Clarkson in his Prize Treatise, has after the Physiologists called the Corpus Mucas & between the Dermis & Epidermis, there is no Fissure or change in the Skin, but an Elevation of about a line (magnified distance) between the fair skin & the black, rising gradually till the two meet together, without a discontinuity of the external surface — The following is his own acct [account] of his Genealogy—his Paternal Grandfather was born in Africa, & his Grandmother was an Indian native of this Country, his Father Issue of this marriage married a Mulattoe born of an African Father & Irish Mother, his Maternal Grandfather was born in Africa — About Feb. 1792 he first began to perceive a change in his Skin, the first appearance was about the roots of his Finger Nails, which extended to the first joints & has gone little further in that direction, about two months after the back of his neck began to change & extended downward & round his body & gradually descended to most parts covered by his Clothes the change was slow for the first year, & more rapid the second year, the Alteration was mostly made during the Summer or Warm Weather, & could not be perceived to make any progress during Winter or cold Weather — He says he came to this City Friday 26th July, and that the African part of his complexion on his Face and Hands has visibly diminished, since he came to Town (this is confirmed by Stephen Paschall & others who saw him at two periods about 13 days apart in which time the difference was abundantly perceptible to the Eye — He says he was shaved this morning by a Barber & did not feel any obstruction to the Razor, where it passed from the white part of his Face to the black or on its return, which must have been at every stroke experienced if there was any discontinuity of the Skin at the Borders — Since the change of his Skin, he feels the heat of the Sun on his Shoulders, much more than formerly & has had Blisters & Freckles raised on every part, which holes in his Clothes exposed to the Action of the Sun, and that he feels the cold much more sensibly than before — I asked him a great number of questions tending to discover, whether any alteration in his mode of life or diet or his Health or cutamous [*sic*] Disorders or Remedies used for their removal or any other Physical cause, had produced the change but nothing satisfactory on this Head could be drawn from his answers—

11 mo. 22 Henry Moss called on me again, I examined his Face, Hands, Breasts, Legs & Thighs & found that the white had considerably increased & the black diminished since I last saw him, so that I have no doubt the change is gradually proceeding & should he live over another Summer or two it will be perfected.

Miers Fisher

New York Historical Society

The Last Words of Abraham Johnstone

Abraham Johnstone was hanged for an unknown offense on July 8, 1797, in Woodbury, New Jersey. Shortly before his execution, he wrote the following address to point out the hypocrisy of those who pay lip service to "natural rights and general freedom" yet continue to inflict the "cruel and ignominious stripes of slavery."

. . . The continual wars and dissentions between the Aborigines and the settlers left the settlers but little time to cultivate their lands, and besides they were too few to carry on husbandry with any success, at least not so extensively as to enable them to benefit themselves by trade in the staple commodities of the country, and Guinea Negroes having some short time before been introduced into the West Indies and found extremely serviceable, they were next introduced into this country for they having tried in vain to make slaves of the Aborigines. but having found all their attempts fruitless they next turned their thoughts to the importation of our colour, particularly to the southward, and it increased astonishingly until the colonies declared their independance, and from that time the importation annually decreased until at last the finishing blow was given to that most inhuman and diabolical trade by an act of Congress, which expressly prohibits the further importation of negroes into any part of the United States, so to that ever memorable era when the doctrine of nonresistance was exploded, the unalienable rights of man were asserted, and the United States of America were declared sovereign free and independent we may ascribe our present dawning hopes of universal freedom. It was then that the prospect of total emancipation from slavery which now begins to brighten upon us had birth, it was then that freedom, liberty, and the natural rights of mankind ennobled every sentiment, banished every slavish regard, and expanded the heart with every thing great noble and beneficient, the generous flame spread with rapidity, and communicated itself to every rank and degree; every bosom glowed with an emanated ardour emulative of its noble and exalted source, and all ages and persons, with transports unspeakable thronged around the standard of liberty—but still my dear brethren we were forgotten, or we were not conceived worthy their regard or attention, being looked on as a different species: Even the patriotic who stood forth the champions of liberty, and in asserting the natural rights of all mankind used the most persuasive eloquence the most powerful rhetoric and choicest language the rich treasury of words could afford, those who undauntedly stood forth day by day the advocates of liberty, at night would be cruel, rigid and inexorable tyrants. How preposterously absurd must an impartial observer think the man whom he sees one moment declaring with a most incredible volubility in favour of natural rights and general freedom, and the next moment with his own hands for some very trivial offence inflicting the cruel and ignominious stripes of slavery, and riveting its shackles—surely in the eyes of any man of sense such conduct must be irreconcilable and just reason to doubt the soundness of his principles as a patriot and a lover of freedom, . . . therefore it justly exposed them to the scoff and derision of their enemies both at home, and abroad,—The New-England states first saw into that, or if they did not see into it first, they were the first that were noble minded, generous and disinterested enough to set all their slaves free. Individuals there, first nobly and generously set the glorious example, which was soon after followed by every individual in their states without the intervention of the legislatures of either, all they have done being the passing laws in each respective state to prohibit slavery in future, and at this time there is not one slave throughout the great populous and flourishing states, that compose New-England, and which states are generally peopled by Presbyterians. New-Jersey was the next that endeavoured to follow the glorious example, the Quaker society therein have manumised and set free all the slaves in their possession or in any wise their property, and the like has been done by many other good characters, and they have uniformly stood our friends, and are now using every effort in their power to render the emancipation of our colour general, and have us admitted to the rights of freedom as citizens in this state, in which truly laudable, and generous design they are now ably seconded in this county by some worthy men of other religious persuasions, whom together with all the friends of freedom, and our colour may God bless and prosper, and grant them health a length of days, fortitude and perseverance to put their designs in execution, and that success may crown their endeavours is my sincere wish and prayer.

From the first bringing of our colour into this country they have been constantly kept to the greatest toil and labour, to drudge incessantly yet without the smallest hopes of a reward, and, oftentimes denied a sufficient portion of food to suffice the cravings of nature, or raiment sufficient to hide their nakedness or shield them from the inclemency of the weather. Yet, labouring under all those hardships and difficulties, the most unheard of cruelties and punishments were daily inflicted on us, for what? for not performing impossibilities, for not doing what was impossible for human nature or strength to have done within the time allotted. And if the most pressing hunger should compel us to take from that master by stealth what we were sure to be denied if we asked, to satisfy our craving appetites, the most wanton and dreadful punishments were immediately inflicted on us even to a degree of inhumanity and cruelty. That I do not exaggerate is I dare say known to many of ye that hear me, or that may hereafter read this address to you, and therefore I appeal to ye, as personal knowledge of the facts I have here stated, I declare myself that I speak from experience—I was born to the southward of here, in the state of Delaware, and a slave, and had five masters before I was free, all of whom liked and loved me, and the last particularly, for having once saved his life when another negro man attempted killing him with a knife, but I instantly throwing myself between, saved my master who did not see the knife the fellow had concealed and endeavoured to stab him with. That together with my being always fond of work, and attentive to his interest gained me his friendship and confidence, and induced him to give me my manumission. When I was a slave I was never treated as rigidly or as cruelly as thousands have been to my own knowledge, yet God knows I have suffered incredible and innumerable hardships—ye ought therefore my dear brethren to account it a very great happiness and to bless God that you are in a country where the laws are wholesome, and where the majority of the leading characters are liberal minded, humane, generous and extremely well disposed to all our colour, and endeavour by a just, upright, sober, honest, and diligently industrious manner of life and a purity of morals to improve that favourable disposition in them, and if possible ripen it into esteem for ye all.

New York Public Library

A Petition on Behalf of Negro Sailors

This petition concerning the treatment received by black seamen in southern ports was sent to the governing body of Massachusetts in 1801.

To the Honorable . . . Court assembled.

The petition of the undersigned shipowners and other citizens of Boston respectfully represents.

That in several of the Southern States when a vessel arrives in their ports with any colored cook, steward or seaman on board, he is taken from the vessel and confined in jail during the whole period of her remaining in port, and the captain before he can be discharged is obliged to pay for his board & other expenses. Many free citizens of Masstts. are in this way subjected to a cruel and wrongful imprisonment, in direct violation of the Constitution of the United States which confers on the citizens of each State the privileges of citizens in every other State. . . .

Your petitioners are persuaded that the objects of this resolve in the protection of our citizens will be more fully effected by having agents for the State in some of the principal Southern ports. They therefore respectfully pray that the governor be directed to appoint an agent for the State to reside for the term of one year in the City of Charleston & one other in the City of New Orleans, who are to ascertain as far as possible the names & number of citizens of Massachusetts who may be imprisoned in those Cities respectively, on account of their color, during their presence there to use such measures at the expense of this State as they may deem expedient to procure their release, and to bring & prosecute one or more suits in behalf of any citizens so imprisoned for the purpose of having the legality of such imprisonment tried & determined by the Courts of the United States.

Samuel E. Sewall's Draft of a Petition.

New York Historical Society

Thomas Jefferson Buys a Slave

The following copy of a bill of sale offers documentary evidence of Thomas Jefferson's attitude toward slavery. Although he purchased the slave John, he did so for only a period of years, after which the man was to be freed.

William Baker To Thomas Jefferson	Bill of Sale Recorded in Liber V. N° 21 folio 30 One of the Land Records of Washington County in the District of Columbia—

Wherein the said William Baker sells to the said Thomas Jefferson for the consideration of four hundred dollars a negro man named John for and during the term of Eleven years from the date of the said Bill of sale, which date is the third day of July 1804. which said Bill of sale is acknowledged before John Oakley a Justice of the Peace—

At the bottom of which Bill of sale is the following—

This is to certify and declare that this paper contains true Copies of two deeds, the originals of which are in my possession which deeds are hereby assented to ratified and confirmed, and the said negro man John therein named is hereby declared to be entitled to his freedom on the 22nd day of July which shall be in the year One thousand eight hundred & fifteen given under my hand this 6th day of October 1804—

Thomas Jefferson

Witness
William A. Burwell

Carter G. Woodson Papers, Library of Congress.

Jefferson's Ideas on Colonization

In August 1800, the first of a series of planned slave insurrections was discovered. Gabriel Prosser, with several thousand followers, had planned an uprising in Virginia. But two house Negroes revealed the plot to their master; the rebels were foiled by a storm, and dozens were arrested. Prosser and at least thirty-four others involved in the insurrection were executed. This incident aroused concern among many of the leading white citizens of Virginia. President Thomas Jefferson suggested that perhaps slaves who were seized as insurgents should be deported to a colony of ex-slaves rather than be executed. At first, Jefferson suggested that a colony be established in the United States for this purpose. By 1802, however, he had apparently changed his mind. In a letter to Rufus King, a prominent Virginia citizen, Jefferson advocated that Negroes found guilty of insurgency be colonized in Africa.

. . . A great disposition to insurgency has manifested itself among them, which, in one instance, in the State of Virginia, broke out into actual insurrection. This was easily suppressed; but many of those concerned (between twenty and thirty, I believe) fell victims to the law. So extensive an execution could not but excite sensibility in the public mind, and beget a regret that the laws had not provided for such cases, some alternative, combining more mildness with equal efficiency. The Legislature of the State . . . took the subject into consideration, and have communicated to me through the Governor of the State, their wish that some place could be provided, out of the limits of the United States, to which slaves guilty of insurgency might be transported; and they have particularly looked to Africa as offering the most desirable receptacle. We might, for this purpose, enter into negotiations with the natives, on some part of the coast, to obtain a settlement; and, by establishing an African company, combine with it commercial operations, which might not only reimburse expenses, but procure profit also. But there being already such an establishment on that coast by the English Sierra Leone Company, made for the express purpose of colonizing civilized blacks to that country, it would seem better, by incorporating our emigrants with theirs, to make one strong, rather than two weak colonies. This would be the more desirable because the blacks settled at Sierra Leone, having chiefly gone from the States, would often receive among those whom we should send, their acquaintances and relatives. The object of this letter is to ask . . . you to enter into conference with such persons, private and public, as would be necessary to give us permission to send thither the persons under contemplation. . . . They are not felons, or common malefactors, but persons guilty of what the safety of society, under actual circumstances, obliges us to treat as a crime, but which their feelings may represent in a far different shape. They will be a valuable acquisition to the settlement, . . . and well calculated to cooperate in the plan of civilization.

. . . The consequences of permitting emancipation to become extensive, unless a condition of emigration be annexed to them, furnish matter of solicitude to the Legislature of Virginia. Although provision for the settlement of emancipated negroes might perhaps be obtained nearer home than Africa, yet it is desirable that we should be free to expatriate this description of people also to the colony of Sierra Leone, if considerations respecting either themselves or us should render it more expedient. I pray you, therefore, to get the same permission extended to the reception of these as well as the [insurgents]. Nor will there be a selection of bad subjects; the emancipations, for the most part, being either of the whole slaves of the master, or of such individuals as have particularly deserved well. The latter are most frequent.

Paul L. Ford (ed.), *The Writings of Thomas Jefferson* (10 vols.; New York, 1892–1899).

A Foreigner Views the Peculiar Institution

Slavery was not practiced to any degree in Europe and, as a result, was one of the institutions in this country of interest to travelers from abroad. The following unusual account of the conditions of slavery was written by a Frenchman who traveled through Louisiana in 1802. It should be noted that the Louisiana Purchase was not made by Thomas Jefferson until 1803 and that the area visited by M. Duvallon was inhabited by many people of French descent.

Nothing can be more simple than the burial of a slave; he is put into the plainest coffin, knocked together by a carpenter of his own colour, and carried unattended by mourners to the neighbouring grave-field. The most absolute democracy, however, reigns there; the planter and slave, confounded with one another, rot in conjunction. *Under ground precedency is all a jest!*

The only cloathing of a slave is a simple woollen garment; it is given to them at the beginning of winter. And will it be believed, that the master, to indemnify himself for this expense, retrenches half an hour from his negro's hours of respite, during the short days of the rigorous season!

Their ordinary food is indian corn, or rice and beans, boiled in water, without fat or salt. To them nothing comes amiss. They will devour greedily racoon, opossum, squirrels, wood-rats, and even the crocodile; leaving to the white people the roebuck and rabbit, which they sell them when they kill those animals.

They raise poultry and hogs, but seldom eat either. . . .

Their smoaky huts admit both wind and rain. An anecdote offers itself to my pen on this subject, which will exhibit the frigid indifference of the colonists of Louisiana towards every thing that interests humanity. Being on a visit at a plantation on the Mississippi, I walked out one fine evening in winter, with some ladies and gentlemen, who had accompanied me from the town, and the planters at whose house we were entertained. We approached the quarter where the huts of the negroes stood. "Let us visit the negroes," said one of the party; and we advanced towards the door of a miserable hut, where an old negro woman came to the threshold in order to receive us, but so decrepit as well as old, that it was painful for her to move.

Notwithstanding the winter was advanced, she was partly naked; her only covering being some old thrown away rags. Her fire was a few chips, and she was parching a little corn for supper. Thus she lived abandoned and forlorn; incapable from old age to work any longer, she was no longer noticed.

But independently of her long services, this negro woman had formerly suckled and brought up two brothers of her master, who made one of our party. She perceived him, and accosting him, said, "My master, when will you send one of your carpenters to repair the roof of my hut? Whenever it rains, it pours down upon my head." The master lifting his eyes, directed them to the roof of the hut, which was within the reach of his hand. "I will think of it," said he,—"You will think of it," said the poor creature. "You always say so, but never do it."—"Have you not," rejoined the masters, "two grandsons who can mend it for you?"—"But are they mine," said the old woman, "do they not work for you, and are you not my son yourself? who suckled and raised your two brothers? who was it but Irrouba? Take pity then on me, in my old age. Mend at least the roof of my hut, and God will reward you for it."

I was sensibly affected; it was *le cri de la bonne nature*. And what repairs did the poor creature's roof require? What was wanting to shelter her from the wind and rain of heaven? A few shingles!—"I will think of it," repeated her master, and departed.

The ordinary punishment inflicted on the negroes of the colony is a whipping. What in Europe would condemn a man to the galleys or the gallows incurs here only the chastisement of the whip. But then a king having many subjects does not miss them after their exit from this life, but a planter could not lose a negro without feeling the privation. . . .

The most common maladies of the negroes are slight fevers in the spring, more violent ones in the summer, dysenteries in autumn, and fluxions of the breast in winter. Their bill of mortality, however, is not very considerable. The births exceed the deaths.

The language of the negro slaves, as well as of a great number of the free mulattoes, is a patois derived from the French, and spoken according to rules of corruption. There are some house-slaves, however, who speak French with not less purity than their masters.

Berquin Duvallon, *Travels in Louisiana and the Floridas, in the Year 1802* (New York, 1806).

Freedom Papers

Free Negroes in the South were often forced to carry papers verifying their status as free men. This document is illustrative of the type issued to many free blacks before the Civil War.

State of North Carolina }
New Hanover County }
Personally appeared
before me W J Harriss a Justice
of the peace in and for said County:
Levi Nichols who being duly sworn
upon the Holy Evangelists of Almighty God:
Says that he is acquainted with B. G. Hazel
a free Coloured person about thirty one
years of age. Stout built and rather
dark. Said Hazel was born of free
pearants and have always passed in
the State of North Carolina as a free
man. he was born in the town of
Wilmington County of New Hanover
and State of North Carolina, and
Sustained a good moral charactor while
in said town. He left Wilmington N. C.
about One year ago

Sworn to & subscribed before
me. 29th day of September
1858. And I certify that
said affiant is a creditable
person.
W J Harriss J P

Levi Nichols

Original in the possession of David W. Hazel, Central State University, Wilberforce, Ohio.

A Negro Woman Petitions to Keep Her Family Together

An early Virginia law required that emancipated Negroes leave the state as soon as they became free. In this document, a black woman petitions for the right of her slave husband to remain in Virginia after his manumission.

Petition Number, 5870,
Southampton County, Dec. 9, 1811.

To the Honorable, the Speaker & house of Delegates of . . . Virginia.

The Petition of Jemima Hunt (a free woman of color) of the County of Southampton, humbly sheweth—that sometime in the month of November, in the Year 1805—Your petitioner entered into a contract with a certain Benj Barrett of said County for the purchase of Stephen a Negro man Slave, the property of said Barrett, & husband to your petitioner, for the sum of ten pounds annually for ten years, and the said Barrett farther bound himself to take the sum of ninety pounds if paid within five years & at the expiration of that time to make a complete bill of sale for the said Negro Stephen, which will appear by reference being made to the obligation entered into between the said Barrett and your petitioner. Your petitioner farther states that she has paid the full amount of the purchase money and has obtained a bill of sale for the said negro Stephen; who (being her husband) she intended to emancipate after she had complyed with her contract,—but in some short time after as your petitioner has been informed an act of Assembly was passed, prohibiting slaves, being emancipated after the law went into operation, from residing in the state—Your petitioner farther states that she has a numerous family of Children by the said Stephen, who are dependent upon the daily labor of herself & husband for a support, & without the assistance of her husband Stephen they must suffer or become burthensome to their county.

Therefore your petitioner humbly prays that the legislature would take her case into consideration & pass a law to permit the said negro Stephen to reside in the State after emancipation, and to enjoy all the privileges that other free people of colour are entitled to & as in duty bound Your Petitioner will ever pray, etc.

Courtesy of the Association for the Study of Negro Life and History.

Negroes in the War of 1812

The War of 1812 brought the United States once again into open conflict with Great Britain. Negroes did not participate as actively as they had done in the Revolution, for two reasons. First, most of the states that contained a large number of free Negroes were not in sympathy with the war. Second, and more significant, there seems to have been an increased mistrust of armed Negroes; therefore, most states were reluctant to use them as combatants.

Negroes did, however, serve in two regiments from New York: in the navy, especially with Perry on Lake Erie; and with Jackson at the Battle of New Orleans. In the following letter addressed to General John Armstrong, a Pennsylvanian is requesting that he be allowed to raise Negro troops in his state. This was not accomplished, but Negroes did give their services in fatigue duty.

INSPECTOR GENERALS OFFICE
3rd M. District
Wednesday August 23rd 1814.

General John Armstrong
Secretary of War, Washington,

Sir I have just been informed by my good friend Col. A. Denniston that you have in contemplation to raise a Regiment of Blacks, should this be the case, I solicit permission to tender my services to assist in Recruiting such a Regiment, confident that in Penns[a] (the place of my nativity) I should be able in a short period to enlist from 3 to 500 men, any information or recommendations you may require respecting me, shall be furnished from the most respectable Military characters in this and the 4th M. District.

Permit me to refer you to the Secretary of the Navy and Richard Rush Esq. who I believe have some knowledge of me,

I am present detailed by the Comdg. Genl. of this district as Acting Inspector General during the Arrest of Col. N. Gray.

Soliciting your attention to my application
I am With sentiments of the highest respect
Sir Your Mo. Obdt. Servt.

P. P. Walter Capt: 32nd I.
Actg. Inspector General 3rd M. District

Magazine of American History, XXII (September 1889).

In Praise of Negro Soldiers

Below are testimonies by members of the United States Congress commending the service of black soldiers during the Revolutionary War and the War of 1812.

Hon. Mr. Burgess of Rhode Island, said on the floor of Congress Jan. 28, 1828:

At the commencement of the Revolutionary War, Rhode Island had a number of this description of people [slaves]. A regiment of them were enlisted into the continental service, and no braver men met the enemy in battle; but not one of them was permitted to be a soldier until he had first been made a freeman.

Said the Hon. Mr. Martindale of New York, in Congress, Jan. 22, 1838:

Blacks who had been slaves, were entrusted as soldiers in the war of the revolution; and I, myself, saw a battalion of them, as fine, martial looking men as I ever saw attached to the northern army in the last war, on its march from Plattsburg to Sackett's Harbor.

Said the Hon. Charles Miner, of Pennsylvania, in Congress, February 7th, 1828:

The African race make excellent soldiers. Large numbers of them were with Perry, and aided to gain the brilliant victory on Lake Erie. A whole battalion of them was distinguished for its soldierly appearance.

The Hon. Mr. Clarke, in the Convention which revised the Constitution of New York, in 1821, said . . .:

In the war of the revolution these people helped to fight your battles by land and by sea. Some of your states were glad to turn out corps of colored men, and to stand shoulder to shoulder with them. In your late war they contributed largely towards your most splendid victories. On Lakes Erie and Champlain, where your fleets triumphed over a foe superior in numbers, and engines of death, they were manned in a large proportion with men of color.

R. B. Lewis, *Light and Truth, Collected from the Bible and Ancient and Modern History: Containing the Universal History of the Colored and the Indian Races from the Creation of the World to the Present Time* (Boston, 1844).

A Free Negro Family Hires a Slave

The Jonathan Roberts family, originally of North Carolina, is one of the oldest Negro families for whom a written record remains. The earliest papers go back to 1734, when the death of a three-year-old child was listed in the family diary. In the following material, it will be seen that this free Negro family engaged in the practice of hiring slave labor.

On demand the 25 of December next, we, Jonathan Roberts and Willis Roberts, promise to pay to Mathias DuBerry, guardian of Martha Haley, the sum of ten dollars and one cent, being for the hire of Negro Eady with one child, until the 25 of December. Witness our hands and seals this 30th day of December 1816.

Witness—William Funnel

Jonathan Roberts
Willis Roberts

We promise to furnish Eady with a summer suit and a winter suit of clothes. Also the usual clothing for the child and a hat and blanket and a pair of shoes for Eady. Witness our hands this 30th.

William

Jonathan Roberts and Family Papers, Library of Congress.

A Black Man's View of Life in the South

Willis Roberts, of the Roberts settlement in Hamilton County, Indiana, decided he could no longer remain in the section of the country to which he had migrated. Upon receiving the news of Willis' determination to return to his native North Carolina, brother James wrote the following sage advice.

After leaving you on the 15th, day of February 1830, I feel it a duty for me to write a few lines to inform you of my mind on what you are going to do, not to try to put you out of your mind for I am willing for every man to be persuaded in his own mind, for I will say if it was my will to go to Africa I will affirm that I would do it if I believed it was right.

It seems very plain to me that you are now going to make one of the worst mistakes that you ever made, in many ways. The first is that you are taking your children to an old country that is worn out and to slave on, where they are in between two fires as I may call them, for it is well known to me that where there is slavery it is not a good place for us to live, for they are the most of them very disagreeable and think themselves above free people of color.

We are always in danger of them doing us injury by some way or other. We are now away from them and I think it the best for me when I am out of such a country to stay away. I want you as a friend to look at these things and remember how times have altered since you could remember. To think that you are a going to take your small children to that place and can't tell how soon you may be taken away from them and they may come under the hands of some cruel slave holder, and you know that if they can get a colored child they will use them as bad again as they will one of their own slaves, it is right that parents should think of this, most especially if they are going to the very place and know it at the same time.

I would not this night, if I had children, take them to such a place and there to stay for the best five farms in three miles around where we came from, for I think I should be going to do something to bring them to see trouble and not enjoy themselves as free men but be in a place where they are not able to speak for their rights, the master takes his servant and makes them come to and do what he will. We dare not say you did so and so or made Negro do so without we can prove it by a white man and many of them will turn their backs when they think they would be witness for us.

I cannot do myself justice to think of living in such a country. When I think of it I can't tell how any man of color can think of going there with small children. It has been my intention ever since I had notice of such if I lived to be a man and God was willing I would leave such a place.

I wish you well and all your family and I hope that you all may do well, as much so as any people I ever saw or ever shall see, and I hope that you may see what you are going to do before it is too late. This is from the heart of one who wishes you well. . . .

James Roberts to Willis Roberts,
State of Indiana

Jonathan Roberts and Family Papers, Library of Congress.

Paul Cuffee's Diary

Paul Cuffee was an exceptional man in his day. Born on the Elizabeth Islands in 1759, he studied and later taught navigation. His family had moved to the Massachusetts mainland while Cuffee was quite young, and he had faced racial discrimination at an early age. While actively resisting taxation without the rights of citizenship in Massachusetts, Cuffee became interested in colonization in Africa. In 1811, he outfitted a ship and, accompanied by a crew of nine Negroes, sailed for Sierra Leone. The following excerpts are from the diary he kept during the expedition.

1mo. 20th. 19 days out from Philadelphia to Sierra Leone.

Our minds were collected together to wait on the Lord notwithstanding we were on the great deep.

2mo. 2. At three A.M. wind and sea struck us down on our beam ends, washed John Masters overboard, but by the help of some loose rigging he regained the ship again.

2mo. 21st. The dust of Africa lodged on our rigging. We judged that land to be about twenty-five leagues off.

2mo. 24th. At 10 A.M. sounded and got bottom for the first ground that we got on the coast of Africa. Sixty-five fathoms.

3mo. 1st. We came to Sierra Leone road.

3mo. 4th. An invitation was given me this day to dine with the Governor, at whose table an extensive observation took place of the slave trade and the unsuccessfulness of the colony of Sierra Leone.

3mo. 5th. Visited the school of 30 girls, which is a pleasing prospect in Sierra Leone.

3mo. 13th. King Thomas came on board to see me. He was an old man, gray headed, appeared to be sober and grave. I treated him with civility, and made him a present of a bible, a history of Elizabeth Webb, a Quaker, and a book of essays on War; together with several other small pamphlets accompanied with a letter of advise from myself, such as appeared to be good to hand to the King for the use and encouragement of the nations of Africa. He and retinue were thirteen in number. I served him with victuals, but it appeared that there was *rum* wanting *but none was given.*

3mo. 14. King George from Bullion Shore sent his messenger on board, with a present of three chickens and invited me over to see him.

3mo. 17. This day being the first day of the week we went ashore to the church, and in the afternoon to the new Methodist.

3mo. 18. This day I went to Bullion Shore in order to visit the King George, King of Bullion, who received and treated us very cordially. I presented the King with a bible, a testament, a treatise of Benjamin Holmes, a history of Elizabeth Webb, and an epistle from the yearly meeting, and a history, or called a short history of a long travel from Babel to Bethel.

3mo. 19. Visiting families on Sierra Leone, found many of them without bibles, and others who had bibles with out the living substance of the spirit.

3mo. 28. I breakfasted with the Governor Columbine and after breakfast had conference with him on the subject of the country, and settling in it—to good satisfaction.

3mo. 31. Attended the church. The Mendingo men have the Scriptures in their tongue, viz the old testament, but deny the new testament. They own Mahomet a prophet.

Cuffee Papers, New Bedford (Massachusetts) Public Library.

The American Colonization Society's Tribute to Paul Cuffee

Cuffee made two trips to Sierra Leone before his death in 1817. As a man of color who regarded colonization as an answer to the Negroes' struggle for equality, he was highly regarded by the American Colonization Society. In the first annual report of the society, this tribute was paid to Cuffee.

The managers cannot omit the testimony of Captain Paul Cuffe so well known in Africa, Europe, and America, for his active and large benevolence, and for his zeal and devoted-ness to the cause of the people of color. The opportunities of Captain Cuffe of forming a correct opinion were superior perhaps to those of any man in America. His judgment was clear and strong, and the warm interest he took in whatever related to the happiness of that class of people is well known. The testimony of such a man is sufficient to out weigh all the unfounded predictions and idle surmises of those opposed to the plan of this society. He had visited twice the coast of Africa, and became well acquainted with the country and its inhabitants. He states that, upon his opinion alone he could have taken to Africa at least two thousand people of color from Boston and its neighborhood. In the death of Paul Cuffe the society has lost a most useful advocate, the people of color a warm and disinterested friend, and society a valuable member. His character alone ought to be sufficient to rescue the people to which he belonged from the unmerited aspersions which have been cast upon them. The plan of the society met with his entire approbation, its success was the subject of his ardent wishes, and the prospect of its usefulness to the native Africans and their decendants in this country was the solace of his declining years, and cheered the last moments of his existence.

American Society for Colonizing the Free People of Color of the United States, *First Annual Report of the American Colonization Society* (Washington, 1818).

Free Negroes Oppose Colonization in Africa

Free Afro-Americans in Richmond, Virginia, agreed to the principle of colonization but desired to be allowed territory for this purpose in the United States. Below is the transcript of a meeting of the Free People of Colour that was held on January 24, 1817.

At a meeting of a respectable portion of the Free People of Colour, of the city of Richmond, on Friday, the 24th of January, 1817, William Bowler was appointed chairman, Ephraim Speed, Moderator, and Lantey Crow, Secretary.

The following Preamble and Resolution was read, unanimously adopted, and ordered to be printed:

Whereas, a Society has been formed at the seat of Government, for the purpose of "colonizing (with their own consent) the Free People of Colour of the United States," therefore, we the Free People of Colour of the city of Richmond, have thought it advisable to assemble together, under the sanction of authority, for the purpose of making a public expression of our sentiments on a question in which we are so deeply interested; We perfectly agree with the society, that it is not only proper, but would ultimately tend to the benefit and advantage of a great portion of our suffering fellow-creatures, to be colonized; but while we thus express our entire approbation of a measure, laudable in its purposes and beneficent in its design, it may not be improper in us to say, we prefer being colonized in the most remote corner of the land of our nativity, to being exiled to a foreign country.

And whereas, The President and Board of Managers of the said Society, have been pleased to leave it to the entire discretion of Congress to provide a suitable place for carrying their laudable intentions in effect—

Be it therefore resolved, That we respectfully submit to the wisdom of Congress, whether it would not be an act of charity to grant us a small portion of their territory, either on the Missouri River, or any place that may seem to them most conducive to the public good, and our future welfare, subject, however, to such rules and regulations as the government of the United States may think proper to adopt.

W. Bowler, Chairman
Ephraim Speed, Moderator
Lantey Crow, Secretary

Jesse Torrey, *A Portraiture of Domestic Slavery in the United States* (Philadelphia, 1817).

A Disillusioned Free Negro Favors Colonization

This excerpt of a letter from a free Negro to the American Colonization Society expresses his reason for favoring colonization.

Lamott, Illinois Territory, July 13th, 1818.

. . . I am a free man of colour, have a family and a large connection of free people of colour residing on the Wabash, who are all willing to leave America whenever the way shall be opened. We love this country and its liberties, if we could share an equal right in them; but our freedom is partial, and we have no hope that it ever will be otherwise here; therefore we had rather be gone, though we should suffer hunger and nakedness for years. Your honour may be assured that nothing shall be lacking on our part in complying with whatever provision shall be made by the United States, whether it be to go to Africa or some other place; we shall hold ourselves in readiness, praying that God (who made man free in the beginning, and who by his kind providence has broken the yoke from every white American) would inspire the heart of every true son of liberty with zeal and pity, to open the door of freedom for us also.

I am, &c.

Abraham Camp.

To:
Elias B. Caldwell, Esq.
Secretary of the Colonization Society of the United States.

Carter G. Woodson (ed.), *The Mind of the Negro: As Reflected in Letters Written during the Crisis, 1800–1860* (Washington, 1926).

The First Issue of *Freedom's Journal*

Freedom's Journal *was first published in 1827 by John B. Russwurm and Samuel E. Cornish. It was the first newspaper in the United States to be both owned and printed by blacks.*

TO OUR PATRONS.

In presenting our first number to our Patrons, we feel all the diffidence of persons entering upon a new and untried line of business. But a moment's reflection upon the noble objects, which we have in view by the publication of this Journal; the expediency of its appearance at this time, when so many schemes are in action concerning our people —encourage us to come boldly before an enlightened publick. For we believe, that a paper devoted to the dissemination of useful knowledge among our brethren, and to their moral and religious improvement, must meet with the cordial approbation of every friend to humanity.

The peculiarities of this Journal, render it important that we should advertise to the world our motives by which we are actuated, and the objects which we contemplate.

We wish to plead our own cause. Too long have others spoken for us. Too long has the publick been deceived by misrepresentations, in things which concern us dearly, though in the estimation of some mere trifles; for though there are many in society who exercise towards us benevolent feelings; still (with sorrow we confess it) there are others who make it their business to enlarge upon the least trifle, which tends to the discredit of any person of colour; and pronounce anathemas and denounce our whole body for the misconduct of this guilty one. We are aware that there [are] many instances of vice among us, but we avow that it is because no one has taught its subjects to be virtuous: many instances of poverty, because no sufficient efforts accommodated to minds contracted by slavery, and deprived of early education have been made, to teach them how to husband their hard earnings, and to secure to themselves comforts.

Education being an object of the highest importance to the welfare of society, we shall endeavour to present just and adequate views of it, and to urge upon our brethren the necessity and expediency of training their children, while young, to habits of industry, and thus forming them for becoming useful members of society. It is surely time that we should awake from this lethargy of years, and make a concentrated effort for the education of our youth. . . .

The civil rights of a people being of the greatest value, it shall ever be our duty to vindicate our brethren, when oppressed, and to lay the case before the publick. We shall also urge upon our brethren, (who are qualified by the laws of the different states) the expediency of using their elective franchise; and of making an independent use of the same. We wish them not to become the tools of party.

And as much time is frequently lost, and wrong principles instilled, by the perusal of works of trivial importance, we shall consider it a part of our duty to recommend to our young readers, such authors as will not only enlarge their stock of useful knowledge, but such as will also serve to stimulate them to higher attainments in science.

We trust also, that through the columns of the *Freedom's Journal,* many practical pieces, having for their bases, the improvement of our brethren, will be presented to them, from the pens of many of our respected friends, who have kindly promised their assistance.

It is our earnest wish to make our Journal a medium of intercourse between our brethren in the different states of this great confederacy: that through its columns an expression of our sentiments, on many interesting subjects which concern us, may be offered to the publick: that plans which apparently are beneficial may be candidly discussed and properly weighed; if worthy, receive our cordial approbation; if not, our marked disapprobation.

Useful knowledge of every kind, and everything that relates to Africa, shall find a ready admission into our columns; and as that vast continent becomes daily more known, we trust that many things will come to light, proving that the natives of it are neither so ignorant nor stupid as they have generally been supposed to be.

And while these important subjects shall occupy the columns of the *Freedom's Journal,* we would not be unmindful of our brethren who are still in the iron fetters of bondage. They are our kindred by all the ties of nature; and though but little can be effected by us, still let our sympathies be poured forth, and our prayers in their behalf, ascend to Him who is able to succour them.

From the press and the pulpit we have suffered much by being incorrectly represented. Men whom we equally love and admire have not hesitated to represent us disadvantageously, without becoming personally acquainted with the true state of things, nor discerning between virtue and vice among us. The virtuous part of our people feel themselves sorely aggrieved under the existing state of things—they are not appreciated.

. . . In the spirit of candor and humility we intend by a simple representation of facts to lay our case before the publick, with a view to arrest the progress of prejudice, and to shield ourselves against the consequent evils. We wish to conciliate all and to irritate none, yet we must be firm and unwavering in our principles, and persevering in our efforts.

If ignorance, poverty and degradation have hitherto been our unhappy lot; has the Eternal decree gone forth, that our race alone, are to remain in this state, while knowledge and civilization are shedding their enlivening rays over the rest of the human family? The recent travels of Denham and Clapperton in the interior of Africa, and the interesting narrative which they have published; the establishment of the republic of Hayti after years of sanguinary warfare; its subsequent progress in all the arts of civilization; and the advancement of liberal ideas in South America, where despotism has given place to free governments, and where many of our brethren now fill important civil and military stations, prove the contrary.

The interesting fact that there are *five hundred thousand* free persons of colour, one half of whom might peruse, and the whole be benefitted by the publication of the Journal; that no publication, as yet, has been devoted exclusively to their improvement—that many selections from approved standard authors, which are within the reach of few, may occasionally be made—and more important still, that this large body of our citizens have no public channel—all serve to prove the real necessity, at present, for the appearance of the *Freedom's Journal.*

It shall ever be our desire so to conduct the editorial department of our paper as to give offence to none of our patrons; as nothing is farther from us than to make it the advocate of any partial views, either in politics or religion. What few days we can number, have been devoted to the improvement of our brethren; and it is our earnest wish that the remainder may be spent in the same delightful service.

In conclusion, whatever concerns us as a people, will ever find a ready admission into the *Freedom's Journal,* interwoven with all the principal news of the day. . . .

Freedom's Journal (New York), March 16, 1827. *New York Public Library.*

An Opponent of Colonization

Soon after founding Freedom's Journal, *John B. Russwurm became an advocate of colonization and went to Liberia. That his actions were not supported by all of his race is indicated by this letter to the editor of* The Liberator.

Sir—Notwithstanding the many preposterous arguments of colonizationists, and their wild and incoherent freaks, in support of their imaginary scheme of civilizing Africa, by draining the people of color from this their original and only home; notwithstanding the many hyperbolical accounts, which they so assiduously and conscientiously circulate about that pestiferous clime;—I never felt so indignant at any of their manœuvres (for every step they take to facilitate their plans, tends but to expose their inconsistency) as at a piece of composition which appeared in the twelfth number of the "Liberia Herald," written by its editor John B. Russworm [*sic*]. This John B. Russworm is known, I presume, to every one of us; his ingratitude is but too deeply stamped on the minds of many, who have been requited in a manner, which neither time nor space will ever obliterate. After he subverted the pledge he made to his colored brethren, he left, to our satisfaction, his country—suffused with shame—and branded with the stigma of disgrace—to dwell in that land for which the temptor *Money* caused him to avow his preferment. He has resided there more than a year, publishing doubtless to the satisfaction of his supporters, their many glorious schemes, and eulogizing to the very skies the prosperity of his goodly Liberia. Not contented with lauding the retreat in which and about which he may flame with impunity, he has the audacity to reprove those with whom he played the traitor. Out of much he said, let this suffice as an example:

'Before God, we know of no other home for the man of color, of republican principles, than Africa. Has he no ambition? Is he dead to everything noble? Is he contented with his condition? Let him remain in America.'

To this we reply, that before God, we know of no surer burial place than Africa, for men of any color; that we will never envy John B. Russworm his ambition; and that we will pray God, that his notions of nobleness may never enter our hearts, and that we will not be contented with our condition, but will make it better in this our native home. R.

Philadelphia, April 8th, 1831.

The Liberator (Boston), April 16, 1831.

Colonization in Liberia

As the controversy over colonization grew more heated, a black American revealed his first-hand report of conditions in Liberia. William Nesbit spent four months in Liberia in 1854. When he returned to the United States, he published an attack on the American Colonization Society and its practices.

. . . They have also laws allowing imprisonment for debt, and the public sale of a debtor to the highest bidder, to work out the amount of his indebtedness. I saw an example of that law, myself. A colonist named Armstrong, who is himself a slave-holder, was sold for debt at Monrovia, and was, at the time I left that place, working out the term of his servitude. And there is nothing more common than to punish offenders at the public whipping-post, and in that way wipe out their crimes; in fact that is the only mode of punishment at all practicable, as there is but one jail in the country, (that at Monrovia.) And numerous other similar specimens of the wisdom of their rulers, and the freedom and magnanimity of their government, are daily exhibited, constituting it as very a tyranny as ever disgraced the earth. Of course, the manner of conducting the government is of an exact piece with all their other impudent pretensions. They assume to be republic, to have copied their forms and laws from the United States. And to give color to it, they pretend to have vested their power and authority in executive, legislative, judicial, and all the other departments, cabinets, and bureaus known in the government of nations; and, however strange it may seem to the reader, it is not the less true, that all this famous government, and all this long list of officers, is in the hands of one man, and that man but a tool in the hands of the Colonization Society. It is true that the President, Vice President, six Senators, and nine representatives, are elected by the people. But a little money and patronage do a great deal with such people; and does any sane man think that the Colonization Society, through its active agent, *President Roberts,* does not use these, in order to have the government harmonize with their *wishes*ʿ I any man would read the long list of officers belonging to the Liberian Government, he would read the name of nearly every man there, and yet all these officers are at the beck and call of President Roberts. He is the main-spring of all this machinery, and on him, through the support and connivance of the Colonization Society, devolves the carrying on and glossing over of as villainous an outrage as ever was perpetrated on a credulous people. And I do not deny the consummate skill and ability of that potentate. This is most emphatically the one-man power. Beside those officers I have mentioned, the people do not even go through the form of electing any others. All the Judges, Sheriffs, Justices, Constables, and every other officer, are appointed by the President. And it is humiliating to me to say it, though it must be said, that the majority of them, even including some of his cabinet officers, *cannot read* and are totally ignorant of the simplest duties belonging to their stations. Every thing is and must be done by the President. He performs the duties of judge, counsellor, justice, and constable. He receives, disburses, and keeps the accounts; in short, he is the government, the embodiment of Liberia; and when you speak of Liberia, you speak of President Roberts. For the reasons herein given, I predict the speedy downfall of this humbug; but as long as it does exist, although he may not always nominally appear as President, still, possessing superior skill and less soul than any other man there, he will continue to be, behind the screen, the pliant tool in the hands of his master, (Rev. J. B. Pinney,) as long as the American public choose to shut their eyes, and contribute their money to the maintenance of this iniquity. . . .

That slavery exists in Liberia, is too true. I would, for the sake of humanity, and the honor of the Colonization Society, that it were otherwise. But slavery as abject, and far more merciless than is to be found almost any where else, exists there universally. There is not one who does not own more or less slaves. They are mostly manumitted slaves themselves, and have felt the blighting effects of slavery here, only to go there to become masters. After my limited powers of description are exhausted, imagination can perhaps finish the picture of the condition of the *Slave's Slave.* A parallel to the Liberian system of slavery is scarcely to be found on the American continent; certainly no where else but on the least favored plantations. Slavery here is severe servitude, generally with plenty to eat; but in Liberia, they have the same tasks to perform, the same stripes to endure, severer masters to please, without sufficient clothing to deserve the name, nor enough rice and casaba, which are the slaves' only food, to satisfy their appetites. They need not, like Oliver Twist, ask for more; their only chance for a full meal, is to steal it; and in that country, theft would be a poor dependence; and as to meat, the slave must content himself if he can catch a monkey, a snake, a crocodile, lizard, rat, or something of this kind, which they often do, and devour it with a gusto, that would astonish and disgust the poorest-fed slaves in the United States. As in the slave states of this country, the slaves occupy small buildings near to their masters' residence, known as the "negro quarters," so their imitators in Liberia, notwithstanding the masters mostly live in bamboo huts themselves, many of them not sufficient to protect the pious patriarchs from the weather, let the colonist himself be barefoot, and three parts naked, let him feel the gnawings of want ever so keenly, still he is never too poor to own slaves, and to have a hut for them at a short distance from his own; and so exact have they been in carrying out the customs and feelings of their exemplers in this country, that the slave is never allowed to eat or sleep in the master's house, or hut, as the case may be. These slaves are generally obtained by purchase from the native parents, after arriving at such size and age as to be able to labor, at prices varying from eight to fifteen dollars. After the private transaction between the master and parents, the courts, at the instance of the master, go through some mummery which fastens the fetters upon the purchased child during his natural life. But I am glad to say that there are many, the laws of Liberia to the contrary, notwithstanding, who run away to the bush; once there, and he is safe. Like the slaves in this country, they run away, re-associate with their brother natives, and defy the powers that would enslave them. Still, there is no lack of slaves; the low price at which they can be bought, makes it a matter of economy to the master, when one of his slaves run away, to buy another, rather than attempt to reclaim the runaway. There is, however, one means much resorted to, to prevent slaves from running away, and its potency is astonishing. I allude to a slave owned by James M'Gill, familiarly called the "second President;" who, though a slave himself, exerts a powerful influence over his native brethren. When a master wishes to obtain the help of this individual, to enable him to retain his slaves, he makes the "second president" a dosh, (gift,) and informs him what he wants him to do. This potent dignitary forthwith gives the slaves a harrangue in their native language, addressing both their hopes and their fears; and being superstitious, this appliance generally accomplishes the object of its design. How long it will require the Liberian colonists to civilize and christianize the idolatrous natives, is yet an unsettled question. It is, however, certain, that if the cruelest slavery on which the sun ever shone —if wars brought on to raise the price of fire-arms and ammunitions—if drunkenness causes them to increase the sale and the price of rum—if all the vices of civilization, without any of its virtues, in any one of these, or all of them combined, can christianize Africa, then the work is in good hands, and I have no doubt will be carried forward; slowly, perhaps, but sure, as that Liberia continues to be a decoy for the colored people of this country.

The colonist once entrapped into this hell on earth, finds, to his dismay, that he cannot return at will, and it is natural that he should try to make the best of a bad bargain; so the manumitted slave, who always thought his master supremely happy, undertakes to procure happiness for himself, by the same means. With a few trinkets, rum, tobacco, &c. he buys a slave, and sets up tyrant on his own hook. They profess to have broken up the foreign slave trade, which is far from the truth; but suppose they had done so, is that *even* a blessing, under the circumstances? I would a thousand times rather be a slave in the United States than in Liberia. . . .

The chances for the poor emigrant to Liberia, are exceedingly slim—he cannot escape the fever—that, is a fixed fact, and it is equally true, that there is no disease to which human flesh is heir, more terrible in its effects. But, suppose he is fortunate, and lives through it—what are his prospects then. At the end of six months he finds himself turned off by the Colonization Society, thrown on his own resources, in a country that can afford him no possible employment, but paddling a canoe at twenty-five cents a day; and it would be at the imminent risk of his life, that he would expose himself to the scorching rays of the sun, and, in the nature of things, he could not have cleared and cultivated any land. He sees that nineteen twentieths of his neighbors are living in the most abject state of misery and want; that he is living in a mean, pusillanimous government, having for its only object, the decoy of the unsuspecting—that he is surrounded by, and must daily mingle with hordes of naked natives, whose habits his children will be sure to imbibe, rendering it certain, that however successful he may be, his children will deteriorate, and finally relapse back to heathenism. Having living witnesses constantly before him of the blighting effects of the climate and food, on the mental, physical, and moral powers, and knowing what he has lost by going there, he becomes dejected and desponding, and realizes that he has cast his lot in a hell on earth. He has no other alternative, but to turn in with those who have preceded him, and by hook and by crook, raise a little rum, tobacco, and cotton cloth, brass trinkets, &c., and start on what is called bush trading. Necessity compels him to leave his conscience behind him, and he soon finds himself stooping to means that he would have scorned before. Many of these poor souls told me with tears in their eyes, that they would gladly return to the worst form of slavery in the United States, rather than remain in that place of torment. A large number of the colonist women have even been reduced to the extremity of marrying, or taking up with naked native men, and are living with them in shameless co-habitation; and to estimate this degradation properly, it is necessary to know, that nothing can exceed the supreme contempt with which the colonists always regard the natives.

Perhaps I cannot better illustrate to the reader, the real condition, mentally and physically, of this class of emigrants, after a few years residence there, than by relating a conversation with Mr. Tucker, of Marshall, who is about a fair sample of old Liberians. He was one of the few who had passed through the ordeal of their horrid diseases, got used to eating casaba, and was, according to the Colonization rule, elevated. He had grown prematurely old and decrepid, and, as will be seen, his mental faculties were not much improved. Being anxious to learn as much of men and things in that country, as possible, one day I asked him: Mr. Tucker, have you been in this country long?

T. Yes, sir, a long time.

N. How many years?

T. About ten or fifteen years.

N. Can't you tell more closely than that, which it is, ten or fifteen?

T. No sir, indeed I can't tell how long I have been here; I was young when I came; I am old now, and you will not find many Liberians who can tell how old they are, or how long they have been here.

After listening to him relate some national affair, in which he had taken part, I questioned him as to what time it occurred. He seemed surprised, that we, who lately came from the States, should be so particular about dates, &c. and with a good deal of feeling, remarked:—"My dear friend, when you have been in this country long enough to have eaten all the bread and meat you brought with you, when anything occurs, you will not be able to remember whether it was last week, last month or last year." . . .

William Nesbit, *Four Months in Liberia, or African Colonization Society Exposed* (Pittsburgh, 1855).

David Walker's *Appeal*

In the late 1820's, a freeborn Negro from North Carolina made his way to Boston, and in 1829, issued an appeal to the people of color. David Walker, who had established a second-hand clothing business, was not content that he should prosper while his fellow slaves were still in bondage. The excerpts from his appeal included here show a prophetic wisdom of what one day would become intense racial strife if Negroes were not given freedom and equal opportunities.

ARTICLE I

. . . Has Mr. Jefferson declared to the world, that we are inferior to the whites, both in the endowments of our bodies and of minds? It is indeed surprising that a man of such great learning, combined with such execellent natural parts, should speak so of a set of men in chains. . . . I know well, that there are some talents and learning among the coloured people of this country, which we have not a chance to develope, in consequence of oppression; but our oppression ought not to hinder us from acquiring all we can.—For we will have a chance to develope them by and by. God will not suffer us, always to be oppressed. Our sufferings will come to an *end,* in spite of all the Americans this side of *eternity*. Then we will want all the learning and talents among ourselves, and perhaps more, to govern ourselves.—"Every dog must have its day," the American's is coming to an end . . .

ARTICLE II

The whites want slaves, and want us for their slaves, but some of them will curse the day they ever saw us. As true as the sun ever shone in its meridian splendor, my colour will root some of them out of the very face of the earth. They shall have enough of making slaves of, and butchering, and murdering us in the manner which they have. No doubt some may say that I write with a bad spirit, and that I being a black, wish these things to occur. Whether I write with a bad or a good spirit, I say if these things do not occur in their proper time, it is because the world in which we live does not exist, and we are deceived with regard to its existence. . . .

ARTICLE III

. . . But the Americans, having introduced slavery among them, their hearts have become almost seared, as with an hot iron, and God has nearly given them up to believe a lie in preference to the truth!!! and I am awfully afraid that pride, prejudice, avarice and blood, will, before long prove the final ruin of this happy republic, or land of *liberty*!!!! Can any thing be a greater mockery of religion than the way in which it is conducted by the Americans? It appears as though they are bent only on daring God Almighty to do his best—they chain and handcuff us and our children and drive us around the country like brutes, and go into the house of the God of justice to return Him thanks for having aided them in their infernal cruelties inflicted upon us. Will the Lord suffer this people to go on much longer, taking his holy name in vain? Will he not stop them, PREACHERS and all? O Americans! Americans!! I call God—I call angels—I call men, to witness, that your DESTRUCTION is *at hand,* and will be speedily consummated unless you REPENT. . . .

ARTICLE IV

. . . God will show the whites what we are, yet. I say, from the beginning, I do not think that we were natural enemies to each other. But the whites having made us so wretched, by subjecting us to slavery, and having murdered so many millions of us, in order to make us work for them, and out of devilishness—and they taking our wives, whom we love as we do ourselves—our mothers, who bore the pains of death to give us birth—our fathers and dear little children, and ourselves, and strip and beat us, one before the other—chain, handcuff, and drag us about like rattlesnakes—shoot us down like wild bears, before each other's faces, to make us submissive to, and work to support them and their families. They know well, if we are *men*—and there is a secret monitor in their hearts which tells them we are—they know, I say, if we *are* men, and see them treating us in the manner they do, that there can be nothing in our hearts but death alone, for them; notwithstanding we may appear cheerful, when we see them murdering our dear mothers and wives, because we cannot help ourselves. Man, in all ages and all nations of the earth, is the same. Man is a peculiar creature—he is the image of his God, though he may be subjected to the most wretched condition upon earth, yet the spirit and feeling which constitute the creature, man, can never be entirely erased from his breast, because the God who made him after his own image, planted it in his heart; he cannot get rid of it. The whites knowing this, they do not know what to do; they know that they have done us so much injury, they are afraid that we, being men, and not brutes, will retaliate, and woe will be to them; therefore, that dreadful fear, together with an avaricious spirit, and the natural love in them, to be called masters, (which term will yet honour them with to their sorrow) bring them to the resolve that they will keep us in ignorance and wretchedness, as long as they possibly can. . . .

And now brethren, having concluded these four Articles, I submit them, together with my Preamble, dedicated to the Lord, for your inspection, in language so very simple, that the most ignorant, who can read at all, may easily understand—of which you may make the best you possibly can. Should tyrants take it into their heads to emancipate any of you, remember that your freedom is your natural right. You are men, as well as they, and instead of returning thanks to them for your freedom, return it to the Holy Ghost, who is our rightful owner. If they do not want to part with your labours, which have enriched them, let them keep you, and my word for it, that God Almighty, will break their strong band. . . .

If any are anxious to ascertain who I am, know the world, that I am one of the oppressed, degraded and wretched sons of Africa, rendered so by the avaricious and unmerciful, among the whites.—If any wish to plunge me into the wretched incapacity of a slave, or murder me for the truth, know ye, that I am in the hand of God, and at your disposal. I count my life not dear unto me, but I am ready to be offered at any moment. For what is the use of living, when in fact I am dead. But remember, Americans, that as miserable, wretched, degraded and abject as you have made us in preceding, and in this generation, to support you and your families, that some of you, (whites) on the continent of America, will yet curse the day that you ever were born. You want slaves, and want us for your slaves!!! My colour will yet, root some of you out of the very face of the earth!!!!!! You may doubt it if you please. I know that thousands will doubt—they think they have us so well secured in wretchedness, to them and their children, that it is impossible for such things to occur. . . .

See the hundreds and thousands of us that are thrown into the seas by Christians, and murdered by them in other ways. They cram us into their vessel holds in chains and in hand-cuffs—men, women and children, all together!! O! save us, we pray thee, thou God of Heaven and of earth, from the devouring hands of the white Christians!!!

David Walker, *Walker's Appeal, in Four Articles; Together with a Preamble, to the Coloured Citizens of the World, but in Particular, and Very Expressly, to Those of the United States of America, Written in Boston, State of Massachusetts, September 28, 1829* (Boston, 1830).

The Denmark Vesey Conspiracy in South Carolina

South Carolina, the scene of many attempted insurrections and small uprisings, was the site of the unsuccessful Denmark Vesey conspiracy in 1822. Vesey, a West Indian free Negro, intended to lead a revolt among the blacks of Charleston. His plans were discovered when one of the members of his group revealed the plot to his master. The following account was written by a white man who was present as the details of the proposed revolt unfolded.

On Thursday, the 30th of May last, about 3 o'clock in the afternoon, the Intendant of Charleston was informed by a gentleman of great respectability, (who, that morning, had returned from the country) that a favourite and confidential slave of his had communicated to him, on his arrival in town, a conversation which had taken place at the market on the Saturday preceding, between himself and a black man; which afforded strong reasons for believing that a revolt and insurrection were in contemplation among a proportion at least of our black population. The Corporation was forthwith summoned to meet at 5 o'clock, for the purpose of hearing the narrative of the slave who had given this information to his master, to which meeting the attendance of His Excellency was solicited; with which invitation he promptly complied. Between, however, the hours of 3 and 5 o'clock, the gentleman who had conveyed the information to the Intendant, having again examined his slave, was induced to believe, that the negro fellow who had communicated the intelligence of the intended revolt to the slave in question, belonged to Messrs. J. & D. Paul, Broad Street, and resided in their premises. Accordingly, with a promptitude worthy of all praise, without waiting for the interposition of the civil authority he applied to the Messrs. Paul's and had the whole of their male servants committed to the Guard-House, until the individual who had accosted the slave of this gentleman, on the occasion previously mentioned, could be identified from among them.

On the assembly of the Corporation at five, the slave of this gentleman was brought before them, having previously identified Mr. Paul's William as the man who had accosted him in the market, he then related the following circumstances:

'On Saturday afternoon last (my master 'being out of town) I went to market; after 'finishing my business I strolled down the 'wharf below the fish market, from which I 'observed a small vessel in the stream with a 'singular flag; whilst looking at this object, 'a black man, (Mr. Paul's William) came up 'to me and remarking the subject which engaged my attention said, I have often seen a 'flag with the number 76 on it, but never with '96, before. After some trifling conversation 'on this point, he remarked with considerable 'earnestness to me. Do you know that something serious is about to take place? To 'which I replied no. Well, said he, there is, 'and many of us are determined to right ourselves! I asked him to explain himself—'when he remarked, why, we are determined 'to shake off our bondage, and for this purpose we stand on a good foundation, many 'have joined, and if you will go with me, I 'will show you the man, who has the list of

' names who will take yours down.—I was so ' much astonished and horror struck at this ' information, that it was a moment or two ' before I could collect myself sufficiently to ' tell him I would have nothing to do with this ' business, that I was satisfied with my condi- ' tion, that I was grateful to my master for his ' kindness and wished no change.—I left him ' instantly, lest, if this fellow afterwards got ' into trouble, and I had been seen conversing ' with him, in so public a place, I might be ' suspected and thrown into difficulty.—I did ' not however remain easy under the burden ' of such a secret, and consequently deter- ' mined to consult a free man of colour ' named ——— and to ask his advice. On ' conferring with this friend, he urged me with ' great earnestness to communicate what had ' passed between Mr. Paul's man and myself ' to my master, and not to lose a moment in ' so doing. I took his advice, and not waiting, ' even for the return of my master to town, I ' mentioned it to my mistress and young mas- ' ter.—On the arrival of my master, he exam- ' ined me as to what had passed, and I stated ' to him what I have mentioned to your- ' selves."

On this witness being dismissed from the presence of Council, the prisoner (William) was examined. The mode resorted to in his examination was to afford him no intimation of the subject of the information which had been lodged against him, as it was extremely desirable in the first place, to have the testimony of the other witness corroborated as to time and place, that, from the confessions of the prisoner himself, it might appear that he was at the fish-market at the period stated, and that a singular flag, flying on board of a schooner, had formed the subject of his observation. After a vast deal of equivocation, he admitted all these facts, but when the rest of his conversation was put home to him, he flatly denied it, but with so many obvious indications of guilt, that it was deemed unwise to discharge him. He was remanded, for the night, to the Guard-House, it having been decided to subject him to solitary confinement in the black-hole of the Work-House, where, on the succeeding morning, he was to be conveyed.

On the morning of the 31st he was again examined by the attending Warden at the Guard-House (having, during the night, made some disclosures to Capt. Dove) on which occasion he admitted all the conversation which he had held at the fish-market, with the witness before mentioned, and stated that he had received his information from Mingo Harth, who was in possession of the muster-roll of the insurgents.

With the hope of still further disclosures William was conveyed to the Work-House and placed in solitary confinement. The individuals (Mingo Harth and Peter Poyas) against whom he gave information, as those who had communicated to him the intelligence of the plot for raising an insurrection, were forthwith taken up by the Wardens and their trunks examined. These fellows behaved with so much composure and coolness, and treated the charge, alleged against them, with so much levity. . . —that the Wardens (Messrs. Wesner & Condy) were completely deceived, and had these men discharged. One of these (Peter Poyas) proved afterwards, as will appear in the sequel, to be one of the principal ringleaders in the conspiracy, on whose courage and sagacity great reliance was placed.

Council being still under the conviction that William Paul was in possession of more information than he had thought proper to disclose, a Committee was appointed to examine him from time to time, with the hope of obtaining further intelligence. Although Peter and Mingo had been discharged, yet it was deemed advisable to have them watched, and consequently spies were employed of their own colour for this purpose, in such a manner as to give advices of all their movements.

Things remained in this state for six or seven days, until about the 8th of June, when William, who had been a week in solitary confinement, and beginning to fear that he would soon be led forth to the scaffold, for summary execution, in an interview with Mr. Napier, (one of the Committee appointed to examine him) confessed, that he had for some time known of the plan, that is was very extensive, embracing an indiscriminate massacre of the whites, and that the blacks were to be headed by an individual, who carried about him a charm which rendered him invulnerable. He stated, that the period fixed for the rising, was on the second Sunday in June. This information was without delay conveyed to his Excellency the Governor, and Council forthwith convened. Whatever faith we might have been disposed to place in the unsupported and equivocal testimony of William, it was not conceived to be a case in which our doubts should influence our efforts for preparation and defence. Measures were consequently promptly taken, to place the City Guard in a state of the utmost efficiency. Sixteen hundred rounds of ball cartridges were provided, and the centinels and patrols ordered on duty with loaded arms. Such had been our fancied security, that the guard had previously gone on duty without muskets, with sheathed bayonets and bludgeons.

Three or four days now elapsed, and notwithstanding all our efforts, we could obtain no confirmation of the disclosure of William, on the contrary, they seemed to have sustained some invalidation, from the circumstance, of one of the individuals (Ned Bennett) whom he named as a person who had information in relation to the insurrection, coming voluntarily to the Intendant, and soliciting an examination, if he was an object of suspicion. In this stage of the business, it was not deemed advisable prematurely to press these examinations, as it might have a tendency to arrest any further developments.

On the night, however, of Friday the 14th, the information of William was amply confirmed, and details infinitely more abundant and interesting afforded. At 8 o'clock on this evening, the Intendant received a visit from a gentleman, who is advantageously known in this community for his worth and respectability.

This gentleman, with an anxiety, which the occasion was well calculated to beget, stated to the Intendant, that, having the most unbounded confidence in a faithful slave belonging to his family, who was distinguished alike for his uncommon intelligence and integrity, he was induced to inform him, that rumors were abroad of an intended insurrection of the blacks, and that it was said, that this movement had been traced to some of the coloured members of Dr. Palmer's church, in which he was known to be a class leader.—On being strongly enjoined to conceal nothing, he, the next day, Friday the 14th, came to his master, and informed him, that the fact was really so, that a public disturbance was contemplated by the blacks, and not a moment should be lost in informing the constituted authorities, as the succeeding Sunday, the 16th, at 12 o'clock, at night, was the period fixed for the rising, which, if not prevented, would inevitably occur at that hour. This slave, it appears, was in no degree connected with the plot, but he had an intimate friend, A— (one of his class) who had been trusted by the conspirators with the secret, and had been solicited by them to join their association; to this A— first appeared to consent, but, on no period absolutely sent in his adhesion. According to the statement which he afterwards made himself to the Court, it would seem that it was a subject of great regret and contrition with him, that he had ever appeared to lend his approbation to a scheme so wicked and atrocious, and that he sought occasion to make atonement, by divulging the plot, which on the 14th he did, to the slave of the gentleman in question, his class leader [Sunday School class leader].

This gentleman, therefore, mentioned, that his servant had informed him, that A—— had stated, that about three months ago, Rolla, belonging to Governor Bennett, had communicated to him the intelligence of the intended insurrection, and had asked him to join—'That he remarked, in the event of their 'rising, they would not be without help, as 'the people from San Domingo and Africa 'would assist them in obtaining their liberty, 'if they only made the motion first them- 'selves. That if A—— wished to know more, 'he had better attend their meetings, where 'all would be disclosed.' After this, at another interview, Rolla informed A——, that 'the 'plan was matured, and that on Sunday night, 'the 16th June, a force would cross from 'James' Island and land on South Bay, march 'up and seize the Arsenal and Guard House, 'that another body at the same time would 'seize the Arsenal on the Neck, and a third 'would rendezvous in the vicinity of his mas- 'ter's mills. They would then sweep the town 'with fire and sword, not permitting a single 'white soul to escape.'

As this account was remarkably coincident with the one given by William (Mr. Paul's slave) as the witnesses could have had no possible communication, or the story have been the result of preconcert and combination, the sum of this intelligence was laid before the Governor by 9 o'clock, and by 10 o'clock the field officers of the regiments of the City militia, convened by his Excellency's order, at the residence of the Intendant. On this and the succeeding afternoon, at another meeting of the same individuals, such measures were determined on by his Excellency, as were deemed best adapted to the approaching exigency of Sunday night.

On Sunday the 16th, at 10 o'clock at night, the following corps were ordered to rendezvous for guard—

Capt. Cattel's Corps of *Hussars*, Capt. Miller's *Light Infantry*, Capt. Martindale's *Neck Rangers*, *Charleston Riflemen*, and *City Guard*.

The whole were organized as a detachment, and placed under the command of Col. R. Y. Hayne [later to be Senator from South Carolina]. Although there was necessarily great excitement, and among the female part of our community much alarm, yet, the night passed off without any thing like commotion or disturbance, and it is peculiarly honorable to the corps on service, that in a populous town, the streets filled until a late hour with persons, uncertain whether it was safe to go to *rest* or *not,* not a single case of false alarm was excited. A steadiness altogether praiseworthy, in troops unaccustomed to guard duty, at least on an occasion involving such deep interest and distressing anxiety.

The conspirators finding the whole town encompassed at 10 o'clock, by the most vigilant patrols, did not dare to show themselves, whatever might have been their plans. In the progress of the subsequent investigation, it was distinctly in proof, that but for these military demonstrations, the effort would unquestionably have been made; that a meeting took place on Sunday afternoon, the 16th, at 4 o'clock, of several of the ringleaders, at Denmark Vesey's, for the purpose of making their preliminary arrangements, and that early in the morning of Sunday, Denmark despatched a courier, to order down some country negroes from Goose Creek, which courier had endeavored in vain to get out of town.

No developement of the plot having been made on Sunday night, and the period having passed, which was fixed on for its explosion, it now became the duty of the civil authority to take immediate steps for the apprehension, commitment, and trial of those against whom they were in possession of information. . . .

On Thursday the 27th, DENMARK VESEY, a free black man, was brought before the Court for trial,

Assisted by his Counsel, G. W. Cross, Esq.

It is perhaps somewhat remarkable, that at this stage of the investigation, although several witnesses had been examined, the *atrocious* guilt of *Denmark Vesey* had not been as yet fully unfolded. From the testimony of most of the witnesses, however, the Court found enough, and amply enough, to warrant the sentence of death, which, on the 28th, they passed on him. But every subsequent step in the progress of the trials of others, lent new confirmation to his overwhelming guilt, and placed him beyond a doubt, on the criminal eminence of having been the individual, in whose bosom the nefarious scheme was first engendered. There is ample reason for believing, that this project was not, with him, of recent origin, for it was said, he had spoken of it for upwards of four years.

These facts of his guilt the journals of the Court will disclose—that no man can be proved to have spoken of or urged the insurrection prior to himself. All the channels of communication and intelligence are traced back to him. His house was the place appointed for the secret meetings of the conspirators, at which he was invariably a leading and influential member; animating and encouraging the timid, by the hopes of prospects of success; removing the scruples of the religious, by the grossest prostitution and perversion of the sacred oracles, and inflaming and confirming the resolute, by all the savage fascinations of blood and booty.

The peculiar circumstances of guilt, which confer a distinction on his case, will be found narrated in the confessions of Rolla, Monday Gell, Frank and Jesse, in the Appendix. He was sentenced for execution on the 2d July.

As Denmark Vesey has occupied so large a place in the conspiracy, a brief notice of him will, perhaps, be not devoid of interest. The following anecdote will show how near he was to the chance of being distinguished in the bloody events of San Domingo. During the revolutionary war, Captain Vesey, now an old resident of this city, commanded a ship that traded between St. Thomas' and Cape Français (San Domingo.) He was engaged in supplying the French of that Island with Slaves. In the year 1781, he took on board at St. Thomas' 390 slaves and sailed for the Cape; on the passage, he and his officers were struck with the beauty, alertness and intelligence of a boy about 14 years of age, whom they made a pet of, by taking him into the cabin, changing his apparel, and calling him by way of distinction *Telemaque*, (which appellation has since, by gradual corruption, among the negroes, been changed to *Denmark,* or sometimes *Telmak.*) On the arrival, however, of the ship at the Cape, Captain Vesey, having no use for the boy, sold him among his other slaves, and returned to St. Thomas'. On his next voyage to the Cape, he was surprised to learn from his consignee that Telemaque would be returned on his hands, as the planter, who had purchased him, represented him unsound, and subject to epileptic fits. According to the custom of trade in that place, the boy was placed in the hands of the king's physician, who decided that he was unsound, and Captain Vesey was compelled to take him back, of which he had no occasion to repent, as Denmark proved, for 20 years, a most faithful slave. In 1800, Denmark drew a prize of $1500 in the East-Bay-Street Lottery, with which he purchased his freedom from his master, at six hundred dollars, much less than his real value. From that period to day of his apprehension he has been working as a carpenter in this city, distinguished for great strength and activity. Among his colour he was always looked up to with awe and respect. His temper was impetuous and domineering in the extreme, qualifying him for the despotic rule, of which he was ambitious. All his passions were ungovernable and, savage; and to his numerous wives and children, he displayed the haughty and capricious cruelty of an Eastern Bashaw. He had nearly effected his escape, after information had been lodged against him. For three days the town was searched for him without success. As early as Monday, the 17th, he had concealed himself. It was not until the night of the 22nd of June, during a perfect tempest, that he was found secreted in the house of one of his wives. It is to the uncommon efforts and vigilance of Mr. Wesner, and Capt. Dove, of the City Guard, (the latter of whom seized him) that public justice received its necessary tribute, in the execution of this man. If the party had been one moment later, he would, in all probability, have effected his escape the next day in some outward bound vessel.

James Hamilton, Jr., *Negro Plot, An Account of the Late Intended Insurrections among a Portion of the Blacks of the City of Charleston, South Carolina* (Boston, 1822).

The Confessions of Nat Turner

In August 1831, the bloodiest slave rebellion in American history occurred in Southampton County, Virginia. Led by the slave Nat Turner, this insurrection resulted in the deaths of more than fifty whites. Turner and his band were later captured, and many of them, including Turner, were hanged. In retaliation, the whites passed a series of stringent laws that restricted the few privileges then available to slaves. While Turner was in jail awaiting execution, he dictated his confession to his court-appointed attorney, Thomas Gray.

SIR,—You have asked me to give a history of the motives which induced me to undertake the late insurrection, as you call it—To do so I must go back to the days of my infancy, and even before I was born. I was thirty-one years of age the 2d of October last, and born the property of Benj. Turner, of this county. In my childhood a circumstance occurred which made an indelible impression on my mind, and laid the ground work of that enthusiasm, which has terminated so fatally to many both white and black, and for which I am about to atone at the gallows. It is here necessary to relate this circumstance—trifling as it may seem, it was the commencement of that belief which has grown with time, and even now, sir, in this dungeon, helpless and forsaken as I am, I cannot divest myself of. Being at play with other children, when three or four years old, I was telling them something, which my mother overhearing, said it had happened before I was born—I stuck to my story, however, and related some things which went in her opinion to confirm it—others being called on were greatly astonished, knowing that these things had happened, and caused them to say in my hearing, I surely would be a prophet, as the Lord had shewn me things that had happened before my birth. And my father and mother strengthened me in this my first impression, saying in my presence, I was intended for some great purpose, which they had always thought from certain marks on my head and breast, . . .

My grand mother, who was very religious, and to whom I was much attached—my master, who belonged to the church, and other religious persons who visited the house, and whom I often saw at prayers, noticing the singularity of my manners, I suppose, and my uncommon intelligence for a child, remarked I had too much sense to be raised, and if I was, I would never be of any service to any one as a slave—To a mind like mine, restless, inquisitive and observant of every thing that was passing, it is easy to suppose that religion was the subject to which it would be directed, and although this subject principally occupied my thoughts—there was nothing that I saw or heard of to which my attention was not directed—The manner in which I learned to read and write, not only had great influence on my mind, as I acquired it with the most perfect ease, so much so, that I have no recollection whatever of learning the alphabet—but to the astonishment of the family, one day, when a book was shewn me to keep me from crying, I began spelling the names of different objects—this was a source of wonder to all in the neighborhood, particularly the blacks—and this learning was constantly improved at all opportunities—when I got large enough to go to work, while employed, I was reflecting on many things that would present themselves to my imagination, and whenever an opportunity occurred of looking at a book, when the school children were getting their lessons, I would find many things that the fertility of my own imagination had depicted to me before; all my time, not devoted to my master's service, was spent either in prayer, or in making experiments in casting different things in moulds made of earth, in attempting to make paper, gunpowder, and many other experiments, that although I could not perfect, yet convinced me of its practicability if I had the means. I was not addicted to stealing in my youth, nor have ever been—Yet such was the confidence of the negroes in the neighborhood, even at this early period of my life, in my superior judgment, that they would often carry me with them when they were going on any roguery, to plan for them. Growing up among them, with this confidence in my superior judgment, and when this, in their opinions, was perfected by Divine inspiration, from the circumstances already alluded to in my infancy, and which belief was ever afterwards zealously inculcated by the austerity of my life and manners, which became the subject of remark by white and black.—Having soon discovered to be great, I must appear so, and therefore studiously avoided mixing in society, and wrapped myself in mystery, devoting my time to fasting and prayer. By this time, having arrived to man's estate, and hearing the scriptures commented on at meetings, I was struck with that particular passage which says: "Seek ye the kingdom of Heaven and all things shall be added unto you." I reflected much on this passage, and prayed daily for light on this subject—As I was praying one day at my plough, the spirit spoke to me, saying "Seek ye the kingdom of Heaven and all things shall be added unto you." *Question*—what do you mean by the Spirit. *Ans.* The Spirit that spoke to the prophets in former days—and I was greatly astonished, and for two years prayed continually, whenever my duty would permit—and then again I had the same revelation, which fully confirmed me in the impression that I was ordained for some great purpose in the hands of the Almighty. Several years rolled round, in which many events occurred to strengthen me in this my belief. At this time I reverted in my mind to the remarks made of me in my childhood, and the things that had been shewn me—and as it had been said of me in my childhood by those by whom I had been taught to pray, both white and black, and in whom I had the greatest confidence, that I had too much sense to be raised and if I was I would never be of any use to any one as a slave. Now finding I had arrived to man's estate, and was a slave, and these revelations being made known to me, I began to direct my attention to this great object, to fulfil the purpose for which, by this time, I felt assured I was intended. Knowing the influence I had obtained over the minds of my fellow servants, (not by the means of conjuring and such like tricks—for to them I always spoke of such things with contempt) but by the communion of the Spirit whose revelations I often communicated to them, and they believed and said my wisdom came from God. I now began to prepare them for my purpose, by telling them something was about to happen that would terminate in fulfilling the great promise that had been made to me—About this time I was placed under an overseer, from whom I ranaway—and after remaining in the woods thirty days, I returned, to the astonishment of the negroes on the plantation, who thought I had made my escape to some other part of the country, as my father had done before. But the reason of my return was, that the Spirit appeared to me and said I had my wishes directed to the things of this world, and not to the kingdom of Heaven, and that I should return to the service of my earthly master—"For he who knoweth his Master's will, and doeth it not, shall be beaten with many stripes, and thus have I chastened you." And the negroes found fault, and murmured against me, saying that if they had my sense they would not serve any master in the world. And about this time I had a vision—and I saw white spirits and black spirits engaged in battle, and the sun was darkened—the thunder rolled in the Heavens, and blood flowed in streams—and I heard a voice saying, "Such is your luck, such you are called to see, and let it come rough or smooth, you must surely bare it." I now withdrew myself as much as my situation would permit, from the intercourse of my fellow servants, for the avowed purpose of serving the Spirit more fully—and it appeared to me, and reminded me of the things it had already shown me, and that it would then reveal to me the knowledge of the elements, the revolution of the planets, the operation of tides, and changes of the seasons. After this revelation in the year 1825, and the knowledge of the elements being made known to me, I sought more than ever to obtain true holiness before the great day of judgment should appear, and then I began to receive the true knowledge of faith. And from the first steps of righteousness until the last, was I made perfect; and the Holy Ghost was with me, and said "Behold me as I stand in the Heavens"—and I looked and saw the forms of men in different attitudes—and there were lights in the sky to which the children of darkness gave other names than what they really were—for they were the lights of the Saviour's hands, stretched forth from east to west, even as they were extended on the cross on Calvary for the redemption of sinners. And I wondered greatly at these miracles, and prayed to be informed of a certainty of the meaning thereof—and shortly afterwards, while labouring in the field, I discovered drops of blood on the corn, as though it were dew from heaven—and I communicated it to many, both white and black, in the neighbourhood—and I then found on the leaves in the woods hieroglyphic characters and numbers, with the forms of men in different attitudes, portrayed in blood, and representing the figures I had seen before in the heavens. —And now the Holy Ghost had revealed itself to me, and made plain the miracles it had shown me—For as the blood of Christ had been shed on this earth, and had ascended to heaven for the salvation of sinners, and was now returning to earth again in the form of dew—and as the leaves on the trees bore the impression of the figures I had seen in the heavens, it was plain to me that the Saviour was about to lay down the yoke he had borne for the sins of men, and the great day of judgment was at hand.—About this time, I told these things to a white man, on whom it had a wonderful effect—and he ceased from his wickedness, and was attacked immediately with a cutaneous eruption, and blood oozed from the pores of his skin, and after praying and fasting nine days, he was healed, and the Spirit appeared to me again, and said, as the Saviour had been baptised, so should we be also—and when the white people would not let us be baptised by the church, we went down into the water together, in the sight of many who reviled us, and were baptised by the Spirit—After this I rejoiced greatly, and gave thanks to God. And on the 12th of May, 1828, I heard a loud noise in the heavens, and the Spirit instantly appeared to me and said the Serpent was loosened, and Christ had laid down the yoke he had borne for the sins of men, and that I should take it on and fight against the Serpent, for the time was fast approaching, when the first should be last and the last should be first. *Ques.* Do you not find yourself mistaken now? *Ans.* Was not Christ crucified? And by signs in the heavens that it would make known to me when I should commence the great work—and until the first sign appeared, I should conceal it from the knowledge of men—And on the appearance of the sign, (the eclipse of the sun last February) I should arise and prepare myself, and slay my enemies with their own weapons. And immediately on the sign appearing in the heavens, the seal was removed from my lips, and I communicated the great work laid out for me to do, to four in whom I had the greatest confidence, (Henry, Hark, Nelson and Sam)—It was intended by us to have begun the work of death on the 4th of July last—Many were the plans formed and rejected by us, and it affected my mind to such a degree, that I fell sick, and the time passed without our coming to any determination how to commence—Still forming new schemes and rejecting them, when the sign appeared again, which determined me not to wait longer.

Since the commencement of 1830, I had been living with Mr. Joseph Travis, who was to me a kind master, and placed the greatest confidence in me; in fact, I had no cause to complain of his treatment to me. On Saturday evening, the 20th of August, it was agreed between Henry, Hark and myself, to prepare a dinner the next day for the men we expected, and then to concert a plan, as we had not yet determined on any. Hark on the following morning, brought a pig, and Henry brandy, and being joined by Sam, Nelson, Will and Jack, they prepared in the woods a dinner, where, about three o'clock, I joined them.

Q. Why were you so backward in joining them.

A. The same reason that had caused me not to mix with them for years before.

I saluted them on coming up, and asked Will how came he there; he answered, his life was worth no more than others, and his liberty as dear to him. I asked him if he thought to obtain it? He said he would, or lose his life. This was enough to put him in full confidence. Jack, I knew, was only a tool in the hands of Hark, it was quickly agreed we should commence at home (Mr. J. Travis') on that night, and until we had armed and equipped ourselves, and gathered sufficient force, neither age nor sex was to be spared, (which was invariably adhered to.) We remained at the feast until about two hours in the night when we went to the house and found Austin; they all went to the cider press and drank, except myself. On returning to the house, Hark went to the door with an axe, for the purpose of breaking it open, as we knew we were strong enough to murder the family, if they were awaked by the noise; but reflecting that it might create an alarm in the neighborhood, we determined to enter the house secretly, and murder them whilst sleeping. Hark got a ladder and set it against the chimney, on which I ascended, and hoisting a window, entered and came down stairs, unbarred the door, and removed the guns from their places. It was then observed that I must spill the first blood. On which armed with a hatchet, and accompanied by Will, I entered my master's chamber; it being dark, I could not give a death blow, the hatchet glanced from his head, he sprang from the bed and called his wife, it was his last word. Will laid him dead, with a blow of his axe, and Mrs. Travis shared the same fate, as she lay in bed. The murder of this family five in number, was the work of a moment, not one of them awoke; there was a little infant sleeping in a cradle, that was forgotten, until we had left the house and gone some distance, when Henry and Will returned and killed it; we got here, four guns that would shoot, and several old muskets, with a pound or two of powder. We remained some time at the barn, where we paraded; I formed them in a line as soldiers, and after carrying them through all the manœuvres I was master of, marched them off to Mr. Salathul Francis', about six hundred yards distant. Sam and Will went to the door and knocked. Mr. Francis asked who was there, Sam replied it was him, and he had a letter for him, on which he got up and came to the door; they immediately seized him, and dragging him out a little from the door, he was dispatched by repeated blows on the head; there was no other white person in the family. We started from there for Mrs. Reese's, maintaining the most perfect silence on our march, where finding the door unlocked, we entered, and murdered Mrs. Reese in her bed, while sleeping; her son awoke, but it was only to sleep the sleep of death, he had only time to say who is that, and he was no more. From Mrs. Reese's we went to Mrs. Turner's, a mile distant, which we reached about sunrise, on Monday morning. Henry, Austin, and Sam, went to the still, where, finding Mr. Peebles, Austin shot him, and the rest of us went to the house; as we approached, the family discovered us, and shut the door. Vain hope! Will, with one stroke of his axe, opened it, and we entered and found Mrs. Turner and Mrs. Newsome in the middle of a room almost frightened to death. Will immediately killed Mrs. Turner, with one blow of his axe. I took Mrs. Newsome by the hand, and with the sword I had when I was apprehended, I struck her several blows over the head, but not being able to kill her, as the sword was dull. Will turning around and discovering it, dispatched her also. A general destruction of property and search for money and ammunition, always succeeded the murders. By this time my company amounted to fifteen, and nine men mounted, who started for Mrs. Whitehead's, (the other six were to go through a by way to Mr. Bryant's, and rejoin us at Mrs. Whitehead's,) as we approached the house we discovered Mr. Richard Whitehead standing in the cotton patch, near the lane fence; we called him over into the lane, and Will, the executioner, was near at hand, with his fatal axe, to send him to an untimely grave. As we pushed on to the house, I discovered some one run round the garden, and thinking it was some of the white family, I pursued them, but finding it was a servant girl belonging to the house, I returned to commence the work of death, but they whom I left, had not been idle; all the family were already murdered, but Mrs. Whitehead and her daughter Margaret. As I came round to the door I saw Will pulling Mrs. Whitehead out of the house, and at the step he nearly severed her head from her body, with his broad axe. Miss Margaret, when I discovered her, had concealed herself in the corner, formed by the projection of the cellar cap from the house; on my approach she fled, but was soon overtaken, and after repeated blows with a sword, I killed her by a blow on the head, with a fence rail. By this time, the six who had gone by Mr. Bryant's, rejoined us, and informed me they had done the work of death assigned them. We again divided, part going to Mr. Richard Porter's, and from thence to Nathaniel Francis', the others to Mr. Howell Harris', and Mr. T. Doyle's. On my reaching Mr. Porter's, he had escaped with his family. I understood there, that the alarm had already spread, and I immediately returned to bring up those sent to Mr. Doyle's, and Mr. Howell Harris'; the party I left going on to Mr. Francis', having told them I would join them in that neighborhood. I met these sent to Mr. Doyle's and Mr. Harris' returning, having met Mr. Doyle on the road and killed him; and learning from some who joined them, that Mr. Harris was from home, I immediately pursued the course taken by the party gone on before; but knowing they would complete the work of death and pillage, at Mr. Francis' before I could get there, I went to Mr. Peter Edwards', expecting to find them there, but they had been here also. I then went to Mr. John T. Barrow's, they had been here and murdered him. I pursued on their track to Capt. Newit Harris', where I found the greater part mounted, and ready to start; the men now amounting to about forty, shouted and hurraed as I rode up, some were in the yard, loading their guns, others drinking. They said Captain Harris and his family had escaped, the property in the house they destroyed, robbing him of money and other valuables. I ordered them to mount and march instantly, this was about nine or ten o'clock, Monday morning. I proceeded to Mr. Levi Waller's, two or three miles distant. I took my station in the rear, and as it was my object to carry terror and devastation wherever we went, I placed fifteen or twenty of the best armed and most to be relied on, in front, who generally approached the houses as fast as their horses could run; this was for two purposes, to prevent their escape and strike terror to the inhabitants—on this account I never got to the houses, after leaving Mrs. Whitehead's until the murders were committed, except in one case. I sometimes got in sight in time to see the work of death completed, viewed the mangled bodies as they lay, in silent satisfaction, and immediately started in quest of other victims —Having murdered Mrs. Waller and ten children, we started for Mr. William Williams'—having killed him and two little boys that were there; while engaged in this, Mrs. Williams fled and got some distance from the house, but she was pursued, overtaken, and compelled to get up behind one of the company, who brought her back, and after showing her the mangled body of her lifeless husband, she was told to get down and lay by his side, where she was shot dead. I then started for Mr. Jacob Williams', where the family were murdered—Here we found a young man named Drury, who had come on business with Mr. Williams—he was pursued, overtaken and shot. Mrs. Vaughan's was the next place we visited—and after murdering the family here, I determined on starting for Jerusalem —Our number amounted now to fifty or sixty, all mounted and armed with guns, axes, swords and clubs—On reaching Mr. James W. Parker's gate, immediately on the road leading to Jerusalem, and about three miles distant, it was proposed to me to call there, but I objected, as I knew he was gone to Jerusalem, and my object was to reach there as soon as possible; but some of the men having relations at Mr. Parker's it was agreed that they might call and get his people. I remained at the gate on the road, with seven or eight; the others going across the field to the house, about half a mile off. After waiting some time for them, I became impatient, and started to the house for them, and on our return we were met by a party of white men, who had pursued our blood-stained track, and who had fired on those at the gate, and dispersed them, which I knew nothing of, not having been at that time rejoined by any of them—Immediately on discovering the whites, I ordered my men to halt and form, as they appeared to be alarmed—The white men eighteen in number, approached us in about one hundred yards, when one of them fired. . . . And I discovered about half of them retreating, I then ordered my men to fire and rush on them; the few remaining stood their ground until we approached within fifty yards, when they fired and retreated. We pursued and overtook some of them who we thought we left dead; . . . after pursuing them about two hundred yards, and rising a little hill, I discovered they were met by another party, and had halted, and were re-loading their guns. . . . As I saw them reloading their guns, and more coming up than I saw at first, and several of my bravest men being wounded, the others became panick struck and squandered over the field; the white men pursued and fired on us several times. Hark had his horse shot under him, and I caught another for him as it was running by me; five or six of my men were wounded, but none left on the field; finding myself defeated here I instantly determined to go through a private way, and cross the Nottoway river at the Cypress Bridge, three miles below Jerusalem, and attack that place in the rear, as I expected they would look for me on the other road, and I had a great desire to get there to procure arms and ammunition. After going a short distance in this private way, accompanied by about twenty men, I overtook two or three who told me the others were dispersed in every direction. After trying in vain to collect a sufficient force to proceed to Jerusalem, I determined to return, as I was sure they would make back to their old neighborhood, where they would rejoin me, make new recruits, and come down again. On my way back, I called at Mrs. Thomas's, Mrs. Spencer's, and several other places, the white families having fled, we found no more victims to gratify our thirst for blood, we stopped at Majr. Ridley's quarter for the night, and being joined by four of his men, with the recruits made since my defeat, we mustered now about forty strong. After placing out sentinels, I laid down to sleep, but was quickly roused by a great racket; starting up, I found some mounted, and others in great confusion; one of the sentinels having given the alarm that we were about to be attacked, I ordered some to ride round and reconnoiter, and on their return the others being more alarmed, not knowing who they were, fled in different ways, so that I was reduced to about twenty again; with this I determined to attempt to recruit, and proceed on to rally in the neighborhood I had left. Dr. Blunt's was the nearest house, which we reached just before day; on riding up the yard, Hark fired a gun. We expected Dr. Blunt and his family were at Maj. Ridley's, as I knew there was a company of men there; the gun was fired to ascertain if any of the family were at home; we were immediately fired upon and retreated leaving several of my men. I do not know what became of them, as I never saw them afterwards. Pursuing our course back, and coming in sight of Captain Harris's, where we had been the day before, we discovered a party of white men at the house, on which all deserted me but two, (Jacob and Nat,) we concealed ourselves in the woods until near night, when I sent them in search of Henry, Sam, Nelson and Hark, and directed them to rally all they could, at the place we had had our dinner the Sunday before, where they would find me, and I accordingly returned there as soon as it was dark, and remained until Wednesday evening, when discovering white men riding around the place as though they were looking for some one, and none of my men joining me, I concluded Jacob and Nat had been taken, and compelled to betray me.—On this I gave up all hope for the present; and on Thursday night, after having supplied myself with provisions from Mr. Travis's, I scratched a hole under a pile of fence rails in a field, where I concealed myself for six weeks, never leaving my hiding place but for a few minutes in the dead of night to get water, which was very near; thinking by this time I could venture out, I began to go about in the night and eaves drop the houses in the neighborhood; pursuing this course for about a fortnight and gathering little or no intelligence, afraid of speaking to any human being, and returning every morning to my cave before the dawn of day. I know not how long I might have led this life, if accident had not betrayed me, a dog in the neighborhood passing by my hiding place one night while I was out, was attracted by some meat I had in my cave, and crawled in and stole it, and was coming out just as I returned. A few nights after, two negroes having started to go hunting with the same dog, and passed that way, the dog came again to the place, and having just gone out to walk about, discovered me and barked, on which thinking myself discovered, I spoke to them to beg concealment. On making myself known, they fled from me. Knowing then they would betray me, I immediately left my hiding place, and was pursued almost incessantly until I was taken a fortnight afterwards by Mr. Benjamin Phipps, in a little hole I had dug out with my sword, for the purpose of concealment, under the top of a fallen tree. On Mr. Phipps discovering the place of my concealment, he cocked his gun and aimed at me. I requested him not to shoot, and I would give up, upon which he demanded my sword. I delivered it to him, and he brought me to prison. During the time I was pursued, I had many hair breadth escapes, which your time will not permit you to relate. I am here loaded with chains, and willing to suffer the fate that awaits me. . . .

The Commonwealth vs. *Nat Turner.* } Charged with making insurrection, and plotting to take away the lives of divers free white persons, &c. on the 22d of August, 1831.

The court composed of ———, having met for the trial of Nat Turner, the prisoner was brought in and arraigned, and upon his arraignment pleaded *Not guilty;* saying to his counsel, that he did not feel so.

On the part of the Commonwealth, Levi Waller was introduced, who being sworn, deposed as follows: *(agreeably to Nat's own Confession.)* Col. Trezvant was then introduced, who being sworn, numerated Nat's Confession to him, as follows: *(His Confession as given to Mr. Gray.)* The prisoner introduced no evidence, and the case was submitted without argument to the court, who having found him guilty, Jeremiah Cobb, Esq. Chairman, pronounced the sentence of the court, in the following words: "Nat Turner! Stand up. Have you any thing to say why sentence of death should not be pronounced against you?"

Ans. I have not. I have made a full confession to Mr. Gray, and I have nothing more to say.

Thomas R. Gray (ed.), *The Confessions of Nat Turner* (Richmond, Va., 1832).

The Self-Defense of the Rev. Peter Williams

In 1834, Benjamin T. Onderdonk was presiding bishop of the New York area for the Episcopal Church. In a letter addressed to the Rev. Peter Williams, first rector of St. Philip's Church in New York, the bishop advised Williams to resign from the American Anti-Slavery Society. Williams made his reply to the bishop through an open letter to the citizens of New York.

College Place, July 12, 1834

Rev. and Dear Sir:

I am sure I need not assure you of the sincere sympathy which I feel for you and your people. . . . Perhaps, however, you have pursued the most prudent course in closing your church.

Let me advise you to resign, at once, your connexion, in every department, with the Anti-Slavery Society, and to make public your resignation. I cannot now give you all my reasons. Let me see you as soon as you can. I can better say than write all I think. Make the within known in any way, and as extensively as you can. "The raging of the sea, and the madness of the people," you know are connected in Holy Writ, and the one might as well be attempted to be stopped as the other. My advice, therefore, is give up at once. Let it be seen that on whichsoever side right may be, St. Philip's Church will be found on the Christian side of meekness, order, and self-sacrifice to common good, and the peace of the community. You will be no losers by it, for the God of peace will be to you also a God of all consolation.

Let me hear from you or see you soon. And believe me to be, with faithful prayer for you and yours, your affectionate brother in Christ.

Benj. T. Onderdonk

* * * * *

Rev. Mr. Williams,
To the Citizens of New York:—

It has always been painful to me to appear before the public. It is especially painful to me to appear before them in the columns of a newspaper, at a time of great public excitement like the present; but when I received Holy orders, I promised "reverently to obey my Bishop, to follow with a glad mind his godly admonitions, and to submit myself to his godly judgment."

My Bishop, without giving his opinions on the subject of Abolition, has now advised me, in order that the Church under my care "may be found on the Christian side of meekness, order, and self-sacrifice to the community," to resign connexion with the Anti-Slavery Society, and to make public my resignation. There has been no instance hitherto, in which I have not sought his advice in matters of importance to the Church, and endeavored to follow it when given; and I have no wish that the present should be an exception.

But in doing this, I hope I shall not be considered as thrusting myself too much upon public attention, by adverting to some facts in relation to myself and the subject of the present excitement, in the hope that when they are calmly considered, a generous public will not censure me for the course I have pursued.

My father was born in Beekman Street in this city, and was never, in all his life, further from it than Albany; nor have I ever been absent from it longer than three months, when I went to Hayti for the benefit of my brethren who had migrated there from this country. In the revolutionary war, my father was a decided advocate for American Independence, and his life was repeatedly jeopardized in its cause. Permit me to relate one instance, which shows that neither the British sword, nor British gold, could make him a traitor to his country. He was living in the state of Jersey, and Parson Chapman, a champion of American liberty, of great influence throughout that part of the country, was sought after by the British troops. My father immediately mounted a horse and rode round among his parishioners, to notify them of his danger, and to call them to help in removing him and his goods to a place of safety. He then carried him to a private place, and as he was returning a British officer rode up to him, and demanded in the most peremptory manner, "where is Parson Chapman?" "I cannot tell," was the reply. On that he drew his sword, and raising it over his head, said "Tell me where he is, or I will instantly cut you down." Again he replied, "I cannot tell." Finding threats useless, the officer put up his sword and drew out a purse of gold, saying, "If you will tell me where he is, I will give you this." The reply still was, "I cannot tell." The officer cursed him and rode off.

This attachment to the country of his birth was strengthened and confirmed by the circumstances that the very day on which the British evacuated this city, was the day on which he obtained his freedom by purchase through the help of some republican friends of the Methodist Church, who loaned him money for that purpose, and to the last year of his life he always spoke of that day as one which gave double joy to his heart, by freeing him from domestic bondage and his native city from foreign enemies.

The hearing him talk of these and similar matters, when I was a child, filled my soul with an ardent love for the American government, and made me feel, as I said in my first public discourse, that it was my greatest glory to be an American.

A lively and growing interest for the prosperity of my country pervaded my whole sole and led to the belief, notwithstanding the peculiarly unhappy condition of my brethren in the United States, that by striving to become intelligent, useful and virtuous members of the community, the time would come when they would all have abundant reason to rejoice in the glorious Declaration of American Independence.

Reared with these feelings, though fond of retirement I felt a burning desire to be useful to my brethren and to my country; and when the last war between this country and Great Britain broke out, I felt happy to render the humble services of my pen, my tongue, and my hands, towards rearing fortifications to defend our shores against invasion. I entreated my brethren to help in the defence of the country, and went with them to the work; and no sacrifice has been considered too great by me, for the benefit of it or them.

These were among the feelings that led me into the ministry, and induced me to sacrifice all my worldly prospects, and live upon the scanty pittance which a colored minister must expect to receive for his labors, and to endure the numerous severe trials peculiar to his situation.

My friends who assisted me in entering into the ministry, know that if the Church with which I am connected as a Pastor, could have been established without my becoming its minister, I should have been this day enjoying the sweets of private life, and there has not been a day since I have entered upon the duties of my office, that I would not have cheerfully retired to earn my living in some humbler occupation, could I have done so consistently with my sense of duty.

By the transaction of last Friday evening, my church is now closed, and I have been compelled to leave my people. Whether I shall be permitted to return to them again, I cannot say, but whether or not, I have the satisfaction of feeling that I have laboured earnestly and sincerely for their temporal and spiritual benefit, and the promotion of the public good.

In regard to my opposition to the Colonization Society it has extended no farther than that Society has held out the idea, that a colored man, however he may strive to make himself intelligent, virtuous and useful, can never enjoy the privileges of a citizen of the United States, but must ever remain a degraded and oppressed being. I could not, and do not believe that the principles of the Declaration of Independence, and of the Gospel of Christ, have not power sufficient to raise him, at some future day, to that rank. I believe that such doctrines tend very much to discourage the efforts which are making for his improvement at home. But whenever any man of color, after having carefully considered the subject, has thought it best to emigrate to Africa, I have not opposed him, but have felt it my duty to aid him, in all my power, on his way, and I have the satisfaction of being able to prove that the most prominent and most useful men in the Colony have been helped there by me.

I helped John B. Russwurm to go to Liberia, and as a token of gratitude for my aid in the case, he sent me his thermometer, which I have now hanging up in my house. . . .

I was anxious that some of our youth should have the opportunity of acquiring a liberal education, and felt that it was my duty to strive to rear up some well qualified colored ministers. I selected two lads of great promise, and made every possible effort to get them a collegiate education. But the Colleges were all closed against them. Anti-Slavery men generously offered to aid us in establishing a Manual Labor College, or High School, for ourselves, and to aid us in all the objects of the Phenix Society. I joined with them in this work heartily, and wished them all success, as I still do in their endeavors, by all means sanctioned by law, humanity and religion, to obtain freedom for my brethren, and to elevate them to the enjoyment of equal rights with the other citizens of the community; but I insisted that while they were laboring to restore us to our rights, it was exclusively our duty to labor to qualify our people for the enjoyment of those rights. . . .

Having given this simple and faithful statement of facts; I now, in conformity to the advice of my Bishop, publicly resign my station as a member of the Board of Managers of the Anti-Slavery Society, and of its executive committee, without, however, passing any opinion respecting the principles on which that society is founded.

I would have offered my resignation long before this, had I not thought that there might be occasions, when by having the privilege of addressing the Board, I might exercise a restraining influence upon measures calculated to advance our people faster than they were prepared to be advanced, and the public feeling would bear. But I am not disposed to blame the members of the Anti-Slavery Society for their measures. I consider them as good men, and good Christians, and true lovers of their country, and of all mankind. I thought they had not an opportunity of knowing my brethren, nor the state of public prejudice against them, as well as myself, and all I supposed that I could do was to aid them in this particular.

I hope that both they and the public generally will judge charitably of this hastily drawn communication.

Peter Williams
Rector of St. Philip's Church, Centre St.

New York, July 14, 1834.

African Repository and Colonial Journal, X (August 1834).

William C. Nell's Account of the "Garrison Mob"

Black abolitionist William C. Nell, in a letter to fellow abolitionist Samuel J. May, gives an account of the day in 1835 when William Lloyd Garrison was mobbed and jailed.

En Route from Philadelphia to Boston,
October 21, 1855

Respected Friend:

Being unavoidably absent from home during your commemoration of the second decade of the Boston or Garrison Mob, I reconciled myself mainly by the fact, that thereby I had the opportunity afforded me of visiting that victim of judicial depotism and slaveholding arbitration, Passmore Williamson.

Twenty years ago this day, William Lloyd Garrison, for promulgating the idea of immediate emancipation, was delivered from the murderous hands of a Boston mob, composed of "gentlemen of property and standing," into Leverett Street Jail; and at this hour, Passmore Williamson endures martyrdom in Moyamensing Prison for his application of immediate emancipation to Jane Johnson and her two boys from her self-styled owner, John H. Wheeler.

My reflections upon the two historical events of 1835 and 1855, induced my noting down the following reminiscences, hoping space may be found for them in your published report.

I well remember the emphatically cloudy day, October 21, 1835, and the various scenes and incidents which characterised it, shrouding with indelible disgrace and infamy my native city.

A friend of mine then boarded at a house in Boylston street, where, at the tea-table that evening, were assembled many Boston merchants. The Abolition Mob was the theme of conversation; and while a majority evinced their pro-slavery spirit by approving of what had occurred, two gentlemen warmly dissented—one of whom, David Tilden, Esq., immediately became a subscriber to *The Liberator,* and so continued until his decease, a few years since.

A sister of the coachman who so adroitly eluded the mob, and landed Mr. Garrison safely at the jail, often alluded to the impression made by that hour upon her brother.

I have obtained the following facts from colored Anti-Slavery friends, whose feelings were deeply moved on the occasion.

John T. Hilton accompanied David H. Ela (a printer in Cornhill, since deceased) to the meeting. They found the stairs impassable, in consequence of the crowd, and an altercation ensued. Mr. Ela was struck a severe blow by a man who rebuked him for upholding Abolitionists and "niggers." He resisted, until the parties were separated by the crowd rushing to seize Garrison in Wilson's Lane. The women came down the stairs amidst the hootings and insults of the mob. Two prominent men were engaged in tearing down the sign. Mr. Hilton heard a printer inform the mob where Garrison was secreted, in the rear of the building, where he (Mr. H.) went with the rest, to do what he could to rescue him, or, at all events, to be at his side. He saw Mr. Garrison dragged into State street, divested of coat and hat, and did not leave until Sheriff Parkman had him in the City Hall.

John Boyer Vashon, of Pittsburg, Pa., was an eye-witness to the terrible scene, which was heart-rending beyond his ability ever afterwards to express, as, of all living men, John B. Vashon loved William Lloyd Garrison most; and this feeling of affection continued, for aught that is known, to the day of his death. When the mob passed along Washington street, shouting and yelling like madmen, the apprehensions of Mr. Vashon became fearfully aroused. Presently there approached a group which appeared even more infuriated than the rest, and he beheld, in the midst of this furious throng, Garrison himself, led on like a beast to the slaughter. He had been on the field of battle, had faced the cannon's mouth, seen its lightnings flash and heard its thunders roar, but such a sight as this was more than the old citizen soldier could bear, without giving vent to a flood of tears. The next day, the old soldier, who had helped to preserve his country's liberty on the plighted faith of security to his own, but who had lived to witness freedom of speech and of the press stricken down by mob violence, and life itself in jeopardy, because that liberty was asked for him and his, with spirits crushed and faltering hopes, called to administer a word of consolation to the bold and courageous young advocate of immediate and universal emancipation. Mr. Garrison subsequently thus referred to this circumstance in his paper:—"On the day of that riot in Boston, he dined at my house, and the next morning called to see me in prison, bringing with him a new hat for me, in the place of one that was cut in pieces by the knives of men of property and standing."

Rev. James E. Crawford, now of Nantucket, boarded in Boston at the time of the mob, and, walking up State street, suddenly encountered the riotous multitude. On learning that Mr. Garrison was mobbed for words and deeds in behalf of the enslaved colored man, his heart and soul became fully dedicated to the cause of immediate emancipation. . . .

Imprisonment is a feature of martyrdom with which Abolitionists in the United States have become familiar, especially Mr. Garrison, who, at the bidding of slavery, was, in 1829, incarcerated in Baltimore. But these persecutions are to be accepted as jewels in their crown, as seals of their devotion to the cause of millions now in the prison-house of bondage.

For whose speedy emancipation, I remain,

Fraternally yours,

William C. Nell

Carter G. Woodson (ed.), *The Mind of the Negro: As Reflected in Letters Written during the Crisis, 1800–1860* (Washington, 1926).

The *Amistad* Affair: A Descriptive Account

In 1839, fifty-three slaves aboard the Amistad *forcibly assumed control of the vessel. They eventually gained their freedom through a decision of the United States Supreme Court. The slaves had been taken from Africa to Havana, Cuba, where they were purchased by two men, Ruiz and Montez. The* Amistad *sailed for Puerto Principe from Havana with the slaves, their owners, and items of cargo on board. It was at this point that the mutiny occurred.*

Following the murder of the Captain and cook, the slaves forced Ruiz and Montez to pilot the ship. By day they navigated toward Africa, and by night toward America. Through this navigational strategy of Ruiz and Montez, they were intercepted by Lieutenant-Commander Gedney aboard the Washington.

At the close of the entire investigation, Judge Judson decided that the Negroes should go free and be turned over to the President for return to Africa. The case was appealed to the Circuit Court and from there to the United States Su-

preme Court. In September 1841, the Supreme Court ruled on the original findings of the lower court.

While this vessel was sounding this day between Gardner's and Montauk Points, a schooner was seen lying in shore off Culloden Point, under circumstances so suspicious as to authorize Lieut. Com. Gedney to stand in to see what was her character—seeing a number of people on the beach with carts and horses, and a boat passing to and fro, a boat was armed and dispatched with an officer to board her. On coming along side, a number of negroes were discovered on her deck, and twenty or thirty more were on the beach—two white men came forward and claimed the protection of the officer. The schooner proved to be the *Amistad,* Capt. Ramonflues, from the Havanah, bound to Guanajah, Port Principe, with 54 blacks and two passengers on board; the former, four nights after they were out, rose and murdered the captain and three of the crew—they then took possession of the vessel, with the intention of returning to the coast of Africa. Pedro Montez, passenger, and José Ruiz, owner of the slaves and a part of the cargo, were only saved to navigate the vessel. After boxing about for four days in the Bahama Channel, the vessel was steered for the Island of St. Andrews, near New Providence—from thence she went to Green Key, where the blacks laid in a supply of water. After leaving this place the vessel was steered by Pedro Montez, for New Providence, the negroes being under the impression that she was steering for the coast of Africa—they would not however permit her to enter the port, but anchored every night off the coast. The situation of the two whites was all this time truly deplorable, being treated with the greatest severity, and Pedro Montez, who had charge of the navigation, was suffering from two severe wounds, one on the head and one on the arm, their lives being threatened every instant. He was ordered to change the course again for the coast of Africa, the negroes themselves steering by the sun in the day time, while at night he would alter their course so as to bring them back to their original place of destination. They remained three days off Long Island, to the eastward of Providence, after which time they were two months on the ocean, sometimes steering to the eastward, and whenever an occasion would permit, the whites would alter the course to the northward and westward, always in hopes of falling in with some vessel of war, or being enabled to run into some port, when they would be relieved from their horrid situation. Several times they were boarded by vessels; once by an American schooner from Kingston; on these occasions the whites were ordered below, while the negroes communicated and traded with the vessels; the schooner from Kingston supplied them with a demijon of water for the moderate sum of one dubloon—this schooner, whose name was not ascertained, finding that the negroes had plenty of money, remained lashed alongside the *Amistad* for twenty-four hours, though they must have been aware that all was not right on board, and probably suspected the character of the vessel—this was on the 18th of the present month [August]; the vessel was steered to the northward and westward, and on the 20th instant, distant from New York 25 miles, the Pilot Boat No. 3 came alongside and gave the negroes some apples. She was also hailed by No. 4: when the latter boat came near, the negroes armed themselves and would not permit her to board them; they were so exasperated with the two whites for bringing them so much out of their way, that they expected every moment to be murdered. On the 24th they made Montauk Light and steered for it in the hope of running the vessel ashore, but the tide drifted them up the bay and they anchored where they were found by the Brig *Washington,* off Culloden Point. The negroes were found in communication with the shore, where they laid in a fresh supply of water, and were on the point of sailing again for the coast of Africa. They had a good supply of money, some of which it is likely was taken by the people on the beach. After disarming and sending them on board from the beach, the leader jumped overboard with three hundred doubloons about him, the property of the Captain, all of which he succeeded in loosing from his person, and then submitted himself to be captured. The schooner was taken in tow by the brig and carried into New London . . .

Cingue [*sic*] having been put on board the *Washington,* displayed much uneasiness, and seemed so very anxious to get on board the schooner, that his keepers allowed him to return. Once more on the deck of the *Amistad,* the blacks clustered around him, laughing, screaming, and making other extravagant demonstrations of joy. When the noise had subsided, he made an address, which raised their excitement to such a pitch, that the officer in command had Cingue led away by force. He was returned to the *Washington,* and was manacled to prevent his leaping overboard. On Wednesday he signified by motions, that if they would take him on board the schooner again, he would show them a handkerchief full of doubloons. He was accordingly sent on board. His fetters were taken off, and he once more went below, where he was received by the Africans in a still more wild and enthusiastic manner than he was the day previous. Instead of finding the doubloons, he again made an address to the blacks, by which they were very much excited. Dangerous consequences were apprehended; Cingue was seized, taken from the hold, and again fettered. While making his speech, his eye was often turned to the sailors in charge; the blacks yelled, leapt about, and seemed to be animated with the same spirit and determination of their leader. Cingue, when taken back to the *Washington,* evinced little or no emotion, but kept his eye steadily fixed on the schooner.

. . . .

At anchor, on board the U.S. cutter *Washington,* commanded by Lieut. Gedney.

New London, Aug. 29, 1839.

His Honor Andrew T. Judson, U.S. District Judge, on the bench, C. A. Ingersol, Esq. appearing for the U.S. District Attorney. The Court was opened by the U.S. Marshal. The clerk then swore Don Pedro Montez, owner of part of the cargo, and three of the slaves, and Don Jose Ruiz, also owner of part of the cargo, and forty-nine of the slaves. These gentlemen then lodged a complaint against Joseph Cingue [*sic*], (the leader in the alledged offense,) Antonio, Simon, Lacis, Peter, Martin, Manuel, Andrew, Edward, Caledonis, Bartholomew, Raymond, Augustine, Evaristo, Casimiro, Mercho, Gabriel, Santaria, Escalastio, Paschal, Estanilaus, Desiderio, Nicholas, Stephen, Thomas, Corsino, Lewis, Bartolo, Julian, Frederick, Saturnio, Lardusolado, Celistino, Epifanio, Tevacio, Genancio, Philip, Francis, Hipiloto, Venito, Tidoro, Vicinto, Dionecio, Apolonio, Ezidiquiel, Leon, Julius, Hippoloto, 2d, and Zinon, or such of the above as might be alive at that time. It was ascertained that Joseph Cingue, and 38 others, were alive, and on the complaint an indictment was framed charging them with murder and piracy on board the Spanish schooner Amistad.

Joseph Cingue, the leader, was brought into the cabin manacled. He had a cord round his neck, to which a snuff box was suspended. He wore a red flannel shirt and duck pantaloons.

Lieut. R. W. Meade, who speaks the Spanish language both elegantly and fluently, acted as an interpreter between the Spaniards and the court.

Several bundles of letters were produced, saved from the Amistad, and such as were unsealed, read. . . .

Many of the events which are detailed in the narrative, were omitted in the evidence as having no bearing on the guilt or innocence of the accused, in the present state of the proceedings.

Senor Don Jose Ruiz was next sworn, and testified as follows. I bought 49 slaves in Havana, and shipped them on board the schooner Amistad. We sailed for Guanaja, the intermediate port for Principe. For the four first days every thing went on well. In the night heard a noise in the forecastle. All of us were asleep except the man at the helm. Do not know how things began; was awoke by the noise. This man Joseph, I saw. Cannot tell how many were engaged. There was no moon. It was very dark. I took up an oar and tried the quell the mutiny; I cried no! no! I then heard one of the crew cry murder. I then heard the captain order the cabin boy to go below and get some bread to throw to them, in hopes to pacify the negroes. I went below and called on Montez to follow me, and told them not to kill me: I did not see the captain killed. They called me on deck, and told me I should not be hurt. I asked them as a favor to spare the old man. They did so. After this they went below and ransacked the trunks of the passengers. Before doing this, they tied our hands. We went on our course—don't know who was at the helm. Next day I missed Captain Ramon Ferrer, two sailors, Manuel Pagilla, and Yacinto ——, and Selestina, the cook. We all slept on deck. The slaves told us next day that they had killed all; but the cabin boy said they had killed only the captain and cook. The other two he said had escaped in the canoe—a small boat. The cabin boy is an African by birth, but has lived a long time in Cuba. His name is Antonio, and belonged to the Captain. From this time we were compelled to steer east in the day: but sometimes the wind would not allow us to steer east, then they would threaten us with death. In the night we steered west, and kept to the northward as much as possible. We were six or seven leagues from land when the outbreak took place. Antonio is yet alive. They would have killed him, but he acted as interpreter between us, as he understood both languages. He is now on board the schooner. Principe is about two days sail from Havana, or 100 leagues, reckoning 3 miles to a league. Sometimes when the winds are adverse, the passage occupies 15 days.

Senor Don Pedro Montez was next sworn. This witness testified altogether in Spanish, Lieut. R. W. Meade, interpreter.

We left Havana on the 28th of June. I owned 4 slaves, 3 females and 1 male. For three days the wind was ahead and all went well. Between 11 and 12 at night, just as the moon was rising, sky dark and cloudy, weather very rainy, on the fourth night I laid down on a matress. Between three and four was awakened by a noise which was caused by blows given to the mulatto cook. I went on deck, and they attacked me. I seized a stick and a knife with a view to defend myself. I did not wish to kill or hurt them. At this time the prisoner wounded me on the head severely with one of the sugar knives, also on the arm. I then ran below and stowed myself between two barrels, wrapped up in a sail. The prisoner rushed after me and attempted to kill me, but was prevented by the interference of another man. I recollect who struck me, but was not sufficiently sensible to distinguish the man who saved me. I was faint from loss of blood. I then was taken on deck and tied to the hand of Ruiz. After this they commanded me to steer for their country. I told them I did not know the way. I was much afraid, and had lost my senses, so I cannot recollect who tied me. On the second day after the mutiny, a heavy gale came on. I still steered, having once been master of a vessel. When recovered, I steered for Havana, in the night by the stars, but by the sun in the day, taking care to make no more way than possible. After sailing fifty leagues, we saw an American merchant ship, but did not speak her. We were also passed by a schooner but were unnoticed. Every moment my life was threatened. I know nothing of the murder of the Captain. All I know of the murder of the mulatto is that I heard the blows. He was asleep when attacked. Next morning the negroes had washed the decks. During the rain the Captain was at the helm. They were all glad, next day, at what had happened. The prisoners treated me harshly, and but for the interference of others, would have killed me several times every day. We kept no reckoning. I did not know how many days we had been out, nor what day of the week it was when the officers came on board. We anchored at least thirty times, and lost an anchor at New Providence. When at anchor we were treated well, but at sea they acted very cruelly towards me. They once wanted me to drop anchor in the high seas. I had no wish to kill any of them, but prevented them from killing each other.

The prisoner was now sent to his quarters, and the Court adjourned to the schooner, that she might be inspected, and that Antonio when making his deposition might recognize those who murdered the Captain and his mulatto cook.

Adjourned investigation on board the Amistad.

John W. Barber (ed.), *A History of the Amistad Captives* (New Haven, Conn., 1840).

A Former Slave Describes His Escape

A revealing story of slavery was told by Jonathan Thomas, an ex-slave from Kentucky who escaped from bondage in the 1840's.

I was born in Kentucky in 1812. My masters name was Henry Beale a wealthy planter in the County of Lexington about 18 miles from Lexington City. Mr. Beale was a kind master & treated me as well as any slave was treated to my knowledge.

My master put me under the care of a Millwright an Englishman . . . with whom I served seven years to learn that trade. I worked with him whenever he could get a job mostly in Kentucky & sometimes in Virginia, Tenesee, Georgia & Ohio.

I became as I thought a good workman and was so esteemed by those who employed me. I earned a great deal of money which I always brought home to my master, who was frequently offered large prices for me but would not sell me.

I always had a desire to be free even when a boy—I made an agreement with my master to buy myself for the sum of $1000 & when my overwork amounted to that sum I was to have my freedom.

I was very diligent & saving & the amount of my overwork wages which I placed in his hands from time to time amounted to nearly $400 last June when he died while I was engaged in building a mill at a distance. When I returned home & found that he was dead I gave the money which I bro't home to my masters son John out of which he gave me only one shilling—now John was a very different person from my old master, he was a reckless fellow a dissipated spendthrift his father would never trust him with any business he would go to northern citys frequently and spend the summer months.

Soon after my masters death John began to sell off slaves the most ready way to get money & I found out from a neighbor that he had sold me to go to Georgia. I reminded him that I had agreed with his father for my freedom for $1000 as soon as my overwork had amt. to that sum & that I had saved up near $400 towards it which I left in his fathers hands for that purpose—he pretended he knew nothing abt that & cared nothing abt it.

I had always dreaded a state of things which was now very apparent—I had always had to be sure a kind master but he was old & I knew not what would become of me when he died & the tho't of it harrassed my mind continually & every year & month & day I saw my fate approaching—I had married a free woman by whom I had two children. For a long time before my masters death we talked of Canada & determined to strike for it but could not screw our courage up to the starting point but when the dreaded event of my old masters death came & his cruel intemperate son John had grasped all my earnings which years of hard toil had saved up in his fathers hands to buy my freedom & the unfeeling & hardened wretch had actually bargained with a Georgia Slave driver who was to have paid $1200 for me who in a few days would forever separate me from my dear wife & children my mind was then fixed on Canada but how to reach it I knew not I had no money—no friends nevertheless I resolved to start at all costs.

There was a Quaker living near by the name of Adam Tucker who altho he would not talk loud talked true he knew that John Beale was intemperate & a great spendthrift & would . . . sell the old mans slaves—he knew my situation too & he gave me good advice—there are many such men as Adam Tucker round Lexington who are becoming more & more bold against slavery & Cassius M. Clay is their mouthpiece.

My wife & children were free—I agreed with a young man my wifes cousin to go with them to Canada & they started in July last & were to stop two days in Buffalo at the house of her cousins father & I was to have started 8 days after they left. I calculated that we all should arrive there near the same time but fate ordered it otherwise—I left the old Plantation near the end of last July stowing some clothes & provisions in my Knapsack strapped to my back—I took the Ohio road & travelled upon it in the night & lay by in the day time—Early in the morning of the third day of my departure I had travelled abt 70 miles & I was still on the great road to Ohio when it was scarcely light enough to see any distant object. I heard the tramp of the horse over the bridge of Smiths Creek behind me & turning round I saw it was my old Masters son John who hallood to me to stop. I quickened my pace but he spurred on his horse & was soon by my side crying out stop! stop! if you don't stop damn you I'll shoot you. I had no belief however that he would shoot me. I went thro the fence & left the road—his horse jumped the fence & followed me. I ran for the swamp & succeeded in getting into the soft ground, he followed close upon me & his horse began to mire & was soon in up to his belly—he drew a pistol from the holsters & fired at me the shot struck me in the ankle of my right foot wounding me very severely & dangerously the shock was so great that I fell upon my hands but soon recovered I unbuckled my knapsack threw it off & ran into a very thick matted & tangled swamp of briars so thick that a dog could scarcely get thro it. I found a little stream of water that parted the thorn bushes & I walked in that little stream a great distance. I finally left the swamp & made for the mountains & reached them about 2 o'clock. On arriving there I sat down to examine my wound which had bled very much filling my boot. I had on a thick pair of boots which broke the force of the shot very much. . . . I picked out 3 shot near my ankle bone & near my shin bone part of which was shot away. I cut a bandage from my shirt & bound it up as well as I could but it soon became very painful—during the short encounter with John he frequently & furiously swore at me to stop but I never answered him a word. I was fully resolved to get clear or die.—he did not follow me into the swamp but sat watching for me to come out—he did not expect I could possibly penetrate it far & I never could had I not found the little stream of water in which I travelled for miles. Sometimes the water was very warm & sometimes very cold when the springs issued out & I have always supposed it was very lucky thing for my wound that it was immersed in the water so long.

I have no idea that John intended to kill me altho I think it very probable that he thot I should die in the swamp—he was an excelent marksman having learned it from me. He intended to shoot the calves of my legs to prevent me from running. A man by the name of Jesse Bingham was with him but he took no part in the fray & never left the road. I was three days in the mountains without any food & travelled then as near as I could judge 40 or 50 miles—I came down from the mountains into the valley still in Kentucky & ate raw corn from the cob in the fields but it did not agree with me it made me sick & dry potatoes & tried to eat them but my appetite had left me I could not eat. I at length found apples peaches & muskmellons which refreshed me very much it was 5 days after I was shot before I entered any house.—I was now in great fear of being over taken & I changed my course from the Ohio road & went into Virginia intending to go to Baltimore because I should not be suspected of taking that route—I passed the white sulphur springs about 40 miles on my right & Staunton, Rockingham, Woodstock & Frederick in Maryland to Baltimore shunning all the public roads & places having travelled 5 or 600 miles. During this long journey I had suffered great pain & distress from my wound. My ankle & leg had swollen so much that I had to cut open my boot & the leg of my pants & lace it up with a string. I thought I should have to loose my foot & leg it seemed to me to be past cure. I dared not show it to any Physician or even white man for fear they would ask me how it came in that terrible situation. I slept in woods, barns & haystacks & begged bread when I came across [some] men who gave bandages for my wound. At Baltimore I went into a little tenement of an old color'd man who asked me to sit down—I was afraid to speak to him, but I wanted to ask him the way to Canada. The old man understood my case the moment I asked him that question—I soon learned that he was my friend indeed—while I was sitting in his hut my leg was in constant & extreme pain & I could not sit still. He noticed my uneasiness & asked what the matter was. I told him I had travelled a great ways & my foot was sore, he looked at it & said that sore didn't come from much travelling—that he could relieve me & take down the swelling—he made a decoction from the root or the leaf of the plant called Apple Peru & applied it upon my leg as warm as I could bear it. I fell asleep under the operation & had a long nap when I awoke the swelling had gone down very much & the pain had nearly subsided. My approach to this old color'd mans hut was by far the most fortunate circumstance to me since I was shot—for he acted the part of the good Samaritan to me. I staid at his hut two days, during which time he paid every attention to me gave me good advice & he went out among the vessels going north & found the Capt of a New Bedford Schooner that was willing to give me free passage to New York where I arrived after a passage of one week. . . .

New York Historical Society

A Free Black Forced into Slavery

Being certified a free person did not always guarantee that a Negro would remain free. Solomon Northup, a free Negro of New York State, was kidnapped in 1841 and forced into slavery on a cotton plantation near the Red River in Louisiana. After twelve years in bondage, he finally regained his freedom. This excerpt from his book describing these experiences tells of the slavepen where Northup was taken shortly after he was kidnapped.

As soon as these formidable whips appeared, I was seized by both of them, and roughly divested of my clothing. My feet, as has been stated, were fastened to the floor. Drawing me over the bench, face downwards, Radburn placed his heavy foot upon the fetters, between my wrists, holding them painfully to the floor. With the paddle, Burch commenced beating me. Blow after blow was inflicted upon my naked body. When his unrelenting arm grew tired, he stopped and asked if I still insisted I was a free man. I did insist upon it, and then the blows were renewed, faster and more energetically, if possible, than before. When again tired, he would repeat the same question, and receiving the same answer, continue his cruel labor. All this time, the incarnate devil was uttering most fiendish oaths. At length the paddle broke, leaving the useless handle in his hand. Still I would not yield. All his brutal blows could not force from my lips the foul lie that I was a slave. Casting madly on the floor the handle of the broken paddle, he seized the rope. This was far more painful than the other. I struggled with all my power, but it was in vain. I prayed for mercy, but my prayer was only answered with imprecations and with stripes. I thought I must die beneath the lashes of the accursed brute. Even now the flesh crawls upon my bones, as I recall the scene. I was all on fire. My sufferings I can compare to nothing else than the burning agonies of hell!

At last I became silent to his repeated questions. I would make no reply. In fact, I was becoming almost unable to speak. Still he plied the lash without stint upon my poor body, until it seemed that the lacerated flesh was stripped from my bones at every stroke. A man with a particle of mercy in his soul would not have beaten even a dog so cruelly. At length Radburn said that it was useless to whip me any more—that I would be sore enough. Thereupon, Burch desisted, saying, with an admonitory shake of his fist in my face, and hissing the words through his firm-set teeth, that if ever I dared to utter again that I was entitled to my freedom, that I had been kidnapped, or any thing whatever of the kind, the castigation I had just received was nothing in comparison with what would follow. He swore that he would either conquer or kill me. With these consolatory words, the fetters were taken from my wrists, my feet still remaining fastened to the ring; the shutter of the little barred window, which had been opened, was again closed, and going out, locking the great door behind them, I was left in darkness as before.

In an hour, perhaps two, my heart leaped to my throat, as the key rattled in the door again. I, who had been so lonely, and who had longed so ardently to see some one, I cared not who, now shuddered at the thought of man's approach. A human face was fearful to me, especially a white one. Radburn entered, bringing with him, on a tin plate, a piece of shriveled fried pork, a slice of bread and a cup of water. He asked me how I felt, and remarked that I had received a pretty severe flogging. He remonstrated with me against the propriety of asserting my freedom. In rather a patronizing and confidential manner, he gave it to me as his advice, that the less I said on that subject the better it would be for me. The man evidently endeavored to appear kind—whether touched at the sight of my sad condition, or with the view of silencing, on my part, any further expression of my rights, it is not necessary now to conjecture. He unlocked the fetters from my ankles, opened the shutters of the little window, and departed, leaving me again alone.

By this time I had become stiff and sore; my body was covered with blisters, and it was with great pain and difficulty that I could move. From the window I could observe nothing but the roof resting on the adjacent wall. At night I laid down upon the damp, hard floor, without any pillow or covering whatever. Punctually, twice a day, Radburn came in, with his pork, and bread, and water. I had but little appetite, though I was tormented with continual thirst. My wounds would not permit me to remain but a few minutes in any one position; so, sitting, or standing, or moving slowly round, I passed the days and nights. I was heart sick and discouraged. Thoughts of my family, of my wife and children, continually occupied my mind. When sleep overpowered me I dreamed of them—

dreamed I was again in Saratoga—that I could see their faces, and hear their voices calling me. Awakening from the pleasant phantasms of sleep to the bitter realities around me, I could but groan and weep. . . .

S. Northup, *Twelve Years a Slave* (New York, n.d.).

Charles Lenox Remond Writes to William Lloyd Garrison

Charles Lenox Remond, son of a former West Indian hairdresser, was born in Salem, Massachusetts, of free parents. None of the Remond family had ever been slaves, but as free people of color they suffered many of the handicaps of their race. In 1838, Remond joined the American Anti-Slavery Society as its first colored lecturer. Until the rise to fame of Frederick Douglass in the 1840's, Remond was probably the best-known man of color in this country.

Because he was so highly regarded by other abolitionists, Remond was frequently in demand as a speaker. In 1842, he took time from his busy schedule to visit the school of Dr. Samuel J. May in Massachusetts. His visit to the school so impressed Remond that he wrote of his experience to William Lloyd Garrison.

Salem, March 5, 1842.

My Very Dear Friend Mr. Garrison:

A line from me has been delayed in the hope of seeing you before this; and since my disappointment, it may not be uninteresting to yourself and others if I intimate that, agreeably to the kind invitation of our mutually esteemed friend, the Rev. Samuel J. May, I visited South Scituate on Tuesday, 22d ultimo, arriving about 3 o'clock in the afternoon. I went immediately to the meeting-house, where I found a large audience assembled, and the children of Mr. May's parish engaged in reciting anti-slavery pieces, with which, I was informed, they had, in a very short time, made themselves acquainted; and my only regret was, that there were not thousands present from a distance to witness for themselves the highly interesting occasion. Many of the pieces were new to me, and never in my life have I seen a juvenile association acquit themselves more creditably. Among the pieces recited, familiar to me, was our friend J. G. Whittier's stanzas, 'Our fellow countrymen in chains,' 'The Yankee Girl,' two or three very pertinent dialogues, the letter of Dr. Rushton to General Washington, &c. The services continued about three hours. At the close of the recitations, I was requested, by friend May, to offer a few remarks; and I frankly confessed the scene was so new in kind and character in our pro-slavery country, that I scarcely knew how to express myself. However, I could not withhold the expression of my thanks, in behalf of the enslaved, to their friend Mr. May, for interesting the children in the worthy cause of suffering millions—and to the parents and friends, for the encouragement they had given by their presence. And what a burning shame it is, that many of the pieces on the subject of slavery and the slave-trade, contained in different school books, have been lost sight of, or been subject to the pruning knife of the slaveholding expurgatorial system! To make me believe that those men, or bodies of men, who have regulated the educational institutions of our country, have humanity in their hearts, is to make me believe a lie; and not less so, in making me believe those christian ministers who profess to love God in words, and hate their brother in works; and I ask, if school committees and schoolmasters,—if christian synods, conventions, ministers and Sabbath-school teachers had resolved and taught, preached and prayed for the proscribed and enslaved colored men, women and children, we should at this time find the rising generation shrinking from the mention of their name—repelling them from the lyceum and lecture room—scouting them from the museum and picture gallery—denying them admission to the white schools, seminaries and colleges—spurning them from the cabin on shipboard, and from artisanship and mechanism on land? I opine otherwise. 'Judicious mothers will always keep in mind, that they are the first book read, and the last put aside, in every child's library: every look, word, tone and gesture, nay, even dress, makes an impression.' [Abbot's Magazine.] And what is true of mothers, I believe also true of fathers, teachers and ministers. I therefore repeat the expression of my gratitude to our long tried friend May, for the excellent example he has set, while I cannot but exclaim, 'Shame on the cant and hypocrisy of those who can teach virtue, preach righteousness, and pray blessings for those only, with skins colored like their own. . . .

Your obliged friend,

C. Lenox Remond

The Liberator (Boston), March 11, 1842.

"I Was Never Reminded of My Complexion": Remond Tells of His Travels Abroad

Because Frederick Douglass overshadowed many abolitionists of equal competence after he arrived on the scene, Remond has not received the recognition that he deserves. In the following address, given in 1842 before the Legislative Committee of the Massachusetts House of Representatives, Remond spoke of his travels abroad and compared them to those he had experienced in this country.

Mr. Chairman, and Gentlemen of the Committee: In rising at this time, and on this occasion, being the first person of color who has ever addressed either of the bodies assembling in this building, I should perhaps, in the first place, observe that, in consequence of the many misconstructions of the principles and measures of which I am the humble advocate, I may in like manner be subject to similar misconceptions from the moment I open my lips in behalf of the prayer of the petitioners for whom I appear, and therefore feel I have the right at least to ask, at the hands of this intelligent Committee, an impartial hearing; and that whatever prejudices they may have imbibed, be eradicated from their minds, if such exist. I have, however, too much confidence in their intelligence, and too much faith in their determination to do their duty as the representatives of this Commonwealth, to presume they can be actuated by partial motives. Trusting, as I do, that the day is not distant, when, on all questions touching the rights of the citizens of this State, men shall be considered great only as they are good—and not that it shall be told, and painfully experienced, that, in this country, this State, aye, this city, the Athens of America, the rights, privileges and immunities of its citizens are measured by complexion, or any other physical peculiarity or conformation, especially such as over which no man has any control. Complexion can in no sense be construed into crime, much less be rightfully made the criterion of rights. Should the people of color, through a revolution of Providence, become a majority, to the last I would oppose it upon the same principle; for, in either case, it would be equally reprehensible and unjustifiable—alike to be condemned and repudiated. It is *Justice* I stand here to claim, and not *Favor* for either complexion. . . .

But it is said we all look alike. If this is true, it is not true that we all behave alike. There is a marked difference; and we claim a recognition of this difference. . . .

Mr. Chairman, the treatment to which colored Americans are exposed in their own country finds a counterpart in no other; and I am free to declare that, in the course of nineteen months' traveling in England, Ireland, and Scotland, I was received, treated and recognized, in public and private society, without any regard to my complexion. From the moment I left the American packet ship in Liverpool, up to the moment I came in contact with it again, I was never reminded of my complexion; and all that know anything of my usage in the American ship, will testify that it was unfit for a brute, and none but one could inflict it. But how unlike that afforded in the British steamer *Columbia!* Owing to my limited resources, I took a steerage passage. On the first day out, the second officer came to inquire after my health; and finding me the only passenger in that part of the ship, ordered the steward to give me a berth in the second cabin; and from that hour until my stepping on shore at Boston, every politeness was shown me by the officers, and every kindness and attention by the stewards; and I feel under deep and lasting obligations to them, individually and collectively.

In no instance was I insulted or treated in any way distinct or dissimilar from other passengers or travelers, either in coaches, railroads, steampackets, or hotels; and if the feeling was entertained, in no case did I discover its existence.

I may with propriety here relate an accident, illustrative of the subject now under consideration. I took a passage ticket at the steampacket office in Glasgow, for Dublin; and on going into the cabin to retire, I found the berth I had engaged occupied by an Irish gentleman and merchant. I enquired if he had not mistaken the number of his berth. He thought not. On comparing tickets, we saw that the clerk had given two tickets of the same number; and it appeared I had received mine first. The gentleman at once offered to vacate the berth, against which I remonstrated, and took my berth in an opposite stateroom. Here, sir, we discover treatment just, impartial, reasonable; and we ask nothing beside. . . .

On my arrival home from England, I went to the railway station, to go to Salem, being anxious to see my parents and sisters as soon as possible—asked for a ticket—paid 50 cents for it, and was pointed to the American designation car. Having previously received information of the regulations, I took my seat peaceably, believing it better to suffer wrong than do wrong. I felt then, as I felt on many occasions prior to leaving home, unwilling to descend so low as to bandy words with the superintendents, or contest my rights with conductors, or any others in the capacity of servants of any stage or steamboat company, or rail-road corporation; although I never, by any means, gave evidence that, by my submission, I intended to sanction usages which would derogate from uncivilized, much less long and loud professing and high pretending America.

Bear with me while I relate an additional occurrence. On the morning after my return home, I was obliged to go to Boston again, and on going to the Salem station I met two friends, who enquired if I had any objection to their taking seats with me. I answered, I should be most happy. They took their seats accordingly, and soon afterwards one of them remarked to me—"Charles, I don't know if they will allow us to ride with you." It was some time before I could understand what they meant, and, on doing so, I laughed—feeling it to be a climax to every absurdity I had heard attributed to Americans. To say nothing of the wrong done those friends, and the insult and indignity offered me by the appearance of the conductor, who ordered the friends from the car in a somewhat harsh manner—they immediately left the carriage.

On returning to Salem some few evenings afterwards, Mr. Chase, the superintendent on this road, made himself known to me by recalling bygone days and scenes, and then enquired if I was not glad to get home after so long an absence in Europe. I told him I was glad to see my parents and family again, and this was the only object I could have, unless he thought I should be glad to take a hermit's life in the great pasture; inasmuch as I never felt to loathe my American name so much as since my arrival. He wished to know my reasons for the remark. I immediately gave them, and wished to know of him, if, in the event of his having a brother with red hair, he should find himself separated while traveling because of this difference, he should deem it just. He could make no reply. I then wished to know if the principle was not the same; and if so, there was an insult implied by his question. . . .

Before sitting down, I owe it to myself to remark, that I was not apprised of the wish of my friends to appear here until passing through Boston, a day or two since; and having been occupied with other matters, I have had no opportunity for preparation on this occasion. I feel much obliged to the Committee for their kind, patient, and attentive hearing.

The Liberator (Boston), February 25, 1842.

Black Militant Henry Highland Garnet

Henry Highland Garnet, a black abolitionist who labored long and courageously, gave this address to a national colored convention in 1843. It illustrates his creativity as well as his militancy.

Brethren and Fellow Citizens:—Your brethren of the North, East, and West have been accustomed to meet together in National Conventions, to sympathize with each other, and to weep over your unhappy condition. In these meetings we have addressed all classes of the free, but we have never, until this time, sent a word of consolation and advice to you. We have been contented in sitting still and mourning over your sorrows, earnestly hoping that before this day your sacred liberty would have been restored. But, we have hoped in vain. Years have rolled on, and tens of thousands have been borne on streams of blood and tears, to the shores of eternity. While you have been oppressed, we have also been partakers with you; nor can we be free while you are enslaved. We, therefore, write to you as being bound with you.

Many of you are bound to us, not only by the ties of a common humanity, but we are connected by the more tender relations of parents, wives, husbands, children, brothers, and sisters, and friends. As such we most affectionately address you.

Slavery has fixed a deep gulf between you and us, and while it shuts out from you the relief and consolation which your friends would willingly render, it affects and persecutes you with a fierceness which we might not expect to see in the fiends of hell. But still the Almighty Father of mercies has left to us a glimmering ray of hope, which shines out like a lone star in a cloudy sky. Mankind are becoming wiser, and better—the oppressor's power is fading, and you, every day, are becoming better informed, and more numerous. . . .

Two hundred and twenty-seven years ago, the first of our injured race were brought to the shores of America. They came not with glad spirits to select their homes in the New World. They came not with their own consent, to find an unmolested enjoyment of the blessings of this fruitful soil. The first dealings they had with men calling themselves Christians, exhibited to them the worst features of corrupt and sordid hearts; and convinced them that no cruelty is too great, no villainy and no robbery too abhorrent for even enlightened men to perform, when influenced by avarice and lust. Neither did they come flying upon the wings of Liberty, to a land of freedom. But they came with broken hearts, from their beloved native land, and were doomed to unrequited toil and deep degradation. Nor did the evil of their bondage end at their emancipation by death. Succeeding generations inherited their chains, and millions have come from eternity into time, and have returned again to the world of spirits, cursed and ruined by American slavery.

The propagators of the system, or their immediate ancestors, very soon discovered its growing evil, and its tremendous wickedness, and secret promises were made to destroy it. The gross inconsistency of a people holding slaves, who had themselves "ferried o'er the wave" for freedom's sake, was too apparent to be entirely overlooked. The voice of Freedom cried, "Emancipate your slaves." Humanity supplicated with tears for the deliverance of the children of Africa. Wisdom urged her solemn plea. The bleeding captive plead his innocence, and pointed to Christianity who stood weeping at the cross. Jehovah frowned upon the nefarious institution, and thunderbolts, red with vengeance, struggled to leap forth to blast the guilty wretches who maintained it. But all was vain. Slavery had stretched its dark wings of death over the land, the Church stood silently by—the priests prophesied falsely, and the people loved to have it so. Its throne is established, and now it reigns triumphant.

Nearly three millions of your fellow-citizens are prohibited by law and public opinion, (which in this country is stronger than law,) from reading the Book of Life. Your intellect has been destroyed as much as possible, and every ray of light they have attempted to shut out from your minds. The oppressors themselves have become involved in the ruin. They have become weak, sensual, and rapacious—they have cursed you—they have cursed themselves—they have cursed the earth which they have trod.

The colonists threw the blame upon England. They said that the mother country entailed the evil upon them, and that they would rid themselves of it if they could. The world thought they were sincere, and the philanthropic pitied them. But time soon tested their sincerity.

In a few years the colonists grew strong, and severed themselves from the British Government. Their independence was declared, and they took their station among the sovereign powers of the earth. The declaration was a glorious document. Sages admired it, and the patriotic of every nation reverenced the God-like sentiments which it contained. When the power of Government returned to their hands, did they emancipate the slaves? No; they rather added new links to our chains. Were they ignorant of the principles of Liberty? Certainly they were not. The sentiments of their revolutionary orators fell in burning eloquence upon their hearts, and with one voice they cried, LIBERTY OR DEATH. Oh what a sentence was that! It ran from soul to soul like electric fire, and nerved the arm of thousands to fight in the holy cause of Freedom. Among the diversity of opinions that are entertained in regard to physical resistance, there are but a few found to gainsay that stern declaration. We are among those who do not.

SLAVERY! How much misery is comprehended in that single word. What mind is there that does not shrink from its direful effects? Unless the image of God be obliterated from the soul, all men cherish the love of Liberty. The nice discerning political economist does not regard the sacred right more than the untutored African who roams in the wilds of Congo. Nor has the one more right to the full enjoyment of his freedom than the other. In every man's mind the good seeds of liberty are planted, and he who brings his fellow down so low, as to make him contented with a condition of slavery, commits the highest crime against God and man. Brethren, your oppressors aim to do this. They endeavor to make you as much like brutes as possible. When they have blinded the eyes of your mind—when they have embittered the sweet waters of life—then, and not till then, has American slavery done its perfect work. . . .

Brethren, it is as wrong for your lordly oppressors to keep you in slavery, as it was for the man thief to steal our ancestors from the coast of Africa. You should therefore now use the same manner of resistance, as would have been just in our ancestors when the bloody foot-prints of the first remorseless soul-thief was placed upon the shores of our fatherland. The humblest peasant is as free in the sight of God as the proudest monarch that ever swayed a sceptre. Liberty is a spirit sent out from God, and like its great Author, is no respecter of persons.

Brethren, the time has come when you must act for yourselves. It is an old and true saying that, "if hereditary bondmen would be free, they must themselves strike the blow." You can plead your own cause, and do the work of emancipation better than any others. . . .

Fellow-men! Patient sufferers! behold your dearest rights crushed to the earth! See your sons murdered, and your wives, mothers and sisters doomed to prostitution. In the name of the merciful God, and by all that life is worth, let it no longer be a debatable question whether it is better to choose *Liberty or death*. . . .

Brethren, arise, arise! Strike for your lives and liberties. Now is the day and the hour. Let every slave throughout the land do this, and the days of slavery are numbered. You cannot be more oppressed than you have been —you cannot suffer greater cruelties than you have already. *Rather die freemen than live to be slaves*. Remember that you are FOUR MILLIONS!

It is in your power so to torment the God-cursed slaveholders that they will be glad to let you go free. If the scale was turned, and black men were the masters and white men the slaves, every destructive agent and element would be employed to lay the oppressor low. Danger and death would hang over their heads day and night. Yes, the tyrants would meet with plagues more terrible than those of Pharaoh. But you are a patient people. You act as though you were made for the special use of these devils. You act as though your daughters were born to pamper the lusts of your masters and overseers. And worse than all, you tamely submit while your lords tear your wives from your embraces and defile them before your eyes. In the name of God, we ask, are you men? Where is the blood of your fathers? Has it all run out of your veins? Awake, awake; millions of voices are calling you! Your dead fathers speak to you from their graves. Heaven, as with a voice of thunder, calls on you to arise from the dust.

Let your motto be resistance! *resistance!* RESISTANCE! No oppressed people have ever secured their liberty without resistance. What kind of resistance you had better make, you must decide by the circumstances that surround you, and according to the suggestion of expediency. Brethren, adieu! . . .

James McCune Smith (ed.), *A Memorial Discourse by Rev. Henry Highland Garnet* (Philadelphia, 1865).

Correspondence between a Master and His Former Slave

This exchange of letters by a former master and his ex-slave offers a striking comparison between the degrees of literacy of the two men.

Bedford, Trimble County, Ky.

Mr. H. Bibb

Dear Sir:—After my respects to you and yours &c., I received a small book which you sent to me that I peroseed [perused] and found it was sent by H. Bibb I am a stranger in Detroit and know no man there without it is Walton H. Bibb if this be the man please write to me and tell me all about that place and the people I will tell you the news here as well as I can your mother is still living here and she is well the people are generally well in this country times are dull and produce low give my compliments to King, Jack, and all my friends in that cuntry I read that book you sent me and think it will do very well—George is sold, I do not know anything about him I have nothing more at present, but remain yours &c

W. H. Gatewood

February 9th, 1844
P.S. You will please to answer this letter.

* * * * *

Dear Sir:—I am happy to inform you that you are not mistaken in the man whom you sold as property, and received pay for as such. But I thank God that I am not property now, but am regarded as a man like yourself, and although I live far north, I am enjoying a comfortable living by my own industry. If you should ever chance to be traveling this way, and will call on me, I will use you better than you did me while you held me as a slave. Think not that I have any malice against you, for the cruel treatment which you inflicted on me while I was in your power. As it was the custom of your country, to treat your fellow men as you did me and my little family, I can freely forgive you.

I wish to be remembered in love to my aged mother, and friends; please tell her that if we should never meet again in this life, my prayer shall be to God that we may meet in Heaven, where parting shall be no more.

You wish to be remembered to King and Jack. I am pleased, sir, to inform you that they are both here, well, and doing well. They are both living in Canada West. They are now the owners of better farms than the men are who once owned them.

You may perhaps think hard of us for running away from slavery, but as to myself, I have but one apology to make for it, which is this: I have only to regret that I did not start at an earlier period. I might have been free long before I was. But you had it in your power to have kept me there much longer than you did. I think it is very probable that I should have been a toiling slave on your plantation today, if you had treated me differently.

To be compelled to stand by and see you whip and slash my wife without mercy, when I could afford her no protection, not even by offering myself to suffer the lash in her place, was more than I felt it to be the duty of a slave husband to endure, while the way was open to Canada. My infant child was also frequently flogged by Mrs. Gatewood, for crying, until its skin was bruised literally purple. This kind of treatment was what drove me from home and family, to seek a better home for them. But I am willing to forget the past. I should be pleased to hear from you again, on the reception of this, and should also be very happy to correspond with you often, if it should be agreeable to yourself. I subscribe myself a friend to the oppressed, and Liberty forever.

Henry Bibb

Detroit, March 23d, 1844

Henry Bibb, *Narrative of the Life and Adventures of Henry Bibb, an American Slave* (New York, 1849).

John Greenleaf Whittier on Expansion

The sympathy of many Americans was aroused when Texans fought a war with Mexico for their independence. However, when Texas began to make overtures toward admission to statehood and the spread of slavery was again likely, opinions became divided. John Tyler, President of the United States from 1841 to 1845, was a southern slaveholder and an expansionist. Therefore, the Massachusetts Anti-Slavery Society and many abolitionists saw the admission of Texas as a threat to their plans. John Greenleaf Whittier, poet and abolitionist, lent his name and actions to the cause against the admission of Texas. This previously unpublished letter, to a member of the society, reveals Whittier's interest in the question of expansion and slavery.

Amesbury 6th 4th Mo. 1844

My Friend Roberts:

In the paper of today I notice an article from the Washington D.C. *Spectator,* imputing to me the authorship of an article in the Boston *Courier* on the Annexation of Texas. I am not the writer of that article. I make this disclaimer however, not because I do not heartily sympathize with its author on this subject, but simply as an act of justice to all parties. There is *truth* as well as *poetry* in the piece.

Permit me to say in this connection that the attempt to weaken the force of the moral and political feeling of the North against the increase of slave-territory, by raising the absurd cry of "Federalism" evinces not only a great lack of sound argument but also of common honesty and common sense. What!—Is it Federalism to seek the emancipation of the enslaved, & make all men in reality free and equal?—Is it Democracy to fasten fetters & facilitate the traffic in human flesh?

But it ill becomes such men as John C. Calhoun and John Tyler to taunt northern abolitionists with Federalism. Let them think of the infamous Post-Office Bill of the former introduced into the Senate in 1836 prohibiting the circulation of "any paper, written or printed touching the subject of Slavery"—shutting the U.S. Mail against all who ventured to speak of the "Southern institution": —a measure every way more oppressive unjust & inexcusable than the worst measure of Federalism—The Sedition Laws!—. . . .

For one I have no sympathy with "Sedition Laws," or Laws like that prepared by J. C. Calhoun against the Liberty of the Press and the freedom of the U.S. Mail. I love my country, & her *free* institutions, *therefore* I detest slavery. I value the Union of these States, *therefore* I oppose the Annexation of Texas.

Thy friend,

John G. Whittier

New York Historical Society

Frederick Douglass and *The North Star*

Frederick Douglass was born a slave in Maryland on February 14, 1817. He escaped when he was 21 years of age and went north to Baltimore, to New York and then to New Bedford, Massachusetts. In 1841, he attended a meeting of the Massachusetts Anti-Slavery Society, where he delivered his first address. After this experience, Douglass used every possible means of communication to spread news of the evils of slavery to the eyes and ears of the world. In 1847, he published the first edition of The North Star, *which he later renamed* Frederick Douglass' Paper. *The following excerpts are from the first issue of* The North Star, *printed December 3, 1847.*

TO OUR OPPRESSED COUNTRYMEN

We solemnly dedicate *The North Star* to the cause of our long oppressed and plundered fellow countrymen. May God bless the offering to your good! It shall fearlessly assert your rights, faithfully proclaim your wrongs, and earnestly demand for you instant and even-handed justice. Giving no quarter to slavery at the South, it will hold no truce with oppressors at the North. While it shall boldly advocate emancipation for our enslaved brethren, it will omit no opportunity to gain for the nominally free, complete enfranchisement. Every effort to injure or degrade you or your cause—originating wheresoever, or with whomsoever—shall find in it a constant, unswerving and inflexible foe.

While our paper shall be mainly Anti-Slavery, its columns shall be freely opened to the candid and decorous discussions of all measures and topics of a moral and humane character, which may serve to enlighten, improve, and elevate mankind. Temperance, Peace, Capital Punishment, Education—all subjects claiming the attention of the public mind may be freely and fully discussed here.

While advocating your rights, the *North Star* will strive to throw light on your duties: while it will not fail to make known your virtues, it will not shun to discover your faults. To be faithful to our foes it must be faithful to ourselves, in all things.

Remember that we are one, that our cause is one, and that we must help each other, if we would succeed. We have drunk to the dregs the bitter cup of slavery; we have worn the heavy yoke; we have sighed beneath our bonds, and writhed beneath the bloody lash; —cruel mementoes of our oneness are indelibly marked in our living flesh. We are one with you under the ban of prejudice and proscription—one with you under the slander of inferiority—one with you in social and political disfranchisement. What you suffer, we suffer; what you endure, we endure. We are indissolubly united, and must fall or flourish together. . . .

Brethren, the first number of the paper is before you. It is dedicated to your cause. Through the kindness of our friends in England, we are in possession of an excellent printing press, types, and all other materials necessary for printing a paper. Shall this gift be blest to our good, or shall it result in our injury? It is for you to say. With your aid, co-operation and assistance, our enterprise will be entirely successful. We pledge ourselves that no effort on our part shall be wanting, and that no subscriber shall lose his subscription—"The *North Star* Shall Live."

The North Star (Rochester, N.Y.), December 3, 1847.

Frederick Douglass' Letter to His Former Master

Probably no other Negro of the nineteenth century has been more quoted and admired than Frederick Douglass. The following letter written to his former master on September 3, 1848 is one of the lesser known documents from the Douglass collection, yet it gives a view of the abolitionist not revealed in his published speeches.

Thomas Auld:

Sir—The long and intimate, though by no means friendly relation which unhappily subsisted between you and myself, leads me to hope that you will easily account for the great liberty which I now take in addressing you in this open and public manner. The same fact may possibly remove any disagreeable surprise which you may experience on again finding your name coupled with mine, in any other way than in an advertisement, accurately describing my person, and offering a large sum for my arrest. In thus dragging you again before the public, I am aware that I shall subject myself to no inconsiderable amount of censure. I shall probably be charged with an unwarrantable, if not a wanton and reckless disregard of the rights and proprieties of private life. There are those North as well as South who entertain a much higher respect for rights which are merely conventional, than they do for rights which are personal and essential. Not a few there are in our country, who, while they have no scruples against robbing the laborer of the hard earned results of his patient industry, will be shocked by the extremely indelicate manner of bringing your name before the public. Believing this to be the case, and wishing to meet every reasonable or plausible objection to my conduct, I will frankly state the ground upon which I justify myself in this instance, as well as on former occasions when I have thought proper to mention your name in public.

All will agree that a man guilty of theft, robbery, or murder, has forfeited the right to concealment and private life; that the community have a right to subject such persons to the most complete exposure. However much they may desire retirement, and aim to conceal themselves and their movements from the popular gaze, the public have a right to ferret them out, and bring their conduct before the proper tribunals of the country for investigation. Sir, you will undoubtedly make the proper application of these generally admitted principles, and will easily see the light in which you are regarded by me, I will not therefore manifest ill temper, by calling you hard names. I know you to be a man of some intelligence, and can readily determine the precise estimate which I entertain of your character. I may therefore indulge in language which may seem to others indirect and ambiguous, and yet be quite well understood by yourself.

I have selected this day on which to address you, because it is the anniversary of my emancipation; and knowing of no better way, I am led to this as the best mode of celebrating that truly important event. Just ten years ago this beautiful September morning, yon bright sun beheld me a slave—a poor, degraded chattel—trembling at the sound of your voice, lamenting that I was a man, and wishing myself a brute. The hopes which I had treasured up for weeks of a safe and successful escape from your grasp, were powerfully confronted at this last hour by dark clouds of doubt and fear, making my person shake and my bosom to heave with the heavy contest between hope and fear. I have no words to describe to you the deep agony of soul which I experienced on that never to be forgotten morning—(for I left by daylight.) I was making a leap in the dark. The probabilities, so far as I could by reason determine them, were stoutly against the undertaking. The preliminaries and precautions I had adopted previously, all worked badly. I was like one going to war without weapons—ten chances of defeat to one of victory. One in whom I had confided, and one who had promised me assistance, appalled by fear at the trial hour, deserted me, thus leaving the responsibility of success or failure solely with myself. You, sir, can never know my feelings. As I look back to them, I can scarcely realize that I have passed through a scene so trying. Trying however as they were, and gloomy as was the prospect, thanks be to the Most High, who is ever the God of the oppressed, at the moment which was to determine my whole earthly career. His grace was sufficient, my mind was made up. I embraced the golden opportunity, took the morning tide at the flood, and a free man, young, active and strong, is the result.

I have often thought I should like to explain to you the grounds upon which I have justified myself in running away from you. I am almost ashamed to do so now, for by this time you may have discovered them yourself. I will, however, glance at them. When yet but a child about six years old, I imbibed the determination to run away. The very first mental effort that I now remember on my part, was an attempt to solve the mystery, Why am I a slave? and with this question my youthful mind was troubled for many days, pressing upon me more heavily at times than others. When I saw the slave-driver whip a slave woman, cut the blood out of her neck, and heard her piteous cries, I went away into the corner of the fence, wept and pondered over the mystery. I had, through some medium, I know not what, got some idea of God, the Creator of all mankind, the black and the white, and that he had made the blacks to serve the whites as slaves. How he could do this and be *good,* I could not tell. I was not satisfied with this theory, which made God responsible for slavery, for it pained me greatly, and I have wept over it long and often. At one time, your first wife, Mrs. Lucretia, heard me singing and saw me shedding tears, and asked of me the matter, but I was afraid to tell her. I was puzzled with this question, till one night, while sitting in the kitchen, I heard some of the old slaves talking of their parents having been stolen from Africa by white men, and were sold here as slaves. The whole mystery was solved at once. Very soon after this my aunt Jinny and uncle Noah ran away, and the great noise made about it by your father-in-law, made me for the first time acquainted with the fact, that there were free States as well as slave States.

From that time, I resolved that I would some day run away. The morality of the act, I dispose as follows: I am myself; you are yourself; we are two distinct persons, equal persons. What you are, I am. You are a man, and so am I. God created both, and made us separate beings. I am not by nature bound to you, or you to me. Nature does not make your existence depend upon me, or mine to depend upon yours. I cannot walk upon your legs, or you upon mine. I cannot breathe for you, or you for me; I must breathe for myself, and you for yourself. We are distinct persons, and are each equally provided with faculties necessary to our individual existence. In leaving you, I took nothing but what belonged to me, and in no way lessened your means for obtaining an *honest* living. Your faculties remained yours, and mine became useful to their rightful owner. I therefore see no wrong in any part of the transaction. It is true, I went off secretly, but that was more your fault than mine. Had I let you into the secret, you would have defeated the enterprise entirely; but for this, I should have been really glad to have made you acquainted with my intentions to leave.

You may perhaps want to know how I like my present condition. I am free to say, I greatly prefer it to that which I occupied in Maryland. I am, however, by no means prejudiced against the State as such. Its geography, climate, fertility and products, are such as to make it a very desirable abode for any man; and but for the existence of slavery there, it is not impossible that I might again take up my abode in that State. It is not that I love Maryland less, but freedom more. You will be surprised to learn that people at the North labor under the strange delusion that if the slaves were emancipated at the South, they would flock to the North. So far from this being the case, in that event, you would see many old and familiar faces back again to the South. The fact is, there are few here who would not return to the South in the event of emancipation. We want to live in the land of our birth, and to lay our bones by the side of our fathers'; and nothing short of an intense love of personal freedom keeps us from the South. For the sake of this, most of us would live on a crust of bread and a cup of cold water.

Since I left you, I have had a rich experience. I have occupied stations which I never dreamed of when a slave. Three out of the ten years since I left you, I spent as a common laborer on the wharves of New Bedford, Massachusetts. It was there I earned my first free dollar. It was mine. I could spend it as I pleased. I could buy hams or herring with it, without asking any odds of any body. That was a precious dollar to me. You remember when I used to make seven or eight, or even nine dollars a week in Baltimore, you would take every cent of it from me every Saturday night, saying that I belonged to you, and my earnings also. I never liked this conduct on your part—to say the best, I thought it a little mean. I would not have served you so. But let that pass. I was a little awkward about counting money in New England fashion when I first landed in New Bedford. I like to have betrayed myself several times. I caught myself saying phip, for fourpence; and at one time a man actually charged me with being a runaway, whereupon I was silly enough to become one by running away from him, for I was greatly afraid he might adopt measures to get me again into slavery, a condition I then dreaded more than death.

I soon, however, learned to count money, as well as to make it, and got on swimmingly. I married soon after leaving you: in fact, I was engaged to be married before I left you; and instead of finding my companion a burden, she was truly a helpmeet. She went to live at service, and I to work on the wharf, and though we toiled hard the first winter, we never lived more happily. After remaining in New Bedford for three years, I met with Wm. Lloyd Garrison, a person of whom you have *possibly* heard, as he is pretty generally known among slaveholders. He put it into my head that I might make myself serviceable to the cause of the slave by devoting a portion of my time to telling my own sorrows, and those of other slaves which had come under my observation. This was the commencement of a higher state of existence than any to which I had ever aspired. I was thrown into society the most pure, enlightened and benevolent that the country affords. Among these I have never forgotten you, but have invariably made you the topic of conversation—thus giving you all the notoriety I could do. I need not tell you that the opinion formed of you in these circles, is far from being favorable. They have little respect for your honesty, and less for your religion.

But I was going on to relate to you something of my interesting experience. I had not long enjoyed the excellent society to which I have referred, before the light of its excellence exerted a beneficial influence on my mind and heart. Much of my early dislike of white persons was removed, and their manners, habits and customs, so entirely unlike what I had been used to in the kitchen-quarters on the plantations of the South, fairly charmed me, and gave me a strong disrelish for the coarse and degrading customs of my former condition. I therefore made an effort so to improve my mind and deportment, as to be somewhat fitted to the station to which I seemed almost providentially called. The transition from degradation to respectability was indeed great, and to get from one to the other without carrying some marks of one's former condition, is truly a difficult matter. I would not have you think that I am now entirely clear of all plantation peculiarities, but my friends here, while they entertain the strongest dislike to them, regard me with that charity to which my past life somewhat entitles me, so that my condition in this respect is exceedingly pleasant.

So far as my domestic affairs are concerned, I can boast of as comfortable a dwelling as your own. I have an industrious and neat companion, and four dear children—the oldest a girl of nine years, and three fine boys, the oldest eight, the next six, and the youngest four years old. The three oldest are now going regularly to school—two can read and write, and the other can spell with tolerable correctness words of two syllables: Dear fellows! they are all in comfortable beds, and are sound asleep, perfectly secure under my own roof. There are no slaveholders here to rend my heart by snatching them from my arms, or blast a mother's dearest hopes by tearing them from her bosom. These dear children are ours—not to work up into rice, sugar and tobacco, but to watch over, regard, and protect, and to rear them up in the nurture and admonition of the gospel—to train them up in the paths of wisdom and virtue, and, as far as we can to make them useful to the world and to themselves. Oh! sir, a slaveholder never appears to me so completely an agent of hell, as when I think of and look upon my dear children. It is then that my feelings rise above my control.

I meant to have said more with respect to my own prosperity and happiness, but thoughts and feelings which this recital has quickened unfits me to proceed further in that direction. The grim horrors of slavery rise in all their ghastly terror before me, the wails of millions pierce my heart, and chill my blood. I remember the chain, the gag, the bloody whip, the death-like gloom overshadowing the broken spirit of the fettered bondman, the appalling liability of his being torn away from wife and children, and sold like a beast in the market. Say not that this is a picture of fancy. You well know that I wear stripes on my back inflicted by your direction; and that you, while we were brothers in the same church, caused this right hand, with which I am now penning this letter, to be closely tied to my left, and my person dragged at the pistol's mouth, fifteen miles, from the Bay side to Easton to be sold like a beast in the market, for the alleged crime of intending to escape from your possession. All this and more you remember, and know to be perfectly true, not only of yourself, but of nearly all of the slaveholders around you.

At this moment, you are probably the guilty

holder of at least three of my own dear sisters, and my only brother in bondage. These you regard as your property. They are recorded on your ledger, or perhaps have been sold to human flesh mongers, with a view to filling your own ever-hungry purse. Sir, I desire to know how and where these dear sisters are. Have you sold them? or are they still in your possession? What has become of them? are they living or dead? And my dear old grandmother, whom you turned out like an old horse, to die in the woods—is she still alive? Write and let me know all about them. If my grandmother be still alive, she is of no service to you, for by this time she must be nearly eighty years old—too old to be cared for by one to whom she has ceased to be of service, send her to me at Rochester, or bring her to Philadelphia, and it shall be the crowning happiness of my life to take care of her in her old age. Oh! she was to me a mother, and a father, so far as hard toil for my comfort could make her such. Send me my grandmother! that I may watch over and take care of her in her old age. And my sisters, let me know all about them. I would write to them, and learn all I want to know of them, without disturbing you in any way, but that, through your unrighteous conduct, they have been entirely deprived of the power to read and write. You have kept them in utter ignorance, and have therefore robbed them of the sweet enjoyments of writing or receiving letters from absent friends and relatives. Your wickedness and cruelty committed in this respect on your fellow-creatures, are greater than all the stripes you have laid upon my back, or theirs. It is an outrage upon the soul—a war upon the immortal spirit, and one for which you must give account at the bar of our common Father and Creator.

The responsibility which you have assumed in this regard is truly awful—and how you could stagger under it these many years is marvellous. Your mind must have become darkened, your heart hardened, your conscience seared and petrified, or you would have long since thrown off the accursed load and sought relief at the hands of a sin-forgiving God. How, let me ask, would you look upon me, were I some dark night in company with a band of hardened villains, to enter the precincts of your elegant dwelling and seize the person of your own lovely daughter Amanda, and carry her off from your family, friends and all the loved ones of her youth—make her my slave—compel her to work, and I take her wages—place her name on my leger as property—disregard her personal rights—fetter the powers of her immortal soul by denying her the right and privilege of learning to read and write—feed her coarsely—clothe her scantily, and whip her on the naked back occasionally; more and still more horrible, leave her unprotected—a degraded victim to the brutal lust of fiendish overseers, who would pollute, blight, and blast her fair soul—rob her of all dignity—destroy her virtue, and annihilate all in her person the graces that adorn the character of virtuous womanhood? I ask how would you regard me, if such were my conduct? Oh! the vocabulary of the damned would not afford a word sufficiently infernal, to express your idea of my God-provoking wickedness. Yet sir, your treatment of my beloved sisters is in all essential points, precisely like the case I have now supposed. Damning as would be such a deed on my part, it would be no more so than that which you have committed against me and my sisters.

I will now bring this letter to a close, you shall hear from me again unless you let me hear from you. I intend to make use of you as a weapon with which to assail the system of slavery—as a means of concentrating public attention on the system, and deepening their horror of trafficking in the souls and bodies of men. I shall make use of you as a means of exposing the character of the American church and clergy—and as a means of bringing this guilty nation with yourself to repentance. In doing this I entertain no malice towards you personally. There is no roof under which you would be more safe than mine, and there is nothing in my house which you might need for your comfort, which I would not readily grant. Indeed, I should esteem it a privilege, to set you an example as to how mankind ought to treat each other.

I am your fellow man, but not your slave.

Frederick Douglass

The Liberator (Boston), September 22, 1848.

The Dred Scott Case

On July 1, 1847, Dred Scott began his legal battle for freedom in Dred Scott *v.* Sandford [*sic*]. *This was the start of the case that was finally ruled on by the United States Supreme Court in 1857. The events leading up to the case began in 1834, when Dred Scott was taken by his master, Dr. John Emerson, from Missouri to Rock Island, Illinois, in free territory, where he lived for two years. In 1836, Scott was taken by his master to Fort Snelling, Minnesota, where slavery was prohibited by the Missouri Compromise. Two years later, they returned to Missouri and Scott established his claim to freedom on the grounds of his past residence in Illinois and the Minnesota territory.*

After the death of his master, Scott and his family were transferred to John F. A. Sanford of New York; subsequently, in an effort to obtain his freedom, he brought suit against Sanford. In 1847, the state circuit court of Missouri rendered judgment in Scott's favor, but the supreme court of the state reversed the decision. Next, the case was taken before a United States circuit court, where judgment again was given in favor of Sanford.

In 1857, a decision was handed down by the United States Supreme Court: seven of the nine justices ruled for Sanford. The decision of the Court was written by Chief Justice Roger B. Taney. The particular significance of this decision was twofold: it declared that Negroes were not to be regarded as citizens, and it held the Missouri Compromise to be unconstitutional.

There are two leading questions presented by the record:

1. Had the Circuit Court of the United States jurisdiction to hear and determine the case between these parties? And

2. If it had jurisdiction, is the judgment it has given erroneous or not? . . .

Before we speak of the pleas in bar, it will be proper to dispose of the questions which have arisen on the plea in abatement.

That plea denies the right of the plaintiff to sue in a court of the United States, for the reasons therein stated. . . . It is suggested, however, that this plea is not before us. . . . We think they [the plea and the judgment of the court upon it] are before us . . . and it becomes, therefore, our duty to decide whether the facts stated in the plea are or are not sufficient to show that the plaintiff is not entitled to sue as a citizen in a court of the United States. . . .

The question is simply this: Can a negro, whose ancestors were imported into this country, and sold as slaves, become a member of the political community formed and brought into existence by the Constitution of the United States, and as such become entitled to all the rights, privileges and immunities, guarantied by that instrument to the citizen? One of which rights is the privilege of suing in a court of the United States in the cases specified in the Constitution. . . .

It is true, every person, and every class and description of persons, who were at the time of the adoption of the Constitution recognized as citizens in the several States, became also citizens of this new political body; but none other; it was formed by them, and for them and their posterity, but for no one else. And the personal rights and privileges guarantied to citizens of this new sovereignty were intended to embrace those only who were then members of the several State communities, or who should afterwards, by birthright or otherwise, become members, according to the provisions of the Constitution and the principles on which it was founded. . . .

It becomes necessary, therefore, to determine who were citizens of the several States when the Constitution was adopted. And in order to do this, we must recur to the Governments and institutions of the thirteen colonies, when they separated from Great Britain and formed new sovereignties, and took their places in the family of independent nations. . . .

In the opinion of the court, the legislation and histories of the times, and the language used in the Declaration of Independence, show, that neither the class of persons who had been imported as slaves, nor their descendants, whether they had become free or not, were then acknowledged as a part of the people, nor intended to be included in the general words used in that memorable instrument. . . .

They had for more than a century before been regarded as beings of an inferior order, and altogether unfit to associate with the white race, either in social or political relations; and so far inferior, that they had no rights which the white man was bound to respect; and that the negro might justly and lawfully be reduced to slavery for his benefit. . . . It cannot be supposed that they intended to secure to them rights, and privileges, and rank, in the new political body throughout the Union, which every one of them denied within the limits of its own dominion. More especially, it cannot be believed that the large slave-holding States regarded them as included in the word citizens, or would have consented to a constitution which might compel them to receive them in that character from another State. . . .

To all this mass of proof we have still to add, that Congress has repeatedly legislated upon the same construction of the Constitution that we have given. . . .

The conduct of the Executive Department of the Government has been in perfect harmony upon this subject with this course of legislation. . . .

And upon a full and careful consideration of the subject, the court is of opinion, that, upon the facts stated in the plea in abatement, Dred Scott was not a citizen of Missouri within the meaning of the Constitution of the United States, and not entitled as such to sue in its courts; and, consequently, that the Circuit Court had no jurisdiction of the case, and that the judgment on the plea in abatement is erroneous. . . .

Now, as we have already said in an earlier part of this opinion, upon a different point, the right of property in a slave is distinctly and expressly affirmed in the Constitution. The right to traffic in it, like an ordinary article of merchandise and property, was guarantied to the citizens of the United States, in every State that might desire it, for twenty years. And the Government in express terms is pledged to protect it in all future time, if the slave escapes from his owner. This is done in plain words—too plain to be misunderstood. And no word can be found in the Constitution which gives Congress a greater power over slave property, or which entitles property of that kind to less protection than property of any other description. The only power conferred is the power coupled with the duty of guarding and protecting the owner in his rights.

Upon these considerations, it is the opinion of the court that the act of Congress which prohibited a citizen from holding or owning property of this kind in the territory of the United States north of the line therein mentioned, is not warranted by the Constitution, and is therefore void; and that neither Dred Scott himself, nor any of his family, were made free by being carried into this territory; even if they had been carried there by the owner, with the intention of becoming a permanent resident. . . .

But there is another point in the case which depends upon State power and State law. And it is contended, on the part of the plaintiff, that he is made free by being taken to Rock

Island, in the State of Illinois, independently of his residence in the territory of the United States; and being so made free, he was not again reduced to a state of slavery by being brought back to Missouri.

Our notice of this part of the case will be very brief; for the principle on which it depends was decided in this court upon much consideration, in the case of *Strader et al.* v. *Graham,* reported in 10th Howard, 82. In that case, the slaves had been taken from Kentucky to Ohio, with the consent of the owner, and afterwards brought back to Kentucky. And this court held that their status or condition, as free or slave, depended upon the laws of Kentucky, when they were brought back into that State, and not of Ohio; and that this court had no jurisdiction to revise the judgment of a State court upon its own laws. . . .

So in this case. As Scott was a slave when taken into the State of Illinois by his owner, and was there held as such, and brought back in that character, his status, as free or slave, depended on the laws of Missouri, and not of Illinois. . . .

Upon the whole, therefore, it is the judgment of this court, that it appears by the record before us, that the plaintiff in error is not a citizen of Missouri, in the sense in which that word is used in the Constitution; and that the Circuit Court of the United States, for that reason, had no jurisdiction in the case, and could give no judgment in it. Its judgment for the defendant must, consequently, be reversed, and a mandate issued, directing the suit to be dismissed for want of jurisdiction.

[Dissenting Opinion of Justice Curtis]

. . . One mode of approaching this question is, to inquire who were citizens of the United States at the time of the adoption of the Constitution.

Citizens of the United States at the time of the adoption of the Constitution can have been no other than the citizens of the United States under the Confederation. . . .

To determine whether any free persons, descended from Africans held in slavery, were citizens of the United States under the Confederation, and consequently at the time of the adoption of the Constitution of the United States, it is only necessary to know whether any such persons were citizens of either of the States under the Confederation at the time of the adoption of the Constitution.

Of this there can be no doubt. At the time of the ratification of the Articles of Confederation, all free native-born inhabitants of the States of New Hampshire, Massachusetts, New York, New Jersey and North Carolina, though descended from African slaves, were not only citizens of those States, but such of them as had the other necessary qualifications possessed the franchise of electors, on equal terms with other citizens. . . .

I can find nothing in the Constitution which, *proprio vigore,* deprives of their citizenship any class of persons who were citizens of the United States at the time of its adoption, or who should be native-born citizens of any State after its adoption; nor any power enabling Congress to disfranchise persons born on the soil of any State, and entitled to citizenship of such State by its constitution and laws. And my opinion is, that, under the Constitution of the United States, every free person born on the soil of a State, who is a citizen of that State by force of its constitution or laws, is also a citizen of the United States. . . .

The Constitution having recognized the rule that persons born within the several States are citizens of the United States, one of four things must be true:

First. That the Constitution itself has described what native-born persons shall or shall not be citizens of the United States; or,

Second. That it has empowered Congress to do so; or,

Third. That all free persons, born within

the several States, are citizens of the United States; or,

Fourth. That it is left to each State to determine what free persons, born within its limits, shall be citizens of such State, and thereby be citizens of the United States. . . .

The conclusions at which I have arrived on this part of the case are:

First. That the free native-born citizens of each State are citizens of the United States.

Second. That as free colored persons born within some of the States are citizens of those States, such persons are also citizens of the United States.

Third. That every such citizen, residing in any State, has the right to sue and is liable to be sued in the federal courts, as a citizen of that State in which he resides.

Fourth. That as the plea to the jurisdiction in this case shows no facts, except that the plaintiff was of African descent, and his ancestors were sold as slaves, and as these facts are not inconsistent with his citizenship of the United States, and his residence in the State of Missouri, the plea to the jurisdiction was bad, and the judgment of the Circuit Court overruling it was correct.

I dissent, therefore, from that part of the opinion of the majority of the court, in which it is held that a person of African descent cannot be a citizen of the United States; . . .

B. C. Howard, *Reports of Cases Argued and Adjudged in the Supreme Court, 1843–1861* (24 vols.; Philadelphia, 1843–1861).

William H. Seward Writes about the Fugitive Slave Act of 1850

William H. Seward, United States senator and former governor of New York, who would later serve as Lincoln's Secretary of State, wrote this letter to a committee of Afro-Americans concerning the Fugitive Slave Act of 1850. Seward had opposed the Compromise of 1850 and later gave to the public the concept of the "irrepressible conflict."

Auburn October 7th 1850

To: William P. Powell & George T. Downing

Gentlemen

On the eve of departure from the City of Washington I received the letter which as a committee of colored citizens you addressed to me on the 27th of September. The incessant occupations incident to the close of the session of Congress prevented my replying at that time, and I avail myself of an early moment of leisure to do so now.

In regard to the true character of the Fugitive Slave Law, I cannot express my views more plainly or even more fully than by referring you to the opinions expressed in my arguments delivered in the Senate in March and in July last. So far as the remedy for the injustice of this act is concerned, the matter rests with the People. I am happy to see that their attention is directed toward it. I trust that it is unnecessary to assure you that I shall remain ready to maintain in the public councils the opinions I have already advocated there.

William H. Seward

Schomburg Collection, New York Public Library.

The Escape of Henry "Box" Brown

One of the most remarkable escapes from slavery was that of Henry "Box" Brown. In the following account, Brown relates his decision to escape and the manner in which it was carried out.

My brother and myself, were in the practice of carrying grain to mill, a few times a year, which was the means of furnishing us with some information respecting other slaves. We often went twenty miles, to a mill owned by a Col. Ambler, in Yansinville county, and used to improve our opportunities for gaining information. Especially desirous were we, of learning the condition of slaves around us, for we knew not how long we should remain in as favorable hands as we were then. On one occasion, while waiting for our grain, we entered a house in the neighborhood, and while resting ourselves there, we saw a number of forlorn-looking beings pass the door, and as they passed, we noticed that they turned and gazed earnestly upon us. Afterwards, about fifty performed the same act, which excited our minds somewhat, as we overheard some of them say, "Look there, and see those two colored men with shoes, vests and hats on," and we determined to obtain an interview with them. Accordingly, after receiving some bread and meat from our hosts, we followed these abject beings to their quarters;—and such a sight we had never witnessed before, as we had always lived on our master's plantation, and this was about the first of our journeys to the mill. They were dressed with shirts made of coarse bagging, such as coffee-sacks are made from, and some kind of light substance for pantaloons, and *no other clothing whatever*. They had on no shoes, hats, vests, or coats, and when my brother asked them why they spoke of our being dressed with those articles of clothing, they said they had "never seen negroes dressed in that way before." They looked very hungry, and we divided our bread and meat among them, which furnished them only a mouthful each. They never had any meat, they said, given them by their masters. My brother put various questions to them, such as, "if they had wives?" "did they go to church?" "had they any sisters?" &c. The one who gave us the information, said they had wives, but were obliged to marry on their own plantation. Master would not allow them to go away from home to marry, consequently he said they were all related to each other, and master made them marry, *whether related or not*. My brother asked this man to show him his sisters; he said he could not tell them from the rest, *they were all his sisters*; and here let me state, what is well known by many people, that no such thing as real marriage is allowed to exist among the slaves. Talk of marriage under such a system! Why, the owner of a Turkish harem, or the keeper of a house of ill-fame, might as well allow the inmates of their establishments to marry as for a Southern slaveholder to do the same. Marriage, as is well known, is the voluntary and perfect union of one man with one woman, without depending upon the will of a third party. This never can take place under slavery, for the moment a slave is allowed to form such a connection as he chooses, the spell of slavery is dissolved. The slave's wife is his, only at the will of her master, who may violate her chastity with impunity. It is my candid opinion that one of the strongest motives which operate upon the slaveholders, and induce them to retain their iron grasp upon the unfortunate slave, is because it gives them such unlimited control in this respect over the female slaves. The greater part of slaveholders are licentious men, and the most respectable and the kindest of masters, keep some of their slaves as mistresses. It is for their pecuniary interest to do so in several respects. Their progeny is so many dollars and cents in their pockets, instead of being a bill of expense to them, as would be the case if their slaves were free; and mulatto slaves command a higher price than dark colored ones; but it is too horrid a subject to describe. Suffice it to say, that no slave has the least certainty of being able to retain his wife or her husband a single hour; so that the slave is placed under strong inducements not to form a union of *love*, for he knows not how soon the chords wound around his heart would be snapped asunder, by the hand of the brutal slave-dealer. Northern people sustain slavery, knowing that it is a system of perfect licentiousness, and yet go to church and boast of their purity and holiness!

On this plantation, the slaves were never allowed to attend church, but managed their religious affairs in their own way. An old slave, whom they called Uncle John, decided upon their piety, and would baptize them during the silent watches of the night, while their master was "taking his rest in sleep." Thus is the slave under the necessity of even "saving his soul" in the hours when the eye of his master, who usurps the place of God over him, is turned from him. Think of it, ye who contend for the necessity of these rites, to constitute a man a Christian! By night must the poor slave steal away from his bed of straw, and leaving his miserable hovel, must drag his weary limbs to some adjacent stream of water, where a fellow slave, as ignorant as himself, proceeds to administer the ordinance of baptism; and as he plunges his comrades into the water, in imitation of the Baptist of old, how he trembles, lest the footsteps of his master should be heard, advancing to their Bethesda,—knowing that if such should be the case, the severe punishment that awaits them all. Baptists, are ye striking hands with Southern churches, which thus exclude so many slaves from the "waters of salvation?"

But we were obliged to cut short our conversation with these slaves, by beholding the approach of the overseer, who was directing his steps towards us, like a bear seeking its prey. We had only time to ask this man, "if they were often whipped?" to which he replied, "that not a day passed over their heads, without some of their number being brutally punished; and," said he, "we shall have to suffer for this talk with you." He then told us, that many of them had been severely whipped that very morning, for having been baptized the night before. After we left them, we looked back, and heard the screams of these poor creatures, suffering under the blows of the hard-hearted overseer, for the crime of talking with us;—which screams sounded in our ears for some time. We felt thankful that we were exempted from such terrible treatment; but still, we knew not how soon we should be subject to the same cruel fate. By this time we had returned to the mill, where we met a young man, (a relation of the owner of this plantation,) who for some time appeared to be eyeing us quite attentively. At length he asked me if I had "ever been whipped," and when I told him I had not, he replied, "Well, you will neither of you ever be of any value, then;" so true is it that whipping is considered a necessary part of slavery. Without this practice, it could not stand a single day. He expressed a good deal of surprise that we were allowed to wear hats and shoes,—supposing that a slave had no business to wear such clothing as his master wore. We had brought our fishing-lines with us, and requested the privilege to fish in his stream, which he roughly denied us, saying, "we do not allow niggers to fish." Nothing daunted, however, by this rebuff, my brother went to another place, and was quite successful in his undertaking, obtaining a plentiful supply of the finny tribe; but as soon as this youngster perceived his good luck, he ordered him to throw them back into the stream, which he was obliged to do, and we returned home without them.

We finally abandoned visiting this mill, and carried our grain to another, a Mr. Bullock's, only ten miles distant from our plantation. This man was very kind to us, took us into his house and put us to bed, took charge of our horses, and carried the grain himself into the mill, and in the morning furnished us with a good breakfast. I asked my brother why this man treated us so differently from our old miller. "Oh," said he, "this man is not a slaveholder!" Ah, that explained the difference; for there is nothing in the southern character averse to gentleness. On the contrary, if it were not for slavery's withering touch, the Southerners would be the kindest people in the land. Slavery possesses the power attributed to one of old, of changing the nature of all who drink of its vicious cup.

"——— ——— ——— Which, as they taste,
Soon as the potion works, their *human* countenance,
The express resemblance of the gods, is changed
Into some brutish form of wolf, or bear,

> Or ounce, or tiger, hog, or bearded goat;
> And they, so perfect is their misery,
> Not once perceive their foul disfigurement,
> But boast themselves more comely than before."

Under the influence of slavery's polluting power, the most gentle women become the fiercest viragos, and the most benevolent men are changed into inhuman monsters. It is true of the northern man who goes South also.

> "*Whoever* tastes, loses his upright shape,
> And downward falls, into a *grovelling swine*."

This non-slaveholder also allowed us to catch as many fish as we pleased, and even furnished us with fishing implements. While at this mill, we became acquainted with a colored man from another part of the country; and as our desire was strong to learn how our brethren fared in other places, we questioned him respecting his treatment. He complained much of his hard fate,—said he had a wife and one child, and begged for some of our fish to carry to his wife; which my brother gladly gave him. He said he was expecting to have some money in a few days, which would be *"the first he ever had in his life!"* . . .

I went to Mr. Allen, and requested of him permission to refrain from labor for a short time, in consequence of a disabled finger; but he refused to grant me this permission, on the ground that my hand was not lame enough to justify him in so doing. Nothing daunted by this rebuff, I took some oil of vitriol, intending to pour a few drops upon my finger, to make it sufficiently sore, to disable me from work, which I succeeded in, beyond my wishes; for in my hurry, a larger quantity than it was my purpose to apply to my finger, found its way there, and my finger was soon eaten through to the bone. The overseer then was obliged to allow me to absent myself from business, for it was impossible for me to work in that situation. But I did not waste my precious furlough in idle mourning over my fate. I armed myself with determined energy, for action, and in the words of one of old, in the name of God, "I leaped over a wall, and run through a troop" of difficulties. After searching for assistance for some time, I at length was so fortunate as to find a friend, who promised to assist me, for one half the money I had about me, which was one hundred and sixty-six dollars. I gave him eighty-six, and he was to do his best in forwarding my scheme. Long did we remain together, attempting to devise ways and means to carry me away from the land of separation of families, of whips and thumbscrews, and auction blocks; but as often as a plan was suggested by my friend, there would appear some difficulty in the way of its accomplishment. Perhaps it may not be best to mention what these plans were, as some unfortunate slaves may thereby be prevented from availing themselves of these methods of escape.

At length, after praying earnestly to Him, who seeth afar off, for assistance, in my difficulty, suddenly, as if from above, there darted into my mind these words, "Go and get a box, and put yourself in it." I pondered the words over in my mind. "Get a box?" thought I; "what can this mean?" But I was "not disobedient unto the heavenly vision," and I determined to put into practice this direction, as I considered it, from my heavenly Father. I went to the depot, and there noticed the size of the largest boxes, which commonly were sent by the cars, and returned with their dimensions. I then repaired to a carpenter, and induced him to make me a box of such a description as I wished, informing him of the use I intended to make of it. He assured me I could not live in it; but as it was dear liberty I was in pursuit of, I thought it best to make the trial.

When the box was finished, I carried it, and placed it before my friend, who had promised to assist me, who asked me if that was to "put my clothes in?" I replied that it was not, but to *"put Henry Brown in!"* He was astonished at my temerity; but I insisted upon his placing me in it, and nailing me up, and he finally consented.

After corresponding with a friend in Philadelphia, arrangements were made for my departure, and I took my place in this narrow prison, with a mind full of uncertainty as to the result. It was a critical period of my life, I can assure you, reader; but if you have never been deprived of your liberty, as I was, you cannot realize the power of that hope of freedom, which was to me indeed, "an anchor to the soul, both sure and steadfast."

I laid me down in my darkened home of three feet by two, and like one about to be guillotined, resigned myself to my fate. My friend was to accompany me, but he failed to do so; and contented himself with sending a telegraph message to his correspondent in Philadelphia, that such a box was on its way to his care.

I took with me a bladder filled with water to bathe my neck with, in case of too great heat; and with no access to the fresh air, excepting three small gimblet holes, I started on my perilous cruise. I was first carried to the express office, the box being placed on its end, so that I started with my head downwards, although the box was directed, "this side up with care." From the express office, I was carried to the depot, and from thence tumbled roughly into the baggage car, where I *happened* to fall "right side up," but no thanks to my transporters. But after a while the cars stopped, and I was put aboard a steamboat, *and placed on my head.* In this dreadful position, I remained the space of an hour and a half, it seemed to me, when I began to feel of my eyes and head, and found to my dismay, that my eyes were almost swollen out of their sockets, and the veins on my temple seemed ready to burst. I made no noise however, determining to obtain *"victory or death,"* but endured the terrible pain, as well as I could, sustained under the whole by the thoughts of sweet liberty. About half an hour afterwards, I attempted again to lift my hands to my face, but I found I was not able to move them. A cold sweat now covered me from head to foot. Death seemed my inevitable fate, and every moment I expected to feel the blood flowing over me, which had burst from my veins. One half hour longer and my sufferings would have ended in that fate, which I preferred to slavery; but I lifted up my heart to God in prayer, believing that he would yet deliver me, when to my joy, I overheard two men say, "We have been here *two* hours and have travelled twenty miles, now let us sit down, and rest ourselves." They suited the action to the word, and turned the box over, containing my soul and body, thus delivering me from the power of the grim messenger of death, who a few moments previously, had aimed his fatal shaft at my head, and had placed his icy hands on my throbbing heart. One of these men inquired of the other, what he supposed that box contained, to which his comrade replied, that he guessed it was the mail. "Yes," thought I, "it is a *male,* indeed, although not the *mail* of the United States."

Soon after this fortunate event, we arrived at Washington, where I was thrown from the wagon, and again as my luck would have it, fell on my head. I was then rolled down a declivity, until I reached the platform from which the cars were to start. During this short but rapid journey, my neck came very near being dislocated, as I felt it crack, as if it had snapped asunder. Pretty soon, I heard some one say, "there is no room for this box, it will have to remain behind." I then again applied to the Lord, my help in all my difficulties, and in a few minutes I heard a gentleman direct the hands to place it aboard, as "it came with the mail and must go on with it." I was then tumbled into the car, my head downwards again, as I seemed to be destined to escape on my head; a sign probably, of the opinion of American people respecting such bold adventurers as myself; that our heads should be held downwards, whenever we attempt to benefit ourselves. Not the only instance of this propensity, on the part of the American people, towards the colored race. We had not proceeded far, however, before more baggage was placed in the car, at a stopping place, and I was again turned to my proper position. No farther difficulty occurred until my arrival at Philadelphia. I reached this place at three o'clock in the morning, and remained in the depot until six o'clock, A.M., at which time, a waggon drove up, and a person inquired for a box directed to such a place, "right side up." I was soon placed on this waggon, and carried to the house of my friend's correspondent, where quite a number of persons were waiting to receive me. They appeared to be some afraid to open the box at first, but at length one of them rapped upon it, and with a trembling voice, asked, "Is all right within?" to which I replied, "All right." The joy of these friends was excessive, and like the ancient Jews, who repaired to the rebuilding of Jerusalem, each one seized hold of some tool, and commenced opening my grave. At length the cover was removed, and I arose, and shook myself from the lethargy into which I had fallen; but exhausted nature proved too much for my frame, and I swooned away.

After my recovery from this fainting fit, the first impulse of my soul, as I looked around, and beheld my friends, and was told that I was safe, was to break out in a song of deliverance, and praise to the most high God, whose arm had been so signally manifest in my escape. Great God, was I a freeman! Had I indeed succeeded in effecting my escape from the human wolves of Slavery? O what . . . joy thrilled through every nerve and fibre of my system! My labor was accomplished, my warfare was ended, and I stood erect before my equal fellow men, no longer a crouching slave, forever at the look and nod of a whimsical and tyrannical slave-owner. Long had seemed my journey, and terribly hazardous had been my attempt to gain my birth-right; but it all seemed a comparatively light price to pay for the precious boon of *Liberty*. . . .

Charles Stearns, *Narrative of Henry Box Brown* (Boston, 1849).

California Manumission Papers

Following the gold rush of 1848, both free and enslaved Negroes migrated to California. These manumission papers found in the archives of that state contain information about the methods used by the slaves to obtain their freedom, as well as the states where they formerly resided.

E. H. Taylor
to
Dennis Aviery

To All Whom It May Concern; This is to certify that Dennis Aviery has been my Slave in the State of Georgia for about the term of eight years but by virtue of money to me in hand paid he is free and Liberated from all allegiance to my authority.

Coloma Eldorado county California Feb. 8, 1851

Witness George Scall

* * * * *

Samuel Grantham
to
Aleck Long
State of California
Eldorado County

Know all men by these presents that I Samuel Grantham of the county and state aforesaid, acting by power of Attorney vested in me by S. Oliver Grantham of St Louis, State of Missouri, acting for and in behalf of said S. Oliver Grantham, and in consideration of the sum of four hundred dollars to me in hand paid the same to receive to the benefit of the said Oliver Grantham have this day liberated, set free and fully and effectually manumitted, Aleck Long. Heretofore a slave for life—the lawful property of the said Thomas Grantham. The description of said Aleck Long, being as follows to wit: about fifty-seven years old; five feet, ten inches in height, gray hair dark complexion with a scar on the inside of the left leg above the ankle.—The said Aleck Long to enjoy and possess now and from hence forth the full exercise of all rights, benefits and privileges of a free man of color free of all or any claim to servitude, slavery or service of the said S. A. Grantham, his heirs, Executors, and assigns and all other persons claiming or to claim forever.

In Testimony of this seal of Manumission, I have this day signed my name and affixed my seal this 2nd day of March 1852.

Samuel A. Grantham
Attorney for State of California

Courtesy of the Association for the Study of Negro Life and History.

The Autobiography of Explorer James P. Beckwourth

Negro adventurer James P. Beckwourth discovered a pass in the Sierra Nevada Mountain Range that facilitated travel for the pioneers during the great westward movement. This account of his unsuccessful efforts to secure remuneration for discovering the pass, along with a description of Beckwourth Valley, California, are contained in his autobiography.

. . . It was the latter end of April when we entered upon an extensive valley at the northwest extremity of the Sierra range. The valley was already robed in freshest verdure, contrasting most delightfully with the huge snow-clad masses of rock we had just left. Flowers of every variety and hue spread their variegated charms before us; magpies were chattering, and gorgeously-plumaged birds were carolling in the delights of unmolested solitude. Swarms of wild geese and ducks were swimming on the surface of the cool crystal stream, which was the central fork of the Rio de las Plumas, or sailed the air in clouds over our heads. Deer and antelope filled the plains, and their boldness was conclusive that the hunter's rifle was to them unknown. Nowhere visible were any traces of the white man's approach, and it is probable that our steps were the first that ever marked the spot. We struck across this beautiful valley to the waters of the Yuba, from thence to the waters of the Truchy, which latter flowed in an easterly direction, telling us we were on the eastern slope of the mountain range. This, I at once saw, would afford the best waggon-road into the American Valley approaching from the eastward, and I imparted my views to three of my companions in whose judgment I placed the most confidence. They thought highly of the discovery, and even proposed to associate with me in opening the road. We also found gold, but not in sufficient quantity to warrant our working it; and, furthermore, the ground was too wet to admit of our prospecting to any advantage.

On my return to the American Valley, I made known my discovery to a Mr. Turner, proprietor of the American Ranch, who entered enthusiastically into my views; it was a thing, he said, he had never dreamed of before. If I could but carry out my plan, and divert travel into that road, he thought I should be a made man for life. Thereupon he drew up a subscription-list, setting forth the merits of the project, and showing how the road could be made practicable to Bidwell's Bar, and thence to Marysville, which latter place would derive peculiar advantages from the discovery. He headed the subscription with two hundred dollars.

When I reached Bidwell's Bar and unfolded my project, the town was seized with a perfect mania for the opening of the route. The subscriptions toward the fund required for its accomplishment amounted to five hundred dollars. I then proceeded to Marysville, a place which would unquestionably derive greater benefit from the newly-discovered route than any other place on the way, since this must be the . . . principal starting-place for emigrants. I communicated with several of the most influential residents on the subject in hand. They also spoke very encouragingly of my undertaking, and referred me before all others to the mayor of the city. Accordingly, I waited upon that gentleman (a Mr. Miles), and brought the matter under his notice, representing it as being a legitimate matter for his interference, and offering substantial advantages to the commercial prosperity of the city. The mayor entered warmly into my views, and pronounced it as his opinion that the profits resulting from the speculation could not be less than from six to ten thousand dollars; and as the benefits accruing to the city would be incalculable, he would insure my expenses while engaged upon it.

I mentioned that I should prefer some guarantee before entering upon my labours, to secure me against loss of what money I might lay out.

"Leave that to me," said the mayor; "I will attend to the whole affair. I feel confident that a subject of so great importance to our interests will engage the earliest attention."

I thereupon left the whole proceeding in his hands, and, immediately setting men to work upon the road, went out to the Truchy to turn emigration into my newly-discovered route. While thus busily engaged I was seized with erysipelas, and abandoned all hopes of recovery; I was over one hundred miles away from medical assistance, and my only shelter was a brush tent. I made my will, and resigned myself to death. Life still lingered in me, however, and a train of waggons came up, and encamped near to where I lay. I was reduced to a very low condition, but I saw the drivers, and acquainted them with the object which had brought me out there. They offered to attempt the new road if I thought myself sufficiently strong to guide them through it. The women, God bless them! came to my assistance, and through their kind attentions and excellent nursing I rapidly recovered from my lingering sickness, until I was soon able to mount my horse, and lead the first train, consisting of seventeen waggons, through "Beckwourth's Pass." We reached the American Valley without the least accident, and the emigrants expressed entire satisfaction with the route. I returned with the train through to Marysville, and on the intelligence being communicated of the practicability of my road, there was quite a public rejoicing. A northern route had been discovered, and the city had received an impetus that would advance her beyond all her sisters on the Pacific shore. I felt proud of my achievement, and was foolish enough to promise myself a substantial recognition of my labours.

I was destined to disappointment, for that same night Marysville was laid in ashes. The mayor of the ruined town congratulated me upon bringing a train through. He expressed great delight at my good fortune, but regretted that their recent calamity had placed it entirely beyond his power to obtain for me any substantial reward. With the exception of some two hundred dollars subscribed by some liberal-minded citizens of Marysville, I have received no indemnification for the money and labour I have expended upon my discovery. The city had been greatly benefited by it, as all must acknowledge, for the emigrants that now flock to Marysville would otherwise have gone to Sacramento. Sixteen hundred dollars I expended upon the road is for ever gone, but those who derive advantage from this outlay and loss of time devote no thought to the discoverer; nor do I see clearly how I am to help myself, for every one knows I cannot roll a mountain into the pass and shut it up. But there is one thing certain: although I recognize no superior in love of country, and feel in all its force the obligation imposed upon me to advance her interests, still, when I go out hunting in the mountains a road for everybody to pass through, and expending my time and capital upon an object from which I shall derive no benefit, it will be because I have nothing better to do.

In the spring of 1852 I established myself in Beckwourth Valley, and finally found myself transformed into a hotel-keeper and chief of a trading-post. My house is considered the emigrant's landing-place, as it is the first ranch he arrives at in the golden state, and is the only house between this point and Salt Lake. Here is a valley two hundred and forty miles in circumference, containing some of the choicest land in the world. Its yield of hay is incalculable; the red and white clovers spring up spontaneously, and the grass that covers its smooth surface is of the most nutritious nature. When the weary, toil-worn emigrant reaches this valley, he feels himself secure; he can lay himself down and taste refreshing repose, undisturbed by the fear of Indians. His cattle can graze around him in pasture up to their eyes, without running any danger of being driven off by the Arabs of the forest, and springs flow before them as pure as any that refreshes this verdant earth. . . .

T. D. Bonner (ed.), *The Life and Adventures of James P. Beckwourth, Mountaineer, Scout, Pioneer, and Chief of the Crow Nation of Indians* (New York, 1892).

Sojourner Truth Turns the Tide

Sojourner Truth, a woman who showed amazing stamina and courage during the Civil War, is remembered well for the speech on woman suffrage that she gave in May 1852. The following graphic account of her appearance at a convention of women seeking the vote is from an article by Frances Gage, in which the author gives her recollections of the event.

. . . Morning, afternoon, and evening exercises came and went. Through all these sessions old Sojourner, quiet and reticent as the "Lybian Statue," sat crouched against the wall on the corner of the pulpit stairs, her sun-bonnet shading her eyes, her elbows on her knees, her chin resting upon her broad, hard palms. At intermission she was busy selling the "Life of Sojourner Truth," a narrative of her own strange and adventurous life. Again and again, timorous and trembling ones came to me and said, with earnestness, "Don't let her speak, Mrs. Gage, it will ruin us. Every newspaper in the land will have our cause mixed up with abolition and niggers, and we shall be utterly denounced." My only answer was, "We shall see when the time comes."

The second day the work waxed warm. Methodist, Baptist, Episcopal, Presbyterian, and Universalist ministers came in to hear and discuss the resolutions presented. One claimed superior rights and privileges for man, on the ground of "superior intellect"; another, because of the "manhood of Christ; if God had desired the equality of woman, He would have given some token of His will through the birth, life, and death of the Saviour." Another gave us a theological view of the "sin of our first mother."

There were very few women in those days who dared to "speak in meeting"; and the august teachers of the people were seemingly getting the better of us, while the boys in the galleries, and the sneerers among the pews, were hugely enjoying the discomfiture, as they supposed, of the "strong-minded." Some of the tender-skinned friends were on the point of losing dignity, and the atmosphere betokened a storm. When, slowly from her seat in the corner rose Sojourner Truth, who, till now, had scarcely lifted her head. "Don't let her speak!" gasped half a dozen in my ear. She moved slowly and solemnly to the front, laid her old bonnet at her feet, and turned her great speaking eyes to me. There was a hissing sound of disapprobation above and below. I rose and announced "Sojourner Truth," and begged the audience to keep silence for a few moments.

The tumult subsided at once, and every eye was fixed on this almost Amazon form, which stood nearly six feet high, head erect, and eyes piercing the upper air like one in a dream. At her first word there was a profound hush. She spoke in deep tones, which, though not loud, reached every ear in the house, . . .

"Wall, chilern, whar dar is so much racket dar must be somethin' out o' kilter. I tink dat 'twixt de niggers of de Souf and de womin at de Norf, all talkin' 'bout rights, de white men will be in a fix pretty soon. But what's all dis here talkin' 'bout?

"Dat man ober dar say dat womin needs to be helped into carriages, and lifted ober ditches, and to hab de best place everywhar. Nobody eber helps me into carriages, or ober mud-puddles, or gibs me any best place!" And raising herself to her full height, and her voice to a pitch like rolling thunder, she asked, "And a'n't I a woman? Look at me! Look at my arm! (and she bared her right arm to the shoulder, showing her tremendous muscular power). I have ploughed, and planted, and gathered into barns, and no man could head me! And a'n't I a woman? I could work as much and eat as much as a man—when I could get it—and bear de lash as well! And a'n't I a woman? I have borne thirteen chilern, and seen 'em mos' all sold off to slavery, and when I cried out with my mother's grief, none but Jesus heard me! And a'n't I a woman?

"Den dey talks 'bout dis ting in de head; what dis dey call it?" ("Intellect," whispered some one near.) "Dat's it, honey. What's dat got to do wid womin's rights or nigger's rights? If my cup won't hold but a pint, and yourn holds a quart, wouldn't ye be mean not to let me have my little half-measure full?" And she pointed her significant finger, and sent a keen glance at the minister who had made the argument. The cheering was long and loud.

"Den dat little man in black dar, he say women can't have as much rights as men, 'cause Christ wan't a woman! Whar did your Christ come from?" Rolling thunder couldn't have stilled that crowd, as did those deep, wonderful tones, as she stood there with outstretched arms and eyes of fire. Raising her voice still louder, she repeated, "Whar did your Christ come from? From God and a woman! Man had nothin' to do wid Him." Oh, what a rebuke that was to that little man.

Turning again to another objector, she took up the defense of Mother Eve. I can not follow her through it all. It was pointed, and witty, and solemn; eliciting at almost every sentence deafening applause; and she ended by asserting: "If de fust woman God ever made was strong enough to turn de world upside down all alone, dese women togedder (and she glanced her eye over the platform) ought to be able to turn it back, and get it right side up again! And now dey is asking to do it, de men better let 'em." Long-continued cheering greeted this. " 'Bleeged to ye for hearin' on me, and now ole Sojourner han't got nothin' more to say."

Amid roars of applause, she returned to her corner, leaving more than one of us with streaming eyes, and hearts beating with gratitude. She had taken us up in her strong arms and carried us safely over the slough of difficulty turning the whole tide in our favor. I have never in my life seen anything like the magical influence that subdued the mobbish spirit of the day, and turned the sneers and jeers of an excited crowd into notes of respect and admiration. Hundreds rushed up to shake hands with her, and congratulate the glorious old mother, and bid her Godspeed on her mission of "testifyin' agin concerning the wickedness of this 'ere people."

Elizabeth Cady Stanton, Susan B. Anthony and Matilda J. Gage (eds.), *History of Woman Suffrage,* I (New York, 1881).

The Underground Railroad in Operation

An actual account of an operator, Seth Concklin, on the underground railroad tells of his initial encounter with a slave family in the South, their subsequent escape and the experiences which followed. Concklin lost his life in an attempt to rescue the family of black abolitionist William Still's brother.

EASTPORT, MISS., FEB. 3, 1851.

TO WM. STILL:—Our friends in Cincinnati have failed finding anybody to assist me on my return. Searching the country opposite Paducah, I find that the whole country fifty miles round is inhabited only by Christian wolves. It is customary, when a strange negro is seen, for any white man to seize the negro and convey such negro through and out of the State of Illinois to Paducah, Ky., and lodge such stranger in Paducah jail, and there claim such reward as may be offered by the master.

There is no regularity by the steamboats on the Tennessee River. I was four days getting to Florence from Paducah. Sometimes they are four days starting, from the time appointed, which alone puts to rest the plan for returning by steamboat. The distance from the mouth of the river to Florence, is from between three hundred and five to three hundred and forty-five miles by the river; by land, two hundred and fifty, or more.

I arrived at the shoe-shop on the plantation, one o'clock, Tuesday, 28th. William and two boys were making shoes. I immediately gave the first signal, anxiously waiting thirty minutes for an opportunity to give the second and main signal, during which time I was very sociable. It was rainy and muddy—my pants were rolled up to the knees. I was in the character of a man seeking employment in this country. End of thirty minutes gave the second signal.

William appeared unmoved; soon sent out the boys; instantly sociable; Peter and Levin at the Island; one of the young masters with them; not safe to undertake to see them till Saturday night, when they would be at home; appointed a place to see Vina, in an open field, that night; they to bring me something to eat; our interview only four minutes; I left; appeared by night; dark and cloudy; at ten o'clock appeared William; exchanged signals; led me a few rods to where stood Vina; gave her the signal sent by Peter; our interview ten minutes; she did not call me "master," nor did she say "sir," by which I knew she had confidence in me.

Our situation being dangerous, we decided that I meet Peter and Levin on the bank of the river early dawn of day, Sunday, to establish the laws. During our interview, William prostrated on his knees, and face to the ground; arms sprawling; head cocked back, watching for wolves, by which position a man can see better in the dark. No house to go to safely, traveled round till morning, eating hoe cake which William had given me for supper; next day going around to get employment. I thought of William, who is a Christian preacher, and of the Christian preachers in Pennsylvania. One watching for wolves by night, to rescue Vina and her three children from Christian licentiousness; the other standing erect in open day, seeking the praise of men.

During the four days waiting for the important Sunday morning, I thoroughly surveyed the rocks and shoals of the river from Florence seven miles up, where will be my place of departure. General notice was taken of me as being a stranger, lurking around. Fortunately there are several small grist mills within ten miles around. No taverns here, as in the North; any planter's house entertains travelers occasionally.

One night I stayed at a medical gentleman's, who is not a large planter; another night at an ex-magistrate's house in South Florence—a Virginian by birth—one of the late census takers; told me that many more persons cannot read and write than is reported; one fact, amongst many others, that many persons who do not know the letters of the alphabet, have learned to write their own names; such are generally reported readers and writers.

It being customary for a stranger not to leave the house early in the morning where he has lodged, I was under the necessity of staying out all night Saturday, to be able to meet Peter and Levin, which was accomplished in due time. When we approached, I gave my signal first; immediately they gave theirs. I talked freely. Levin's voice, at first, evidently trembled. No wonder, for my presence universally attracted attention by the lords of the land. Our interview was less than one hour; the laws were written. I to go to Cincinnati to get a rowing boat and provisions; a first class clipper boat to go with speed. To depart from the place where the laws were written, on Saturday night of the first of March. I to meet one of them at the same place Thursday night, previous to the fourth Saturday from the night previous to the Sunday when the laws were written. We to go down the Tennessee river to some place up the Ohio, not yet decided on, in our row boat. Peter and Levin are good oarsmen. So am I. . . .

Came from Florence to here Sunday night by steamboat. Eastport is in Mississippi. Waiting here for a steamboat to go down; paying one dollar a day for board. Like other taverns here, the wretchedness is indescribable; no pen, ink, paper or newspaper to be had; only one room for everybody, except the gambling rooms. It is difficult for me to write. Vina intends to get a pass for Catharine and herself for the first Sunday in March.

The bank of the river where I met Peter and Levin is two miles from the plantation. I have avoided saying I am from Philadelphia. Also avoided talking about negroes. I never talked so much about milling before. I consider most of the trouble over, till I arrive in a free State with my crew, the first week in March; then will I have to be wiser than Christian serpents, and more cautious than doves. I do not consider it safe to keep this letter in my possession, yet I dare not put it in the post-office here; there is so little business in these post-offices that notice might be taken.

I am evidently watched; everybody knows me to be a miller. I may write again when I get to Cincinnati, if I should have time. The ex-magistrate, with whom I stayed in South Florence, held three hours' talk with me, exclusive of our morning talk. Is a man of good general information; he was exceedingly inquisitive. "I am from Cincinnati, formerly from the *State of New York*." I had no opportunity to get anything to eat from seven o'clock Tuesday morning till six o'clock Wednesday evening, except the hoe cake, and no sleep.

Florence is the head of navigation for small steamboats. Seven miles, all the way up to my place of departure, is swift water, and rocky. Eight hundred miles to Cincinnati. I found all things here as Peter told me, except the distance of the river. South Florence contains twenty white families, three warehouses of considerable business, a post-office, but no school. McKiernon is here waiting for a steamboat to go to New Orleans, so we are in company.

[Seth Concklin]

* * * * *

PRINCETON, GIBSON COUNTY, INDIANA,
FEB. 18, 1851.

TO WM. STILL:—The plan is to go to Canada, on the Wabash, opposite Detroit. There are four routes to Canada. One through Illinois, commencing above and below Alton; one through to North Indiana, and the Cincinnati route, being the largest route in the United States.

I intended to have gone through Pennsylvania, but the risk going up the Ohio river has caused me to go to Canada. Steamboat traveling is universally condemned; though many go in boats, consequently many get lost.

Going in a skiff is new, and is approved of in my case. After I arrive at the mouth of the Tennessee river, I will go up the Ohio seventy-five miles, to the mouth of the Wabash, then up the Wabash, forty-four miles to New Harmony, where I shall go ashore by night, and go thirteen miles east, to Charles Grier, a farmer, (colored man), who will entertain us, and next night convey us sixteen miles to David Stormon[t], near Princeton, who will take the command, and I be released.

David Stormon estimates the expenses from his house to Canada, at forty dollars, without which, no sure protection will be given. They might be instructed concerning the course, and beg their way through without money. If you wish to do what should be done, you will send me fifty dollars, in a letter, to Princeton, Gibson county, Inda., so as to arrive there by the 8th of March. Eight days should be estimated for a letter to arrive from Philadelphia.

The money to be State Bank of Ohio, or State Bank, or Northern Bank of Kentucky, or any other Eastern bank. Send no notes larger than twenty dollars.

Levi Coffin had no money for me. I paid twenty dollars for the skiff. No money to get back to Philadelphia. It was not understood that I would have to be at any expense seeking aid.

One half of my time has been used in trying to find persons to assist, when I may arrive on the Ohio river, in which I have failed, except Stormon.

Having no letter of introduction to Stormon from any source, on which I could fully rely, I traveled two hundred miles around, to find out his stability. I have found many Abolitionists, nearly all who have made propositions, which themselves would not comply with, and nobody else would. Already I have traveled over three thousand miles. Two thousand and four hundred by steamboat, two hundred by railroad, one hundred by stage, four hundred on foot, forty-eight in a skiff.

I have yet five hundred miles to go to the plantation, to commence operations. I have been two weeks on the decks of steamboats, three nights out, two of which I got perfectly wet. If I had had paper money, as McKim desired, it would have been destroyed. I have not been entertained gratis at any place except Stormon's. I had one hundred and twenty-six dollars when I left Philadelphia, one hundred from you, twenty-six mine.

Telegraphed to station at Evansville, thirty-three miles from Stormon's, and at Vinclure's, twenty-five miles from Stormon's. The Wabash route is considered the safest route. No one has ever been lost from Stormon's to Canada. Some have been lost between Stormon's and the Ohio. The wolves have never suspected Stormon. Your asking aid in money for a case properly belonging east of Ohio, is detested. If you have sent money to Cincinnati, you should recall it. I will have no opportunity to use it.

SETH CONCKLIN,
Princeton, Gibson county, Ind.

P.S. First of April, will be about the time Peter's family will arrive opposite Detroit. You should inform yourself how to find them there. I may have no opportunity. . . .

* * * * *

EVANSVILLE, INDIANA,
MARCH 31st, 1851.

WM. STILL: *Dear Sir,*—On last Tuesday I mailed a letter to you, written by Seth Concklin. I presume you have received that letter. It gave an account of his rescue of the family of your brother. If that is the last news you have had from them, I have very painful intelligence for you. They passed on from near Princeton, where I saw them and had a lengthy interview with them, up north, I think twenty-three miles above Vincennes, Ind., where they were seized by a party of men, and lodged in jail. Telegraphic dispatches were sent all through the South. I have since learned that the Marshall of Evansville received a dispatch from Tuscumbia, to look out for them. By some means, he and the master, so says report, went to Vincennes and claimed the fugitives, chained Mr. Concklin and hurried all off. Mr. Concklin wrote to Mr. David Stormon, Princeton, as soon as he was cast into prison, to find bail. So soon as we got the letter and could get off, two of us were setting off to render all possible aid, when we were told they all had passed, a few hours before, through Princeton, Mr. Concklin in chains. What kind of process was had, if any, I know not. I immediately came down to this place, and learned that they had been put on a boat at 3 P.M. I did not arrive until 6. Now all hopes of their recovery are gone. No case ever so enlisted my sympathies. I had seen Mr. Concklin in Cincinnati. I had given him aid and counsel. I happened to see them after they landed in Indiana. I heard Peter and Levin tell their tale of suffering, shed tears of sorrow for them all; but now, since they have fallen a prey to the unmerciful blood-hounds of this state, and have again been dragged back to unrelenting bondage, I am entirely unmanned. And poor Concklin! I fear for him. When he is dragged back to Alabama, I fear they will go far beyond the utmost rigor of the law, and vent their savage cruelty upon him. It is with pain I have to communicate these things. But you may not hear them from him. I could not get to see him or them, as Vincennes is about thirty miles from Princeton, where I was when I heard of the capture.

I take pleasure in stating that, according to the letter he (Concklin) wrote to Mr. D. Stewart, Mr. Concklin did not abandon them, but risked his own liberty to save them. He was not with them when they were taken; but went afterwards to take them out of jail upon a writ of Habeas Corpus, when they seized him too and lodged him in prison.

I write in much haste. If I can learn any more facts of importance, I may write you. If you desire to hear from me again, or if you should learn any thing specific from Mr. Concklin, be pleased to write me at Cincinnati, where I expect to be in a short time. If curious to know your correspondent, I may say I was formerly Editor of the "New Concord Free Press," Ohio. I only add that every case of this kind only tends to make me abhor my (no!) *this* country more and more. It is the Devil's Government, and God will destroy it.

Yours for the slave, N. R. JOHNSTON.

P.S. I broke open this letter to write you some more. The foregoing pages were written at night. I expected to mail it next morning before leaving Evansville; but the boat for which I was waiting came down about three in the morning; so I had to hurry on board, bringing the letter along. As it now is I am not sorry, for coming down, on my way to St. Louis, as far as Paducah, there I learned from a colored man at the wharf that, that same day, in the morning, the master and the family of fugitives arrived off the boat, and had then gone on their journey to Tuscumbia, but that the "white man" (Mr. Concklin) had "got away from them," about twelve miles up the river. It seems he got off the boat some way, near, or at Smithland, Ky., a town at the mouth of the Cumberland River. I presume the report is true, and hope he will finally escape, though I was also told that they were in pursuit of him. Would that the others had also escaped. Peter and Levin could have done so, I think, if they had had resolution. One of them rode a horse, he not tied either, behind the coach in which the others were. He followed apparently "contented and happy." From report, they told their master, and even their pursuers, before the master came, that Concklin had decoyed them away, they coming unwillingly. I write on a very unsteady boat.

Yours, N. R. JOHNSTON.

William Still, *The Underground Rail Road* (Philadelphia, 1872).

Frederick Douglass' Independence Day Address

A poignant and eloquent speech was delivered by Frederick Douglass on July 5, 1852, in Rochester, New York. Note especially the last paragraph, in which Douglass discusses the meaning of the Fourth of July to a slave.

Fellow-citizens, pardon me, allow me to ask, why am I called upon to speak here to-day? What have I, or those I represent, to do with your national independence? Are the great principles of political freedom and of natural justice, embodied in that Declaration of Independence, extended to us? And am I, therefore, called upon to bring our humble offering to the national altar, and to confess the benefits and express devout gratitude for the blessings resulting from your independence to us?

Would to God, both for your sakes and ours, that an affirmative answer could be truthfully returned to these questions! Then would my task be light, and my burden easy and delightful. For *who* is there so cold, that a nation's sympathy could not warm him? Who so obdurate and dead to the claims of gratitude, that would not thankfully acknowledge such priceless benefits? Who so stolid and selfish, that would not give his voice to swell the hallelujahs of a nation's jubilee, when the chains of servitude had been torn from his limbs? I am not that man. In a case like that, the dumb might eloquently speak, and the "lame man leap as an hart."

But such is not the state of the case. I say it with a sad sense of the disparity between us. I am not included within the pale of this glorious anniversary! Your high independence only reveals the immeasurable distance between us. The blessings in which you, this day, rejoice are not enjoyed in common. The rich inheritance of justice, liberty, prosperity and independence, bequeathed by your fathers, is shared by you, not by me. The sunlight that brought light and healing to you, has brought stripes and death to me. This Fourth July is *yours,* not *mine. You* may rejoice, *I* must mourn. To drag a man in fetters into the grand illuminated temple of liberty, and call upon him to join you in joyous anthems, were inhuman mockery and sacrilegious irony. Do you mean, citizens, to mock me, by asking me to speak to-day? If so, there is a parallel to your conduct. And let me warn you that it is dangerous to copy the example of a nation whose crimes, towering up to heaven, were thrown down by the breath of the Almighty, burying that nation in irrevocable ruin! I can to-day take up the plaintive lament of a peeled and woe-smitten people!

"By the rivers of Babylon, there we sat down. Yea! We wept when we remembered Zion. We hanged our harps upon the willows in the midst thereof. For there, they that carried us away captive, required of us a song; and they who wasted us required of us mirth, saying, Sing us one of the songs of Zion. How can we sing the Lord's song in a strange land? If I forget thee, O Jerusalem, let my right hand forget her cunning. If I do not remember thee, let my tongue cleave to the roof of my mouth."

Fellow-citizens, above your national, tumultuous joy, I hear the mournful wail of millions! whose chains, heavy and grievous yesterday, are, to-day, rendered more intolerable by the jubilee shouts that reach them. If I do forget, if I do not faithfully remember those bleeding children of sorrow this day, "may my right hand forget her cunning, and may my tongue cleave to the roof of my mouth!" To forget them, to pass lightly over their wrongs, and to chime in with the popular theme, would be treason most scandalous and shocking, and would make me a reproach before God and the world. My subject, then, fellow-citizens, is AMERICAN SLAVERY. I shall see this day and its popular characteristics from the slave's point of view. Standing there identified with the American bondman, making his wrongs mine, I do not hesitate to declare, with all my soul, that the character and conduct of this nation never looked blacker to me than on this 4th of July! Whether we turn to the declarations of the past, or to the professions of the present, the conduct of the nation seems equally hideous and revolting. America is false to the past, false to the present, and solemnly binds herself to be false to the future. Standing with God and the crushed and bleeding slave on this occasion, I will, in the name of humanity which is outraged, in the name of liberty which is fettered, in the name of the constitution and the Bible which are disregarded and trampled upon, dare to call in question and to denounce, with all the emphasis I can command, everything that serves to perpetuate slavery—the great sin and shame of America! "I will not equivocate; I will not excuse"; I will use the severest language I can command; and yet not one word shall escape me that any man, whose judgment is not blinded by prejudice, or who is not at heart a slaveholder, shall not confess to be right and just.

But I fancy I hear some one of my audience say, "It is just in this circumstance that you and your brother Abolitionists fail to make a favorable impression on the public mind. Would you argue more, and denounce less; would you persuade more, and rebuke less; your cause would be much more likely to succeed." But, I submit, where all is plain there is nothing to be argued. What point in the anti-slavery creed would you have me argue? On what branch of the subject do the people of this country need light? Must I undertake to prove that the slave is a man? That point is conceded already. Nobody doubts it. The slaveholders themselves acknowledge it in the enactment of laws for their government. They acknowledge it when they punish disobedience on the part of the slave. There are seventy-two crimes in the State of Virginia which, if committed by a black man (no matter how ignorant he be), subject him to the punishment of death; while only two of the same crimes will subject a white man to the like punishment. What is this but the acknowledgment that the slave is a moral, intellectual, and responsible being? The manhood of the slave is conceded. It is admitted in the fact that Southern statute books are covered with enactments forbidding, under severe fines and penalties, the teaching of the slave to read or to write. When you can point to any such laws in reference to the beasts of the field, then I may consent to argue the manhood of the slave. When the dogs in your streets, when the fowls of the air, when the cattle on your hills, when the fish of the sea, and the reptiles that crawl, shall be unable to distinguish the slave from a brute, *then* I will argue with you that the slave is a man!

For the present, it is enough to affirm the equal manhood of the Negro race. Is it not astonishing that, while we are ploughing, planting, and reaping, using all kinds of mechanical tools, erecting houses, constructing bridges, building ships, working in metals of brass, iron, copper, silver and gold; that, while we are reading, writing and ciphering, acting as clerks, merchants and secretaries, having among us lawyers, doctors, ministers, poets, authors, editors, orators and teachers; that, while we are engaged in all manner of enterprises common to other men,—digging gold in California, capturing the whale in the Pacific, feeding sheep and cattle on the hill-side, living, moving, acting, thinking, planning, living in families as husbands, wives and children, and, above all, confessing and worshipping the Christian's God, and looking hopefully for life and immortality beyond the grave—, we are called upon to prove that we are men!

Would you have me argue that man is entitled to liberty? That he is the rightful owner of his own body? You have already declared it. Must I argue the wrongfulness of slavery? Is that a question for Republicans? Is it to be settled by the rules of logic and argumentation, as a matter beset with great difficulty, involving a doubtful application of the principle of justice, hard to be understood? How should I look to-day, in the presence of Americans, dividing and subdividing a discourse, to show that men have a natural right to freedom? speaking of it relatively and positively, negatively and affirmatively. To do so, would be to make myself ridiculous, and to offer an insult to your understanding.—There is not a man beneath the canopy of heaven who does not know that slavery is wrong *for him.*

What, am I to argue that it is wrong to make men brutes, to rob them of their liberty, to work them without wages, to keep them ignorant of their relations to their fellow men, to beat them with sticks, to flay their flesh with the lash, to load their limbs with irons, to hunt them with dogs, to sell them at auction, to sunder their families, to knock out their teeth, to burn their flesh, to starve them into obedience and submission to their masters? Must I argue that a system thus marked with blood, and stained with pollution, is wrong? No! I will not. I have better employment for my time and strength than such arguments would imply.

What, then, remains to be argued? Is it that slavery is not divine; that God did not establish it; that our doctors of divinity are mistaken? There is blasphemy in the thought. That which is inhuman, cannot be divine! *Who* can reason on such a proposition? They that can, may; I cannot. The time for such argument is past.

At a time like this, scorching irony, not convincing argument, is needed. O! had I the ability, and could I reach the nation's ear, I would, to-day, pour out a fiery stream of biting ridicule, blasting reproach, withering sarcasm, and stern rebuke. For it is not light that is needed, but fire; it is not the gentle shower, but thunder. We need the storm, the whirlwind, and the earthquake. The feeling of the nation must be quickened; the conscience of the nation must be roused; the propriety of the nation must be startled; the hypocrisy of the nation must be exposed; and its crimes against God and man must be proclaimed and denounced.

What, to the American slave, is your 4th of July? I answer; a day that reveals to him, more than all other days in the year, the gross injustice and cruelty to which he is the constant victim. To him, your celebration is a sham; your boasted liberty, an unholy license; your national greatness, swelling vanity; your sounds of rejoicing are empty and heartless; your denunciation of tyrants, brass fronted impudence; your shouts of liberty and equality, hollow mockery; your prayers and hymns, your sermons and thanksgivings, with all your religious parade and solemnity, are, to him mere bombast, fraud, deception, impiety, and hyprocrisy—a thin veil to cover up crimes which would disgrace a nation of savages. There is not a nation on the earth guilty of practices more shocking and bloody than are the people of the United States, at this very hour.

Go where you may, search where you will, roam through all the monarchies and despotisms of the Old World, travel through South America, search out every abuse, and when you have found the last, lay your facts by the side of the every-day practices of this nation, and you will say with me, that, for revolting barbarity and shameless hypocrisy, America reigns without a rival. . . .

Carter G. Woodson (ed.), *Negro Orators and Their Orations* (Washington, 1925).

"Suffer the Little Children to Come unto Me" But Do Not Educate Them

Two trials that were noteworthy in the pre-Civil War period revolved around women. Prudence Crandall, a teacher in Connecticut, opened her school to Negro girls in 1833. Her actions were not only roundly condemned by her contemporaries, but she was arrested, tried and found guilty of breaking a law that had been passed after she admitted her first black student. In 1853, Mrs. Margaret Douglass was convicted of breaking a Virginia law that forbade the teaching of free Negroes. The following is the decision of the Virginia judge who sentenced Mrs. Douglass to one month in prison.

Upon an indictment found against you for assembling with Negroes to instruct them to read and write, and for associating with them in an unlawful assembly, you were found guilty, and a mere nominal fine imposed, on the last day of this court held in the month of November.

At the time the jury came in and rendered their verdict, you were not in court, and the court, being about to adjourn for the purpose of attending to other official duties in a distant part of the state, it was necessary and proper, under the law, to award a *capias* against you, returnable to the present adjourned term, so that the judgment and sentence of the law may be fulfilled. The court is not called on to vindicate the policy of the law in question, for so long as it remains upon the statute book, and unrepealed, public and private justice and morality require that it should be respected and sustained.

There are persons, I believe, in our community opposed to the policy of the law in question. They profess to believe that universal intellectual culture is necessary to religious instruction and education, and that such culture is suitable to a state of slavery, and there can be no misapprehension as to your opinions on this subject, judging from the indiscreet freedom with which you spoke of your regard for the colored race in general. Such opinions in the present state of our society I regard as manifestly mischievous.

It is not true that our slaves cannot be taught religious and moral duty without being able to read the Bible and use the pen. Intellectual and religious instruction often go hand in hand, but the latter may well exist without the former; and the truth of this is abundantly vindicated by the well-known fact that in many parts of our own commonwealth, as in other parts of the country in which among the whites one-fourth or more are entirely without a knowledge of letters, respect for the law, and for moral and religious conduct and behavior, are justly and properly appreciated and practised.

A valuable report, or document, recently published in the city of New York by the Southern Aid Society sets forth many valuable and important truths upon the condition of the Southern slaves, and the utility of moral and religious instruction, apart from a knowledge of books. I recommend the careful perusal of it to all whose opinions concur with your own. It shows that a system of catechetical instruction, with a clear and simple exposition of Scripture, has been employed with gratifying success; that the slave population of the South are peculiarly susceptible of good religious influences. Their mere residence among a Christian people has wrought a great and happy change in their condition: they have been raised from the night of heathenism to the light of Christianity, and thousands of them have been brought to a saving knowledge of the Gospel.

Of the 100 million of the Negro race, there cannot be found another so large a body as the 3 million slaves in the United States, at once so intelligent, so inclined to the Gospel, and so blessed by the elevating influence of civilization and Christianity. Occasional instances of cruelty and oppression, it is true, may sometimes occur, and probably will ever continue to take place under any system of laws; but this is not confined to wrongs committed upon the Negro. Wrongs committed and cruelly practised in a like degree by the lawless white man upon his own color; and while the Negroes of our town and state are known to be surrounded by most of the substantial comforts of life, and invited both by precept and example to participate in proper moral and religious duties, it argues, it seems to me, a sickly sensibility toward them to say their persons, and feelings, and interests are not sufficiently respected by our laws, which, in effect, tend to nullify the act of our legislature passed for the security and protection of their masters.

The law under which you have been tried and found guilty is not to be found among the original enactments of our legislature. The first legislative provision upon this subject was introduced in the year 1834, immediately succeeding the bloody scenes of the memorable Southampton insurrection; and that law, being found not sufficiently penal to check the wrongs complained of, was reenacted with additional penalties in the year 1848, which last mentioned act, after several years' trial and experience, has been reaffirmed by adoption and incorporated into our present code.

After these several and repeated recognitions of the wisdom and propriety of the said act, it may well be said that bold and open opposition to it is a matter not to be slightly regarded, especially as we have reason to believe that every Southern slave state in our country, as a measure of self-preservation and protection, has deemed it wise and just to adopt laws with similar provisions. There might have been no occasion for such enactments in Virginia, or elsewhere, on the subject of Negro education but as a matter of self-defense against the schemes of Northern incendiaries and the outcry against holding our slaves in bondage.

Many now living well remember how and when and why the antislavery fury began, and by what means its manifestations were made public. Our mails were clogged with Abolition pamphlets and inflammatory documents, to be distributed among our Southern Negroes to induce them to cut our throats. Sometimes, it may be, these libelous documents were distributed by Northern citizens professing Southern feelings, and at other times by Southern people professing Northern feelings. These, however, were not the only means resorted to by the Northern fanatics to stir up insubordination among our slaves. They scattered, far and near, pocket handkerchiefs and other similar articles with frightful engravings and printed over with antislavery nonsense, with the view to work upon the feeling and ignorance of our Negroes, who otherwise would have remained comfortable and happy. Under such circumstances there was but one measure of protection for the South, and that was adopted.

Teaching the Negroes to read and write is made penal by the laws of our state. The act imposes a fine not exceeding $100, to be ascertained by the jury, and imprisonment not exceeding six months, to be fixed and ascertained by the court. And, now, since the jury in your case has in my opinion properly settled the question of guilt, it devolves on me, under the law, to ascertain and decide upon the quantum of imprisonment under the circumstances of your trial; and I exceedingly regret that, in being called on for the first time to act under the law in question, it becomes my duty to impose the required punishment upon a female, apparently of fair and respectable standing in the community. The only mitigating circumstance in your case, if in truth there be any, according to my best reason and understanding of it, is that to which I have just referred, namely, you being a female.

Under the circumstances of this case, if you were of a different sex, I should regard the full punishment of six months' imprisonment as eminently just and proper. Had you taken the advice of your friends and of the court and had employed counsel to defend you, your case, no doubt, would have been presented in a far more favorable light, both to the court and to the jury. The opinions you advanced, and the pertinacity and zeal you manifested in behalf of the Negroes, while they indicated perfect candor and sincerity on your part, satisfied the court, and must have satisfied all who heard you, that the act complained of was the settled and deliberate purpose of your mind, regardless of consequences, however dangerous to your peace.

In conformity with these views, I am impelled by a feeling of common honesty to say that this is not a case in which a mere formal judgment should be announced as the opinion of the court. Something more substantial under the circumstances of this case, I think, is demanded and required. The discretionary power to imprison for the term of six months or less, in good sense and sound morality, does not authorize a mere minimum punishment, such as imprisonment for a day or week, in a case in which the question of guilt is free from doubt, and there are many facts and circumstances of aggravation. A judgment of that sort, therefore, in this case, would doubtless be regarded by all true advocates of justice and law as mere mockery. It would be no terror to those who acknowledge no rule of action but their own evil will and pleasure, but would rather invite to still bolder incendiary movements.

For these reasons, as an example to all others in like cases disposed to offend, and in vindication of the policy and justness of our laws, which every individual should be taught to respect, the judgment of the court is, in addition to the proper fine and costs, that you be imprisoned for the period of one month in the jail of this city.

John D. Lawson (ed.), *American State Trials*, VII (St. Louis, 1917).

Robert Purvis on His Rights As a Citizen

Born in Charleston, South Carolina, of a white father, and educated in New England, where he frequently associated with abolitionists, Robert Purvis became active in the antislavery struggle. It is said that Purvis aided over nine thousand fleeing slaves on the underground railroad in Philadelphia before the Civil War. These letters written by Purvis illustrate his militancy in the matter of paying taxes for benefits he could not receive.

Byberry, Pa., Nov. 5th, 1853

Friend Burleigh: Amid the animating and encouraging signs of the times, occurrences there are which seem to dash our hopes, and drive us into the very darkness of despair. The recent outrage upon Misses Remond and Wood, and my son, at the Franklin Exhibition —Alderman Mitchell's decision in the case, when, too, he had, previously to the suit being brought before him, properly characterized it as most brutal and infamous—the continued high-handed exclusion of my children from the Public School in this Township, against law, justice and decency, perplexes and excites a spirit of belligerancy, at war with the peace of my soul and body. It seemed impossible to bear any longer this robbery of my rights and property, by those miserable serviles to the slave power, the Directors of the Public Schools for this Township, and feeling it impossible, I wrote the following letter to the collector of taxes, which you may publish in the *Freeman*, should you deem proper.

Yours, very truly,

Robert Purvis

* * * * *

Byberry, Nov. 4th, 1853

Mr. Jos. J. Butcher—*Dear Sir:* You called yesterday for the tax upon my property in this Township, which I shall pay, excepting the "School Tax." I object to the payment of this tax, on the ground that my rights as a citizen, and my feelings as a man and a parent, have been grossly outraged in depriving me, in violation of law and justice, of the benefits of the school system which this tax was designed to sustain. I am perfectly aware that all that makes up the character and worth of the citizens of this township look upon the proscription and exclusion of my children from the Public School as illegal, and an unjustifiable usurpation of my right. I have borne this outrage ever since the innovation upon the usual practice of admitting *all* the children of the Township into the Public Schools, and at considerable expense, have been obliged to obtain the services of private teachers to instruct my children, while my school tax is greater, with a single exception, than that of any other citizen of the township. It is true, (and the outrage is made but the more glaring and insulting,) I was informed by a *pious Quaker* director, with a sanctifying grace, imparting, doubtless, an unctuous glow to his *saintly* prejudices, that a school in the village of Mechanicsville was appropriated for "*thine*." The miserable shanty, with all its appurtenances, on the very line of the township, to which this *benighted* follower of George Fox alluded, is, as you know, the most flimsy and ridiculous sham which any tool of a skin-hating aristocracy could have resorted to, to cover or protect his servility. To submit by voluntary payment of the demand is too great an outrage upon nature, and, with a spirit, thank God, unshackled by this, or any other wanton and cowardly act, I shall resist this tax, which, before the unjust exclusion, had always afforded me the highest gratification in paying. With no other than the best feeling towards yourself, I am forced to this unpleasant position, in vindication of my rights and personal dignity against an encroachment upon them as contemptibly mean as it is infamously despotic.

Yours, very respectfully,

Robert Purvis

The Liberator (Boston), September 16 and December 16, 1853.

The Banishment of Manumitted Negroes

According to the law in Virginia, a Negro who was freed had to leave the state within one year after securing his freedom. Ironically, the man was free but not able to choose his own domicile.

[See document below.]

Carter G. Woodson Papers, Library of Congress.

27

To the Sheriff of Norfolk County, *Greeting.*

YOU ARE HEREBY COMMANDED TO SUMMON Bill Portlett a free negro, being a slave emancipated since the first day of May in the year 1806, being twenty one years of age at the time of his emancipation

witness Major Herbert

to appear before the Circuit Court of Norfolk county, at the Court House of said County, on the first day of September Term next, to ~~testify and the truth to say on behalf of~~ to shew cause if any he can why an Information should not be filed upon a certain presentment made by the Grand Jury at april term 1853 against him, for remaining in the Commonwealth for more than twelve months after his right to freedom accrued without having obtained leave according to law, to wit: from the first day of ~~in a certain matter of controversy in our said Court, depending and undetermined between~~ April in the year 1849, to the present time, continually in the County of Norfolk and within the jurisdiction of this Court contrary to law ~~and this shall in no wise omit, under the penalty of $300~~: and have then and there this Summons. *Witness*, Arthur Emmerson, Clerk of our said Court, at his Office, this 27th day of August, 1853; in the 78th year of the Commonwealth.

Copy Left

Arthur Emmerson C[lk]

A Slave Trader on the Domestic Slave Trade

The following information was given to Harriet Beecher Stowe by Captain Austin Bearse, a shipmaster in Boston. Bearse, a native of Barnstable, Cape Cod, participated in the slave trade and compared the American system of slavery unfavorably with his experiences elsewhere in the world.

I am a native of the State of Massachusetts. Between the years 1818 and 1830, I was, from time to time, mate on board of different vessels engaged in the coasting-trade on the coast of South Carolina.

It is well known that many New England vessels are in the habit of spending their winters on the southern coast in pursuit of this business. Our vessels used to run up the rivers for the rough rice and cotton of the plantations, which we took to Charleston.

We often carried gangs of slaves to the plantations, as they had been ordered. These slaves were generally collected by slave-traders in the slave-pens in Charleston—brought there by various causes, such as the death of owners and the division of estates, which threw them into the market. Some were sent as punishment for insubordination, or because the domestic establishment was too large, or because persons moving to the North or West preferred selling their slaves to the trouble of carrying them. We had on board our vessels, from time to time, numbers of these slaves—sometimes two or three, and sometimes as high as seventy or eighty. They were separated from their families and connexions with as little concern as calves and pigs are selected out of a lot of domestic animals.

Our vessels used to lie in a place called Poor Man's Hole, not far from the city. We used to allow the relations and friends of the slaves to come on board and stay all night with their friends, before the vessel sailed.

In the morning it used to be my business to pull off the hatches and warn them that it was time to separate; and the shrieks and heart-rending cries at these times were enough to make anybody's heart ache.

In the year 1828, while mate of the brig "Milton," from Boston, bound to New Orleans, the following incident occurred, which I shall never forget:—

The traders brought on board four quadroon men in handcuffs, to be stowed away for the New Orleans market. An old negro woman, more than eighty years of age, came screaming after them, "My son, O my son, my son!" She seemed almost frantic, and when we had got more than a mile out in the harbour we heard her screaming yet.

When we got into the Gulf Stream, I came to the men, and took off their handcuffs. They were resolute fellows, and they told me that I would see that they would never live to be slaves in New Orleans. One of the men was a carpenter, and one a blacksmith. We brought them into New Orleans, and consigned them over to the agent. The agent told the captain afterwards that in forty-eight hours after they came to New Orleans they were all dead men, having every one killed themselves, as they said they should. One of them, I know, was bought for a fireman on the steamer "Post Boy," that went down to the Balize. He jumped over, and was drowned.

The others—one was sold to a blacksmith, and one to a carpenter. The particulars of their death I didn't know, only that the agent told the captain that they were all dead.

There was a plantation at Coosahatchie, back of Charleston, S. C., kept by a widow lady, who owned eighty negroes. She sent to Charleston, and bought a quadroon girl, very nearly white, for her son. We carried her up. She was more delicate than our other slaves, so that she was not put with them, but was carried up in the cabin.

I have been on the rice-plantations on the river, and seen the cultivation of the rice. In the fall of the year, the plantation hands, both men and women, work all the time above their knees in water in the rice-ditches, pulling out the grass, to fit the ground for sowing the rice. Hands sold here from the city, having been bred mostly to house-labour, find this very severe. The plantations are so deadly that white people cannot remain on them during the summer time, except at a risk of life. The proprietors and their families are there only through the winter, and the slaves are left in the summer entirely under the care of the overseers. Such overseers as I saw were generally a brutal, gambling, drinking set.

I have seen slavery, in the course of my wanderings, in almost all the countries in the world. I have been to Algiers, and seen slavery there. I have seen slavery in Smyrna, among the Turks. I was in Smyrna when our American consul ransomed a beautiful Greek girl in the slave-market. I saw her come aboard the brig "Suffolk," when she came on board to be sent to America for her education. I have seen slavery in the Spanish and French ports, though I have not been on their plantations.

My opinion is, that American slavery, as I have seen it in the internal slave-trade, as I have seen it on the rice and sugar plantations, and in the city of New Orleans, is full as bad as slavery in any country of the world, heathen or Christian. People who go for visits or pleasure through the Southern States cannot possibly know those things which can be seen of slavery by shipmasters who run up into the back plantation of countries, and who transport the slaves and produce of plantations.

In my past days the system of slavery was not much discussed. I saw these things as others did, without interference. Because I no longer think it right to see these things in silence, I trade no more south of Mason & Dixon's line.

Harriet Beecher Stowe, *The Key to Uncle Tom's Cabin* (Boston, 1853).

A Slave's Attempt to Convert His Master

James L. Orr was a member of the United States House of Representatives from South Carolina. One of his slaves, known to us only as Alfred, expressed an uncommon desire to convert his master to Christianity. Although Alfred was interested in Orr's salvation, it is possible that he also hoped his own freedom would be forthcoming as a result of the conversion.

Greenville [S.C.]
29 June, 1856

Dear Master,

You will pardon your servant Alfred, for . . . writing to you. You have done me much kindness and I hope that I feel thankful to you for it. But as I owe you all my service I cannot express how much good I wish you unless you allow me to speak of a good that is more precious than any service my hands can render.

I think of you often and I feel concerned for you; not that the world don't show you honor, nor that you are in want of the friendship of man, or the love of kind friends; but this is the thing most concerns me; for you to seek to be honored as a child of God; to have your name witness in the Saintshood of life—that you may take the friendship of God and that you may be a companion of the Saints. Now you know that I would not dare to teach; but I hope you will allow me to remind you that after all the honors and friendships of this world are gone that you will need what God above can give you, even his friendship and love, & you know that these things must be gained before you die, and when I think how much you are engaged for the good of the country & how such things call the mind away from religion, I feel very uneasy about you. Do don't let Jesus miss you. & when I think of the sickness you are exposed to constantly where there are so many people, from every part of the world, & when I think of the dangers that are all around you, from the malice of your enemies, & when I think of the dangers of travelling on water & on land I am uneasy—I am afraid that you might be cut off from this life before you are prepared. Then all your life would be lost to yourself. Let not these things be so—But I desire you 'to seek the Lord where he may be found & to call upon him while he is near.' Let your humble servant beg you to make peace with God, then you will be stronger to serve the country & you will be safe from all harm & you will be helped. I would rather you would be a Christian than to be king & would rather you had the friendship of God if the whole world pressed upon you. Do this 'Seek first the Kingdom of God & his righteousness.' For Christ says 'What shall it profit a man, should he gain the whole world & lose his own soul, & what shall a man give in exchange for his soul?' My Dear Master accept these few words as the sincere love of Alfred for I do want you to be happy in a hereafter.

May God help you with bounteous good wishes & prayer for you. I am your unworthy servant

Alfred

To My Master
James L. Orr Washington City, District of Columbia

Orr-Patterson Papers, in the Southern Historical Collection, University of North Carolina Library.

Charlotte Forten's Diary

One of the most interesting female personalities in the years preceding the Civil War was Charlotte Forten, daughter of a wealthy Philadelphia merchant and granddaughter of James Forten, Negro sailmaker of the post-Revolutionary War era. Born as she was, into an educated and respected family, Miss Forten began keeping a diary. In the following excerpt from her diary, she describes her reaction to a visit by the poet John Greenleaf Whittier.

Monday, Aug. 10. [1857]. I scarcely know myself tonight;—a great and sudden joy has completely dazzled—overpowered me. This evening Miss R[emond] sent for me in haste saying a gentleman wished to see me. I went wondering who it *could* be, and found—Whittier! one of the few men whom I truly reverence for their great minds and greater hearts. I cannot *say* all that I *felt*—even to *thee,* my Journal! I stood like one bewildered before the noble poet, whose kindly, earnest greeting *could* not increase my love and admiration for him;—my heart was full, but I *could* not speak, though constantly tormented by the thought that *he* would think me very stupid, very foolish;—but after a few simple words from him I felt more at ease, and though I still could say but very little, and left the talking part to Miss R[emond] who can *always talk,* it was such a pleasure to listen to *him,* to have *him* before me, to watch that noble, spiritual face, those glorious eyes—there are no eyes like them—that I felt *very, very* happy. —The memory of this interview will be a lifelong happiness to me.—Shall I try to tell thee, my Journal, *something* of what he said? First we spoke of my old home and my present home. He asked me if I liked N[ew] E[ngland]—it was *such* a pleasure to tell him that I loved it well,—to see the approving smile, the sudden lighting of those earnest eyes! In comparing P[ennsylvani]a and N[ew] E[ngland] he spoke of the superior richness of the soil of the former, but said that here, though there were fewer and smaller farms, larger crops were raised on the same extent of ground, because vastly more labor and pains were bestowed upon its cultivation. Then I remembered that the poet was also a *farmer.* By some strange transition we got from *agriculture* to *spiritualism.* Whittier said that he too (having read them) thought that Prof. F[elton's] views were most uncharitable. Though *he* cannot believe in it; he thinks it wrong and unjust to condemn all interested in it.—The transition from this subject to that of the "future life" was easy. I shall never forget how earnestly, how beautifully the poet expressed his *perfect faith,* that faith so evident in his writings, in his holy and consistent life—. . . .

The poet gave me a cordial invitation to visit him and his sister at their home. God Bless him! This is a day to be marked with a white stone. . . .

Charlotte L. Forten, *The Journal of Charlotte L. Forten: A Free Negro in the Slave Era,* ed. Ray Allen Billington (New York, 1962).

An Escaped Slave Corresponds with His Former Mistress

Perhaps one of the most unusual incidents that was ever recorded between slave and master is presented below. Jarm Loguen escaped from slavery and became a minister in Syracuse, New York. In 1860, before the outbreak of war, his former mistress wrote him demanding that he purchase his freedom or return to be sold. Mr. Loguen replied with a caustic attack on the institution of slavery as it personally affected him.

Maury County, State of Tennessee,
Feb. 20, 1860.

To Jarm:—I now take my pen to write you a few lines, to let you know how we all are. I am a cripple, but I am still able to get about. The rest of the family are all well. Cherry is as well as common. I write you these lines to let you know the situation we are in,—partly in consequence of your running away and stealing Old Rock, our fine mare. Though we got the mare back, she never was worth much after you took her;—and, as I now stand in need of some funds, I have determined to sell you, and I have had an offer for you, but did not see fit to take it. If you will send me one thousand dollars, and pay for the old mare, I will give up all claim I have to you. Write to me as soon as you get these lines, and let me know if you will accept my proposition. In consequence of your running away, we had to sell Abe and Ann and twelve acres of land; and I want you to send me the money, that I may be able to redeem the land that you was the cause of our selling, and on receipt of the above-named sum of money, I will send you your bill of sale. If you do not comply with my request, I will sell you to some one else, and you may rest assured that the time is not far distant when things will be changed with you. Write to me as soon as you get these lines. Direct your letter to Bigbyville, Maury County, Tennessee. You had better comply with my request.

I understand that you are a preacher. As the Southern people are so bad, you had better come and preach to your old acquaintances. I would like to know if you read your Bible. If so, can you tell what will become of the thief if he does not repent? and, if the blind lead the blind, what will the consequence be? I deem it unnecessary to say much more at present. A word to the wise is sufficient. You know where the liar has his part. You know that we reared you as we reared our own children; that you was never abused, and that shortly before you ran away, when your master asked you if you would like to be sold, you said you would not leave him to go with any body.

Sarah Logue

* * * * *

Syracuse, [N.Y.] March 28, 1860

Mrs. Sarah Logue: Yours of the 20th of February is duly received, and I thank you for it. It is a long time since I heard from my poor old mother, and I am glad to know that she is yet alive, and, as you say, "as well as common." What that means, I don't know. I wish you had said more about her.

You are a woman; but, had you a woman's heart, you never could have insulted a brother by telling him you sold his only remaining brother and sister, because he put himself beyond your power to convert him into money.

You sold my brother and sister, Abe and Ann, and twelve acres of land, you say, because I ran away. Now you have the unutterable meanness to ask me to return and be your miserable chattel, or, in lieu thereof, send you $1000 to enable you to redeem the *land,* but not to redeem my poor brother and sister! If I were to send you money, it would be to get my brother and sister, and not that you should get land. You say you are a *cripple,* and doubtless you say it to stir my pity, for you knew I was susceptible in that direction. I do pity you from the bottom of my heart. Nevertheless, I am indignant beyond the power of words to express, that you should be so sunken and cruel as to tear the hearts I love so much all in pieces; that you should be willing to impale and crucify us all, out of compassion for your poor *foot* or *leg.* Wretched woman! Be it known to you that I value my freedom, to say nothing of my mother, brothers and sisters, more than your whole body; more, indeed, than my own life; more than all the lives of all the slaveholders and tyrants under heaven.

You say you have offers to buy me, and that you shall sell me if I do not send you $1000, and in the same breath and almost in the same sentence, you say, "You know we raised you as we did our own children." Woman, did you raise your *own children* for the market? Did you raise them for the whipping-post? Did you raise them to be driven off, bound to a coffle in chains? Where are my poor bleeding brothers and sisters? Can you tell? Who was it that sent them off into sugar and cotton fields, to be kicked and cuffed, and whipped, and to groan and die; and where no kin can hear their groans, or attend and sympathize at their dying bed, or follow in their funeral? Wretched woman! Do you say *you* did not do it? Then I reply, your husband did, and *you* approved the deed—and the very letter you sent me shows that your heart approved it all. Shame on you!

But, by the way, where is your husband? You don't speak of him. I infer, therefore, that he is dead; that he has gone to his great account, with all his sins against my poor family upon his head. Poor man! gone to meet the spirits of my poor, outraged and murdered people, in a world where Liberty and Justice are *Masters.*

But you say I am a thief, because I took the old mare along with me. Have you got to learn that I had a better right to the old mare, as you call her, than Mannasseth Logue had to me? Is it a greater sin for me to steal his horse, than it was for him to rob my mother's cradle, and steal me? If he and you infer that I forfeit all my rights to you, shall not I infer that you forfeit all your rights to me? Have you got to learn that human rights are mutual and reciprocal, and if you take my liberty and life, you forfeit your own liberty and life? Before God and high heaven, is there a law for one man which is not a law for every other man?

If you or any speculator on my body and rights, wish to know how I regard my rights, they need but come here, and lay their hands on me to enslave me. Did you think to terrify me by presenting the alternative to give my money to you, or give my body to slavery? Then let me say to you, that I meet the proposition with unutterable scorn and contempt. The proposition is an outrage and an insult. I will not budge one hair's breadth. I will not breathe a shorter breath, even to save me from your persecutions. I stand among a free people, who, I thank God, sympathize with my rights, and the rights of mankind; and if your emissaries and venders come here to re-enslave me, and escape the unshrinking vigor of my own right arm, I trust my strong and brave friends, in this city and State, will be my rescuers and avengers.

Yours, &c.,

J. W. Loguen

The Liberator (Boston), April 27, 1860.

SECTION II

Oh, wasn't that a wide river,
river of Jordan, Lord? wide river!
There's one more river to cross.

Oh, the river of Jordan is so wide,
One more river to cross;
I don't know how to get on the other side;
One more river to cross.

I have some friends before me gone,
One more river to cross;
By the grace of God I'll follow on;
One more river to cross.

Shout, shout, Satan's about,
One more river to cross;
Shut your door and keep him out;
One more river to cross.

Old Satan is a snake in the grass,
One more river to cross;
If you don't mind he'll get you at last;
One more river to cross.

New York Public Library

The torch of freedom.

Tell Them We Are Rising

WHEN JOHN BROWN led his raiding party at Harpers Ferry in 1859, the black man in America began to sense the presence of freedom. As the approaching winds of civil war gathered over the horizon, John Copeland, one of five Negroes who participated in the raid, wrote to his brother in Oberlin, Ohio, that although he stood at the threshold of death, freedom was in the air. Copeland felt that both the raid and his own death were worth the sacrifice.

The onslaught of civil war between the two sections of the nation did not bring immediately the long-awaited freedom to blacks, however, as many forces regarding their status came into play. Most historians concede that the issue of slavery was dominant in starting the conflict, but once the guns of the South fired on Fort Sumter, the restoration of the Union became the major objective of the Lincoln administration. Thus, in tragic irony, the slave was forgotten momentarily while armies were recruited and sent into the battlefields in large numbers both in the North and in the South, while the southern forces established a new government, and while both sections garnered funds with which to conduct the war.

The philosophy of Abraham Lincoln toward the status of the Negro is an enigma. At one time, he favored colonization in Haiti or some other remote spot because he did not believe that the two races could live harmoniously with each other if freedom came for the slaves. Later, in an effort to reunite the country, Lincoln swayed between compensated emancipation for the blacks and retention of the slave system as it existed. As the war continued and morale in the North began to decline, Lincoln's political senses latched onto the issue of emancipation as a moral issue by which the North could unify itself. Lincoln, the Commander-in-Chief, also came to see the value of using black troops in the field as a means of increasing his forces and as a psychological weapon against the South.

Although the Emancipation Proclamation was issued in 1863, and blacks were recruited into the Union forces in large numbers beginning in that year, they had long been active in supporting the war and anxious to participate in it. In fact, those Negroes who remained loyal to their southern ties were, in some instances, already on the battlefields serving their masters before the northern armies finally settled the issue in favor of Negro troops. Prior to the end of the conflict, General Robert E. Lee also advocated the use of armed black troops in defense of the South, but his advice fell upon deaf ears within the Confederate hierarchy.

At this period, the unifying theme of Negro life was the desire to be free, to be equal and to achieve the concepts embodied in the American dream. At the close of the Civil War, it seemed for a time that these aspirations would be realized, when blacks tasted the fruits of democracy in operation during the Reconstruction era. Two Negro U.S. Senators served their nation; a third was elected but was not allowed to take his seat. Other Negroes were elected to the U.S. House of Representatives and to local legislatures within their own states. Constitutional amendments were passed that guaranteed freedom, promised equality and ensured the franchise. In addition, a liberal Congress passed civil rights laws which re-enforced the amendments. The Freedmen's Bureau was established during the war, and with Reconstruction came into its own as a vehicle for improving the lot of the ex-slave through education, financial assistance and law enforcement.

Some southerners began to reconcile themselves to the inevitable, while others sought and eventually found new ways to subjugate the blacks. The birth of the Ku Klux Klan *c.* 1865, the gradual rebirth of southern aristocratic power and the changing political nature of the nation combined to bring an end to Reconstruction in 1877—and the beginning of a new reign of terror for Negroes in the South.

Although blacks had aided in the writing and adoption of progressive state constitutions during Reconstruction, it was not long before the whites who returned to power reversed this trend and new laws were passed that placed Negroes in positions not far removed from slavery. Those who were able psychologically, educationally and financially began an exodus from the oppressive South, only to find that conditions favored them little more when they reached "the promised land." Hostility to the black man was not confined to the former Confederacy.

The main impetus of the westward movement was reaching its peak, following a break in migration during the Civil War. Here, too, blacks made their contributions. As the white settlers advanced across the country in their covered wagons, they were accompanied and often led by blacks. Beckwourth Pass, in the Sierra Nevada Mountains, California, was discovered by Negro James Beckwourth. Black cowboys roamed the prairies along with whites, while others panned gold and silver in their search for a strike and instant wealth.

Although the periods of war and peace in the nineteenth century did not solve the problems of race relations in the United States, they did produce leaders who left a legacy for those who followed and who created a base on which others could build. The first Negro graduate of West Point, Henry O. Flipper, came to a questionable end in his career, but he was soon followed by John Alexander, who served with commendation in his capacity of cavalry commander. In tribute to Lieut. Alexander's capable performance, a camp in Virginia was named for him by the United States Army. Frederick Douglass, the noted abolitionist, expanded his horizons following the war and became the virtual spokesman for his people, until the rise of Booker T. Washington later in the century.

Negro women continued to make contributions to their race—through the work of such individuals as Harriet Tubman and Sojourner Truth—and to the beginnings of mass involvement by the organization of women's groups. Although Douglass dominated the scene to a large extent, men like Richard T. Greener, a Harvard graduate; John B. Rayner, of the Populist tradition in Texas; Isaac Myers, labor leader; and hundreds of unnamed blacks worked for the entrance of their people into the mainstream of American life following the oppressive centuries of bondage.

When the Supreme Court issued its famous decision in the case of Homer Plessy in 1896, it only served to illuminate the storm that had formed from a dark cloud gathering on the horizon in the wake of Reconstruction. Professor Rayford W. Logan refers to this period in Negro history as the "Nadir," and no one who reads the facts can challenge him.

No more auction block for me, no more
Many thousands gone.

No more slavery chains for me, no more
Many thousands gone.

"Could I Die in a More Noble Cause?"
—John A. Copeland

John A. Copeland, who was with John Brown during the raid on Harpers Ferry, wrote the following letter before he was executed at Charlestown, Virginia. One of five blacks with Brown, Copeland was condemned to death, at the age of twenty-five, for taking part in the raid.

Charlestown, Va., Dec. 10, 1859

My Dear Brother:—

I now take my pen to write you a few lines to let you know how I am, and in answer to your kind letter of the 5th instant. Dear brother, I am, it is true, so situated at present, as scarcely to know how to commence writing; not that my mind is filled with fear or that it has become shattered in view of my near approach to death. Not that I am terrified of the gallows which I see staring me in the face, and upon which I am so soon to stand and suffer death for doing what George Washington, the so-called father of this great but slavery-cursed country, was made a hero for doing, while he lived, and when dead his name was immortalized, and his great and noble deeds in behalf of freedom taught by parents to their children. And now, brother, for having lent my aid to a general no less brave, and engaged in a cause no less honorable and glorious, I am to suffer death. Washington entered the field to fight for the freedom of the American people—not for the white man alone, but for both black and white. Nor were they white men alone who fought for the freedom of this country. The blood of black men flowed as freely as that of white men. Yes, the *very best* blood that was spilt was that of a negro. It was the blood of that heroic man, (though black he was), Cyrus Attuck [Crispus Attucks]. And some of the *very last* blood shed was that of black men. To the truth of this, history, though prejudiced, is compelled to attest. It is true that black men did an equal share of the fighting for American Independence, and they were assured by the whites that they should share equal benefits for so doing. But after having performed their part honorably, they were by the whites most treacherously deceived,—they refusing to fulfill their part of the contract. But this you know as well as I do, and I will therefore say no more in reference to the claims which we, as colored men, have on the American people.

It was a sense of the wrongs which we have suffered that prompted the noble but unfortunate Captain Brown, and his associates, to attempt to give freedom to a small number, at least, of those who are now held by cruel and unjust laws, and by no less cruel and unjust men. To this freedom they were entitled by every known principle of justice and humanity, and for the enjoyment of it God created them. And now, dear brother, could I die in a more noble cause? . . .

Dear brother, I want you, and all of you, to meet me in Heaven. Prepare your souls for death. Be ready to meet your God at any moment, and then, though we meet no more on earth, we shall meet in Heaven, where parting is no more. Dear William and Fred, be good boys—mind your mother and father—love and honor them—grow up to be good men, and fear the Lord thy God. Now, I want you, dear brothers, to take this advice and follow it; remember, it comes from your own brother, and is written under most peculiar circumstances. Remember it is my dying advice to you, and I hope you will, from the love you have for me, receive it.

You may think I have been treated very harshly since I have been here, but it is not so. I have been treated exceedingly well—far better than I expected to be. My jailor is a most kind-hearted man, and has done all he could consistent with duty to make me and the rest of the prisoners comfortable. Capt. John Avis is a gentleman who has a heart in his bosom as brave as any other. He met us at the Ferry and fought us as a brave man would do. But since we have been in his power he has protected us from insult and abuse which cowards would have heaped upon us. He has done as a brave man and a gentleman only would do. Also one of his aids, Mr. John Sheats, has been very kind to us and has done all he could to serve us. And now, Henry, if fortune should ever throw either of them in your way and you can confer the least favor on them, do it for my sake. Give my love to all my friends. And now my dear brothers, one and all, I pray God we may meet in Heaven.

Good bye. I am now and shall remain, your affectionate brother.

John A. Copeland

Original in the possession of David W. Hazel, Central State University, Wilberforce, Ohio.

Garrison's Message on the Haitian Colonization Scheme

Soon after the outbreak of the Civil War, the noted abolitionist William Lloyd Garrison was contacted regarding the feasibility of American Negroes accepting an offer by the Haitian government to migrate to Haiti. A meeting was called by several prominent black citizens of New York for the purpose of discussing the Haitian proposal. Garrison, who was invited, could not attend but sent the following message regarding his opinion of the matter.

Boston, May 13, 1861

Messrs. George T. Downing, John V. De Grasse, and Robert Morris:

Gentlemen — You apprise me of a meeting to be held this evening in the Joy Street Church, in this city, by our colored fellow-citizens, with reference to the Haytian emigration scheme, and desire me to express my views respecting it. This I must do very briefly, for want of time to go into the consideration of the subject with that thoroughness which its importance demands.

. . . in many cases there will be good success; in others, disappointment and loss. Everything will depend upon the character and spirit of the emigrants. In all lands, some never fail to thrive; others are ever poor and shiftless. In such cases, generally, the cause is organic, and no change of circumstances can essentially alter it. Thus far, the emigrants appear to be satisfied with the change they have made, with a few exceptions.

If you desire to know whether, as a general rule, I would advise colored persons to emigrate to Hayti, even on the generous terms proposed by its government, my reply is, decidedly, no. Hence it is that I have given no encouragement to that scheme, or to any other similar scheme, in the columns of the *Liberator*. One unavoidable evil attending it is to unsettle the minds of the colored people themselves in regard to their future destiny; to inspire the mischievous belief in the minds of the white people that they can yet be effectually "got rid of"; and to keep law and custom unfriendly to them, so as to induce their departure to a foreign land. In proportion to the magnitude and success of the scheme will be this evil. A few thousands may be colonized without any perceptible effect of this kind; but plans for a general exodus, I believe, would have a very injurious effect upon the cause of the enslaved, and those already free.

This is their native land. Here they are to remain, as a people, as long as men are left to tread upon the soil; here they are gradually, but surely, to rise in the scale of civilization and improvement; here their fetters are to be broken, and their rights restored. All the signs of the times indicate that a death-blow has been given to the accursed slave system; and when that shall be abolished, the way will be opened for a glorious redemption. Complexional prejudice shall swiftly disappear, injurious distinctions cease, and peace and good will everywhere reign. Though I have no word of censure to bestow upon any one emigrating to Hayti, but, on the contrary, wish him all possible success, yet I specially honor the colored man who cherishes this faith in the future, and is willing to stand firmly in his lot here, even though it be a hard one, manfully laboring for "the good time coming," at whatever present cost to himself, and bearing his cross which in due time a just God shall change into a crown of glory.

Your faithful and untiring advocate,

Wm. Lloyd Garrison

Original in the possession of the Rev. Howard Asbury, Jamaica, Long Island, N.Y.

Address to the Patrons and Friends of Colored Schools

Although in December 1861 the war was the issue of primary importance, a small group of Afro-American teachers met in Ohio to promote education among their race. They realized that, whatever the outcome of the Civil War, free men would need the benefits of education.

Friends and Patrons of Our Schools:—In the language of necessity we address you. Through a generous provision of our state government, schools are being established throughout the state; and the colored schools are not behind in the process of multiplication. Though they are not as prolific or good as the white schools, this, nevertheless, is attributable in part to matters beyond our control; but the cause which mostly obstructs the progress and efficiency of our schools is in our own hands. The day has passed for man to be used as a mere machine. He must reflect the light of his own moral and intellectual development—must either shine in the effulgence of his own wisdom, or sink to poverty and wretchedness by his own ignorance. . . .

Recent accounts show that there are in this state nearly 14,000 colored youth, between 5 and 21 years of age. Of this number, about 7,000 have been enrolled in the schools during the year. The daily average attendance is not more than 3,500. The number of colored schools is known to be 160. The number of colored teachers about 150. In the light of these considerations, the condition of our people calls on you to educate them. The voice of unborn generations calls out to you from the bosom of the future; and the duty which you owe to your children enjoins it upon you.

It is a question with many to understand *why* we should spend so much time and money in educating our children, when it is known they are not allowed to fill the places of lawyers, senators, judges or presidents. . . . Never can we become an influential or enlightened people in these United States, Canada, Liberia, Hayti, or any other country, unless we educate ourselves.

Parents, teach your children that it is not disgraceful to labor. Give them a good education, and they will exert an influence which will be felt in the world. Every age and generation have their peculiar wants. Every year brings us nearer the golden era, when we shall exult in the glory of our mental acquisitions, or discover to ourselves the painful truth of being insufficient for the work before us. The truth of this will become more mortifying to us when we reflect that everything is receiving the impress of improvement. No matter how circumscribed by adverse circumstances, no matter how oppressed by inexorable law; if an opportunity is afforded, *we must educate*. . . .

Let us, then, acknowledge the claim, and mutually strive to meet it. Let the work of human education be made more efficient, until society shall brighten by our acquisitions, and a light of intellectual glory pervade the earth.

JOHN G. MITCHELL
THO'S J. FERGUSON
BENJ. K. SAMPSON
Committee on Address

Transactions of the First Annual Meeting of the Colored Teachers' Association, Springfield, Ohio, December 25 and 26, 1861 (MS in the Virginia State College Library, Petersburg, Va.).

William Wells Brown Urges the Use of Black Troops

When the firing on Fort Sumter marked the beginning of the Civil War, Negroes from both the North and the South were anxious to take part in the struggle for freedom. Prominent Negroes such as William Wells Brown led the movement for full participation of people of color. Using as an example his own progress following his escape from slavery, Brown exhorted the federal government to give Negroes the opportunity to serve in the Union Army. This excerpt is from a speech given in New York on May 6, 1862, to the American Anti-Slavery Society.

. . . One of the first things that I heard when I arrived in the free States—and it was the strangest thing to me that I heard—was, that the slaves cannot take care of themselves. I came off without any education. Society did not take me up; I took myself up. I did not ask society to take me up. All I asked of the white people was, to get out of the way, and give me a chance to come from the South to the North. That was all I asked, and I went to work with my own hands. And that is all I demand for my brethren of the South to-day—that they shall have an opportunity to exercise their own physical and mental abilities.

Now, Mr. President, I think that the present contest has shown clearly that the fidelity of the black people of this country to the cause of freedom is enough to put to shame every white man in the land who would think of driving us out of the country, provided freedom shall be proclaimed. I remember well, when Mr. Lincoln's proclamation went forth, calling for the first 75,000 men, that among the first to respond to that call were the colored men. A meeting was held in Boston, crowded as I never saw a meeting before; meetings were held in Rhode Island and Connecticut, in New York and Philadelphia, and throughout the West, responding to the President's call. Although the colored men in many of the free States were disfranchised, abused, taxed without representation, their children turned out of the schools, nevertheless, they went on, determined to try to discharge their duty to the country, and to save it from the tyrannical power of the slaveholders of the South. But the cry went forth—"We won't have the Negroes; we won't have anything to do with them; we won't fight with them; we won't have them in the army, nor about us." Yet scarcely had you got into conflict with the South, when you were glad to receive the news that contrabands brought. The first telegram announcing any news from the disaffected district commences with—"A contraband just in from Maryland tells us" so much. The last telegram, in to-day's paper, announces that a contraband tells us so much about Jefferson Davis and Mrs. Davis and the little Davises. The nation is glad to receive the news from the contraband. We have an old law with regard to the mails, that a Negro shall not touch the mails at all; and for fifty years the black man has not had the privilege of touching the mails of the United States with his little finger; but we are glad enough now to have the Negro bring the mail in his pocket! The first thing asked of a contraband is—"Have you got a newspaper?—what's the news?" And the news is greedily taken in, from the lowest officer or soldier in the army, up to the Secretary of War. They have tried to keep the Negro out of the war, but they could not keep him out, and now they drag him in, with his news, and are glad to do so. General Wool says the contrabands have brought the most reliable news. Other Generals say their information can be relied upon. The Negro is taken as a pilot to guide the fleet of General Burnside through the inlets of the South. The black man welcomes your armies and your fleets, takes care of your sick, is ready to do anything, from cooking up to shouldering a musket; and yet these would-be patriots and professed lovers of the land talk about driving the Negro out!

The Liberator (Boston), May 16, 1862.

Thomas Wentworth Higginson on Negro Participation in the Civil War

Early in 1862, Major General David Hunter tried to establish a regiment composed of ex-slaves in South Carolina. After Hunter resigned because his efforts were opposed by the Lincoln administration, his replacement, General Rufus Saxton, continued the organization of the 1st South Carolina Volunteers by bringing in Thomas Wentworth Higginson of Massachusetts to lead the regiment. Higginson, who had just assumed his command, recorded one of his early experiences with the Negro troops.

December 1, 1862

How absurd is the impression bequeathed by Slavery in regard to these Southern blacks, that they are sluggish and inefficient in labor! Last night, after a hard day's work (our guns and the remainder of our tents being just issued), an order came from Beaufort that we should be ready in the evening to unload a steamboat's cargo of boards, being some of those captured by them a few weeks since, and now assigned for their use. I wondered if the men would grumble at the night-work; but the steamboat arrived by seven, and it was bright moonlight when they went at it. Never have I beheld such a jolly scene of labor. Tugging these wet and heavy boards over a bridge of boats ashore, then across the slimy beach at low tide, then up a steep bank, and all in one great uproar of merriment for two hours. Running most of the time, chattering all the time, snatching the boards from each other's backs as if they were some coveted treasure, getting up eager rivalries between different companies, pouring great choruses of ridicule on the heads of all shirkers, they made the whole scene so enlivening that I gladly stayed out in the moonlight for the whole time to watch it. And all this without any urging or any promised reward, but simply as the most natural way of doing the thing. The steamboat captain declared that they unloaded the ten thousand feet of boards quicker than any white gang could have done it; and they felt it so little, that, when, later in the night, I reproached one whom I found sitting by a campfire, cooking a surreptitious oppossum, telling him that he ought to be asleep after such a job of work, he answered, with the broadest grin,—

"O no, Cunnel, da's no work at all, Cunnel; dat only jess enough *for stretch we.*"

Thomas Wentworth Higginson, *Army Life in a Black Regiment* (Boston, 1882).

An Escaped Slave Aids the Union

Although officially not allowed to participate in military service, many slaves left their masters to offer help to the advancing federal armies. This letter to Military Governor Andrew Johnson of Tennessee advises that an escaped slave has proved of substantial aid to the troops stationed in Nashville and that he is requesting permission to stay with the Union forces rather than be returned to his owner.

Nashville Aug 21st 1862

Gov Johnson
——Dear Sir
the Barrer has Come to me and gave me his name desiring to be pressed he has worked three days and is well satisfied. his Mistress Mrs Creaghead is coming to you to day in order to try and get him Back you will pleas not to let him go for he is a good hand
——Yours Respectfouly. R. J. Wood
In charge of Contrabands

Andrew Johnson Papers, Library of Congress.

Abraham Lincoln Urges Andrew Johnson to Employ Black Troops

After President Lincoln's Emancipation Proclamation became effective, on January 1, 1863, he sought to increase the recruiting of black soldiers into the Union armies. The following letter was written to Andrew Johnson, who was then the military governor of Tennessee.

Executive Mansion.
Washington—March 26. 1863.

Private—
Hon. Andrew Johnson.

My Dear Sir.

I am told you have at least *thought* of raising a negro military force. In my opinion the country now needs no specific thing so much as some man of your ability, and position to go to this work. When I speak of your position, I mean that of an eminent citizen of a slave-state, and himself a slave-holder. The colored population is the great *available* and yet *unavailed of,* force for restoring the Union. The bare sight of fifty-thousand armed, and drilled black soldiers on the banks of the Mississippi, would end the rebellion at once. And who doubts that we can present that sight, if we but take hold in earnest? If you *have* been thinking of it please do not dismiss the thought.

Yours truly
A. Lincoln

Andrew Johnson Papers, Library of Congress.

"The Yankees Would Kill Me I Would Better Stay"

In an effort to frighten their slaves into subjugation, many Confederate citizens painted lurid pictures of the advancing Yankee invaders.

When i was liveing whith White People i was tide down hand and foot and they tide me to the Post and whip me till i Could not stand up and they tide my Close over my head and whip me much as they want and they took my Brother and sent him to Richmond to stay one year And sent my Aunt my Sister my farther away too and said if he did not go away they would kill him they said they was Goin to Put me in Prisens But the light has come the Rebles is put down and Slavry is dead God Bless the union Forever more and they was puting people in tubs and they stead [scared] me to Death and i hope slavly shall be no more and they said that the yankees had horns and said that the yankees was Goin to kill us and somthing told me not to Believe them and somthing told me not to Be afraid and when they Come hare they would not let me Come out to see them and when i was out in the Street they was Stead i would go away from them and they said I Better stay whith them for the yankees would kill me I would Better stay

Charlotte Ann Jackson

Henry L. Swint, *Dear Ones at Home* (Nashville, Tenn., 1966), from original in the American Antiquarian Society, Worcester, Mass.

The Plight of a Free Negro Family during the New York Draft Riots

During the New York Draft Riots in 1863, many prominent Afro-Americans were viciously attacked by bands of whites who roved the city. Albro Lyons, who ran a home for colored seamen and a seaman's clothing store, encountered threats and violence three times before he was forced to seek refuge in a police station. Lyons had been active in the underground railroad and is said to have aided more than one thousand slaves escape to freedom. This letter from the police precinct where Lyons obtained help illustrates the plight of Lyons and his family.

METROPOLITAN POLICE DISTRICT,
Precinct No. 4
New York, July 17th. 1863

Mr. & Mrs. Lyons

You had better leave your Clothing here, for a day, or two, and every thing will be Settled, then you Can come here yourselves, and take Charge of them. they are all Safe here. I will call over and see you this afternoon and then you can come over with me if you want to. I now remain your friend

John W. Rode
Sergt. 4th Precinct
No 9 Oak St.
N.Y.

P.S.
I have got three policemen watching your House to prevent fire & c [etc.]

Schomburg Collection, New York Public Library.

A Black Mother Seeks an Education for Her Children

The Albro Lyons family moved from New York to Rhode Island following the draft riots in 1863. When Mrs. Mary Lyons tried to enter her children in school, she met with the familiar problem of discrimination. While war raged about her, Mary Lyons acted as a mother whose only interest is the welfare of her children. In this undated letter to the governor of Rhode Island, she sought aid in securing an education for them.

Hon. James M. Smith, Gov. State of Rhode Island

Sir

I hope you will forgive the liberty I take in addressing you, when you know that it is about the education of my children.

In the month of June last, having recently removed to this city and purchased a humble house in "A" Street, I applied for admission to the neighboring district school, of two children, aged respectively 11 & 14 years. I was refered by the teacher to the Superintendent of the schools, who denied my application on the ground that my children were of colored complexion, and he also refused an older child admittance in the High School.

Friends, who have examined the case with more ability than I can command, assure me that this denial is contrary to the laws of the state . . . as well as a shameful oppression of innocent children.

If the laws of the state guarantee to my children an equal education with others, your Excellency will see that I naturally appeal to you, as the Executive of the State to secure to me the right most precious, for a good education is all I can give to the young being it has pleased God to place under my care.

If, however, the laws of the State do not secure for my children equal educational rights, then must I also appeal to your Excellency to suggest to the Legislature such alteration of the laws as will grant the right . . . this one point of plain duty we have—to educate every soul. Every native and every foreign child, that is cast on our coast; shall be taught at the public cost; the rudiments of knowledge, and at last the richest results of art and science.

Mary Josephe Lyons

Schomburg Collection, New York Public Library.

A Black Union Soldier Writes a Letter from a South Carolina Battlefield

Bravery and restraint are seen in this letter written to his wife by a black soldier who fought in the bloody battle of Fort Wagner.

Morris Island. S.C. July 20 [1863]

My Dear Amelia: I have been in two fights, and am unhurt. I am about to go in another I believe to-night. Our men fought well on both occasions. The last was desperate we charged that terrible battery on Morris Island known as Fort Wagoner, and were repulsed with a loss of 3 killed and wounded. I escaped unhurt from amidst that perfect hail of shot and shell. It was terrible. I need not particularize the papers will give a better than I have time to give. My thoughts are with you often, you are as dear as ever, be good enough to remember it as I no doubt you will. As I said before we are on the eve of another fight and I am very busy and have just snatched a moment to write you. I must necessarily be brief. Should I fall in the next fight killed or wounded I hope to fall with my face to the foe.

If I survive I shall write you a long letter. . . .

This regiment has established its reputation as a fighting regiment not a man flinched, though it was a trying time. Men fell all around me. A shell would explode and clear a space of twenty feet, our men would close up again, but it was no use we had to retreat, which was a very hazardous undertaking. How I got out of that fight alive I cannot tell, but I am here. My Dear girl I hope again to see you. I must bid you farewell should I be killed. Remember if I die I die in a good cause. I wish we had a hundred thousand colored troops we would put an end to this war. Good Bye to all Your own loving

Lewis

Carter G. Woodson Papers, Library of Congress.

A Letter from Camp Saxton

Anxious to serve his country and to be a good soldier, a Negro recruit wrote the following letter to his commanding officer. The soldier wished to purchase an Army regulations book, even if it cost him a whole month's wages, so that he might be fully informed of his duties.

At Camp saxton Feb 20th [18]63

My dear Colonel I have inform in here About so doing: According to the different in Rule in wish how: I stand now: for I dont know if it is Right for me to have one of the Armies Regulation Books: so sir that is the reason I had come to you to know: and if you think that it is right for me to have one I Like to have one: if it cost me one Months wages: for I Am wittness that it will in Prove and give me A wittness: in so doing: it from sergt Wm Brunson Co A

Carter G. Woodson Papers, Library of Congress.

Controversy over the Use of Black Soldiers in the Civil War

In 1863, a letter to the editor appeared in the Boston Journal *concerning the use of Afro-American troops by the Union Army. Included was an excerpt from a letter written by General David Hunter, who had long advocated the employment of Negro troops. Before receiving official command to do so, Hunter experimented with the use of Negroes as soldiers and found them well equipped for the job. The letter to the editor also included testimony from a Union field officer who had personally witnessed Negroes in action as Confederate soldiers.*

To the Editor of the Boston Journal:

The extract below, from a private letter from Gen. Hunter, shows that the movement for arming the Negro is going vigorously forward.

Louis Napoleon, the shrewdest of military men, has shown his appreciation of the necessity of using the black race for making war in southern climates; and if anything else were wanting, the accumulating evidence of the use made by the rebels of Negroes as soldiers, ought to convince the most doubting.

Let any such read . . . the letter of Capt. Walter Davis, one of our own fellow citizens, whose evidence will be conclusive with his brother soldiers of the Cadets, and with all who have watched his course through the hard-fought fields of Virginia.

Let us have done with our old prejudices and join heartily in giving the Negro a chance to fight for his race and ours.

Congress has passed the conscription bill for black and white soldiers. The days are fast passing in which to organize the force which must keep our southern possession to us during the coming summer, and which, if promptly raised, will be a notice to European inter-meddlers that we have an acclimated army nearer than Egypt.

Audax

* * * * *

[Extract from a private letter written by General David Hunter]

Hilton Head, S.C., Feb. 11, 1863.

Finding that the able bodied Negroes did not enter the military service as rapidly as could be wished, I have resolved, and so ordered, that all who are not regularly employed in the Quartermaster's Department, or as officers' servants, shall be drafted. In this course I am sustained by the views of all the more intelligent amongst them. . . .

In drafting them I was actuated by several motives—the controlling one being that I regard their services as a military necessity, if this war is to be ended in the triumph of the Union arms. Subordinate to this consideration, I regard the strict discipline of military life as the best school in which this people can be gradually lifted toward our higher civilization; and their enrollment in the Negro brigade will have the further good effect of rendering mere servile insurrection, unrestrained by the laws and usages of war, less likely. If any further argument were needed to justify my course it would be found in my deep conviction that Freedom (like all other blessings) can never be justly appreciated except by men who have been taught the sacrifices which are its price. In this course, let me add, I expect to be sustained by all the intelligent and practically minded friends of the enfranchised bondmen.

* * * * *

[Extract from a private letter written by Capt. W. S. Davis]

Dear Sir: In answer to your inquiry, I would state that after the battle of West Point, I walked over the field and saw the dead bodies of four Negroes dressed in Confederate uniforms, and wearing their cartridge boxes and roundabouts.

I have heard Confederate prisoners acknowledge that the blacks are used as soldiers, and they argue that they are willing to fight against us.

At Yorktown, I saw myself plainly the Negroes working the enemies' heavy guns.

I have not the slightest doubt, from my own observation and from conversation with our returned prisoners and captured enemies, that the Negroes are extensively used by the enemy.

I have no doubt the Negro will fight, and I saw a Negro servant in the thickest of the fight, at Fredericksburg, who fired away sixty rounds, and was as cool as any man on the field.

Very respectfully, your obedient servant,

W. S. Davis, Capt.

New York Public Library

General Lee Urges the Confederacy to Recruit Negroes

Negroes had been used in the Confederate Army throughout the Civil War, usually as aides to their masters and in building fortifications. After the tide turned against the South and Lee's army began to suffer extreme losses, an effort was made to recruit Negroes for full military participation. While the Confederate Congress debated the advisability of arming Negroes, General Lee urged their recruitment.

1st 2n U.S. Armies
30th March 1865

[To:]
Lt. Gen. N. S. Ewell

General,

General Lee directs me to acknowledge the receipt of your letter of the 29th inst: and to say that he regrets very much to learn that owners refuse to allow their slaves to enlist. He deems it of great moment that some of this force should be put in the field as soon as possible, believing that they will remove all doubts as to the expediency of the measure. He regrets it the more in the case of the owners about Richmond, inasmuch as the example would be extremely valuable, and the present posture of military affairs renders it almost certain that if we do not get these men, they will soon be in arms against us, and perhaps relieving white Federal soldiers from guard duty in Richmond. He desires you to press this view upon the owners.

He says that he regards it as very important that immediate steps be taken to put the recruiting in operation, and has so advised the Department. He desires to have you placed in general charge of it if agreeable to you, as he thinks nothing can be accomplished without energetic and intelligent effort by someone who fully appreciates the vital importance of the duty. He has written to the Dept to that effect, and also requesting compliance with your suggestion with reference to Col Otey & Adjt Cowardin. He thinks that if the conscript be fit to command, it would be well to accept the offer of the 100 men. He will recommend any suitable persons to be employed on recruiting duty that you may name, who can be spared, and thinks they should be sent out at once. He expects greater results if suitable persons be authorized to raise companies, battalions & even regiments, than from mere recruiting officers, as contemplated in Gen. Order No. 14.

Prompt action is all important, and the General only wants to receive your suggestions.

Very respt
Your obt servt

Charles Marshall
Lt. Col & Adjt

Robert E. Lee Papers, Library of Congress.

The Freedmen's Bureau

Following the Civil War and emancipation, new problems faced the freedmen. The adjustment in the South, for black and white alike, was one of tremendous uncertainty. The newly freed Negroes sought jobs to replace the bonds of slavery. Former owners who were used to the old system often sought to re-enslave the Negroes by means of physical brutality and fright. The Freedmen's Bureau established a policy of investigating claims brought by the freedmen regarding the indignities heaped upon them by white persons.

United States
vs.
Nathan Bastine

State of Georgia
County of Columbia

Before one George W. Pease Capt. 136th USC Infty personally appeared Dick Bastine (col'd) who being duly Sworn deposeth and Saith that on or about the eight (8) day of October 1865, Nathan Bastine of Columbia Co State of Ga did violently assault the afforsaid Dick Bastin, Striking him once with his fist and Struck him twice on the head with a Stick of Wood, Severely wounding him and injuring his Constitution and physical Strength.

Furthermore the afforsaid Nathan Bastine did Say to the Afforsaid Dick Bastine that he was not a "freeman" and that he belonged to him (Nathan Bastine) as much as he ever did.

Furthermore that if he Dick Bastine should report to the authorities how he had been abused he would hier men to bring him Dick Bastine back and he would then most severely punish him.

Dick Bastine
his
X
mark

Sworn and Subscribed to before me this 18th day of October 1865.

G. W. Pease
Capt. 136 USC Inftry

* * * * *

Office Sub. Com. F. Bureau
Augusta, Ga, Nov 27, 1865

Warren County
State of Georgia

Before me, Thos. Nichols, Lt; and Act Sub. Apt. Com. F. Bureau, Dist of Augusta; personally appeared; Harriet Battles (col) having been first duly sworn deposes and says that: her husband had made a contract with Mr. Battle, for her and her husband to work until Christmas; she further states that Mr. Battle had a grudge against her husband, so he went to work, and tied him up with ropes, and nearly whipped him to death, at least had him whipped, for it was the overseer that whipped him "named John Sprinks" She also says that, she went to take up for him, and the overseer (John Sprinks) threatened to kill her, and at the same time said that "none of the niggers were free and that he would whip them, as much as he wanted to, and that he was not afraid of Capt. Bryant, or any of the damned Yankees. Being threatened to be whipped to death, she, was forced to leave the place, Without pay or shelter, leaving her 3 children behind.

her
Harriet X Battles
Mark

Sworn and Subscribed to before me this 27 day of Nov. 1865
Thos. Nichols
Lt and Act. Sub. Apt. Com.
F. Bureau

Witnesses
Jy
Lucy
Penelepy

Records of the Bureau of Refugees, Freedmen, and Abandoned Lands, Record Group 105, National Archives.

A White Southerner Records His Views of Post-Civil War Life

With General Sherman's march through Georgia to the sea came the decline of the Confederacy and the end of the war. The war-ravaged South was left with little but bitter memories of four years of turmoil and strife. Expressing the experiences of many slaveholders, John A. Inglis of South Carolina wrote a letter to his niece in the North. This letter is probably typical of the attitude of many southerners regarding their ex-slaves and the problems which confronted the South at that time.

Cheraw, S.C. June 28, 1865.

My Dear Carrie!

. . . The Negroes were plundered equally with myself—their clothes, cooking utensils etc. were taken out of their houses, their money, shoes, coats etc. off their persons. Notwithstanding which, Toney, Kent, Horace, Emeline, Julia, Jinny, and the two Philips went off or were carried off with the Federal Army. Kent and perhaps the Philips went against their will, the others gladly. I trust they are satisfied by this time. Philip, however, (Ann's or Roberts) has returned. He says he was carried as far as Washington City, and there turned loose and told to go back to his master and go to work as before. They gave him transportation on railroads and steamboat to Fayettesville and from there he walked. They supplied him also with rations for his return. He was separated from the rest of our people at Cheraw and never saw any of them since. King, to whom Emeline was married last Christmas, went off, and she went, I suppose, with *him*. For reasons which you will understand, I did not regret it and could not blame her much. The last news I have had of them, they were in Wilmington, but expecting to *spend the summer in Washington City*!!! I hope she may be taken care of, for with her faults, and in spite of them she was a good servant. Julia, Jinny and Philip when last heard from were at Wilmington, *all* working for a Mr. Worth, on wages. Kent and Horace were at Goldborough—I dont know how employed. I have never heard anything of Tony, and I dont care much ever to hear of him, unless it were to make him take his old mother Lizzette, and support her. I regret that the army of Sherman did not take all the rest, except Robert's and Nelly's families with them. You know the rest well enough to understand that they will be only a burden and expensive to me, or starve in freedom, more likely the former. . . .

About 500 negroes left this District with the Federal army, of whom only *very* few have returned. Some of them were forced away. Most of them were borne off by a kind of wild excitement, destined to become wiser when the stir had subsided. Generally those left who had been treated with the most kindness. The men who have the reputation of being most severe and even cruel masters lost none. Maj. M'Queen lost 60—and Mr. Campbell 40. . . . Those who remained have thus far been behaving very well. There may be some few exceptions. But this gigantic folly & wrong, emancipation, is playing havoc with the social & industrial interests of the Country. Every one who knows the negro is well aware that he will not work except under the constant stimulus of an overseer's watchfulness—he is essentially idle and lazy. The presence of a Federal garrison and the tendering of written contracts for labor is the signal for disorder. I must not be understood to mean that the Garrisons are intentionally responsible for such disorder or that they encourage it. On the contrary, so far as I know, they directly discourage and promptly & vigorously repress it, using far more severity than Southern owners could or would do. But the negroes have come to regard their late owners and the Federal Army as occupying antagonistic positions, and themselves as the subject matter of strife, and at once, suppose that the garrison has come specially to take their part against their late owners and vindicate their freedom. Now the particular in which the negro regards his master as his enemy is that he will make him work which he dont want to do. His notion of freedom is that he is to be relieved entirely from this control and to be left to work or not, as he pleases and when he pleases. And this kind of freedom he thinks it is the special mission of the garrison to secure him in. As soon, therefore, as a garrison appears the negroes in the neighborhood leave their places and flock to headquarters. . . . Then when you propose to them to sign an agreement, they think that is signing away their liberty, and as the agreement of course, obliges them to labor constantly and faithfully—they refuse to come. . . . The negroes in this neighborhood have not yet been tried in this way.

Our own people (the whites) in this region have been thus far very orderly. There is much suffering for want of food, for never was a region more utterly stripped and peeled, wasted and desolated than was Chesterfield District by our loving friends & brethren who followed the humane & chivalric Sherman. Imagination cannot conceive it and if it could, neither pen or pencil could produce the picture. It is distressing beyond expressing to see the crowds of pale faced, emaciated women who crowd the Depot daily begging for a passage to the more favored section below in Darlington & Marion, where they go seeking bread. . . .

Affectionately yours

John A. Inglis

John A. Inglis Papers, Library of Congress.

Southern Hostility at the Close of the War

Not all southerners vented their frustrations by writing letters to relatives. When the Civil War had finally drawn to an end, many in the rebellious and bitter South settled down to the problem of finding a new method for subjugating the Negroes. An example of the various means used is included in this unidentified newspaper clipping. The article is attributed to Miss Lucy Chase, who was one of the many northerners who went to the South during the war to aid the freedmen.

Norfolk, Va., June 25, 1865.

"The days of bayonets are passed!" is the bullying street-cry of the returned rebel soldiers in Norfolk and Portsmouth, as they fearlessly assume the once-familiar knife and pistol. At the corners, and in the market-place, many have been heard to say, "We'll kill every nigger, or drive 'em all out of town." Civil power is established here, and the military command is restricted. But Gen. Howard, commandant of the small military force retained here, has said, "There is one thing I *will* do; I *will* protect the colored people."

On Thursday last, two or three Southern gentlemen succeeded in infusing Southern sentiments into the hearts of some of the New York 13th Artillery by dosing them with drugged whiskey; and, leading themselves, they encouraged the soldiers to destroy the wares on the stand of a colored man. On from the stand, crying, "Clear out all the niggers," they passed to a ball-room, through which they dashed, driving all before them, and destroying whatever came in their way. On Friday night, a body of colored men, wishing to see a circus performance, deemed it prudent to go in a body, and, protecting themselves with canes, they went forth quietly, but were fired upon as they drew near the circus. Two or three were shot; and all withdrew without offering resistance. Colored men were attacked, that night, in various parts of the city. One man was hung upon a lamp-post. Another, going home from a mission house with a letter which had been written for him there, was seized and put into prison, where he remained until the next day, when his kind amanuensis obtained his release. A worthy exhorter was knocked down, and severely injured, on his way home from church. Another was woefully bruised, while crossing the street from the house of a sick sister to his own home. On Saturday night, the wood-wharf men were attacked, and the stores of two Union white men were broken into, and much of the property destroyed. Finding the declaration, "I am a Union man," no defence against the attack of New York soldiers, one man resorted to his pistol, and, after wounding two of his assailants, succeeded in making his escape. Last night many shots were fired in Portsmouth. The demonstrations there are more violent than here.

On Sunday, two colored men were found hanging dead upon trees, this side of Suffolk. And a young man leaving a church in this city, was shot through the side, and robbed. He still lies, a panting sufferer, on an attic floor; bare of every comfort, save the inestimable one of a devoted mother, who leaves him neither night nor day. "He might have gone to the hospital," his mother said; "but I want him where I can be with him, and do for him all the time." My sister and I well remember when the mother and son came from their master to Norfolk. "We won't stay upon government one moment," the mother said. "Uncle Sam is very good, but he has too much to do; and we don't want to trouble any one. I'll get a little room, and I reckon we can scrub along." And from that little room, for months, they have gone out to their little work, coming back at night to peace and independence; never dreaming of one to molest or make them afraid.

I have just come from the bedsides of two wounded men. One of them was quietly passing to his home, when three soldiers run after him and fired three shots, neither of which took effect. They then cried "Halt!" but, as the man knew their order was not to be respected, he walked on. Another shot fired, and the ball passed through his mouth. "Finish him, finish him," some one cried. Two men overtook him, and each pointed a revolver at his breast; he turned their hands aside, and said, "You don't shoot me again." "Very well," they said, "come into the guardhouse." There he was received without investigation. In the morning, when the officer of the guard came, he inquired what brought him there, and after hearing the man's story, he said: "Pity they did not kill you." The other man is badly wounded in the leg. He was hobbling home from his day's work at the government commissary when he was overtaken by a howling crowd. His co-laborers were with him, and eleven shots were fired at them. Only one took effect. "You must fight it out, I can do nothing for you," the Mayor of Norfolk said to a committee of colored men who sought his protection. The rioters are taking advantage of the divided, and somewhat obscurely defined, responsibilities resting upon the associated military and civil authorities; responsibilities which the civil authorities shirk, when the interests of the colored man or of Union citizens are at stake. The Mayor of Portsmouth, whose city is more disturbed than our own, requests Col. Howard to "relieve Portsmouth of its military guard!" Col. Howard is abroad, with the will of an army in his breast, and we are confident he will speedily restore quiet again. The disturbance is maintained through the daytime.

Henry L. Swint, *Dear Ones at Home* (Nashville, Tenn., 1966).

John Sella Martin at the Paris Anti-Slavery Conference

John Sella Martin was one of the most versatile men of his period. An escaped slave, he eventually went to Massachusetts, where he served as a pastor in Lawrence and then in Boston. He was active in the abolition movement in this country and traveled to Europe several times to gain support for his cause. In 1870, Martin became editor of the Washington, D.C., New Era *(later the* New National Era) *and active in organizing Negro labor. These excerpts are from a speech Martin made before the Paris Anti-Slavery Conference in August 1867.*

Mr. President, Ladies and Gentlemen: Mr. Garrison justly rejoices that the statute-books of his country have been cleansed from the thousand clauses that sanctioned its greatest crime and curse; and even I, as a Negro, can rejoice with him that it is not now as it formerly was, when every white man who escaped persecution did so by carrying a lie in his right hand. Looking at the results of emancipation from the standpoint of a white man, there are many things to make the flush of triumph deepen into a blush of shame.

The Negroes are free as to their chains, but everywhere their prospects are darkened by prejudice and proscription, which Fred Douglass forcibly calls the shadow of Slavery. And this fact shows how deeply corrupted the Americans were by that system which they deliberately made their own, in defiance of every claim of justice for those who helped them to win the battle of national independence, and who, in their generous confidence, came again to the rescue when these same breakers of faith were sinking in the waters of strife upon which they had so confidently entered at the beginning of the late war. There is, nevertheless, a hopeful sign about the present state of things, and that is, that even those who used to vilify the Negro are now beginning to apologize for his present state. Yet I undertake to say that the Negro needs no apology. What is the Negro? Why, the popular notion is that he is a coward. Yet he has proved that he will fight, though for one I have no high eulogy to pass upon him for doing that which is the last resort of a cur that cannot run away. I know the whites have another measurement for brute force. While the Negro behaved like a Christian—like the old English slaves who waited for the advance of civilization to gradually melt rather than to break their chains—the whites called him a brute, too degraded to wish for freedom or try to win it. But as soon as he began to act like a brute and to revel in the dreadful orgies of war, then they called him a man. Wendell Phillips truly says that the Negro race is the only one in history which, unaided, broke its chains of bondage. I do not know what gradual emancipation would have brought with it. . . . But I know this: we did not get gradual emancipation, and that the slaveholders refused to have it; and I know, also, that such emancipation as the Negro has got was won partly by his wisdom in waiting till those who had united in oppressing him got too far apart even to join their weapons in putting down a Negro insurrection, and partly by a bravery equal to his brethren of St. Domingo. When events justified the Negro in joining the contest, his ready submission to discipline, his fidelity in helping those who, through necessity only, had become his friends, and his willing assault upon strongholds in which he had to walk over hidden torpedoes, which was considered rather hard walking for white men, made him a place in history that needs no apology. Whatever, therefore, may be the value of physical courage, he is entitled to it.

The Negro, too, is a man that will work. Wise men would have excused him if the first days of his freedom had been spent in visiting the cities which slavery never allowed him to see. Had he feasted his eyes upon the fine things—for which, it is said, he has a taste—displayed in the shop windows, he would have followed very elegant examples. There would have been no wonder in his desire and effort to leave a form of labour which suggested even the most painful reminiscences of murdered kindred, ruined wives and daughters, and degrading submission. And yet whenever they could get work the majority have remained to do it. When they could get paid for their work they have worked to profit; and when they have made money, they have learned to save it. Nobody with any sense denies that there may be a large number of lazy Negroes who will not work; the carrion from which the vultures of the pro-Slavery press get their food; and it would be a sad thing for commerce if there were no lazy Negroes, for the race would have to be removed from the American Continent and the cultivation of cotton, for fear of being corrupted into laziness and vagabondage by the too numerous examples of the white race. But this I do contend for: that for a people ignorant of the laws of contract, and beneath the general stimulus to industry which long habit of enterprise, and long enjoyment of the fruits of labour bring for them, to rise from the conditions of bondage, and without any system of constraint, under great uncertainty of getting paid, cheated by those whom they often take at first for their best friends—for such a people to give the world from their industry, in four years after the unparalleled devastation of the late war, within two-thirds the amount of cotton it got before the war began, is to prove beyond question their capacity and willingness to work. Why, Sir, on the Sea Islands, one year's labour by a few thousand freedmen gave the United States Government, which employed them, 1,000,120 francs' profit, and three years of labour made the Negroes the largest purchasers of the abandoned lands which were sold for unpaid taxes on these very islands, where, only two years before, they were held as slaves. . . .

The Negro will learn. He has been denied the capacity for it; and in cases where the falsehood could not be dodged, as it could not in the case of Toussaint and Christophe, the pure Negro rulers of Hayti, it has been contended that they were exceptions. As though anybody took Lord Brougham, or the Emperor Napoleon, or Longfellow, Bryant and Beecher, as the rule among the white race as to capacity. Cannot they learn? Why, sir, one of the meanest men I ever saw was a black man; he was a Negro slaveholder, and he kept only the company of white men. The simple fact is this; prejudice and proscription in free society during the time of slavery kept the white people away from the Negroes, so that they knew, and still know, but little of colored people; and the slaveholder, though knowing better, found it to his interest to keep his knowledge to himself; or else it would have been known, that in New York and Boston, in New Orleans and Mobile, there are to be found some of the most accomplished colored men and women to be found anywhere, some of them of such unmixed African blood that they cannot be robbed of their virtues and attainments by that Anglo-Saxon pride of race which believes in no blood it has not corrupted by the vices of amalgamation.

But a new phase—many new phases of Negro capacity are being developed by the opportunities of this transition state of the freedmen, and by the efforts of the various Freedmen's Societies. . . .

The American Missionary Association has in the field nearly 500 teachers, who teach not less than 150,000 scholars. And from every one of them we have the strongest testimony of the most uniform character, that the Negroes, old and young, are eager and apt scholars, and that a great many of them are endowed with most extraordinary natural powers. Whatever the philanthropy of a country may do, governments are made up of elements too neutralizing to each other for them to be carried away by mere sentiment . . . [and] it must be taken as the best of all proofs of Negro capacity that the Freedmen's Bureau of Washington has gone on from year to year, spending its 25,000,000 of francs per annum in aid of the Freedmen, much of which goes towards education.

The Negro can be elevated. He has a moral nature that shrinks from bloodshed, and his imitative power is the chief feature of difference between him and the race which has perished from its own native soil, because the instinct of revenge could never be subdued in it; no excuse for the white race, whose every act of intercourse with the poor red men has been as treacherous and as bloody as the policy and code of these poor savages. The Negro is a lover of family and home and some of the most touching records of this transition state are to be found in the efforts of husbands to find the wives, and wives their husbands, that slavery tore from them, and for parents to find their children, and children their parents. . . .

We are not unmindful of the advantages to the world that are to grow out of the civilization and Christianization of the Freedmen in commercial, social and political points of view. Europe and the north will get better cotton and more of it from free men than they did from slaves, and the corresponding increase of their export trade to clothe and satisfy these people, whose daughters must dress, and whose wives will demand luxuries, will not be the least of their gains. We know that a people who can defy the semi-tropical climate of the Southern States, and who possess the secret of the culture of that staple in which the whole world takes such an interest, if they are once educated will put the supply of cotton on a basis of permanency that no white laborers can put it upon for many generations; and we know, too, if the Negro is educated and made prosperous that he must be the main link of binding the South to the North. His gratitude for his freedom and his love of home and country, along with his love of peace, guarantees permanency in our political relations to the South, more surely than would a colony of New Englanders. But, Sir, above all these considerations with us, there arises this one, that a civilized and converted population of Africans in America means the civilization, in no very distant day, of Africa itself. England and France spend every year their millions to maintain squadrons on the coast of Africa, but the slave-trade still goes on. The whole civilized world has sent missionaries to Christianize the Africans, and but little headway has been made in the work, because of the deadly nature of the climate to the white. But if our labors are aided, as they ought to be, by the good people of every country, we shall send educated Christian coloured men from America proof against the deadly diseases of the climate, possessing a claim to the confidence of the natives in sameness of complexion, and carrying the principles of truth against those of error to an ardent-natured people, with natures of their own as ardent to dry up the fountain-head of the slave-trade, and so stop the stream for ever, and to attack superstition with the strongest weapon next to truth itself—the ability to live where it prevails, and to command the confidence and sympathy of the natives.

Carter G. Woodson, *Negro Orators and Their Orations* (Washington, 1925).

"This Country Is Where I Intend to Live, Where I Expect to Die"—John R. Lynch

Black Congressman John R. Lynch spoke on the floor of the United States House of Representatives for the enactment of a civil rights bill in 1875. The bill, which passed in 1875, was the forerunner of and similar to those introduced and passed in the twentieth century.

I will now endeavor to answer the arguments of those who have been contending that the passage of this bill is an effort to bring about social equality between the races. That the passage of this bill can in any manner affect the social status of any one seems to me to be absurd and ridiculous. I have never believed for a moment that social equality could be brought about even between persons of the same race. I have always believed that social distinctions existed among white persons the same as among colored people. But those who contend that the passage of this bill will have a tendency to bring about social equality between the races virtually and substantially admit that there are no social distinctions among white people whatever, but that all white persons, regardless of their moral character, are the social equals of each other; for if by conferring upon colored people the same rights and privileges that are now exercised and enjoyed by whites indiscriminately will result in bringing about social equality between the races, then the same process of reasoning must necessarily bring us to the conclusion that there are no social distinctions among whites, because all white persons, regardless of their social standing, are permitted to enjoy these rights. See then how unreasonable, unjust, and false is the assertion that social equality is involved in this legislation. I cannot believe that gentlemen on the other side of the House mean what they say when they admit, as they do, that the immoral, the ignorant and the degraded of their own race are the social equals of themselves, and their families. If they do, then I can only assure them that they do not put as high an estimate upon their own social standing as respectable and intelligent colored people place upon theirs; for there are hundreds and thousands of white people of both sexes whom I know to be the social inferiors of respectable and intelligent colored people. I can then assure that portion of my democratic friends on the other side of the House whom I regard as my social inferiors that if at any time I should meet any one of you at a hotel and occupy a seat at the same table with you, or the same seat in a car with you, do not think that I have thereby accepted you as my social equal. Not at all. But if any one should attempt to discriminate against you for no other reason than because you are identified with a particular race or religious sect, I would regard it as an outrage; as a violation of the principles of republicanism; and I would be in favor of protecting you in the exercise and enjoyment of your rights by suitable and appropriate legislation.

No, Mr. Speaker, it is not social rights that we desire. We have enough of that already. What we ask is protection in the enjoyment of public rights. Rights which are or should be accorded to every citizen alike. Under our present system of race distinctions a white woman of a questionable social standing, yea, I may say, of an admitted immoral character, can go to any public place or upon any public conveyance and be the recipient of the same treatment, and the same courtesy, and the same respect that is usually accorded to the most refined and virtuous; but let an intelligent, modest, refined colored lady present herself and ask that the same privileges be accorded to her that have just been accorded to her social inferior of the white race, and in nine cases out of ten, except in certain portions of the country, she will not only be refused, but insulted for making the request.

Mr. Speaker, I ask the members of this House in all candor, is this right? I appeal to your sensitive feelings as husbands, fathers, and brothers, is this just? You who have affectionate companions, attractive daughters and loving sisters, is this just? If you have any of the ingredients of manhood in your composition you will answer the question most emphatically, No! What a sad commentary upon our system of government, our religion, and our civilization! Think of it for a moment; here am I, a member of your honorable body, representing one of the largest and wealthiest districts in the State of Mississippi, and possibly in the South; a district composed of persons of different races, religions, and nationalities; and yet, when I leave my home to come to the capital of the nation, to take part in the deliberations of the House and to participate with you in making laws for the government of this great Republic, in coming through the God-forsaken States of Kentucky and Tennessee, if I come by the way of Louisville or Chattanooga, I am treated, not as an American citizen, but as a brute. Forced to occupy a filthy smoking-car both night and day, with drunkards, gamblers, and criminals; and for what? Not that I am unable or unwilling to pay my way; not that I am obnoxious in my personal appearance or disrespectful in my conduct; but simply because I happen to be of a darker complexion. If this treatment was confined to persons of our own sex we could possibly afford to endure it. But such is not the case. Our wives and our daughters, our sisters and our mothers are subjected to the same insults and to the same uncivilized treatment. You may ask why we do not institute civil suits in the State courts. What a farce! Talk about instituting a civil-rights suit in the State courts of Kentucky, for instance, where the decision of the judge is virtually rendered before he enters the court-house, and the verdict of the jury substantially rendered before it is impaneled. The only moments of my life when I am necessarily compelled to question my loyalty to my Government or my devotion to the flag of my country is when I read of outrages having been committed upon innocent colored people and the perpetrators go unwhipped of justice, and when I leave my home to go traveling.

Mr. Speaker, if this unjust discrimination is to be longer tolerated by the American people, which I do not, cannot, and will not believe until I am forced to do so, then I can only say with sorrow and regret that our boasted civilization is a fraud; our republican institutions a failure; our social system a disgrace; and our religion a complete hypocrisy. But I have an abiding confidence—(though I must confess that that confidence was seriously shaken a little over two months ago)—but still I have an abiding confidence in the patriotism of this people, in their devotion to the cause of human rights, and in the stability of our republican institutions. I hope that I will not be deceived. I love the land that gave me birth; I love the Stars and Stripes. This country is where I intend to live, where I expect to die. To preserve the honor of the national flag and to maintain perpetually the Union of the States hundreds, and I may say thousands, of noble, brave, and true-hearted colored men have fought, bled, and died. And now, Mr. Speaker, I ask, can it be possible that that flag under which they fought is to be a shield and a protection to all races and classes of persons except the colored race? God forbid!

Congressional Record, 43rd Congress, 1st Session (Washington, 1867).

Wendell Phillips Advises Robert Purvis

In 1867, President Andrew Johnson offered to appoint Robert Purvis of Philadelphia commissioner of the Freedmen's Bureau to replace General Oliver Otis Howard. This same position had been offered to Frederick Douglass and to John M. Langston but had been declined by both men. This probably was a political move on Johnson's part to further divide the radical Republicans. Purvis, in doubt as to whether he should accept the proposal, wrote to abolitionist Wendell Phillips for advice. In the following letter, Phillips offered his views.

Sept. 13 '67

My dear Purvis

Yours of the 9th inst. reached me day before yesterday. I took a day to chew on the subject—the more willingly as the papers say there will be nothing done in Howard's case for the present.

Believe me nothing could give me more pleasure than to see you in such a national & commanding position. I think I would give a year of life for the sight—this feeling *tempts* me to see the matter in that light. But on the soberest thought I am *decided* that you should refuse.

Before giving my reasons, let me remind you that it is an important decision & you must make it *for yourself;* not allowing any of us to influence you too much—our reasons are conjectures after all—& your *instincts* may be truer.

The first, & to me sufficient reason, is that this move—offering the office to colored men—is only a cunning trick. Johnson wishes just now to confuse & divide the loyal sentiment.

In making these official changes—which are substantially rebel & treasonable—he confuses *for a time* (& that is all he needs) public opinion by not appointing McLellan [*sic*] or Steadman or one of his tools Secretary of War *at first;* but lets the country down to it gradually by putting Grant there for a while—this breaks the brunt, takes off the edge of public indignation—a month *accustoms* us to the move & we are less roused when its finally made.

Johnson is playing the same game with Howard's office.

Grant should have checkmated the intrigue by *at once* refusing to play a part in it. It will be highly honorable to the colored men if, wiser & more consistent than Grant, they all refuse to be made cats paws of—their refusal stamps Johnson as a traitor to their race more emphatically than any words can do. Further for a loyal man to accept *just* now Howard's office, out of which he has been turned out for his virtues not for his faults, strengthens Johnson—a thing not to be done.

2 I am as confident as I can be of anything in the future that, if it be possible & lawful, Congress will not confirm the appointment but will consider the office still to belong to Howard. You should not stand, in November, opposed, as it would seem, to Congress, thrown out of office by it. In that battle between Johnson & Congress such a position would not be the right one for you.

3rd I doubt much whether Johnson, after playing with these offers, will ever actually appoint a colored man. He gets almost all he wants by these *reports* of offers to Douglass & Langston—& by the action of the colored people naming candidates to him, &c. &c.

He will never, in *my judgment,* actually appoint one. The man who consents to accept the place will find himself befooled. The south, Johnson's ally, will never allow a colored man in that place. Half the officers would refuse to serve under him. Johnson will never peril his chances, for which he is now risking impeachment, by offending the south in this way, even by a temporary appointment. Such is my very *confident opinion* but even if a colored man be appointed, he will be allowed no power & very soon some pretence will be made for removing him, (that officers refuse to serve &c &c) & probably the pretence adopted will be one to discredit him & try to show his race incapable. You see by formally appointing you & then having two or three southern statesmen remonstrate & a dozen officers refuse to serve under you Johnson *gets* all the *credit* of a radical—"he has appointed R. P. to office"—but he hurts nobody except you, since assigning these obstructions as his reason, he in a week or two removes you. Then the acct. will stand thus

1. Johnson is a patent radical—he *wanted* a colored man in office.

2. But it couldn't be

3. Colored men were quick to snatch at office even if it did help their enemy.

Dont give too much weight to these reasons, which you see are only *my conjectures.* Judge for yourself. I know you will intend the most honorable & singlehearted service to the "cause" whichever course you take.

The office takes charge of the welfare of the victim race, anything honorable is allowable that will save them from the cruelty they are exposed to in these months of crisis.

I appreciate these considerations, fully I hope, but my conviction is that one in your position should refuse the poor victims you'd not be allowed to protect.

With kindest regards to your family & sincere congratulations that the hour has at last come when a politician thinks he strengthens himself—& does strengthen himself—by coquetting with colored men in this way,

I am yours
cordially

Wendell Phillips

Weston Papers, Boston Public Library.

Francis L. Cardozo on the "Infernal Plantation System"

After the Civil War, Francis L. Cardozo became the first Negro to serve as secretary of state in South Carolina. At the South Carolina constitutional convention of 1868, he decried the plantation system in the South.

One of the greatest of slavery bulwarks was the infernal plantation system, one man owning his thousand, another his twenty, another fifty thousand acres of land. This is the only way by which we will break up that system, and I maintain that our freedom will be of no effect if we allow it to continue. What is the main cause of the prosperity of the North. It is because every man has his own farm and is free and independent. Let the lands of the South be similarly divided. I would not say for one moment they should be confiscated, but if sold to maintain the war, now that slavery is destroyed, let the plantation system go with it. We will never have true freedom until we abolish the system of agriculture which existed in the Southern States. It is useless to have any schools while we maintain the stronghold of slavery as the agricultural system of the country. . . .

Walter L. Fleming (ed.), *Documentary History of Reconstruction* (2 vols.; Cleveland, 1906–1907).

Frederick Douglass on Woman Suffrage

Two movements for suffrage ran parallel in the nineteenth century: one for Negro enfranchisement and the other for voting rights for women. Frederick Douglass was an active sympathizer for women's rights, having participated in the 1848 Seneca Falls Convention, which was the first meeting of the suffragettes. However, when he was approached in 1868 by Josephine Griffing to lecture on woman suffrage, he refused her request and justified his position in the following letter.

Rochester Sept. 27, 1868

My dear Friend:

I am impelled by no lack of generosity in refusing to come to Washington to speak in behalf of woman's suffrage. The right of woman to vote is as sacred in my judgment as that of man, and I am quite willing at anytime to hold up both my hands in favor of this right. It does not however follow that I can come to Washington or go elsewhere to deliver lectures upon this special subject. I am now devoting myself to a cause not more sacred, [but] certainly more urgent, because it is life and death to the long-enslaved people of this country; and this is: Negro suffrage. While the Negro is mobbed, beaten, shot, stabbed, hanged, burnt, and is the target of all that is malignant in the North and all that is murderous in the South, his claims may be preferred by me without exposing in any wise myself to the imputation of narrowness or meanness towards the cause of woman. As you very well know, woman has a thousand ways to attach herself to the governing power of the land and already exerts an honorable influence on the course of legislation. She is the victim of abuses, to be sure, but it cannot be pretended I think that her cause is as urgent as that of ours. I never suspected you of sympathizing with Miss Anthony and Mrs. Stanton in their course. Their principle is: that no Negro shall be enfranchised while woman is not. Now, considering that white men have been enfranchised always, and colored men have not, the conduct of these white women, whose husbands, fathers and brothers are voters, does not seem generous.

very truly yours,

Fred Douglass

Josephine S. W. Griffing Papers, Columbia University Library.

Charles Lenox Remond Seeks Employment

Following the Civil War, abolitionist Charles Lenox Remond was faced with a perplexing problem. His earlier income-producing years had been spent in the cause of freedom while he worked for the American Anti-Slavery Society. Therefore, when the slaves were freed, he found it necessary to find new employment. With this in mind, he wrote the following letter to George Downing.

Greenwood, March 23, 1869

My dear friend
Geo. T. Downing, Esq.

Don't think I have a mania for letter writing, but I have this moment learned that yourself and Mr. Douglass and other gentlemen contemplate starting a paper on an early day in Washington. If so please acquaint me with the design and your plans. And make me if you can a party in some way to the undertaking. You are aware I have no money to put in (as I wish I had) but I can render perhaps good service in other directions. I am bound to do something that shall place my wife and children above want and suffering. Of my chances on the subject embraced in my last letter, you can better judge than myself. I only desire to say I mean business of some kind. Permit me to hear from you on your earliest convenience & oblige.

Yours Truly,

C. Lenox Remond

Original in the possession of the Rev. Howard Asbury, Jamaica, Long Island, N.Y.

Isaac Myers and the Negro Labor Movement

The first conference to organize blacks into an effective labor union was held in Washington, D.C., in December 1869. The following year, Isaac Myers, one of the early active members of the Negro National Labor Union, addressed a group of about twelve hundred assembled workers in Richmond, Virginia, urging them to organize for their own protection.

. . . Is there a necessity for the colored mechanics and laborers of the United States organizing? My answer is, there is the greatest necessity, and unless you do organize in a few short years the trades will pass from your hands—you become the servants of servants, the sweeper of shavings, the scrapers of pitch, and the carriers of mortar and why do I make such a broad and positive assertion? It is because I do not find the colored men organized for protection and because I know if you do organize you will preserve your labor, command employment, and educate your children in the trades.

The New Era (Washington), April 21, 1870.

Charles Sumner on Equal Rights for Negroes

Although a civil rights bill had been passed in 1866, there were many phases of constitutional rights that it did not include. Some Republican leaders, among them Senator Charles Sumner, worked most of their political lives to bring equality in all areas of American life to the Negro. From 1870 on, Sumner and others devoted themselves to the enactment of a comprehensive civil rights bill. Regarding this effort, Sumner wrote these two letters to George T. Downing, his friend and co-worker in the struggle for equal rights.

Private
Washington 28th Dec. '71

My dear Sir,

All possible help is needed to secure the passage of the Bill for Equal Rights. Besides petitions & letters there must be a strong committee to visit every Republican Senator. Not a vote must be lost. Now is the time. In the talk for amnesty I insist upon Justice—& so I shall cry to the end. But there must be help.

Faithfully yours,

Charles Sumner

* * * * *

Senate Chamber
8th April '72

Dear Mr. Downing,

Just after you left me yesterday Prof. Langston called on me, & in the course of conversation, requested me to address him a letter in answer to his inquiry,—what the Convention should do? Yielding to his request, I wrote a brief note, embodying what in my judgment should be the special work of the Convention,—touching on the points to which I called your attention.

The more I reflect upon the Convention, I see the important part it can perform. It can settle the great question of Equal Rights, by making all parties accept them. But it must be positive & firm—without compromise. It must insist upon the full recognition of Equal Rights as the condition of support. Whether in one Convention or another other things may be in issue, but Equal Rights must no longer be in issue anywhere. They must be recognized & accepted by all. I hope Mr. Douglass will help secure this great victory. He may then dismiss me to private life.

Ever yours,

Charles Sumner

Original in the possession of the Rev. Howard Asbury, Jamaica, Long Island, N.Y.

Ulysses S. Grant Declines an Invitation

As President of the United States, Ulysses S. Grant faced the awesome task of economically and politically rebuilding the South, placating the North and aiding the freedmen. That he did not measure up to his responsibilities is well known. He was, however, in sympathy with the plight of the Negro. In 1872, his waning interest was expressed when he declined to attend a meeting of black citizens who were seeking civil rights for the freedmen. He sent the following reply to their invitation.

Executive Mansion,
Washington D.C. May 9th 1872

Gentlemen:

I am in receipt of your invitation extended to me to attend a mass meeting to be held for the purpose of aiding in securing civil rights for the colored citizens of our country. I regret that a previous engagement will detain me at the Executive Mansion this evening, and that I shall not be able to participate with you in person in your efforts to further the cause in which you are laboring.

I beg to assure you, however, that I sympathize most cordially in any effort to secure for all our people of whatever race, nativity or color, the exercise of those rights to which every citizen should be entitled.

I am very respectfully

U. S. Grant

Schomburg Collection, New York Public Library.

DOWNING HELD SUMNER'S HAND AT DEATH

Letter in Possession of Mrs. M. R. DeMortie Proves George T. Downing Had the Honor Claimed by White Senator—Was Written to His Family the Day of Charles Sumner's Death—Tribute by His Son.

LETTER OF MR. DOWNING VERBATIM ET LITTERATIM.

The Editor of the Guardian was shown, last week, a letter of which the following is an exact co[illegible] It was on stationery with picture of U. S. [illegible] in upper [illegible]

Schomburg Collection, New York Public Library

George T. Downing's Grief on the Death of Charles Sumner

George T. Downing had aided Senator Sumner in his crusade for civil rights. When Sumner died in March 1874, nearly a year before the Civil Rights Bill of 1875 was passed, Downing expressed his grief in a letter to his wife and children.

Forty-third Congress U.S.,
House of Representatives,
Washington, D.C., March 11, 1874

Dear Wife & Children—

I had just returned to the Capital; tears run down my cheek, I have just helped to close the eyes and fit the mouth of Charles Sumner, I mist him from his seat in the Senate yesterday, but did not know he was sick until I took up the paper this morning I went to his house and remained with him until his death which took place at 13 minute before 3 o. c. I had hold of his hand when he died. He spoke to me and of me several times, he did not say much, he was in pain but repeated and repeated do not let the civil rights bill fail. He asked me how came I to know he was sick, Senator Schurts asked him if he knew him, he replied yes and Mr. Downing too. He had on spasm, I strove to open his hand. There was present in the room when he died, a doctor, his private secretary Stryker and myself, I would write more but can not now—Love to all,

Your true husband,

Geo. T. Downing.

Original in the possession of the Rev. Howard Asbury, Jamaica, Long Island, N.Y.

Blanche K. Bruce, the Black Man's Senator

Blanche K. Bruce was born in Virginia in 1841. A man of limited education, in 1868 he became a planter in Mississippi. Later, he served in several local offices, and in 1847 he became the first Negro to be elected for a full term in the United States Senate. As soon as Bruce was elected, his mail overflowed with requests for aid in securing appointments. The following letters taken from Bruce's correspondence contain such requests as well as information about the plight of Negroes in the South.

Superintendent of Education
Shannon, Lee Co. Miss.
November 17th, 1875

Hon. B. K. Bruce,—
Dear Sir:
I am anxious through you to procure a Federal appointment, I have not only been threatened, but attacked so often recently, and in some of the encounters I have been so much worsted, that I prefer not risking my life much longer among our confederate victors. On the night after our recent so called election my office was to a considerable degree demolished, and a salute of small arms was fired by a company of self constituted regulators in front of my residence. I have been informed I was hung in effigy in a number of places during the next few days. In politics I have been a Republican without departures. I was a union man and went north during the latter portion of the rebellion. I was never in the Confederate service. I supported Alcorn when he was our nominee. I was on the Grant electoral ticket in 1872. I canvassed North Miss with and for Ames in the last Gubernatorial race and was for Buchanan for Treasurer in the recent gov't. I was appointed Assessor of this County by Alcorn when he was Gov, and I have been Superintendent of Education for this county for near two years. Neither of these positions have paid me anything over a living. You will remember I am minus one arm, which I lost in a personal situation. I am a poor man and have aged parents dependent on me for a support. I am a good business man, and could prosper here but for persecution. Tell the President I will gladly accept a paying position anywhere on earth. You may forward this to him with such endorsement as you see proper to make.

With great respect yours &c

Wm. F. Simonton

* * * * *

Custom House, Vicksburg, Miss.,
Collector's Office, March 2nd, 1877.

Hon. B. K. Bruce
Senate Chamber
Washington, D.C.

Sir:—I have the honor to write to you requesting that you have the kindness to interceed for my retention in to the office of Collection of Customs for the Port of Vicksburg Miss. I have been requested to respectfully ask you to act thus, and to have me retained in said office, as I am the only colored man in Miss. who is holding federal appointment, and as I have acted satisfactory to all; they pray to have me retained as such collector. there are some white republicans who desire a white man to be appointed and I understand that one Mr. Wm. Muller is that white man. please let me hear from you soon, and greatly oblige

I am your obedient servant
with much respect etc.

P. C. Hall
Collector of Customs etc

Fears that he will lose his place

You shall stay

[The above notations, by two different hands, appear at the bottom of the last page of the letter.]

Moorland Foundation, Howard University Library.

Senator Bruce Speaks Out for Pinchback

In 1876, Senator Bruce spoke in the United States Senate on behalf of admitting P. B. S. Pinchback, who had been elected a senator by the Louisiana legislature. The body of the Senate refused to admit Pinchback even though Bruce argued his case convincingly.

When I entered upon my duties here as Senator from Mississippi, the question ceased to be novel, and had already been elaborately and exhaustively discussed. So far as opportunity has permitted me to do so, I have dispassionately examined the question in the light of the discussion, and I venture my views now with the diffidence inspired by my limited experience in the consideration of such questions and by a just appreciation of the learning and ability of the gentlemen who have already attempted to elucidate and determine this case.

I believe, Mr. President, whatever seeming informalities may attach to the manner in which the will of the people was ascertained, Mr. Pinchback is the representative of a majority of the legal voters of Louisiana, and is entitled to a seat in the Senate. In the election of 1872, the white population of the state exceeded, by the census of 1872, the colored population by about two thousand, including in the white estimate 6,300 foreigners, only half of whom were naturalized. This estimate, at the same ratio in each race, would give a large majority of colored voters. The census and registration up to 1872 substantially agree, and both sustain this conclusion. The census of 1875, taken in pursuance of an article of the State constitution, gives, after including the foreign population (naturalized and unnaturalized) in the white aggregate, a majority of 45,695 colored population.

This view of the question is submitted not as determining the contest, but as an offset to the allegation that Mr. Pinchback does not fairly represent the popular will of the State, and as a presumption in favor of the legal title of the assembly that elected him. . . .

In my judgment, this question shall at this juncture be considered and decided not on abstract but practical grounds. Whatever wrongs have been done and mistakes made in Louisiana by either party, the present order of things is accepted by the people of the State and by the nation, and will be maintained as final settlement of the political issues that have divided the people there; and no changes in the administration of public affairs can or will be made except by the people, through the ballot, under the existing government and laws of the Commonwealth.

Under these circumstances, holding the question in abeyance is, in my judgment, an unconstitutional deprivation of a State, and a provocation of popular disquietude; and in the interest of goodwill and good government, the most judicious and consistent course is to admit the claimant to his seat.

I desire, Mr. President, to make a personal reference to the claimant. I would not attempt one or deem one proper were it not that his personal character has been assailed.

As a father, I know him to be affectionate; as a husband, the idol of a pleasant home and cheerful fireside; as a citizen, loyal, brave, and true. And in his character and success we behold an admirable illustration of the excellence of our republican institutions.

Carter G. Woodson, *Negro Orators and Their Orations* (Washington, D.C., 1925).

Henry O. Flipper's Memories of Life at West Point

In 1877, Henry O. Flipper became the first Afro-American to graduate from West Point. He was not the first Negro to enroll; at the time of his admittance another cadet of color, James W. Smith, was at the Point. In his memoirs, Flipper revealed some of the difficulties in being a colored cadet at West Point.

It may not be inappropriate to give in this place a few—as many as I can recall—of the incidents, more or less humorous, in which I myself have taken part or have noticed at the various times of their occurrence. First, then, an adventure on "Flirtation."

During the encampment of 1873—I think it was in July—Smith and myself had the—for us—rare enjoyment of a visit made us by some friends. We had taken them around the place and shown and explained to them every thing of interest. We at length took seats on "Flirtation," and gave ourselves up to pure enjoyment such as is found in woman's presence only. The day was exceedingly beautiful; all nature seemed loveliest just at that time, and our lone, peculiar life, with all its trials and cares, was quite forgotten. We chatted merrily, and as ever in such company were really happy. It was so seldom we had visitors—and even then they were mostly males—that we were delighted to have some one with whom we could converse on other topics than official ones and studies. While we sat there not a few strangers, visitors also, passed us, and almost invariably manifested surprise at seeing us.

But O fate! Anon a cadet, whose perfectly fitting uniform of matchless gray and immaculate white revealed the symmetry of his form in all its manly beauty, saunters leisurely by, his head erect, shoulders back, step quick and elastic, and those glorious buttons glittering at their brilliant points like so many orbs of a distant stellar world. Next a plebe strolls wearily along, his drooping shoulders, hanging head, and careless gait bespeaking the need of more squad drill. Then a dozen or more "Picnicers," all females, laden with baskets, boxes, and other et ceteras, laughing and playing, unconscious of our proximity, draw near. The younger ones tripping playfully in front catch sight of us. Instantly they are hushed, and with hands over their mouths retrace their steps to disclose to those in rear their astounding discovery. In a few moments all appear, and silently and slowly pass by, eyeing us as if we were the greatest natural wonder in existence. They pass on till out of sight, face about and "continue the motion," passing back and forth as many as five times. Wearied at length of this performance, Smith rose and said, "Come, let's end this farce," or something to that effect. We arose, left the place, and were surprised to find a moment after that they were actually following us.

The "Picnicers," as they are called in the corps, begin their excursions early in May, and continue them till near the end of September. They manage to arrive at West Point at all possible hours of the day, and stay as late as they conveniently can. In May and September, when we have battalion drills, they are a great nuisance, a great annoyance to me especially. The vicinity of that flank of the battalion in which I was, was where they "most did congregate." It was always amusing, though most embarrassing, to see them pointing me out to each other, and to hear their verbal accompaniments, "There he is, the first"—or such—"man from the right"—"or left." "Who?" "The colored cadet."

"Haven't you seen him? Here, I'll show him to you," and so on *ad libitum*. . . .

There is an article in the academic regulations which provides or declares that no citizen who has been a cadet at the Military Academy can receive a commission in the regular army before the class of which he was a member graduates, unless he can get the written consent of his former classmates.

A classmate of mine resigned in the summer of '75, and about a year after endeavored to get a commission. A friend and former classmate drew up the approval, and invited the class to his "house" to sign it. When half a dozen or more had signed it, it was sent to the guard-house, and the corporal of the guard came and notified me it was there for my consideration. I went to the guard-house at once. A number of cadets were sitting or standing around in the room. As soon as I entered they became silent and remained so, expecting, no doubt, I'd refuse to sign it, because of the treatment I had received at their hands. They certainly had little cause to expect that I would add my signature. Nevertheless I read the paper over and signed it without hesitation. Their anxiety was raised to the highest possible pitch, and scarcely had I left the room ere they seized the paper as if they would devour it. I heard some one who came in as I went out ask, "Did he sign it?"

Henry Ossian Flipper, *The Colored Cadet at West Point* (New York, 1878).

Flipper Seeks Aid from Booker T. Washington

Henry O. Flipper later was dishonorably discharged from the army after a charge of embezzlement was leveled against him. In an effort to obtain dismissal of the charge, which he rebutted, and to regain his status as a commissioned officer, Flipper sought the aid of such Negro leaders as Booker T. Washington in getting a bill passed on his behalf in Congress.

Sante Fe, N. Mex.
December 12, 1898.

Prof. Booker T. Washington,
Tuskegee Normal and Industrial Institute,
Tuskegee, Ala.

My Dear Sir:—

Your esteemed favor of the 5th inst. enclosing copies of letters from Senator Hawley and Hon. John A. T. Hull, reached me this morning and I hasten to thank you for your efforts in my behalf.

Recent events show, and it has been apparent for some time, that my bill would fail, unless an extraordinary effort were made to have it passed. The disgraceful conduct of the colored volunteers in the south has reduced my chances at least fifty per cent. In Macon, Georgia, a soldier of one of these regiments went into a place of business and asked to be served. He was refused. He went to camp and got about half a hundred of his comrades, came back and undertook to get revenge. Now, in my opinion, this was wholly uncalled for. He was simply inviting trouble instead of trying to avoid it. This statement of the case may not be true, but it is the one published to the country and believed by those to whom we have to look for assistance in such cases as mine. This conduct on the part of the colored volunteers is making the putting of more colored men in the reorganized Army extremely problematical. These soldiers have seemed to think that because they wore the government's uniform they were at liberty to avenge all the wrongs they conceive the white people of the South have ever done to them. The colored officers with them seem to have shared these ideas.

There seems to be no disposition on the part of any one to interest himself in my bill, though they all say I have a strong case and ought to be restored to the service. Mr. Hull, above all others, is the man to push this bill, but he seems to be afraid of it. I have no doubt it would readily be passed, if he would father it. The bill must be passed at this session or not at all. The new Army bill will be passed at this session and before I could get another bill introduced and passed, if at all, by the 56th Congress, the Army will have been reorganized and there would be no place for me. In this view of the case, it seems to me that my only hope is to bring such influence to bear upon Mr. Hull as will induce him to push the bill. This can be done through the President. President McKinley's position is such now that any bill he wants passed will be passed. Can you not see the President, in one of your trips north, lay this matter before him in this light and ask him to endorse the bill and ask Mr. Hull to push it? An intimation of this character from the President will, no doubt, secure the passage of the bill. I am convinced that this is my only chance and hope. I shall ask Hon. Judson W. Lyons, the Register of the Treasury, to do the same thing. You two gentlemen are the only men of our race who can make such a request of the President with any promise of success, and for this reason I appeal to you. Will you do this? I have asked Register Lyons to hand a copy of my brief to the President.

This is the situation as it appears to me and my only hope of success lies along the line I have herein indicated.

With best wishes to yourself and yours, I have the honor to be,

Very truly yours,

Henry O. Flipper

Booker T. Washington Papers, Library of Congress.

Frederick Douglass Criticizes the Exodus to Kansas

As the South gradually regained its political autonomy, the leaders of the old order once again sought to gain control. By the mid-1870's, the Afro-American was losing the few rights he had gained, politically, economically and socially. Many blacks became disillusioned with their future in the South and sought new locations in the United States. During this period, a movement was started to emigrate to Kansas. The leader of this Exodus, as it was called, was Benjamin "Pap" Singleton, who was responsible for establishing eleven colonies in Kansas between 1873 and 1880.

The rush of people from the South to the "promised land" was so great that the Negro population increased from 2 slaves and 625 free blacks in 1860 to 43,107 blacks by 1880. Rumors of free transportation and land ran rampant. Hundreds of Negroes left behind what little they possessed and blindly rushed to the western states seeking a haven in the wilderness. Upon their arrival, however, they found very little of the promised opportunity; and when the influx reached its peak, relief societies were formed to ward off starvation while plans were formulated for caring for the destitute. Eventually, conditions became so bad that a congressional investigation was made to determine what factors were involved in the initial promotion of the Exodus.

Before the problems of the Exodus became widely known, many black leaders became concerned with the migration to Kansas. Attitudes among the leaders differed as to whether Negroes should emigrate or remain in the South to gradually assume their proper place in that society. Frederick Douglass felt that migration was a mistake, and in the following address, read before the American Social Science Association in September 1879, at Saratoga Springs, N.Y., he defended his stand.

. . . While necessity often compels men to migrate; to leave their old homes and seek new ones; to sever old ties and create new ones; to do this the necessity should be obvious and imperative. It should be a last resort and only adopted after carefully considering what is against the measure as well as what is in favor of it. There are prodigal sons everywhere, who are ready to demand the portion of goods that would fall to them and betake themselves to a strange country. Something is ever lost in the process of migration, and much is sacrificed at home for what is gained abroad. A world of wisdom is in the saying of Mr. Emerson, "that those who made Rome worth going to stayed there." . . . The colored people of the South, just beginning to accumulate a little property, and to lay the foundation of families, should not be in haste to sell that little and be off to the banks of the Mississippi. The habit of roaming from place to place in pursuit of better conditions of existence is by no means a good one. A man should never leave his home for a new one till he has earnestly endeavored to make his immediate surroundings accord with his wishes. The time and energy expended in wandering about from place to place, if employed in making him comfortable where he is, will, in nine cases out of ten, prove the best investment. No people ever did much for themselves or for the world, without the sense and inspiration of native land; of a fixed home; of familiar neighborhood, and common associations. The fact of being to the manor born has an elevating power upon the mind and heart of a man. It is a more cheerful thing to be able to say, "I was born here and know all the people," than to say, "I am a stranger here and know none of the people." It cannot be doubted, that in so far as this Exodus tends to promote restlessness in the colored people of the South, to unsettle their feelings of home and to sacrifice positive advantages where they are, for fancied ones in Kansas or elsewhere, it is an evil. Some have sold their little homes at a sacrifice, their chickens, mules and pigs, to follow the Exodus. Let it be understood that you are going, and you advertise the fact that your mule has lost half his value—for your staying with him makes half his value. Let the colored people of Georgia offer their six millions worth of property for sale, with the purpose to leave Georgia, and they will not realize half its value. Land is not worth much where there are no people to occupy it, and a mule is not worth much where there is no one to use it.

It may safely be asserted that, whether advocated and commended to favor on the ground that it will increase the political power of the Republican party, and thus help to make a solid North against a solid South; or upon the ground that it will increase the power and influence of the colored people as a political element, and enable them the better to protect their rights, and ensure their moral and social elevation, the Exodus will prove a disappointment, a mistake and a failure . . .

As an assertion of power by a people hitherto held in bitter contempt; as an emphatic and stinging protest against high-handed, greedy and shameless injustice to the weak and defenceless; as a means of opening the blind eyes of oppressors to their folly and peril, the Exodus has done valuable service. Whether it has accomplished all of which it is capable in this particular direction for the present, is a question which may well be considered. With a moderate degree of intelligent leadership among the laboring class at the South, properly handling the justice of their cause, and wisely using the Exodus example, they can easily exact better terms for their labor than ever before. Exodus is medicine, not food; it is for disease, not health; it is not to be taken from choice, but necessity. In anything like a normal condition of things the South is the best place for the Negro. Nowhere else is there for him a promise of a happier future. Let him stay there if he can, and save both the South and himself to civilization. While, however, it may be the highest wisdom under the circumstances for the freedmen to stay where they are, no encouragement should be given to any measures of coercion to keep them there. The American people are bound, if they are or can be bound to anything, to keep the North gate of the South open to black and white, and to all the people. The time to assert a right, Webster says, is when it is called in question. If it is attempted by force or fraud to compel the colored people to stay, then they should by all means go; go quickly, and die, if need be, in the attempt. Thus far and to this extent any man may be an emigrationist. In no case must the Negro be "bottled up" or "caged up." He must be left free, like every other American citizen, to choose his own local habitation, and to go where he shall like. Though it may not be for his interest to leave the South, his right and power to leave it may be his best means of making it possible for him to stay there in peace. Woe to the oppressed and destitute of all countries and races if the rich and powerful are to decide when and where they shall go or stay. The deserving hired man gets his wages increased when he can tell his employer that he can get better wages elsewhere. And when all hope is gone from the hearts of the laboring classes of the old world, they can come across the sea to the new. If they could not do that their crushed hearts would break under increasing burdens. The right to emigrate is one of the most useful and precious of all rights. But not only to the oppressed, to the oppressor also, is the free use of this right necessary. To attempt to keep these freedmen in the South, who are spirited enough to undertake the risks and hardships of emigration, would involve great possible danger to all concerned. Ignorant and cowardly as the Negro may be, he has been known to fight bravely for his liberty. He went down to Harper's Ferry with John Brown, and fought as bravely and died as nobly as any. There have been Nathaniel Turners and Denmark Veseys among them in the United States, Joseph Cinques, Madison Washingtons and Tillmans on the sea, and Toussaint L'Ouvertures on land. Even his enemies, during the late war, had to confess that the Negro is a good fighter, when once in a fight. If he runs, it is only as all men will run, when they are whipped.

This is no time to trifle with the rights of men. All Europe today is studded with the material for a wild conflagration. Every day brings us news of plots and conspiracies against oppressive power. . . . It will not be wise for the Southern slaveholders and their successors to shape their policy upon the presumption that the Negro's cowardice or forbearance has no limit. The fever of freedom is already in the Negro's blood. He is not just what he was fourteen years ago. To forcibly dam up the stream of emigration would be a measure of extreme madness as well as oppression. It would be exposing the heart of the oppressor to the pistol and dagger, and his home to fire and pillage. The cry of "Land and Liberty," the watchword of the Nihilistic party in Russia, has a music in it sweet to the ear of all oppressed peoples, and well it shall be for the landholders of the South if they shall learn wisdom in time and adopt such a course of just treatment towards the landless laborers of the South in the future as shall make this popular watchword uncontagious and unknown among their laborers, and further stampede to the North wholly unknown, indescribable and impossible.

Frederick Douglass, "The Negro Exodus from the Gulf States," *Journal of Social Science,* XI (May 1880).

Richard T. Greener Supports the Exodus

At the same American Social Science Association meeting where Douglass argued against migration from the South, another leader offered his views in favor of the movement. Richard T. Greener, who was the first Afro-American to graduate from Harvard University, argued that the Exodus was necessary if Negroes were ever to achieve their full rights in this country. In the following speech, Greener outlined the unhappy lot of the Negroes in the South and the advantages they would gain in seeking new opportunities elsewhere.

. . . After the war it was difficult to purchase land because the old master was not disposed to sell. With the downfall of reconstruction a new lease of life was given to Southern barbarity and lawlessness. As usual, the Negro was the principal sufferer. Negro representation went first; next the educational system, which the carpet-bagger had brought to the South, was crippled by insufficient appropriations. Majorities were overcome by shot-gun intimidation, or secretly by the tissue ballot. Radical office-holders were forced to resign, robbed of their property by "due process of law," and driven North. The jury-box and representation the Negro was forced to give up; but after enduring all this, he found himself charged exorbitantly for the most necessary articles of food. His land was rented to him at fabulous prices. His cabin was likely to be raided at any time, whenever capricious lust, or a dreadful thirst for blood was roused. He saw his crop dwindling day by day; he saw himself growing poorer and getting into debt; his labor squandered between exacting landlords and rapacious store-keepers. It was then the Negro resolved to give up the fruitless contest so long and hopelessly waged, and try his fortune in the great West, of which he had heard and read so much during the past ten years.

To quote from the St. Louis Memorial: "The story is about the same, in each instance; great privation and want from excessive rent exacted for land; connected with the murder of colored neighbors and friends, and threats of personal violence to themselves; the tenor of which statement is that of suffering and terror. Election days and Christmas, by the concurrent testimony, seem to have been preferred for killing the 'smart man,' while robbery and personal violence, in one form and another, seem to have run the year around. Here they are in multitudes, not often alone, but women and children, old and middle-aged and young, and with common consent, leaving their old home for an unnatural climate, and facing storms and unknown dangers to go to northern Kansas. Why? Among them little is said of hope in the future; it is all of fear in the past. They are not drawn by the attractions of Kansas, they are driven by the terrors of Mississippi and Louisiana." The thriftless habits of work, endangered by southern life; the utter lack of foresight found in white and black alike, are powerful agents in bringing about the Exodus. The universal credit system is fostered by the planters, and kept up by the wily store-keeper; the insecurity of the holdings (long leases being unknown), is such that, if the Negro succeeds in raising a good crop, he has no guaranty that he can keep his patch the next year. The prices charged for the necessaries of life may be noticed. These are copied from the original documents brought by the refugees: $1.50 per lb. for tobacco; molasses, $1.50 per gallon; filling out a contract, $2.50; meal, per bushel, $2.00, not worth more than $1; pork, per barrel, $30.

"Again, the political differences of opinion which exists in the South is another important cause. There, political convictions rank with religious opinions in intensity. The over-production of cotton is another cause, by the low price of that staple. Then the fact that the Negro owns neither land, nor presses, cotton-gin, and implements, but buys mules, rents land, and purchases his provisions at an advance, often thirty and forty per cent., is sufficient cause for the Exodus. If we add that the landlord has a first claim on the crop, a law which is identical with the Scotch law of hypotheca, we shall see reasons enough for a failure, and for the disposition to seek a happier home elsewhere. It can not be denied that there are instances where the Negroes find themselves hopelessly involved; and seeing no propect of any compensation, have at once repudiated their contracts and their country. This, of course, does not apply to those who have mules, carts, implements, and other utensils, which keep them attached closer to the soil. The law protects the landlord, and his claim always has the precedence. It is a punishable offence to remove any portion of the crop from the plantation before the landlord's claim is met. Next comes the store-keeper with his bill of six months. If anything were left for the poor Negro when all these demands are satisfied, it would partake of the nature of a genuine miracle."

This emigration will benefit the Negro, who is now too much inclined to stay where he is put. At the South he never knows his own possibilities. Then again, the South is a wretched place for any people to develop in, and this is especially true of the Negro; because, like all subject races, he imitates the life about him. The Negro of the South is in a demoralized condition, and no jury will convict for political offences committed against him. . . . District attorneys are appointed at the recommendation of known rebels and sympathizers and assassins. Of course, they will not do their duty; hence, the Negro dares not look for justice in the courts —once proudly called the palladium of English liberty. . . . I need not enumerate the demoralizing features of Southern life, the reckless disregard for human life, the lack of thrift, drinking customs, gaming, horse-racing, etc. The Negro needs contact with all that is healthful and developing in modern civilization, and by emigration the Negro will learn to love thrift, and unlearn many bad habits and improvident notions acquired from preceding generations.

The exclusive devotion of the Negro to the culture of cotton and rice is demoralizing to him. They drag women and children into the field, with no commissioner of labor to look out for outraged childhood and impaired maternity. I do not expect this argument to find favor with those who think the Negro has no other future before him than to cultivate sugar, cotton and rice. On the politico-economic side a partial Exodus will benefit those who remain, by raising the wage fund, increasing the demand, and insuring better treatment to those who are left; the fact of the Exodus being a preventive check, if I may borrow a phrase from Mr. Malthus. It will remove the Negro from the incessant whirl of politics, in which, like all dark races, he is governed more by feeling than selfish interest.

At present the Negro stands in the way of his own advancement, by reason of political fidelity, and the very excess of population, not diminished since the war, and yet not so systematically diffused and employed. Even Senator Butler, of South Carolina, says: "We have too much cheap Negro labor in the South." As to wages, the average Negro can earn higher wages and live more comfortably at the North, even if confined to humble employments, than he can at the South. When we add such trifles as protection, school privileges, free suffrage and Christian influences, we transcend the limits of legitimate comparison. . . .

There are few opponents of the Exodus. Most of them are only negative objectors. The only class positively objecting is the planting class. At Vicksburg, and in Washington County (Miss.), they objected vehemently and loudly. Foreign labor, they say, would cost money. Not one planter in ten is able to make further outlay. During the change of laborers, even, they would go to rack and ruin. The Negro is the only one who can do their work. To go now will ruin the cotton crop, and, hence affect the North as well as the South.

No one disputes the right of the Negro to go West, now that he is free. We accord to all men the rights to improve their condition by change of residence or employment. Nearly all of the objectors, white and black, have grave doubts as to our ability to stand this severe Northern climate. They fear we may not find work adapted to our limited peculiar powers; may not meet with kind friends and genial sympathy. We must endure privations and meet with ostracism at the North. Mechanics will not work with Negroes. The Negro remembers Slavery, Black Codes, Ku-Klux, Sister Sallie's plan, tissue ballots, the murder of Dr. Dostie and Randolph in South Carolina, Caldwell and Dixon in Mississippi, and says: "My relatives and friends who have gone North since the war tell a different story. They have held no offices, but they are free. They sleep in peace at night; what they earn is paid them, if not, they can appeal to the courts. They vote without fear of the shot-gun, and their children go to school.

The most important opponent of the Exodus is Marshal Frederick Douglass, my distinguished antagonist in this discussion, who, I sincerely regret, is not here to lend to his able and ingenious argument the magic of his presence and the influence of his eloquent voice. The greatest Negro whom America has produced, having suffered all that our race could endure, and having been elevated higher than any other Negro, he cannot lack sympathy with any movement which concerns his race, and hence, any objection coming from him challenges attention, and demands to be answered. Age, long service, and a naturally keen and analytic mind would presume a soundness of view on almost any topic of national importance or race interest. It is, therefore, with the highest regard for the honesty of Mr. Douglass's views that I venture to reply to some of his objections. Mr. Douglass has not been an inactive opponent. He has written elaborate resolutions, made at least six speeches, spoken at the Methodist Conference, and been interviewed on the Exodus. While time has modified his extreme views, and more recent events have blunted the edge of his sarcasm, and while most of his objections are of the negative rather than the positive order, against the methods and men who seek to help the movement, rather than against the Exodus itself, still the morale of his influence is in opposition.

The little rill has started on its course toward the great sea of humanity. It moves slowly on by virtue of the eternal law of gravitation, which leads peoples and individuals toward peace, protection and happiness. Today it is a slender thread and makes way with difficulty amid the rocks and tangled growth; but it has already burst through serious impediments, showing itself possessed of a mighty current. It started in Mississippi, but it is even now being rapidly fed by other rills and streams from the territory through which it flows. Believing that it comes from God, and feeling convinced that it bears only blessings in its course for that race so long tossed, so ill-treated, so sadly misunderstood, I greet its tiny line, and almost see in the near future its magnificent broad bosom, bearing proudly onward, until at last, like the travel-worn and battle-scarred Greeks of old, there bursts upon its sight the sea, the broad sea of universal freedom and protection.

Richard T. Greener, "The Emigration of Colored Citizens from the Southern States," *Journal of Social Science,* XI (May 1880).

Booker T. Washington on Tuskegee

On July 4, 1881, soon after his arrival at Tuskegee, Alabama, Booker T. Washington wrote the following description of the school and the conditions he found in the rural South.

. . . I arrived here four weeks ago. Instead of finding my work in a low marshy country as I expected, I find Tuskegee a beautiful little town, with a high and healthy location. It is a town such as one rarely sees in the South. Its quiet shady streets and tasteful and rich dwellings remind one of a New England village. After my arrival I had one week in which to prepare for the opening of the Normal School. I utilized this time in seeing the teachers and others who wished to enter the school, and in getting a general idea of my work and the people. Sunday I spoke in both churches to the people about the school, and told all who wished to enter to come and see me at my boarding place during the week. About thirty persons called and had their names enrolled, others called whose names for various reasons, I could not enroll. With the young people many of their parents came. I was particularly impressed with the desire of the parents to educate their children, whatever might be the sacrifice.

On Friday I rode about fourteen miles into the country to visit the closing exercises of one of the teachers. From this trip I got some idea of the people in the country. Never was I more surprised and moved than when I saw at one house, two boys thirteen or fourteen years old, perfectly *nude*. They seemed not to mind their condition in the least. Passing on from house to house, I saw many other children five and six years old in the same condition. It was very seldom that I saw children anything like decently dressed. If they wore clothing it was only one garment, and this so black and greasy that it did not resemble cloth. As a rule, the colored people all through this section are very poor and ignorant, but the one encouraging thing about it is that they see their weakness and are desirous of improving. The teachers in this part of Alabama have had few advantages, many of them having never attended school themselves. They know nothing of the improved methods of teaching. They hail with gladness, the Normal School, and most of them will be among its students. If there is any place in the world where a good Normal School is needed, it is right here. What an influence for good, first on the teachers, and from them on the children and parents!

I opened school last week. At present I have over forty students, anxious and earnest young men and women. I expect quite an increase in September and October. The school is taught, at present, in one of the colored churches, which they kindly let us have for that purpose. This building is not very well suited to school purposes, and we hope to be able to move to a more commodious place in a short time. The place referred to is on a beautiful and conveniently located farm of one hundred acres, which we have contracted to buy for $500. The state pays for tuition. The farm I hope to pay for by my own exertions and the help of others here. As a rule, the colored people in the South are not and will not be able for years to board their children in school at ten or twelve dollars per month, hence my object is, as soon as possible, to get the school on a labor basis, so that earnest students can help themselves and at the same time learn the true dignity of labor. An institution for the education of colored youths can be but a *partial* success without a boarding department. In it they can be taught those correct habits which they fail to get at home. Without this part of the training they go out into the world with untrained intellects and their morals and bodies neglected. After the land is paid for, we hope to get a boarding department on foot as soon as possible.

The good will manifested towards the school by both white and colored is a great encouragement to me to push the work forward. I have had many kind words of encouragement from the whites, and have been well treated by them in every way. The Trustees seem to be exceptional men. Whether I have met the colored people in their churches, societies, or homes, I have received their hearty cooperation and a "God bless you." Even the colored preachers seem to be highly in favor of the work, and one of the pastors here, fifty years old, is one of my students. . . .

Southern Workman, X (September 1881).

John Alexander's Military Experiences

Lieutenant John Alexander, the second Negro to graduate from West Point, was destined to have a more successful career than his predecessor, Henry O. Flipper. Assigned to the cavalry for duty in the West, Alexander kept a diary of his daily activities in his new command. Alexander was a true soldier who took his leadership of the 9th Cavalry seriously. He performed in such a fashion as to be remembered after his death in the annals of military history. In 1918, a fort in Virginia was named for him as a memorial to his outstanding performance in the army.

Trip of "M" troop from Fort Washakie, Wyo. to Ft. Du Chesne, Utah

Lauder, Wyo. June 11, 1888.
17 miles from Ft. Washakie, Wyo.
First day's march.

Left Ft. Washakie this morning at 7:40 & marched here about 12:25 P.M. Have a passable camping place. Had quite a pleasant leave taking of the Post. We march in fighting time with 200 rounds of ammunition per man. Have along 5 freight wagons & three carriages containing families. Went up town visiting friends this afternoon. Took tea with Miss Roberts. My first experience in practical field service is very pleasant. I mess with my Captain.

* * * * *

In Camp on Beaver Creek
June 13, 1888
12 miles from Lemon's Ranch
Third day's march

Got in Camp at 10 o'clock this morning. Freight trains got in Camp five hours later. Pull was terrible up Tweed's Hill out of Red Canyon and up Twin Creek Hill. Went back a couple of miles on "Red" bareback to find out what the matter with trains. Splendid camping place. Do not feel very tired. Athletics in camp with Captain and the boys. Mosquitoes very bad. Have had sore throat last three days but am over it now. Beautiful scenery along the march & especially in Red Canyon. The days are hot but the nights are very cold. Camp is right on summit of mountains & snow is seen on the side of the ridges surrounding us. Did not sleep this afternoon.

* * * * *

In Camp on Little Sandy River
June 16
15 miles from Dry Sandy C
6th day's march.

Broke camp at 5:00 A.M. and arrived here at 9:00. Very easy march. Good grass & water but no wood. . . . Saw lots of antelope on the road and got a shot at one. Had a good swim in the River. Was very much refreshed as the day has been very warm. Slept all afternoon. Passed a bunch of Oregon horses on the way to Kansas. Couple of emigrants families going west are camping near us on the River. Wonder what is going on in the outside world.

* * * * *

Ft. Du Chesne Utah
June 27
30 miles from Sibley
17th day's march.

I had a terrible duty mean march to-day. . . . Not a dwelling on line of travel & no water. Reached our coveted Du Chesne and find it a terrible dusty, windy hot post, very uninviting at the first glance. Find the officers of my own reg. & the 16th Troop very genial men. Met Grant & Ballou whom I knew at the Point. Burnett seems to be a much more affable man than I had thought him. Met with no sort of reception. Not sufficient quarters so I am camped out as usual. Not comfortable these hot days in a tent.

* * * * *

Delaware, O. [Ohio]
Mch. 28, 1894

To:
Prof. W. S. Scarborough
Wilberforce University,
Wilberforce, O.

Dear Sir:

Your thoughtful note in behalf of your Univ. Faculty reached me this evening, and I hasten to reply.

It will be almost impossible for me, on account of the opening of the Spring term here and for other reasons, to be present at the funeral of Lieut. Alexander, which, you write me, is to take place tomorrow. I very deeply regret this, as I had a sincere regard for Lieut. Alexander and I was greatly shocked and grieved to learn of his sudden and untimely death.

He entered West Point in 1883, graduating four years later, No. 32 in an exceptionally bright class of 64 members. This class originally numbered about 132, being cut down in four years to 64, by reason of its members being unable to keep up!

When Lt. Alexander graduated, such was his popularity that he was applauded by the audience present more than any other graduate; he was the second colored man to graduate from the Academy. I was with Alexander at West Point during the two years, 1885–1887, and saw much in his character and behavior to admire and respect.

At graduation in 1887 he was assigned to the 9th U.S. Cavalry, and served almost continuously for seven years in Utah and Nebraska. I have been told that he was well liked and respected by his regiment, and bore the reputation of being capable, efficient, and gentlemanly officer.

Believe me that I sincerely sympathize with both his family and your University in his loss.

Thanking you for your kind invitation to be present, and again regretting my inability to comply.

Believe me, Sincerely yours,

C. D. Rhodes
2nd Lieut. 6th U.S. Calvary
Prof. Mil. Science and Tactics

* * * * *

Headquarters, Port of
Embarkation
Newport News, Virginia

August 15, 1918.

General Orders
No. 294.

The Stevedore Cantonment and the Labor Encampments in the vicinity of North Newport News will hereafter be known collectively as CAMP ALEXANDER, Newport News, Va.

The above designation is in honor of the late Lieutenant John H. Alexander, 9th U.S. Cavalry, a colored graduate of the United States Military Academy who served from the time of his graduation until his death as an officer of the army; a man of ability, attainments and energy,—who was a credit to himself, to his race and to the service.

By command of
Brigadier General Hutcheson:
Daniel Van Voorhis,
Colonel, General Staff,
Chief of Staff.

John H. Alexander Papers, Henry E. Huntington Library, San Marino, Calif.

Booker T. Washington on the Plight of the Negro Tenant Farmer

In a letter to George W. Cable, dated October 8, 1889, Booker T. Washington describes the plight of the Negro tenant farmer after emancipation.

. . . when the [Civil] war ended the colored people had nothing much on which to live. . . . They had to get the local merchant or someone else to supply the food for the family to eat while the first crop was being made. For every dollar's worth of provisions so advanced the local merchant charged from 12 to 30 per cent interest. In order to be sure that he secured his principal and interest a mortgage or lien was taken on the crop, in most cases not then planted. Of course the farmers could pay no such interest and the end of the first year found them in debt—the 2nd year they tried again, but there was the old debt and the new interest to pay, and in this way the "mortgage system" has gotten a hold on everything that it seems impossible to shake off. Its evils have grown instead of decreasing, until it is safe to say that ⅚ of the colored farmers mortgage their crops every year. Not only their crops before, in many cases, they are actually planted, but their wives sign a release from the homestead law and in most every case mules, cows, wagons, plows and often all household furniture is covered by the lien.

At a glance one is not likely to get the full force of the figures representing the amount of interest charged. Example, if a man makes a mortgage with a merchant for $200 on which to "run" during the year the farmer is likely to get about $50 of this amount in February or March, $50 May, $50 in June or July and the remainder in Aug. or Sept. By the middle of September the farmer begins returning the money in cotton and by the last of Oct. whatever he can pay the farmer has paid, but the merchant charges as much for the money gotten in July or Aug. as for that gotten in Feb. The farmer is charged interest on all for the one year of 12 months. And as the "advance" is made in most cases in provisions rather than cash, the farmer, in addition to paying the interest mentioned, is charged more for the same goods than one buying for cash. If a farmer has 6 in a family, say wife and 4 children, the merchant has it in his power to feed only those who work and sometimes he says to the farmer if he sends his children to school no rations can be drawn for them while they are attending school.

After a merchant has "run" a farmer for 5 or 6 years and he does not "pay out" or decides to try mortgaging with another merchant the first merchant in such cases usually "cleans up" the farmer, that is takes everything, mules, cows, plows, chicken's fodder—everything except wife and children. . . .

The result of all this is seen in the "general run down" condition of ⅘ of the farms in Alabama—houses unpainted—fences tumbling down, animals poorly cared for, and the land growing poorer every year. Many of the colored farmers have almost given up hope and do just enough work to secure their "advances." One of the strongest things that can be said in favor of the colored people is, that in almost every community there are one or two who have shaken off this yoke of slavery and have bought farms of their own and are making money—and there are a *few* who rent land and "mortgage" and still do something. . . .

Journal of Negro Education, XVII (April 1948).

The Convict Lease System in Arkansas

When it was no longer possible to govern blacks through the plantation system, southerners devised a new means of availing themselves of cheap labor. Negroes who were unemployed or who committed minor misdemeanors were sentenced to prison terms. Once in prison, along with unfortunate poor whites, they were leased to private individuals who forced them to labor in the fields and mines, to do whatever work was most distasteful and for which a labor gap existed. This excerpt from The Cleveland Gazette *describes the sordid conditions in the Arkansas penitentiary.*

Last year the Board of Penitentiary Commissioners of Arkansas, consisting of the Governor, Secretary of State and Attorney General, investigated the treatment of the prisoners by the lessees of the penitentiary. They found near Coal Hill 149 convicts in a convict camp, 120 of whom worked in the mines. In a building ninety feet long by eighteen feet wide, all the convicts, black and white, sick and well, were huddled together at night in one room, on filthy straw, with but one flimsy blanket apiece, the beds reeking with vermin, and the stench overpowering.

They had worked all winter in water and the poisonous air of a coal mine, and slept in wet clothing. One of the wardens had whipped as many as seventy-five men in one night until the blood ran in a stream from their bodies. Some had been beaten to death. They found scores of men whose backs were covered with sores and frightfully mutilated. One colored man who had failed to accomplish his task had been shot dead in the mines. Another had been chained up by the neck, and left suspended until he was dead. . . .

The Cleveland Gazette, April 19, 1890.

John B. Rayner and the Rural Negroes

While many Negroes viewed their plight on the farm as one of serfdom, John B. Rayner of Texas foresaw Negroes returning to the rural areas because of equally poor or worse conditions in the cities. In this undated manuscript, Rayner wrote of the philosophy of education at Landonia College, Texas, which was similar to that advocated by Booker T. Washington at Tuskegee Institute in Alabama.

. . . The college is out of debt: but needs nine buildings to do the work the college can do. R. L. Smith the president of this college and president of The Farmer's Improvement Society is doing more for the moral, industrial and mental uplift of his race than any other Negro in Texas. R. L. Smith is wise, cautious & meek in his life and positive enough to make a good executive in his leadership.

The best lesson which the Landonia School teaches is the great necessity of being polite, truthful, honest, virtuous and industrious. . . .

The school also teaches how to make the farm a Modern Paradise. The Farmers Improvement Society believe that the farm is the best place for the Negro to evolve the highest order of good citizenship. The Negro on the farm is a King, in the city he is menial, or a loafer, or a professional. The white man's labor union, will soon drive the Negro laborers from the industries of the cities; from the saw mill plant, and from the coal mines, and then the Negro will be forced to return to his first love—the farm. The sheriffs and constables can not afford to protect the Negro laborers when white labor unions mob them, because the members of the white labor unions vote in the white man's primary and nominate these officers and the Negro can not. Back to the farms means a step forward into peace and prosperity. The worthy Negroes have not been noticed because they give the white man no trouble. . . .

Schomburg Collection, New York Public Library.

Frederick Douglass Seeks Aid for Hallie Quinn Brown

Hallie Quinn Brown was one of the few silver-tongued female orators of her day. Known as an elocutionist in the late nineteenth century, she lectured in the United States and Canada on behalf of her fellow Negroes. As professor of speech at Wilberforce College in Ohio, Miss Brown undertook to raise funds for the addition of a library to the school. When Miss Brown decided to travel to Europe to raise funds, Frederick Douglass wrote the following letter of introduction for her to his friends in Great Britain.

Cedar Hill
Washington, D.C.
October 5, 1894

To My British friends:

In writing you a few lines to introduce to your favorable consideration, Miss Hallie Q. Brown, the bearer of this paper, I assume that your interest in the cause of my much oppressed and persecuted people is unabated, and that you desire to do anything you can to improve their condition. Miss Brown has a laudable object in view, which she will lay before you. Namely: the founding of a library for the use of Wilberforce College, an institution which was originated by the colored people themselves more than forty years ago and which has been of great service in training colored youths of both sexes for upright and useful lives. It has sent forth many teachers, preachers and practical workers in the cause of mental, moral, religious and social progress among our people, and the prospect is that its efficiency in this work will go on with increasing vigor and success hereafter. The institution is in excellent hands and I feel sure that whatever you may be moved to donate towards the library in question will be wisely and honestly applied to that object. I think this is the last call for help. I shall even write to my transatlantic friends. Nearly fifty years ago you were asked to ransom one from American slavery and you did it and I have employed the liberty you bought for me in the cause of my people and I hope with your approval.

Truly yours,

Frederick Douglass

Hallie Q. Brown Collection, Central State University, Wilberforce, Ohio.

Negro Women: "Let Us Confer Together"

Sensing a need for unity in the struggle for equality, black women joined together in a national conference held in Boston in July 1895. This early conference resulted in the eventual formation of one of the oldest continuing organizations in Negro life, the National Association of Colored Women's Clubs. Included here is the call for the first meeting, which went out from Boston in 1895.

The coming together of our women from all over the country for consultation, for conference, for the personal exchange of greetings, which means so much in the way of encouragement and inspiration, has been a burning desire in the breasts of the colored women in every section of the United States.

The matter has been discussed and re-discussed. Of some things all are convinced—the need of such a conference is great, the benefit to be derived inevitable and inestimable. In view of this, we, the women of the Woman's Era Club of Boston, send forth, a call to our sisters all over the country, members of all clubs, societies, associations, and circles to take immediate action, looking towards the sending of delegates to this convention.

Boston has been selected as a meeting place because it has seemed to be the general opinion that here, and here only, can be found the atmosphere which would best interpret and represent us, our position, our needs, and our aims. One of the pressing needs of our cause is the education of the public to a just appreciation of us, and only here can we gain the attention upon which so much depends.

It is designed to hold the convention three days, the first of which will be given up to business, the second and third to the consideration of vital questions concerning our moral, mental, physical and financial growth and well-being, these to be presented through addresses by representative women.

Although this matter of a convention has been talked over for some time, the subject has been precipitated by a letter to England, written by a southern editor, and reflecting upon the moral character of all colored women; this letter is too indecent for publication, but a copy of it is sent with this call to all the women's bodies throughout the country. Read this document carefully and use discriminately and decide if it be not time for us to stand before the world and declare ourselves and our principles.

The time is short, but everything is ripe and remember, earnest women can do anything.

A circular letter will be sent you . . ..

Elizabeth Lindsay Davis, *Lifting As We Climb* (Chicago, 1933).

Booker T. Washington's Atlanta Exposition Speech

One of the most controversial speeches ever given by a black leader was the 1895 Atlanta Exposition Address of Booker T. Washington.

Here, for the first time in print, is the address as spoken by Mr. Washington before the large, integrated audience in Atlanta. The address, as prepared, was given to the press for publication. It was also recorded when delivered, and though the deviations from the printed copy are slight, it is interesting to read the address as it was actually heard on that day in 1895. The speech set off a controversy in Negro thought which has continued through the twentieth century. Ironically, the portion of the printed speech that urged Negroes to enter the vocational and trade areas, so highly criticized by Du Bois and others, was omitted from the spoken version.

Mr. President and Gentlemen of the Board of Directors and Citizens:

One-third of the population of the South is of the Negro race. No enterprise seeking the material, civil, or moral welfare of this section can disregard this element of our population and reach the highest success. I but convey to you, Mr. President and Directors, the sentiment of the masses of my race when I say that in no way have the value and manhood of the American Negro been more fittingly and generously recognized than by the managers of this magnificent exposition at every stage of its progress. It is a recognition that will do more to cement the friendship of the two races than any occurrence since the dawn of our freedom.

Not only this, but the opportunity here afforded will awaken among us a new era of industrial progress. Ignorant and inexperienced, it is not strange that in the first years of our new life we began at the top instead of at the bottom; that a seat in Congress or the state legislature was more sought than real estate or industrial skill; that the political convention or stump speaking had more attractions than starting a dairy farm or a truck garden.

A ship lost at sea for many days suddenly sighted a friendly vessel. From the mast of the unfortunate vessel was seen a signal, "Water, water; we die of thirst!" The answer from the friendly vessel at once came back, "Cast down your buckets where you are." A second time the signal, "Water, water; send us water!" ran up from the distressed vessel, and was answered, "Cast down your buckets where you are." A third and fourth signal for water was answered, "Cast down your buckets where you are." The captain of the distressed vessel, at last heeding the injunction, cast down his bucket, and it came up full of fresh, sparkling water from the mouth of the Amazon River. To those of my race who depend on bettering their condition in a foreign land or who underestimate the importance of cultivating friendly relations with the Southern white man, who is their next-door neighbor, I would say: "Cast down your bucket where you are"—cast it down in making friends in every manly way of the people of all races by whom we are surrounded.

To those of the white race who look to the incoming of those of foreign birth and strange tongue and habits for the prosperity of the South, were I permitted I would repeat what I say to my own race, "Cast down your bucket where you are." Cast it down among the eight millions of Negroes whose habits you know, whose fidelity and love you have tested in days when to have proved treacherous meant the ruin of your firesides. Cast down your bucket among these people who have, without strikes and labor wars, tilled your fields, cleared your forests, builded your railroads and cities, and brought forth treasures from the bowels of the earth, and helped make possible this magnificent representation of the progress of the South. Casting down your bucket among my people, helping and encouraging them as you are doing on these grounds, and to education of head, hand, and heart, you will find that they will buy your surplus land, make blossom the waste places in your fields, and run your factories. While doing this, you can be sure in the future, as in the past, that you and your families will be surrounded by the most patient, faithful, law-abiding, and unresentful people that the world has seen. As we have proved our loyalty to you in the past, in nursing your children, watching by the sick-bed of your mothers and fathers, and often following them with tear-dimmed eyes to their graves, so in the future, in our humble way, we shall stand by you with a devotion that no foreigner can approach, ready to lay down our lives, if need be, in defense of yours, interlacing our industrial, commercial, civil, and religious life with yours in a way that shall make the interests of both races one. In all things that are purely social we can be as separate as the fingers, yet one as the hand in all things essential to mutual progress.

There is no defense or security for any of us except in the highest intelligence and development of all. If anywhere there are efforts tending to curtail the fullest growth of the Negro, let these efforts be turned into stimulating, encouraging, and making him the most useful and intelligent citizen. Effort or means so invested will pay a thousand per cent interest. These efforts will be twice blessed—"blessing him that gives and him that takes."

There is no escape through law of man or God from the inevitable:—

> The laws of changeless justice bind
> Oppressor with oppressed;
> And close as sin and suffering joined
> We march to fate abreast.

Nearly sixteen millions of hands will aid you in pulling the load upward, or they will pull against you the load downward. We shall constitute one-third and more of the ignorance and crime of the South, or one-third its intelligence and progress; we shall contribute one-third to the business and industrial prosperity of the South, or we shall prove a veritable body of death, stagnating, depressing, retarding every effort to advance the body politic.

Gentlemen of the Exposition, as we present to you our humble effort at an exhibition of our progress, you must not expect overmuch. Starting thirty years ago with ownership here and there in a few quilts and pumpkins and chickens (gathered from miscellaneous sources), remember the path that has led from these to the inventions and production of agricultural implements, buggies, steam-engines, newspapers, books, statuary, carving, paintings, the management of drugstores and banks, has not been trodden without contact with thorns and thistles. While we take pride in what we exhibit as a result of our independent efforts, we do not for a moment forget that our part in this exhibition would fall far short of your expectations but for the constant help that has come to our educational life, not only from the southern states, but especially from northern philanthropists, who have made their gifts a constant stream of blessing and encouragement.

The wisest among my race understand that the agitation of questions of social equality is the extremest folly, and that progress in the environment of all the privileges that will come to us must be the result of severe and constant struggle rather than of artificial forcing. No race that has anything to contribute to the markets of the world is long in any degree ostracized. It is important and right that all privileges of the law be ours, but it is vastly more important that we be prepared for the exercises of these privileges. The opportunity to earn a dollar in a factory just now is worth infinitely more than the opportunity to spend a dollar in an opera house.

In conclusion, may I repeat that nothing in thirty years has given us more hope and encouragement and drawn us so near to you of the white race, as this opportunity offered by the Exposition; and here bending, as it were, over the altar that represents the results of the struggles of your race and mine, both starting practically empty-handed three decades ago, I pledge that in your effort to work out the great and intricate problem which God has laid at the doors of the South, you shall have at all times the patient, sympathetic help of my race. Only let this be constantly in mind: that, while from representations in these buildings of the product of field, of forest, of mine, of factory, letters, and art much good will come, yet far above and beyond material benefits will be that higher good, that, let us pray God, will come, in a blotting out of sectional differences and racial animosities and suspicions, in a determination to administer absolute justice, in a willing obedience among all classes to the mandates of law. This, coupled with our material prosperity, will bring into our beloved South a new heaven and a new earth.

Tape recording of the original RCA record, in the possession of the editor.

Susan B. Anthony Writes to Booker T. Washington

This letter was written by the famed suffragette Susan B. Anthony to Booker T. Washington following the visit of President William McKinley to Tuskegee Institute. Miss Anthony, who gained notoriety for her role in the woman suffrage movement, was also active in the struggle for Negro suffrage.

Dec. 19, 1898.

Mr. and Mrs. Booker T. Washington,
Tuskegee, Ala.

My Dear Friends:—

I am despatching to you a set of my biography, both for yourself and for the library of your splendid school.

I should very much like to have been present when you were escorting the President through the different departments of your institution. It must have made him and the members of his cabinet realize something of the work you are doing for the education and elevation of the colored people of the South.

You have of course noticed the proscription of the Chinese and Japanese from citizenship in the proposed government of the new Territory of Hawaii, and I hope you have also noticed the invidious shutting out of all women from the right to vote or to hold office there. Both propositions, I hope, will be repudiated by Congress, and if not I shall hope that President McKinley will veto the bill on the ground of the preliminary constitution violation of the fundamental principles of our government.

I trust that you are well, and that your family and your school are all prospering. Please accept my kind regards and Christmas greetings for all who abide with you.

Very sincerely yours,

Susan B. Anthony

Booker T. Washington Papers, Library of Congress.

Harriet Tubman Seeks a Pension

Harriet Tubman, one of the most courageous women of her time, was a conductor on the Underground Railroad prior to the Civil War. During the war, she served as scout, nurse and adviser to the Union Army. In 1898, thirty-three years after her service had ended, she petitioned the United States government for her bonus pay based on the services she had performed.

I am about 75 years of age. I was born and reared in Dorchester County, Md. My maiden name was Araminta Ross. Sometime prior to the late War of the Rebellion I married John Tubman who died in the State of Maryland on the 30th day of September, 1867. I married Nelson Davis, a soldier of the late war, on the 18th day of March, 1869, at Auburn, N.Y.

I furnished the original papers in my claim to one Charles P. Wood, then of Auburn, N.Y., who died several years ago. Said Wood made copies of said original papers which are herewith annexed. I was informed by said Wood that he sent said original papers to one James Barrett, an attorney on 4½ Street, Washington, D.C., and I was told by the wife of said Barrett that she handed the original papers to the Hon. C. D. MacDougall, then a member of the House of Representatives.

My claim against the U.S. is for three years' service as nurse and cook in hospitals, and as commander of several men (eight or nine) as scouts during the late War of the Rebellion, under directions and orders of Edwin M. Stanton, Secretary of War, and of several Generals.

I claim for my services above named the sum of eighteen hundred dollars. The annexed copies have recently been read over to me and are true to the best of my knowledge, information and belief.

Earl Conrad, "The Charles P. Wood Manuscripts of Harriet Tubman," *Negro History Bulletin,* XIII (January 1950).

Plessy v. *Ferguson*

A "black" man who was seven-eighths white was arrested for riding on a Louisiana train in a section reserved for "whites only." Homer Plessy was the man, and he symbolized a turning point in American Negro history. Protected on paper by the Fourteenth Amendment, blacks had not long enjoyed their constitutional privileges before new and more subtle means of segregation were found to limit their liberties. This shift in attitudes eventually found its way to the Supreme Court of the United States. In 1896, seven justices (with one not voting) upheld the Louisiana conviction of Plessy and further ruled that segregation could be practiced if the facilities were "separate but equal." The lone dissenter, Justice John Marshall Harlan, in a prophetic statement envisioned the trend that would follow this lawful separation of the races.

It was said in argument that the statute of Louisiana does not discriminate against either race, but prescribes a rule applicable alike to white and colored citizens. But this argument does not meet the difficulty. Every one knows that the statute in question had its origin in the purpose, not so much to exclude white persons from railroad cars occupied by blacks, as to exclude colored people from coaches occupied by or assigned to white persons. Railroad corporations of Louisiana did not make discrimination among whites in the matter of accommodation for travellers. The thing to accomplish was, under the guise of giving equal accommodation for white and blacks, to compel the latter to keep to themselves while travelling in railroad passenger coaches. No one would be so wanting in candor as to assert the contrary. The fundamental objection, therefore, to the statute is that it interferes with the personal freedom of citizens. "Personal liberty," it has been well said, "consists in the power of locomotion, of changing situations, or removing one's person to whatsoever places one's own inclination may direct, without imprisonment or restraint, unless by due course of law." If a white man and a black man choose to occupy the same public conveyance on a public highway, it is their right to do so, and no government, proceeding alone on grounds of race, can prevent it without infringing the personal liberty of each.

It is one thing for railroad carriers to furnish, or to be required by law to furnish, equal accommodations for all whom they are under a legal duty to carry. It is quite another thing for government to forbid citizens of the white and black races from travelling in the same public conveyance, and to punish officers of railroad companies for permitting persons of the two races to occupy the same passenger coach. If a State can prescribe, as a rule of civil conduct, that whites and blacks shall not travel as passengers in the same railroad coach, why may it not so regulate the use of the streets of its cities and towns as to compel white citizens to keep on one side of a street and black citizens to keep on the other? Why may it not, upon like grounds, punish whites and blacks who ride together in street cars or in open vehicles on a public road or street? Why may it not require sheriffs to assign whites to one side of a court-room and blacks to the other? And why may it not also prohibit the commingling of the two races in the galleries of legislative halls or in public assemblages convened for the consideration of the political questions of the day? Further, if this statute of Louisiana is consistent with the personal liberty of citizens, why may not the State require the separation in railroad coaches of native and naturalized citizens of the United States, or of Protestants and Roman Catholics? . . .

The white race deems itself to be the dominant race in this country. And so it is, in prestige, in achievements, in education, in wealth and in power. So, I doubt not, it will continue to be for all time, if it remains true to its great heritage and holds fast to the principles of constitutional liberty. But in view of the Constitution, in the eye of the law, there is in this country no superior, dominant, ruling class of citizens. There is no caste here. Our Constitution is color-blind, and neither knows nor tolerates classes among citizens. In respect of civil rights, all citizens are equal before the law. The humblest is the peer of the most powerful. The law regards man as man, and takes no account of his surroundings or of his color when his civil rights as guaranteed by the supreme law of the land are involved. It is, therefore, to be regretted that this high tribunal, the final expositor of the fundamental law of the land, has reached the conclusion that it is competent for a State to regulate the enjoyment by citizens of their civil rights solely upon the basis of race.

In my opinion, the judgment this day rendered will, in time, prove to be quite as pernicious as the decision made by this tribunal in the *Dred Scott* case. It was adjudged in that case that the descendants of Africans who were imported into this country and sold as slaves were not included nor intended to be included under the word "citizens" in the Constitution, and could not claim any of the rights and privileges which that instrument provided for and secured to citizens of the United States; that at the time of the adoption of the Constitution they were "considered as a subordinate and inferior class of beings, who had been subjugated by the dominant race and, whether emancipated or not, yet remained subject to their authority, and had no rights or privileges but such as those who held the power and the government might choose to grant them." The recent amendments of the Constitution, it was supposed, had eradicated these principles from our institutions. But it seems that we have yet, in some of the States, a dominant race—a superior class of citizens, which assumes to regulate the enjoyment of civil rights, common to all citizens, upon the basis of race. The present decision, it may well be apprehended, will not only stimulate aggressions, more or less brutal and irritating, upon the admitted rights of colored citizens, but will encourage the belief that it is possible, by means of state enactments, to defeat the beneficent purposes which the people of the United States had in view when they adopted the recent amendments of the Constitution, by one of which the blacks of this country were made citizens of the United States and of the States in which they respectively reside, and whose privileges and immunities, as citizens, the States are forbidden to abridge. Sixty millions of whites are in no danger from the presence here of eight millions of blacks. The destinies of the two races, in this country, are indissolubly linked together, and the interests of both require that the common government of all shall not permit the seeds of race hate to be planted under the sanction of law. What can more certainly arouse race hate, what more certainly create and perpetuate a feeling of distrust between these races, than state enactments, which, in fact, proceed on the ground that colored citizens are so inferior and degraded that they cannot be allowed to sit in public coaches occupied by white citizens? That, as all will admit, is the real meaning of such legislation as was enacted in Louisiana.

The sure guarantee of the peace and security of each race is the clear, distinct, unconditional recognition by our governments, National and State, of every right that inheres in civil freedom, and of the equality before the law of all citizens of the United States without regard to race. State enactments, regulating the enjoyment of civil rights, upon the basis of race, and cunningly devised to defeat legitimate results of the war, under the pretence of recognizing equality of rights, can have no other result than to render permanent peace impossible, and to keep alive a conflict of races, the continuance of which must do harm to all concerned. This question is not met by the suggestion that social equality cannot exist between the white and black races in this country. That argument, if it can be properly regarded as one, is scarcely worthy of consideration; for social equality no more exists between two races when travelling in a passenger coach or a public highway than when members of the same races sit by each other in a street car or in the jury box, or stand or sit with each other in a political assembly, or when they use in common the streets of a city or town, or when they are in the same room for the purpose of having their names placed on the registry of voters, or when they approach the ballot-box in order to exercise the high privilege of voting.

There is a race so different from our own that we do not permit those belonging to it to become citizens of the United States. Persons belonging to it are, with few exceptions, absolutely excluded from our country. I allude to the Chinese race. But by the statute in question, a Chinaman can ride in the same passenger coach with white citizens of the United States, while citizens of the black race in Louisiana, many of whom, perhaps, risked their lives for the preservation of the Union, who are entitled, by law, to participate in the political control of the State and nation, who are not excluded, by law or by reason of their race, from public stations of any kind, and who have all the legal rights that belong to white citizens, are yet declared to be criminals, liable to imprisonment, if they ride in a public coach occupied by citizens of the white race. It is scarcely just to say that a colored citizen should not object to occupying a public coach assigned to his own race. He does not object, nor, perhaps, would he object to separate coaches for his race, if his rights under the law were recognized. But he objects, and ought never to cease objecting to the proposition, that citizens of the white and black races can be adjudged criminals because they sit, or claim the right to sit, in the same public coach on a public highway.

The arbitrary separation of citizens, on the basis of race, while they are on a public highway, is a badge of servitude wholly inconsistent with the civil freedom and the equality before the law established by the Constitution. It cannot be justified upon any legal grounds.

If evils will result from the commingling of the two races upon public highways established for the benefit of all, they will be infinitely less than those that will surely come from state legislation regulating the enjoyment of civil rights upon the basis of race. We boast of the freedom enjoyed by our people above all other peoples. But it is difficult to reconcile that boast with a state of the law which, practically, puts the brand of servitude and degradation upon a large class of our fellow-citizens, our equals before the law. The thin disguise of "equal" accommodations for passengers in railroad coaches will not mislead any one, nor atone for the wrong this day done.

The result of the whole matter is, that while this court has frequently adjudged, and at the present term has recognized the doctrine, that a State cannot, consistently with the Constitution of the United States, prevent white and black citizens, having the required qualifications for jury service, from sitting in the same jury box, it is now solemnly held that a State may prohibit white and black citizens from sitting in the same passenger coach on a public highway, or may require that they be separated by a "partition," when in the same passenger coach. May it not now be reasonably expected that astute men of the dominant race, who affect to be disturbed at the possibility that the integrity of the white race may be corrupted, or that its supremacy will be imperilled, by contact on public highways with black people, will endeavor to procure statutes requiring white and black jurors to be separated in the jury box by a "partition," and that, upon retiring from the court room to consult as to their verdict, such partition, if it be a moveable one, shall be taken to their consultation room, and set up in such way as to prevent black jurors from coming too close to their brother jurors of the white race? If the "partition" used in the court room happens to be stationary, provision could be made for screens with openings through which jurors of the two races could confer as to their verdict without coming into personal contact with each other. I cannot see but that, according to the principles this day announced, such state legislation, although conceived in hostility to, and enacted for the purpose of humiliating citizens of the United States of a particular race, would be held to be consistent with the Constitution.

I do not deem it necessary to review the decisions of state courts to which reference was made in argument. Some, and the most important, of them are wholly inapplicable, because rendered prior to the adoption of the last amendments of the Constitution, when colored people had very few rights which the dominant race felt obliged to respect. Others were made at a time when public opinion, in many localities, was dominated by the institution of slavery; when it would not have been safe to do justice to the black man; and when, so far as the rights of blacks were concerned, race prejudice was, practically, the supreme law of the land. Those decisions cannot be guides in the era introduced by the recent amendments of the supreme law, which established universal civil freedom, gave citizenship to all born or naturalized in the United States and residing here, obliterated the race line from our systems of governments, National and State, and placed our free institutions upon the broad and sure foundation of the equality of all men before the law.

I am of opinion that the statute of Louisiana is inconsistent with the personal liberty of citizens, white and black, in that State, and hostile to both the spirit and letter of the Constitution of the United States. If laws of like character should be enacted in the several States of the Union, the effect would be in the highest degree mischievous. Slavery, as an institution tolerated by law would, it is true, have disappeared from our country, but there would remain a power in the States, by sinister legislation, to interfere with the full enjoyment of the blessings of freedom; to regulate civil rights, common to all citizens, upon the basis of race; and to place in a condition of legal inferiority a large body of American citizens, now constituting a part of the political community called the People of the United States, for whom, and by whom through representatives, our government is administered. Such a system is inconsistent with the guarantee given by the Constitution to each State of a republican form of government, and may be stricken down by Congressional action, or by the courts in the discharge of their solemn duty to maintain the supreme law of the land, anything in the constitution or laws of any State to the contrary notwithstanding.

For the reasons stated, I am constrained to withhold my assent for the opinion and judgment of the majority.

Plessy v. *Ferguson,* 163 U.S. 537 (1896).

SECTION III

March on, and you shall gain the victory,
March on, and you shall gain the day.

Way over in the Egypt land,
You shall gain the victory;
Way over in the Egypt land,
You shall gain the day.

When Peter was preaching at the Pentecost,
You shall gain the victory;
He was endowed with the Holy Ghost,
You shall gain the day.

When Peter was fishing in the sea,
You shall gain the victory;
He dropped his net and followed me,
You shall gain the day.

King Jesus on the mountain top,
You shall gain the victory;
King Jesus speaks and the chariot stops,
You shall gain the day.

THE CRISIS

A RECORD OF THE DARKER RACES

Volume One | NOVEMBER, 1910 | Number One

Edited by W. E. BURGHARDT DU BOIS, with the co-operation of Oswald Garrison Villard, J. Max Barber, Charles Edward Russell, Kelly Miller, W. S. Braithwaite and M. D. Maclean.

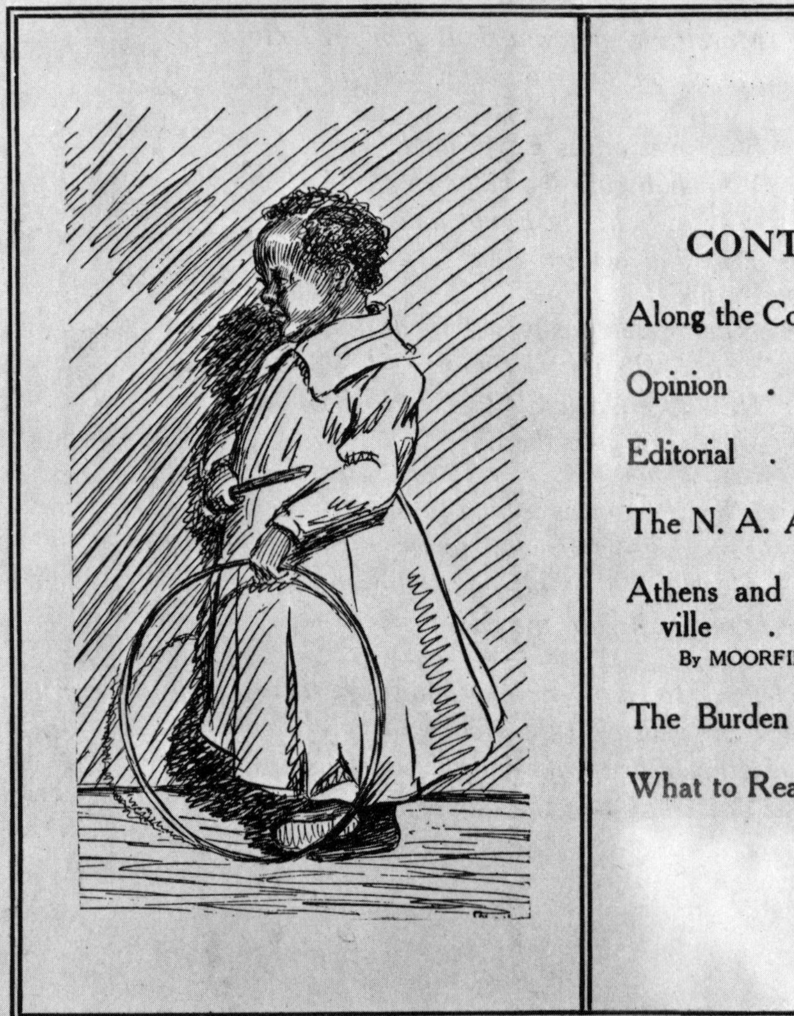

CONTENTS

PUBLISHED MONTHLY BY THE

National Association for the Advancement of Colored People

AT TWENTY VESEY STREET NEW YORK CITY

ONE DOLLAR A YEAR TEN CENTS A COPY

Library of Congress

I Have a Dream

IN THE TWENTIETH CENTURY, there were new voices raised in protest as a new breed of abolitionist joined with the black man in his quest for the guarantees he had long been promised but denied as basically the same theme prevailed in this country—that of prejudice and discrimination.

As events at the opening of the century swirled around the black population in the United States, a controversy developed within its ranks. Booker T. Washington, President of Tuskegee Institute in Alabama, had come to be considered by many as the spokesman for his race. The interpretation placed on his actions in this capacity was questioned by a growing number of Negroes who regarded themselves as better equipped to lead their people. Among them were William E. B. Du Bois, a recent graduate of Harvard and the University of Berlin, and Monroe Trotter, a militant Boston journalist. It is not the function of this volume to evaluate either Washington or Du Bois, but it should be noted that recent historiography indicates that Washington was not the "Uncle Tom" alleged by his detractors. The documentation for this point of view awaits the publication of Washington's voluminous works, now in process under the editorship of Professor Louis R. Harlan. Therefore, the sections represented in this volume merely reflect the attitudes of Du Bois and Trotter, based on their interpretation of Washington's philosophy.

The positive result that developed from the controversy between Washington and Du Bois was the growing sense of security that Negroes felt within their own group since they were permitting divisions to occur within the ranks. However, the dissident voices did little to advance the status of the black man, as it maintained its all-time low since the gaining of freedom.

Conditions in the South were still barely tolerable for most Negroes. The rise of the sharecropping system, which was the white man's response to the abolition of slavery, rarely allowed the blacks to maintain a subsistence level of existence. Often women and children worked in the fields, with or without a man in the family, to stave off the pangs of hunger that did not adjust to the Negro's "place" in society.

The public education system, which had been established by the Reconstruction governments, operated on the principle established in the *Plessy* v. *Ferguson* decision—"separate but equal." The operation of this arrangement provided that separation be firmly enforced, but not equality. If black children attended school at all, they were usually herded together in a one-room broken-down shack with a teacher who had also been a product of the separate and unequal educational system.

In the North, as more and more blacks were learning, things were not much better. There was the lurking hostility of the white workers toward the immigrant blacks from the South and the subtle prejudices that kept Negroes confined to ghetto areas; and the slogan popularized during the Depression—"last hired, first fired"—had long been in operation as an established policy.

Black men followed in the tradition of their predecessors and continued to serve their country on the battlefields and in military service in both World Wars. Prejudice followed the same tradition—and the fruits of strife were borne in race riots at locations where black soldiers were stationed. The opening of the twentieth century, however, had seen the rise of new and more enduring organizations that were destined to play a major role in the later chapters of Negro history. The National Association for the Advancement of Colored People, a biracial group founded in 1909, and the Urban League, also composed of whites and blacks to help migrating Negroes find homes and jobs, were the beginnings of a formalized activity that developed into permanent institutions. Splinter groups and leaders held the spotlight for a brief period, advocating the black unity concept advanced by Marcus Garvey and the "heavens" of Father Divine. When race relations reached a particular low point, local groups often formed societies based on protecting one another from the verbal and physical assaults of whites.

The need for recording the past achievements, as well as the indignities of blacks, was recognized by Carter G. Woodson, who organized the Association for the Study of Negro Life and History in 1915. Woodson, a guiding light in the preservation of the records of free and literate Negroes, began a trend that gathered momentum as the civil rights movement began in American life.

The growth of the nation's economic system in the 1920's provided jobs for blacks and created mass migrations to major northern cities. The blight of the Depression caught all Americans off guard, but Negroes, because they were not just poor but also black, were the major recipients of the Depression's misery. The election of Franklin D. Roosevelt, and his subsequent New Deal programs, brought an end to the Depression and, furthermore, a new beginning to the progress of the Negro in the United States.

Soon after the New Deal started to become effective, the country again engaged in a world war, the second of the century. The first one, fought "to make the world safe for democracy," had accomplished little toward that end, especially where blacks were concerned. The second war, however, resulted in new concepts and brought peoples together in a more united way as they sought to save their nation from invasion and attack. From it all emerged a new philosophy. Granted that this philosophy was mostly articulated, rather than implemented, Negroes had by now sufficiently overcome their quasi-slavery attitude, and they listened to the new voices of democracy and equality with ears attuned to the same strains of freedom that their forefathers heard when the guns sounded at Fort Sumter.

The political leadership of the country heard their protests, and a new mood gradually developed in the country. This resulted in a concerted effort that involved people of all complexions to overcome the existing racial barriers and to work, for a time at least, toward the "one world" idea advanced by Wendell Willkie in the 1940's. Legislation, however, was passed, grimly representative of the types enacted during Reconstruction, but the Supreme Court assumed the role that had been abdicated by Congress and eliminated the dual "separate but equal" concepts of education. The Court was not able to abolish the reality of these principles, however, and they continued to be practiced in much the same way as before the Brown case was heard.

New and more militant civil rights groups evolved, led by men who would not be threatened into submission. For a time, it seemed as if the struggle had been won and the Negro was to be free at last. Many martyrs were made in the midst of the civil rights revolution, but, like John Copeland, they felt they had not died in vain. Probably the most prominent leader since the days of Frederick Douglass, Martin Luther King, Jr., became a legend in American history by the way he lived and died for his people. But even King's sacrifice was not enough; blacks became disenchanted with the gains they felt should rightfully be theirs, while whites grew tired of the many demands made upon them—not realizing the depth of the poverty and privation, emotional, financial and educational, that blacks still suffered. A lack of communication seemed to be developing between the two races as members of the far right in each group became the most articulate.

While the civil rights revolution has been raging, however, a large black middle class has emerged. More Negroes are going to college than ever before; more are moving out of the ghetto to better housing; and lynching—the dreaded word of the first half of the twentieth century—is almost nonexistent. Opportunities for jobs in dignified positions have opened; the military has changed its restrictive policies and eliminated segregation among its troops. Teachers, ministers and other members of the black middle class have reached back into the ghetto in an attempt to touch the lives of those they left behind, and a black senator once more sits in Congress, and sixteen Negroes serve in the House. The cycle of Negro history, from the Reconstruction period to the present, is complete.

Freedom! Freedom! Oh freedom over me
Before I'd be a slave,
I'd be buried in my grave
And go home to my maker and be free.

A Southern Negro Woman on Her Life in the South

This anonymous letter written by a black woman in the South depicts the harsh and degrading conditions under which many Negro families were forced to live.

. . . I am a colored woman, wife and mother. I have lived all my life in the South, and have often thought what a peculiar fact it is that the more ignorant the Southern whites are of us the more vehement they are in their denunciation of us. They boast that they have little intercourse with us, never see us in our homes, churches or places of amusement, but still they know us thoroughly.

They also admit that they know us in no capacity except as servants, yet they say we are at our best in that single capacity. What philosophers they are! The Southerners say we Negroes are a happy, laughing set of people, with no thought of tomorrow. How mistaken they are! The educated, thinking Negro is just the opposite. There is a feeling of unrest, insecurity, almost panic among the best class of Negroes in the South. In our homes, in our churches, wherever two or three are gathered together, there is a discussion of what is best to do. Must we remain in the South or go elsewhere? Where can we go to feel that security which other people feel? Is it best to go in great numbers or only in several families? These and many other things are discussed over and over. . . .

I know of houses occupied by poor Negroes in which a respectable farmer would not keep his cattle. It is impossible for them to rent elsewhere. All Southern real estate agents have "white property" and "colored property." In one of the largest Southern cities there is a colored minister, a graduate of Harvard, whose wife is an educated, Christian woman, who lived for weeks in a tumble-down rookery because he could neither rent nor buy in a respectable locality.

Many colored women who wash, iron, scrub, cook or sew all the week to help pay the rent for these miserable hovels and help fill the many small mouths, would deny themselves some of the necessaries of life if they could take their little children and teething babies on the cars to the parks of a Sunday afternoon and sit under the trees, enjoy the cool breezes and breathe God's pure air for only two or three hours; but this is denied them. Some of the parks have signs, "No Negroes allowed on these grounds except as servants." Pitiful, pitiful customs and laws that make war on women and babes! There is no wonder that we die; the wonder is that we persist in living.

Fourteen years ago I had just married. My husband had saved sufficient money to buy a small home. On account of our limited means we went to the suburbs, on unpaved streets, to look for a home, only asking for a high, healthy locality. Some real estate agents were "sorry, but had nothing to suit," some had "just the thing," but we discovered on investigation that they had "just the thing" for an unhealthy pigsty. Others had no "colored property." One agent said that he had what we wanted, but we should have to go to see the lot after dark, or walk by and give the place a casual look; for, he said, "all the white people in the neighborhood would be down on me." Finally we bought this lot. When the house was being built we went to see it. Consternation reigned. We had ruined this neighborhood of poor people; poor as we, poorer in manners at least. The people who lived next door received the sympathy of their friends. When we walked on the street (there were no sidewalks) we were embarrassed by the stare of many unfriendly eyes.

Two years passed before a single woman spoke to me, and only then because I helped one of them when a little sudden trouble came to her. Such was the reception, I a happy young woman, just married, received from people among whom I wanted to make a home. Fourteen years have now passed, four children have been born to us, and one has died in this same home, among these same neighbors. Although the neighbors speak to us, and occasionally one will send a child to borrow the morning's paper or ask the loan of a pattern, not one woman has ever been inside of my house, not even at the times when a woman would doubly appreciate the slightest attention of a neighbor. . . .

A noble man, who has established rescue homes for fallen women all over the country, visited a Southern city. The women of the city were invited to meet him in one of the churches. The fallen women were especially invited and both good and bad went. They sat wherever they could find a seat, so long as their faces were white; but I, a respectable married woman, was asked to sit apart. A colored woman, however respectable, is lower than the white prostitute. The Southern white woman will declare that no Negro women are virtuous, yet she places her innocent children in their care. . . .

White agents and other chance visitors who come into our homes ask questions that we must not dare ask their wives. They express surprise that our children have clean faces and that their hair is combed. . . .

We were delighted to know that some of our Spanish-American heroes were coming where we could get a glimpse of them. Had not black men helped in a small way to give them their honors? In the cities of the South, where these heroes went, the white school children were assembled, flags were waved, flowers strewn, speeches made, and "My Country, 'tis of Thee, Sweet Land of Liberty," was sung. Our children who need to be taught so much, were not assembled, their hands waved no flags, they threw no flowers, heard no thrilling speech, sang no song of their country. And this is the South's idea of justice. Is it surprising that feeling grows more bitter, when the white mother teaches her boy to hate my boy, not because he is mean, but because his skin is dark? I have seen very small white children hang their black dolls. It is not the child's fault, he is simply an apt pupil. . . .

"The Negro Problem: How It Appears to a Southern Colored Woman," *Independent,* LIV (September 18, 1902).

Du Bois on Washington: A Controversy

At the turn of the century, a controversy developed between Booker T. Washington and the younger black intellectuals, notably, W. E. B. Du Bois. The latter took issue with Washington on several matters regarding relations between the races. In the following excerpt from Dusk of Dawn, *Du Bois explains his point of view.*

Since the controversy between myself and Mr. Washington has become historic, it deserves more careful statement than it has had hitherto, both as to the matters and the motives involved. There was first of all the ideological controversy. I believed in the higher education of a Talented Tenth who through their knowledge of modern culture could guide the American Negro into a higher civilization. I knew that without this the Negro would have to accept white leadership, and that such leadership could not always be trusted to guide this group into self-realization and to its highest cultural possibilities. Mr. Washington, on the other hand, believed that the Negro as an efficient worker could gain wealth and that eventually through his ownership of capital he would be able to achieve a recognized place in American culture and could then educate his children as he might wish and develop his possibilities. For this reason he proposed to put the emphasis at present upon training in the skilled trades and encouragement in industry and common labor.

These two theories of Negro progress were not absolutely contradictory. I recognized the importance of the Negro gaining a foothold in trades and his encouragement in industry and common labor. Mr. Washington was not absolutely opposed to college training, and sent his own children to college. But he did minimize its importance, and discouraged the philanthropic support of higher education; while I openly and repeatedly criticized what seemed to me the poor work and small accomplishment of the Negro industrial school. Moreover, it was characteristic of the Washington statesmanship that whatever he or anybody believed or wanted must be subordinated to dominant public opinion and that opinion deferred to and cajoled until it allowed a deviation toward better ways. This is no new thing in the world, but it is always dangerous.

But beyond this difference of ideal lay another and more bitter and insistent controversy. This started with the rise at Tuskegee Institute, and centering around Booker T. Washington, of what I may call the Tuskegee Machine. Of its existence and work, little has ever been said and almost nothing written. The years from 1899 to 1905 marked the culmination of the career of Booker T. Washington. In 1899 Mr. Washington, Paul Laurence Dunbar, and myself spoke on the same platform at the Hollis Street Theatre, Boston, before a distinguished audience. Mr. Washington was not at his best and friends immediately raised a fund which sent him to Europe for a three months' rest. . . .

Returning to America he became during the administrations of Theodore Roosevelt and William Taft, from 1901 to 1912, the political referee in all Federal appointments or action taken with reference to the Negro and in many regarding the white South. In 1903 Andrew Carnegie made the future of Tuskegee certain by a gift of $600,000. There was no question of Booker T. Washington's undisputed leadership of the ten million Negroes in America, a leadership recognized gladly by the whites and conceded by most of the Negroes.

But there were discrepancies and paradoxes in this leadership. It did not seem fair, for instance, that on the one hand Mr. Washington should decry political activities among Negroes, and on the other hand dictate Negro political objectives from Tuskegee. At a time when Negro civil rights called for organized and aggressive defense, he broke down that defense by advising acquiescence or at least no open agitation. During the period when laws disfranchising the Negro were being passed in all the Southern states, between 1890 and 1909, and when these were being supplemented by "Jim Crow" travel laws and other enactments making color caste legal, his public speeches, while they did not entirely ignore this development, tended continually to excuse it, to emphasize the shortcomings of the Negro, and were interpreted widely as putting the chief onus for his condition upon the Negro himself.

All this naturally aroused increasing opposition among Negroes and especially among the younger classes of educated Negroes, who were beginning to emerge here and there, especially from Northern institutions. This opposition began to become vocal in 1901 when two men, Monroe Trotter, Harvard 1895, and George Forbes, Amherst 1895, began the publication of the Boston *Guardian*. The *Guardian* was bitter, satirical, and personal; but it was well-edited, it was earnest, and it published facts. It attracted wide attention among colored people; it circulated among them all over the country; it was quoted and discussed. I did not wholly agree with the *Guardian,* and indeed only a few Negroes did, but nearly all read it and were influenced by it.

This beginning of organized opposition, together with other events, led to the growth at Tuskegee of what I have called the Tuskegee Machine. It arose first quite naturally. Not only did presidents of the United States consult Booker Washington, but governors and congressmen; philanthropists conferred with him, scholars wrote to him. Tuskegee became a vast information bureau and center of advice. It was not merely passive in these matters but, guided by a young unobtrusive minor official who was also intelligent, suave and far-seeing, active efforts were made to concentrate influence at Tuskegee. After a time almost no Negro institution could collect funds without the recommendation or acquiescence of Mr. Washington. Few political appointments were made anywhere in the United States without his consent. Even the careers of rising young colored men were very often determined by his advice and certainly his opposition was fatal. How much Mr. Washington knew of this work of the Tuskegee Machine and was directly responsible, one cannot say, but of its general activity and scope he must have been aware.

Moreover, it must not be forgotten that this Tuskegee Machine was not solely the idea and activity of black folk at Tuskegee. It was largely encouraged and given financial aid through certain white groups and individuals in the North. This Northern group had clear objectives. They were capitalists and employers and yet in most cases sons, relatives, or friends of the abolitionists who had sent teachers into the new Negro South after the war. These younger men believed that the Negro problem could not remain a matter of philanthropy. It must be a matter of business. These Negroes were not to be encouraged as voters in the new democracy, nor were they to be left at the mercy of the reactionary South. They were good laborers and they might be better. They could become a strong labor force and properly guided they would restrain the unbridled demands of white labor, born of the Northern labor unions and now spreading to the South.

One danger must be avoided and that was to allow the silly idealism of Negroes, half-trained in Southern missionary "colleges," to mislead the mass of laborers and keep them stirred-up by ambitions incapable of realization. To this school of thought, the philosophy of Booker Washington came as a godsend and it proposed by building up his prestige and power to control the Negro group. The control was to be drastic. The Negro intelligentsia was to be suppressed and hammered into conformity. The process involved some cruelty and disappointment, but that was inevitable. This was the real force back of the Tuskegee Machine. It had money and it had opportunity, and it found in Tuskegee tools to do its bidding. . . . Contrary to most opinion, the controversy as it developed was not entirely against Mr. Washington's ideas, but became the insistence upon the right of other Negroes to have and express their ideas. Things came to such a pass that when any Negro complained or advocated a course of action, he was silenced with the remark that Mr. Washington did not agree with this. . . .

It was this point, and not merely disagreement with Mr. Washington's plans, that brought eventually violent outbreak. It was more than opposition to a program of education. It was opposition to a system and that system was part of the economic development of the United States at the time. The fight cut deep: it went into social relations; it divided friends; it made bitter enemies. I can remember that years later, when I went to live in New York and was once invited to a social gathering among Brooklyn colored people, one of the most prominent Negroes of the city refused to be present because of my former attitude toward Mr. Washington.

When the *Guardian* began to increase in influence, determined effort was made to build up a Negro press for Tuskegee. Already Tuskegee filled the horizon so far as national magazines and the great newspapers were concerned. In 1901 the *Outlook,* then the leading weekly, chose two distinguished Americans for autobiographies. Mr. Washington's "Up from Slavery" was so popular that it was soon published and circulated all over the earth. Thereafter, every magazine editor sought articles with his signature and publishing houses continued to ask for books. A number of talented "ghost writers," black and white, took service under Tuskegee, and books and articles poured out of the institution. An annual letter "To My People" went out from Tuskegee to the press. Tuskegee became the capital of the Negro nation. Negro newspapers were influenced and finally the oldest and largest was bought by white friends of Tuskegee. Most of the other papers found it to their advantage certainly not to oppose Mr. Washington, even if they did not wholly agree with him. Negroes who sought high positions groveled for his favor.

I was greatly disturbed at this time, not because I was in absolute opposition to the things that Mr. Washington was advocating, but because I was strongly in favor of more open agitation against wrongs and above all I resented the practical buying up of the Negro press and choking off of even mild and reasonable opposition to Mr. Washington in both the Negro press and the white. . . .

[Later], I received an invitation to join Mr. Washington and certain prominent white and colored friends in a conference to be held in New York. The conference was designed to talk over a common program for the American Negro and evidently it was hoped that the growing division of opinion and opposition to Mr. Washington within the ranks of Negroes would thus be overcome. I was enthusiastic over the idea. It seemed to me just what was needed to clear the air.

There was difficulty, however, in deciding what persons ought to be invited to the conference, how far it should include Mr. Washington's extreme opponents, or how far it should be composed principally of his friends. There ensued a long delay and during this time it seemed to me that I ought to make my own position clearer than I had hitherto. I was increasingly uncomfortable under the statements of Mr. Washington's position: his depreciation of the value of the vote; his evident dislike of Negro colleges; and his general attitude which seemed to place the onus of blame for the status of Negroes upon the Negroes themselves rather than upon the whites. And above all, I resented the Tuskegee Machine.

I had been asked sometime before by A. C. McClurg and Company of Chicago if I did not have some material for a book; I planned a social study which should be perhaps a summing up of the work of the Atlanta Conferences, or at any rate, a scientific investigation. They asked, however, if I did not have some essays that they might put together and issue immediately, mentioning my articles in the *Atlantic Monthly* and other places. I demurred because books of essays almost always fall so flat. Nevertheless, I got together a number of my fugitive pieces. I then added a chapter, "Of Mr. Booker T. Washington and Others," in which I sought to make a frank evaluation of Booker T. Washington. I left out the more controversial matter: the bitter resentment which young Negroes felt at the continued and increasing activity of the Tuskegee Machine. I concentrated my thought and argument on Mr. Washington's general philosophy. As I read that statement now, a generation later, I am satisfied with it. I see no word that I would change. The *Souls of Black Folk* was published in 1903 and is still selling today.

My book settled pretty definitely any further question of my going to Tuskegee as an employee. But it also drew pretty hard and fast lines about my future career. Meantime, the matter of the conference in New York dragged on until finally in October, 1903, a circular letter was sent out setting January, 1904, as the date of meeting. The conference took place accordingly in Carnegie Hall, New York. About fifty persons were present, most of them colored and including many well-known persons. There was considerable plain speaking but the whole purpose of the conference seemed revealed by the invited guests and the tone of their message. Several white persons of high distinction came to speak to us, including Andrew Carnegie and Lyman Abbott. Their words were lyric, almost fulsome in praise of Mr. Washington and his work, and in support of his ideas. Even if all they said had been true, it was a wrong note to strike in a conference of conciliation. The conferences ended with two speeches by Mr. Washington and myself, and the appointment of a Committee of Twelve in which we were also included.

The Committee of Twelve which was thus instituted was unable to do any effective work as a steering committee for the Negro race in America. First of all, it was financed, through Mr. Washington, probably by Mr. Carnegie. This put effective control of the committee in Mr. Washington's hands. It was organized during my absence and laid down a plan of work which seemed to me of some value but of no lasting importance and having little to do with the larger questions and issues. I, therefore, soon resigned so as not to be responsible for work and pronouncements over which I would have little influence. . . .

W. E. B. Du Bois, *Dusk of Dawn* (New York, 1968).

Monroe Trotter Criticizes Booker T. Washington

In 1903, Booker T. Washington called for a conference of men of both races, from both the North and the South, to discuss the racial problems of the day. Monroe Trotter, another outspoken critic of Washington, questioned the need for such a meeting in his newspaper, The Guardian.

WHAT DOES BOOKER WANT WITH A CONFERENCE?

It is hard to say whether it is through fate, or the folly of his own foolhardiness that Mr. Booker Washington seems always doomed to come forth at the wrong juncture, yet it is a fact that the very untimeliness of that man in appearing at the wrong season is indeed most regular, and like the irregular movements of a comet can be told beforehand by computation. Said the great Athenian orator: "Is there anything in agitation for the interests of the country? Aeschines is mute. Does anything go wrong and disappoint expectations? Forth comes Aeschines; as old fractures and sprains annoy us afresh the moment the body is stricken with disease." Change the name of Aeschines to Booker Washington and the description is perfect. Of course it was not to be expected that after Secretary Root's pronouncement that the amendments have failed, Washington would maintain . . . silence. . . . He must now rush in. . . . And this he did thus in his New York speech Monday night.

"The age for settling great questions either social or national, with the shotgun, the torch, and by lynchings has passed. An appeal to such methods is unworthy of either race. I believe the time has come, and I believe it is a perfectly practical thing, when a group of representative southern white men, and northern white men, and Negroes, should meet and consider with the greatest calmness and business sagacity the whole subject as viewed from every standpoint."

Now everybody will say amen to the end of shotgun rule and lynching, for the plain reason that they never obtain anywhere where laws are made and enforced. But what of the conference of "representative southern and northern whites and colored men"? What would the conference do? . . .

The southern states were readmitted into the Union on the fundamental condition that the grant of universal suffrage should never be revoked or taken out of their constitution, and these conditions are still binding and obligatory. What then besides advertising Washington's schemes could such a conference do? Not one thing! For Booker Washington and all the rest of the self-seekers might as well understand now as at any time that the Colored people will never consent to have their rights, which are already imbedded in the national constitution, become a subject for the academic palaver and sentimental whining of a gang of busy-bodies, know-nothings.

Washington has already endorsed Jim Crow cars; he has already endorsed disfranchisement; and now, the coward that he is, having skulked all his life far from the field of combat, he comes running up asking for a conference over the prostrate body of his disfranchised brother! Conference! What, oh heaven and earth, do you want with a conference? Leave us alone to die, at least, in peace!

Go ahead with the building of your Tuskegee, the monument to the short-lived liberty of the Negro in America, and when you have finished let some future Simonides fitly describe it:

> Stranger, go tell the world that
> Within this pile, the hard-earned freedom
> Of his race was laid.

The Guardian (Boston), February 28, 1903.

The Du Bois Credo

In July 1905, at a meeting held near Niagara Falls, Canada, the Niagara Movement was founded. This movement, or organization, was made up of Negro professional people and was the forerunner of the NAACP. W. E. B. Du Bois was instrumental in calling these concerned Negroes together. Some months earlier, he had written a credo, expressing his philosophy of life and his racial attitudes.

I believe in God who made of one blood all races that dwell on earth. I believe that all men, black and brown, and white, are brothers, varying, through Time and Opportunity, in form and gift and feature, but differing in no essential particular, and alike in soul and in the possibility of infinite development.

Especially do I believe in the Negro Race; in the beauty of its genius, the sweetness of its soul, and its strength in that meekness which shall inherit this turbulent earth.

I believe in pride of race and lineage itself; in pride of self so deep as to scorn injustice to other selves; in pride of lineage so great as to despise no man's father; in pride of race so chivalrous as neither to offer bastardy to the weak nor beg wedlock of the strong, knowing that men may be brothers in Christ, even though they be not brothers-in-law.

I believe in Service—humble reverent service, from the blackening of boots to the whitening of souls; for Work is Heaven, Idleness Hell, and Wages is the "Well done!" of the Master who summoned all them that labor and are heavy laden, making no distinction between the black sweating cotton-hands of Georgia and the First Families of Virginia, since all distinction not based on deed is devilish and not divine.

I believe in the Devil and his angels, who wantonly work to narrow the opportunity of struggling human beings, especially if they be black; who spit in the faces of the fallen, strike them that cannot strike again, believe the worst and work to prove it, hating the image which their Maker stamped on a brother's soul.

I believe in the Prince of Peace. I believe that War is Murder. I believe that armies and navies are at bottom the tinsel and braggadacio of oppression and wrong; and I believe that the wicked conquest of weaker and darker nations by nations white and stronger but foreshadows the death of that strength.

I believe in Liberty for all men; the space to stretch their arms and their souls; the right to breathe and the right to vote, the freedom to choose their friends, enjoy the sunshine and ride on the railroads, uncursed by color; thinking, dreaming, working as they will in a kingdom of God and love.

I believe in the training of children black even as white; the leading out of little souls into the green pastures and beside the still waters, not for pelf or peace, but for Life lit by some large vision of beauty and goodness and truth; lest we forget, and the sons of the fathers, like Esau, for mere meat barter their birthright in a mighty nation.

Finally, I believe in Patience—patience with the weakness of the Weak and the strength of the Strong, the prejudice of the Ignorant and the ignorance of the Blind; patience with the tardy triumph of Joy and the mad chastening of Sorrow—patience with God.

W. E. B. Du Bois, "Credo," *Independent*, LVII (October 6, 1904).

The Brownsville Affair

In 1906, a group of Negro soldiers who had been treated in a discriminatory manner disobeyed military orders by participating in a small conflict with local citizens in Brownsville, Texas. This resulted in the death of one white man and slight destruction of property. The members of the entire regiment chose to face disciplinary action rather than report those of the regiment who were guilty. The following news release discusses the results of their action.

By order of President Roosevelt, acting upon a report made to him by Brig-Gen. E. A. Garlington, Inspector-General of the Army, every man of companies B, C, and D of the Twenty-Fifth Infantry, the Afro-American regiment, will be discharged without honor from the army and forever debarred from reenlisting in the army or the navy, as well as from employment by the Government in any civil capacity.

The action is one of the most drastic ever taken by the President and is sure to cause a sensation throughout the service. The refusal of members of the battalion to give Gen. Garlington or their immediate superiors the names of the men implicated in the shooting of citizens at Brownsville, Texas, near Fort Brown, on August 13, led the Inspector-

General to recommend the discharge of all the men and the President concurred. . . .

The Afro-American soldiers were heroic in refusing to betray their comrades to an unfair trial and certain death. . . . It is said the soldiers have entered into a compact never to divulge the evidence.

New York *Age,* November 8, 1906.

Mary Church Terrell Writes of Her Meeting with Secretary of War Taft

Mary Church Terrell, one of the most prominent Negro women of her era, became active in a campaign to aid the troops President Roosevelt had ordered discharged without honor as a result of the Brownsville, Texas, incident. In the Independent, *two years after she had visited Secretary of War Taft and urged him to intercede on behalf of the Negro troops, she wrote of her experiences that day.*

Waiting three or four hours to see a Cabinet officer with whom one wishes to intercede in behalf of three companies of soldiers who are about to be dismissed without honor from the Army, is an experience which a woman does not easily forget. This is particularly true, if during a large portion of the tedious wait one fears she may not be able to see the officer at all. The morning I went to see Secretary Taft I did not know just what I should say to him, even if it were possible to get an audience with him. Whether Secretary Taft could do anything for the soldiers, even if he wished to, after the order to dismiss them had actually been issued by the President and was about to be executed, I did not know. I did know, however, that something desperate should be done immediately in the soldiers' behalf, if the innocent ones were to be saved from disgrace. In the midst of a fit of depression as disheartening and as all enveloping as I have ever experienced, the 'phone rang and somebody in New York began to talk to me. . . . When I hung up the receiver, I was determined to see Secretary Taft and make a plea in behalf of the soldiers who were about to be discharged, if he and I lived thru that day. When I reached the War Department, Mr. Carpenter, Mr. Taft's secretary, told me it would be impossible for me to see Mr. Taft, because he had just returned from a long journey, was about to start on another the next morning, and had more business to transact than he could finish. I heard Mr. Carpenter tell a number of people who wished to see Secretary Taft the same thing. I did not press my case unduly, but I sat quietly in the office, until the minutes had made several hours. Convinced that I was determined to remain, Mr. Carpenter asked me why I was so eager to see Mr. Taft. Fearing that my chances of seeing the Secretary would be slimmer than ever if I disclosed the object of my visit, I hesitated to answer the question, till it occurred to me that my prospects could not be much gloomier than they were, and then I hinted broadly what the nature of my errand was. After a moment's reflection, Mr. Carpenter promised to arrange an audience with Mr. Taft for me, if I was willing to wait till the Secretary had attended to some very pressing matters and had seen the newspaper men. When I was finally ushered into Secretary Taft's presence as the afternoon was drawing to a close, I wasted not a second with preamble or preliminary. I urged him to do something for the three companies of colored soldiers who were about to be discharged without honor with all the earnestness, intensity and ardor of which I am capable. "What do you want me to do, Mrs. Terrell?" asked Mr. Taft. "All I want you to do, Mr. Secretary," I replied, "is to withhold the execution of the order to dismiss the soldiers without honor until they can have a trial, so that the innocent ones, many of whom have had excellent records in the Army, shall not be sent forth branded as murderers." "All you want me to do," quoted Mr. Taft with a merry twinkle in his eye, "is to withhold the execution of that order. Is that all you want me to do?" inquired Mr. Taft, with such emphasis upon the word "all" that I realized for the first time what a tremendous request I had preferred and how difficult it would be to change the status of the soldiers' case. Briefly I referred to the splendid record which many of the soldiers who were about to be discharged had made, particularly those who had served many years, like Mingo Saunders. When I had finished, Mr. Taft replied with an intensity and a sympathy which I shall not soon forget: "I do not wonder that you are proud of the record of your soldiers. They have served their country well." Less than half an hour after I had left Secretary Taft he had cabled the President, who was on his way to Panama, that he would withhold the execution of the order to dismiss without honor the three companies of the Twenty-Fifth Infantry until he heard from him—or words to that effect. In spite of my keen disappointment I try to be reasonable. I shall never cease to be grateful to Mr. Taft for the effort he made in the colored soldiers' behalf. I know that when he withheld the execution of the President's order thirty-six hours in response to my plea for the discharged soldiers he did what no other cabinet officer has ever done since the Declaration of Independence was signed. So far as I have been able to ascertain no other cabinet officer has withheld the execution of a Presidential order thirty-six seconds. There was nobody in Secretary Taft's office but himself and myself. The interest he manifested in the colored soldiers and the tribute he paid them were not the flowery words of a politician, uttered to serve personal ends, but they were the genuine expressions of an honest, generous-hearted man, who meant what he said and who intended to do what he could in their behalf. The effort he made was commendable and it required great courage, too.

Mary Church Terrell, "Secretary Taft and the Negro Soldiers," *Independent*, LXV (July 23, 1908).

The National Negro Committee Is Formed

Following the initial organizational attempts of the Niagara Movement, which did not meet the expectations of its founders, a group of prominent citizens, black and white, formed the National Negro Committee.

In 1909, this committee adopted a platform from which they hoped to assault the color line, which Du Bois had predicted would be the major problem of the twentieth century.

We denounce the ever-growing oppression of our 10,000,000 colored fellow citizens as the greatest menace that threatens the country. Often plundered of their just share of the public funds, robbed of nearly all part in the government, segregated by common carriers, some murdered with impunity, and all treated with open contempt by officials, they are held in some States in practical slavery to the white community. The systematic persecution of law-abiding citizens and their disfranchisement on account of their race alone is a crime that will ultimately drag down to an infamous end any nation that allows it to be practiced, and it bears most heavily on those poor white farmers and laborers whose economic position is most similar to that of the persecuted race.

The nearest hope lies in the immediate and patiently continued enlightenment of the people who have been inveigled into a campaign of oppression. The spoils of persecution should not go to enrich any class or classes of the population. Indeed persecution of organized workers, peonage, enslavement of prisoners, and even disfranchisement already threaten large bodies of whites in many Southern States.

We agree fully with the prevailing opinion that the transformation of the unskilled colored laborers in industry and agriculture into skilled workers is of vital importance to that race and to the nation, but we demand for the Negroes, as for all others, a free and complete education, whether by city, State or nation, a grammar school and industrial training for all and technical, professional, and academic education for the most gifted.

But the public schools assigned to the Negro of whatever kind of grade will never receive a fair and equal treatment until he is given equal treatment in the Legislature and before the law. Nor will the practically educated Negro, no matter how valuable to the community he may prove, be given a fair return for his labor or encouraged to put forth his best efforts or given the chance to develop that efficiency that comes only outside the school until he is respected in his legal rights as a man and a citizen.

We regard with grave concern the attempt manifest South and North to deny black men the right to work and to enforce this demand by violence and bloodshed. Such a question is too fundamental and clear even to be submitted to arbitration. The late strike in Georgia is not simply a demand that Negroes be displaced, but that proven and efficient men be made to surrender their long-followed means of livelihood to white competitors.

As first and immediate steps toward remedying these national wrongs, so full of peril for the whites as well as the blacks of all sections, we demand of Congress and the Executive:

(1) That the Constitution be strictly enforced and the civil rights guaranteed under the Fourteenth Amendment be secured impartially to all.

(2) That there be equal educational opportunities for all and in all the States, and that public school expenditure be the same for the Negro and white child.

(3) That in accordance with the Fifteenth Amendment the right of the Negro to the ballot on the same terms as other citizens be recognized in every part of the country.

NAACP Papers, Library of Congress.

The Formation of the NAACP

In 1909, a permanent organization was formed as an outgrowth of the National Negro Committee. A preliminary committee on permanent organization was established to draw up the aims and policies of this new organization, The National Association for the Advancement of Colored People. The following report of the committee became the basis for the NAACP.

TO THE NATIONAL NEGRO COMMITTEE:

Your Committee herewith submits the following plan of a permanent organization for your consideration:

ORGANIZATION:

The organization shall be known as The National Association for the Advancement of Colored People; its object to be equal rights and opportunities for all.

The National Association to be composed of a National Committee of 100 members, with an Executive Committee, to be elected from the members of the National Committee, of thirty members; 15 resident in New York City and 15 resident elsewhere; with an auxiliary membership as hereafter described.

The National Headquarters to be in New York City.

The Auxiliary Membership to be made up as follows:

(a) Members paying dues of $100 per year. Such members shall be entitled to receive, free of all other cost, the Proceedings, publications, and other literature published by the National Association. They shall have the privilege of voting at all elections and of attending all meetings, public and private, held under the auspices of the National Association;

(b) Members paying dues of $10 per year. Such members shall be entitled to receive, free of all other cost, the Annual Proceedings of the National Association. They shall have the privilege of voting at all elections, and of attending all public and private meetings held under the auspices of the National Association; and

(c) Members paying dues of $2 per year. Such members shall be entitled to receive, free from all other cost, the Annual Proceedings of the Association. They shall have the privilege of voting at all elections, and of attending all public meetings held under the auspices of the National Association.

ACTIVITIES:

It is recommended that the activities of the National Association be as follows:

(a) Public Meetings: A series of meetings to be held in the various cities in which the National Association is or shall be organized, at such intervals as may be determined at which Peonage, Public Education, Lynching, Injustices in the Courts, etc., will be presented and discussed; such meetings to be given the widest possible publicity and their Proceedings published by the National Association and widely circulated.

(b) Investigation: Your Committee deems it advisable that such department be instituted as soon as the funds can be secured; and that the whole time of at least one person be taken up with this work.

While the effort is being made to raise funds, it is proposed to undertake immediately a campaign involving a minimum of expense; i.e., simply the net cost of compiling such data as is already within easy reach of some of our members, or others who might be prevailed upon to undertake this work at cost. It is hoped that some of the members of the organization, and others outside, may have enough time to spare aside from their regular employments, to be willing to bring together for us as much data as can be readily collected, on the questions that interest us—such as Peonage, Public Education, Lynching, Injustice in the Courts, etc.—at cost to themselves in time and money. In this way it will not be necessary, or desirable, to carry on any work of original investigation at the present moment, or until the funds are secured for a permanent investigator.

(c) Publicity: The same policy as above would apply to a permanent worker in this field, for the present. It is more than probable that a part of our collected material would be so novel and interesting that it could be sold to periodicals and newspapers, and in this manner compensate those of our members who should be disposed to write it up. It is recommended, however, that some individual from the Committee should be appointed especially to undertake at least a part of this work, and to secure the cooperation of others. All articles so appearing shall, on the approval of a Press Committee of the National Association, be given the widest possible circulation by the Committee.

As to the proposed Legal Aid Bureau, it is recommended that the work of the Constitution League be endorsed as filling the need in this direction at present.

The foregoing activities will necessitate a permanent headquarters and the services of a secretary to organize the membership, and there will also be expenses of postage, printing, etc.

It is recommended that our first effort be directed to securing funds for this purpose, and as many members as possible in those places where we have already secured a foothold—i.e. Boston, Philadelphia, Chicago, and Washington, in order that (a) meetings of our National Committee resident in those cities may be held, (b) a general meeting of members be arranged for those cities and (c) public meetings be held in these cities as well as New York City.

It is further recommended that the naming of the place of meeting for the coming year be left to the Executive Committee in order that it may be held in such place where the public interest seems to be most promising at that time.

Respectfully Submitted

Preliminary Committee on Permanent Organization

Oswald G. Willard
Edwin R. A. Seligman
W. E. B. Du Bois
Charles Edward Russell
John H. Milholland
William English Walling

NAACP Papers, Library of Congress.

The First Editorial of the *Crisis*

Following the establishment of The National Association for the Advancement of Colored People, W. E. B. Du Bois was chosen to edit an official publication for the organization, which was to be called the Crisis. *The first editorial, in the November 1910 issue, explains the purpose of the periodical.*

The object of this publication is to set forth those facts and arguments which show the danger of race prejudice, particularly as manifested today toward colored people. It takes its name from the fact that the editors believe that this is a critical time in the history of the advancement of men. Catholicity and tolerance, reason and forbearance can to-day make the world-old dream of human brotherhood approach realization, while bigotry and prejudice, emphasized race consciousness and force can repeat the awful history of the contact of nations and groups in the past. We strive for this higher and broader vision of Peace and Good Will.

The policy of the *Crisis* will be simple and well defined:

It will first and foremost be a newspaper: it will record important happenings and movements in the world which bear on the great problem of inter-racial relations, and especially those which affect the Negro-American.

Secondly, it will be a review of opinion and literature, recording briefly books, articles, and important expressions of opinion in the white and colored press on the race problem.

Thirdly, it will publish a few short articles.

Finally, its editorial page will stand for the rights of men, irrespective of color or race, for the highest ideals of American democracy, and for reasonable but earnest and persistent attempts to gain these rights and realize these ideals. The magazine will be the organ of no clique or party and will avoid rancor of all sorts. In the absence of proof to the contrary it will assume honesty of purpose on the part of all men, North and South, white and black.

Crisis, I (November 1910).

The First Minutes of the Association for the Study of Negro Life and History

These minutes were recorded at the first meeting held for the purpose of organizing the Association for the Study of Negro Life and History.

9/9/15

A meeting called by Dr. [Carter G.] Woodson for the purpose of considering definite plans for the organization of a society, which should publish a magazine devoted to the study of the Negro, was held in the office of the Executive Secretary of the Wabash Avenue Department of the Chicago Y.M.C.A. Those present were C. G. Woodson, G. C. Hall, A. L. Jackson, W. B. Hartgrove, and J. E. Stamps. Dr. Hall was elected temporary chairman, J. E. Stamps, temporary secretary. The proposed constitution was read, and after alterations adopted. A permanent organization was formed, and the following officers were elected: Dr. G. C. Hall, President; J. E. Moorland, Secretary-Treasurer; C. G. Woodson, Director of Research and Editor.

In addition to the above named officers the Executive Council will be J. A. Bigham, A. L. Jackson, Miss S. P. Breckinridge, and G. N. Grisham.

The editorial staff will consist of six or eight persons to be selected by the Editor and approved by the Executive Council.

A motion prevailed that in a reply to a request from Dr. Moorland we offer to cooperate with Howard University along lines satisfactory to the Executive Council.

J. E. Stamps

Original in the possession of James E. Stamps, Chicago, Illinois.

The Formation of a Mutual Protective Society in Philadelphia

In a letter written to Carter G. Woodson, founder of the Association for the Study of Negro Life and History, African Methodist Episcopal Bishop Levi J. Coppin related the founding of a protective association among Negroes in Philadelphia. Race riots, instigated by whites and directed against blacks, grew to serious proportions during the second decade of this century. Having no recourse in the law, in many cases, because of police sympathy for the whites, Negroes sought protection from their own groups.

Philadelphia, Pa. Oct. 24th, 1918

Mr. Carter G. Woodson
Washington, D.C.

My dear Mr. Woodson:

I have your letter and I quite agree with you, that if our soldiers are to be segregated into separate units, they should be given credit for what they do.

The democracy for which we are fighting remains yet to be fully established, certainly as it relates to us in many ways.

After the race riot in Phila. we were moved to organize a Colored Protective Association and raised a fund for the prosecution of policemen and others who took part in the mob. We have made the organization permanent for just such things as your letter calls attention to.

What we need as a people is organization and cooperation.

The Society for the Advancement of Colored People is doing a much needed work in a general way, or, nationally, but could not possibly cover the whole field locally, hence our organization.

Our Association seeks to organize all the churches, but we cooperate with the local NAACP. I am a member of both associations. Dr. R. R. Wright, Jr., 631 Pine Street Philadelphia is President of the CPA, you might correspond with him.

I think we all might find a common ground for cooperation, and for this I can be depended upon.

Yours very truly,

L. J. Coppin

Carter G. Woodson Papers, Library of Congress.

Kelly Miller on the Houston Riot

As the United States became directly involved in the struggle to "make the world safe for democracy" in World War I, Negroes became more insistent on obtaining the fruits of democracy at home. A group of Afro-American troops stationed in Houston, Texas, were heckled in a manner similar to those soldiers in Brownsville, and they too rebelled. Again, the government reacted toward the black troops in a way that was not according to military tradition.

The treatment received by those who participated in the Houston riot was quite different from that received by whites involved in a bloody riot against Negroes in East St. Louis a month before. As mentioned in the following letter written by Professor Kelly Miller of Howard University, no action had been taken as a result of the deplorable behavior of the whites who rioted in East St. Louis.

Honorable Newton D. Baker
The Secretary of War
Washington D.C.

My dear Mr. Baker:

I deem it a patriotic duty to focus and to express the feeling of the colored race over the deplorable outbreak at Houston, Texas, and the direful tragedy resulting therefrom. I realize the necessity of patriotic reticence in time of national peril, but the government has a right to know, through free and untrammelled utterance, the effect of its policy upon the feeling and attitude of loyal and patriotic citizens.

The Houston outbreak was a most deplorable occurrence and calculated to frustrate the desired good feeling between the races as well as to impair the Negro's chances as a military factor in the United States Army. But it did not seem wise to indulge in public discussion while the case was under adjudication by the Federal authorities.

The execution of thirteen of the participants and life sentence upon forty-one others has fallen like a pall over the spirit of the colored race. I am undertaking to explain, as briefly as possible, the nature and cause of this depression of spirit.

1. The Negro has no just cause to complain when the perpetrators of outrage meet with just punishment at the hands of the law. The black man is the accustomed and expected victim of lawlessness. His righteous plea is that the majesty of the law should be upheld. Every murderous rioter and every participant in lynching should die the death decreed by law. . . .

2. The Negro has no just ground for complaint against the finding of the court-martial. The culprits were, doubtless, proved guilty of offence which, according to the technical exactions of the laws of war, merited capital punishment.

3. But it was universally conceded by North and South, white and black alike, that the soldiers were incited to lawless action by strong provocative circumstances. . . . When drunk with the malignant passion of race passion, the erstwhile good citizen defies the law and overrides the judge, and even the pious priest looks impotently or complacently on, while the Negro victim swings from the limb or burns at the stake. The black race is usually the victim and the white the perpetrator. . . . As the civil law is usually impotent to restrain the whites under these circumstances, in this instance, unfortunately, military discipline was not able to restrain the fury of the blacks. The whites, whose aggravative conduct undoubtedly precipitated the outbreaks, suffered the heavier toll of fatality. . . .

In view of all the circumstances involved in and the complex issues growing out of the deplorable outbreak, the Negro race had a right to expect that before the findings of the court-martial were put into execution, the War Department would have required or requested that they be reviewed by the commander-in-chief of the United States Army. From a broader and more comprehensive viewpoint, he, doubtless, would have given consideration and weight to the mitigating circumstances which the court-martial was estopped from considering by the technical exactions of the code of war. A statement from the highest authority based upon all of the factors involved would, doubtless, have led to an enlightened understanding of the compelling reasons for such drastic action. During the Civil War, when the nation was surrounded by a cloud of enemies, many a victim, justly condemned to die by military authority, was spared that fare by the humanitarian promptings of the great heart of the great commander-in-chief.

4. The Negro is mystified by the nature of the secrecy with which this case was surrounded. It is easy to understand how secrecy of procedure may become a military necessity. But why was the lid of secrecy lifted the moment the victims were executed? It would

seem that the evident purpose was, on the one hand, to prevent the Negro race from appealing the case to the Secretary of War and to the President; and, on the other hand, to appease the spirit of vengeance of the afflicted community. If secrecy were necessary in order to keep the case disentangled from popular commotion, why might it not have been maintained until the end of the war?

5. In consonance with this view it was reported that the sheriff at Houston was a witness of the military execution, but no Negro civilian was permitted to be present at that solemn hour.

6. As the case now stands, there is not the slightest indication that the provoking conduct of the white people of Houston has received the slightest rebuke on the part of the Federal authorities. On the other hand, in the absence of any express or implied condemnation, it would appear that such conduct has received the stamp of Federal sanction.

7. The Negro believes that this punishment involves an element of race vengeance and that its purpose was to intimidate and terrrify the black man's spirit. It still remains unexplained why these men were not given the privilege of being shot like soldiers rather than being hanged like dastards. . . . These men went singing to their doom as if conscious of righteous guilt. In the minds of many Negroes these men stand as martyrs who were crucified upon the cross of race passion. No patriotic purpose is served when an act of the government produces martyrs in the estimation of loyal and patriotic citizens.

Although there have been thousands of victims of race riot and passion during the past half century, scarcely a white man has suffered the legal penalty of death. Even the Negro, by legal process, is bearing the brunt of the penalty of the horrors of East St. Louis although his race was the victim of its fury. This case has increased the strength of appeal of the Negro as his blood crieth from the ground unto the conscience of the nation.

Although the Houston incident, in its present phase, has a morbid effect upon the Negro race, it will not be permitted to impair its patriotic morale and devotion to country in this hour of serious peril. The Negro is of the long-suffering and forgiving nature. I sometimes feel that one petition of the Lord's Prayer is calculated to meet the peculiarities of his character: "Forgive us our trespasses, as we forgive those who trespass against us." Although the white race enslaved the Negro and for 250 years exacted his unrequited toil and bestialized his nature, and by discriminating laws and proscriptive regulations holds him in despite, the Negro is willing to overlook and forgive all if the white man will even now allow him the semblance of a square deal. . . . I am anxious, as a loyal and patriotic citizen, to do my full share to assist you and the nation in the tremendous task in which we are involved. . . .

Yours truly,

Kelly Miller

NAACP Papers, Library of Congress.

Charles Young, Black Graduate of West Point

Colonel Charles Young, a Negro graduate of West Point, became the highest-ranking officer of his race before his death in 1922. His career was one of frustration combined with perseverance. He was stationed in many parts of the world, including Haiti, the Philippines and Africa. In the following letter to a member of his West Point graduating class, Young refers to the blackwater fever, which eventually killed him, and to his work in Africa.

While at West Point, Colonel Young had difficulty with some of his course work. In order to graduate and receive his commission, he had to be tutored. General George W. Goethals, engineer of the Panama Canal, wrote Young's mother following the Colonel's death of his experience in helping the young Negro receive his degree.

Charles Young's appointment to West Point in 1884.

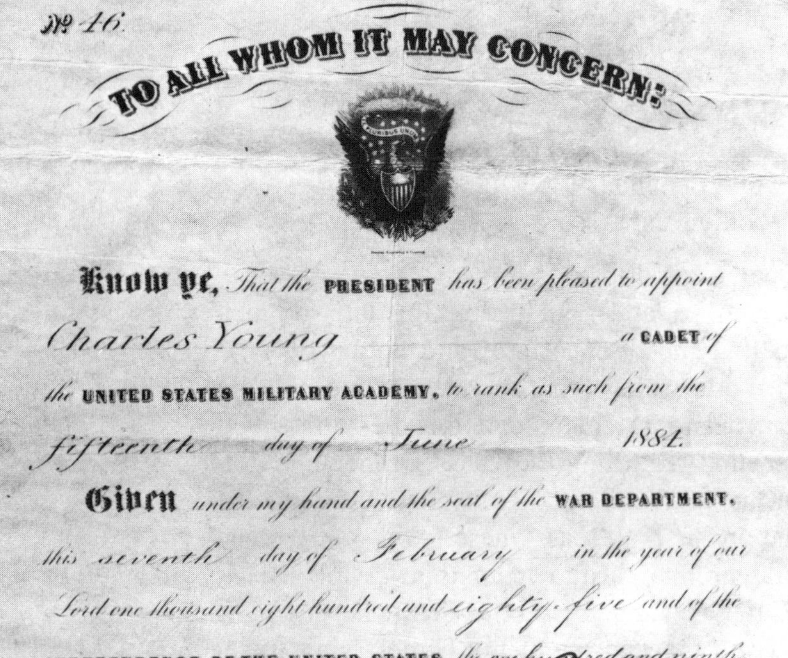

No. 46.

TO ALL WHOM IT MAY CONCERN:

Know ye, That the PRESIDENT has been pleased to appoint Charles Young a CADET of the UNITED STATES MILITARY ACADEMY, to rank as such from the fifteenth day of June 1884.

Given under my hand and the seal of the WAR DEPARTMENT, this seventh day of February in the year of our Lord one thousand eight hundred and eighty-five and of the INDEPENDENCE OF THE UNITED STATES the one hundred and ninth.

Secretary of War

UNITED STATES MILITARY ACADEMY

Be it known that Cadet Charles Young, of the State of Ohio, having been carefully examined on all the Branches of the ARTS, SCIENCES and of LITERATURE taught at the United States Military Academy has been judged worthy to receive the Degree required by LAW preparatory to his advancement in the U.S. Army. In testimony whereof and by Virtue of authority vested in the Academic Staff We do confer upon Him this Diploma and recommend him to the President for Promotion in Cavalry or Infantry

Given at West Point in the STATE of New York this thirty first day of August in the Year of our Lord One thousand Eight Hundred and eighty-nine.

John M. Wilson Colonel of Engineers, Superintendent

The diploma presented to Cadet Charles Young upon graduation from the United States Military Academy.

AMERICAN LEGATION
MONROVIA, LIBERIA, AFRICA

July 26, 1915

Capt. Alexander Piper
Brooklyn, New York

Dear Capt. Piper:
I've got "a late"—an inexcusable late so much so that an absence total and cold would be far better than trying to get into line, if I did not desire to thank you for the letters you sent me regarding the Class Dinner and Reunion at the Point. Your first letter passed me on the high seas, where I was going home in search of health from this terrible Black Water Fever [*sic*] of the West Coast. Your second reached me at my home trying to recuperate but far from being able to handle a pen. I thought to answer afterward and tell you how Liberia called again to duty—it was mislaid then forgot; then I returned and into the boiling pot of hard work I was immediately forced. Indeed, the Brochure setting forth the transactions both in New York and West Point, and sent me by Schermerhorn, meets me here in the jungle about 75 miles from Monrovia, making a road thru the said jungle to the hinterland, to help in some permanent work here for my people before the Manchu Law calls me back to duty with our own troops in the U.S. Army.

We have succeeded in organizing a decent Frontier Force, in making a working system of Reports and Returns, and Regulations, a Map of the Republic, and when this road of possibly 150 miles is finished with a Central Mil[itary] Station at its further end my work that I laid out at the Army War College before coming over here will be finished. The American officers that I brought with me have been loyal and worked well. The troops are natives, not Liberians. They are not one whit inferior in the soldier spirit to our best black troops of our own Army, which as you know is saying much.

But I set out to thank you all, of the Class who remembered me, both while getting up the Reunion, during and since.

While West Point was pretty hard pulling for me, still the roughness was relieved by the sympathy of many of my classmates, to whom I shall ever be grateful and among [whom] I shall remember you.

Chas. Young

* * * * *

George W. Goethals
CONSULTING ENGINEER
40 WALL STREET
NEW YORK

May 8, 1922

Mrs. Ada M. Young,
Youngsholme, R.F.D. No. 5,
Xenia, Ohio.

My dear Mrs. Young:

Yours of the 24th ultimo was received during my absence.

I regret to state that I know little about Colonel Young's career at West Point outside of the Section Room in Civil and Military Engineering. He had considerable difficulty with the course and was deficient in it but was not so declared by the Academic Board at the June examination of his graduating year. The Board decided to give him until September to see if he could then qualify. I was leaving West Point, intending to remain there during the summer; my sympathies were aroused, and I offered to give him a certain amount of time daily in order to assist him in preparation for the examination which he was to take the last of August. This I did and subsequently learned that he had successfully passed it.

I regret that I can give you no incidents of his cadet life as I am not familiar with them.

Very truly yours,

Geo. W. Goethals

Original in the possession of the Charles N. Young heirs, Xenia, Ohio.

An Account by Black Militant Marcus Garvey

Marcus Garvey, twentieth-century forerunner of the Black Nationalists, started a "back-to-Africa" campaign before 1920. Concerned about the seemingly endless racial strife in the United States, Garvey solicited funds to establish the Black Star [shipping] Line. Money poured in from Negroes who were interested in the movement, and for a brief moment in history, Garvey was overwhelmed with success. His scheme failed, however, when financial ruin came to the Black Star Line. Garvey was convicted of using the United States mails to commit fraud and was sentenced to prison in 1925. After two years, he was pardoned by President Coolidge and deported to Jamaica. The following account written by Garvey tells about his early years, his attitudes on race and his story of the Universal Negro Improvement Association.

I was born in the Island of Jamaica, British West Indies, on August 17, 1887. My parents were black Negroes. My father was a man of brilliant intellect and dashing courage. He was unafraid of consequences. He took human chances in the course of life, as most bold men do, and he failed at the close of his career. He once had a fortune; he died poor. My mother was a sober and conscientious Christian, too soft and good for the time in which she lived. She was the direct opposite of my father. He was severe, firm, determined, bold and strong, refusing to yield even to superior forces if he believed he was right. My mother, on the other hand, was always willing to return a smile for a blow, and ever ready to bestow charity upon her enemy. Of this strange combination I was born thirty-six years ago, and ushered into a world of sin, the flesh and the devil.

I grew up with other black and white boys. I was never whipped by any, but made them all respect the strength of my arms. I got my education from many sources—through private tutors, two public schools, two grammar or high schools and two colleges. My teachers were men and women of varied experiences and abilities; four of them were eminent preachers. They studied me and I studied them. With some I became friendly in after years, others and I drifted apart, because as a boy they wanted to whip me, and I simply refused to be whipped. I was not made to be whipped. It annoys me to be defeated; hence to me, to be once defeated is to find cause for an everlasting struggle to reach the top.

I became a printer's apprentice at an early age, while still attending school. My apprentice master was a highly educated and alert man. In the affairs of business and the world he had no peer. He taught me many things before I reached twelve, and at fourteen I had enough intelligence and experience to manage men. I was strong and manly, and I made them respect me. I developed a strong and forceful character, and have maintained it still.

To me, at home in my early days, there was no difference between white and black. One of my father's properties, the place where I lived most of the time, was adjoining that of a white man. He had three girls and two boys; the Wesleyan minister, another white man, whose church my parents attended, also had property adjoining ours. He had three girls and one boy. All of us were playmates. We romped and were happy children playmates together. The little white girl whom I liked most knew no better than I did myself. We were two innocent fools who never dreamed of a race feeling and problem. As a child, I went to school with white boys and girls, like all other Negroes. We were not called Negroes then. I never heard the term Negro used once until I was about fourteen.

At fourteen my little white playmate and I parted. Her parents thought the time had come to separate us and draw the color line. They sent her and another sister to Edinburgh, Scotland, and told her that she was never to write or try to get in touch with me, for I was a "nigger." It was then that I found for the first time that there was some difference in humanity, and that there were different races, each having its own separate and distinct social life. I did not care about the separation after I was told about it, because I never thought all during our childhood association that the girl and the rest of the children of her race were better than I was; in fact, they used to look up to me. So I simply had no regrets.

After my first lesson in race distinction, I never thought of playing with white girls any more, even if they might be next door neighbors. At home my sister's company was good enough for me, and at school I made friends with the colored girls next to me. White boys and I used to frolic together. We played cricket and baseball, ran races and rode bicycles together, took each other to the river and to the sea beach to learn to swim, and made boyish efforts while out in deep water to drown each other, making a sprint for shore crying out "shark, shark, shark." In all our experiences, however, only one black boy was drowned. He went under on a Friday afternoon after school hours, and his parents found him afloat half eaten by sharks on the following Sunday afternoon. Since then we boys never went back to sea. . . .

At eighteen I had an excellent position as manager of a large printing establishment, having under my control several men old enough to be my grandfathers. But I got mixed up with public life. I started to take an interest in the politics of my country, and then I saw the injustice done to my race because it was black, and I became dissatisfied on that account. I went traveling to South and Central America and parts of the West Indies to find out if it was so elsewhere, and I found the same situation. I set sail for Europe to find out if it was different there, and again I found the stumbling-block—"You are black." I read of the conditions in America. I read "Up From Slavery," by Booker T. Washington, and then my doom—if I may so call it—of being a race leader dawned upon me in London after I had traveled through almost half of Europe. . . .

Becoming naturally restless for the opportunity of doing something for the advancement of my race, I was determined that the black man would not continue to be kicked about by all the other races and nations of the world, as I saw it in the West Indies, South and Central America and Europe, and as I read of it in America. My young and ambitious mind led me into flights of great imagination. I saw before me then, even as I do now, a new world of black men, not peons, serfs, dogs and slaves, but a nation of sturdy men making their impress upon civilization and causing a new light to dawn upon the human race. I could not remain in London any more. My brain was afire. There was a world of thought to conquer. I had to start ere it became too late and the work be not done. Immediately I boarded a ship at Southampton for Jamaica, where I arrived on July 15, 1914. The Universal Negro Improvement Association and African Communities (Imperial) League was founded and organized five days after my arrival, with the program of uniting all the Negro peoples of the world into one great body to establish a country and Government absolutely their own.

Where did the name of the organization come from? It was while speaking to a West Indian Negro who was a passenger on the ship with me from Southampton, who was returning home to the West Indies from Basutoland with his Basuto wife, that I further learned of the horrors of native life in Africa. He related to me in conversation such horrible and pitiable tales that my heart bled within me. Retiring from the conversation to my cabin, all day and the following night I pondered over the subject matter of that conversation, and at midnight, lying flat on my back, the vision and thought came to me that I should name the organization the Universal Negro

Improvement Association and African Communities (Imperial) League. Such a name I thought would embrace the purpose of all black humanity. Thus to the world a name was born, a movement created, and a man became known.

I really never knew there was so much color prejudice in Jamaica, my own native home, until I started the work of the Universal Negro Improvement Association. We started immediately before the war. I had just returned from a successful trip to Europe, which was an exceptional achievement for a black man. The daily papers wrote me up with big headlines and told of my movement. But nobody wanted to be a Negro. "Garvey is crazy; he has lost his head. Is that the use he is going to make of his experience and intelligence?" —such were the criticisms passed upon me. Men and women as black as I, and even more so, had believed themselves white under the West Indian order of society. I was simply an impossible man to use openly the term "Negro"; yet every one beneath his breath was calling the black man a Negro. . . .

. . . I made my first political enemies in Harlem. They fought me until they smashed the first organization and reduced its membership to about fifty. I started again, and in two months built up a new organization of about 1,500 members. Again the politicians came and divided us into two factions. They took away all the books of the organization, its treasury and all its belongings. At that time I was only an organizer, for it was not then my intention to remain in America, but to return to Jamaica. The organization had its proper officers elected, and I was not an officer of the New York division, but President of the Jamaica branch.

On the second split in Harlem thirteen of the members conferred with me and requested me to become President for a time of the New York organization so as to save them from the politicians. I consented and was elected President. There then sprung up two factions, one led by the politicians with the books and the money, and the other led by me. My faction had no money. I placed at their disposal what money I had, opened an office for them, rented a meeting place, employed two women secretaries, went on the street of Harlem at night to speak for the movement. In three weeks more than 2,000 new members joined. By this time I had the association incorporated so as to prevent the other faction using the name, but in two weeks the politicians had stolen all the people's money and had smashed up their faction.

The organization under my Presidency grew by leaps and bounds. I started *The Negro World.* Being a journalist, I edited this paper free of cost for the association, and worked for them without pay until November, 1920. I traveled all over the country for the association at my own expense, and established branches until in 1919 we had about thirty branches in different cities. By my writings and speeches we were able to build up a large organization of over 2,000,000 by June, 1919, at which time we launched the program of the Black Star Line.

To have built up a new organization, which was not purely political, among Negroes in America was a wonderful feat, for the Negro politician does not allow any other kind of organization within his race to thrive. We succeeded, however, in making the Universal Negro Improvement Association so formidable in 1919 that we encountered more trouble from our political brethren. They sought the influence of the District Attorney's office of the County of New York to put us out of business. Edwin P. Kilroe, at that time an Assistant District Attorney, on the complaint of the Negro politicians, started to investigate us and the association. . . .

During my many tilts with Mr. Kilroe, the question of the Black Star Line was discussed. He did not want us to have a line of ships. I told him that even as there was a White Star Line, we would have, irrespective of his wishes, a Black Star Line. On June 27, 1919, we incorporated the Black Star Line of Delaware, and in September we obtained a ship.

The following month (October) a man by the name of Tyler came to my office at 56 West 135th Street, New York City, and told me that Mr. Kilroe had sent him to "get me," and at once fired four shots at me from a .38-calibre revolver. He wounded me in the right leg and the right side of my scalp. I was taken to the Harlem Hospital, and he was arrested. The next day it was reported that he committed suicide in jail just before he was to be taken before a City Magistrate.

The first year of our activities for the Black Star Line added prestige to the Universal Negro Improvement Association. Several hundred thousand dollars worth of shares were sold. Our first ship, the steamship *Yarmouth,* had made two voyages to the West Indies and Central America. The white press had flashed the news all over the world. I, a young Negro, as President of the corporation, had become famous. My name was discussed on five continents. The Universal Negro Improvement Association gained millions of followers all over the world. By August, 1920, over 4,000,000 persons had joined the movement. A convention of all the Negro peoples of the world was called to meet in New York that month. Delegates came from all parts of the known world. Over 25,000 persons packed the Madison Square Garden on Aug. 1 to hear me speak to the first International Convention of Negroes. It was a record-breaking meeting, the first and the biggest of its kind. The name of Garvey had become known as a leader of his race.

Such fame among Negroes was too much for other race leaders and politicians to tolerate. My downfall was planned by my enemies. They laid all kinds of traps for me. They scattered their spies among the employes of the Black Star Line and the Universal Negro Improvement Association. Our office records were stolen. Employes started to be openly dishonest; we could get no convictions against them; even if on complaint they were held by a Magistrate, they were dismissed by the Grand Jury. The ships' officers started to pile up thousands of dollars of debts against the company without the knowledge of the officers of the corporation. Our ships were damaged at sea, and there was a general riot of wreck and ruin. Officers of the Universal Negro Improvement Association also began to steal and be openly dishonest. I had to dismiss them. They joined my enemies, and thus I had an endless fight on my hands to save the ideals of the association and carry out our program for the race. My Negro enemies, finding that they alone could not destroy me, resorted to misrepresenting me to the leaders of the white race, several of whom, without proper investigation, also opposed me.

With robberies from within and from without, the Black Star Line was forced to suspend active business in December, 1921. While I was on a business trip to the West Indies in the Spring of 1921, the Black Star Line received the blow from which it was unable to recover. A sum of $25,000 was paid by one of the officers of the corporation to a man to purchase a ship, but the ship was never obtained and the money was never returned. The company was defrauded of a further sum of $11,000. Through such actions on the part of dishonest men in the shipping business, the Black Star Line received its first setback. This resulted in my being indicted for using the United States mails to defraud investors in the company. I was subsequently convicted and sentenced to five years in a Federal penitentiary. My trial is a matter of history. I know I was not given a square deal, because my indictment was the result of a "frame-up" among my political and business enemies. I had to conduct my own case in court because of the peculiar position in which I found myself. I had millions of friends and a large number of enemies. I wanted a colored attorney to handle my case, but there was none I could

THE FIGHT

Between MARCUS GARVEY

THE CHAMPION OF NEGRO LIBERTY

AND

The Black Parasites

WHO HAVE LIVED OFF THE INNOCENCE OF THE NEGRO RACE FOR THE LAST FIFTY YEARS,

IS ON

A NUMBER OF SO-CALLED NEGRO LEADERS, MEMBERS OF SOCIALISTS AND ALLEGED ADVANCEMENT ASSOCIATIONS, HAVE BEEN TRYING TO FOOL THE PEOPLE ABOUT

GARVEY AND THE KU KLUX KLAN

THESE REPTILES KNOW THAT GARVEY IS THE MOST FEARLESS CHAMPION AND DEFENDER OF THE NEGRO RACE, BUT FOR THE SAKE OF DECEIVING THE PEOPLE THEY HAVE BEEN CONDUCTING A CAMPAIGN AGAINST GARVEY TO FEATHER THEIR OWN NESTS.

THE LAZY, FROTHY DEMAGOGUES HAVE NEVER DONE ANYTHING FOR THE RACE

THEY HAVE BEEN TALKING AND WRITING FOR MANY YEARS AND HAVE ACCOMPLISHED NOTHING. SEE WHAT GARVEY HAS DONE ALL OVER AMERICA AND THE WORLD. THESE ENVIOUS AND MALICIOUS GAS-BAGS HAVE ONLY FOMENTED LYNCHING IN THE SOUTH. THEY HAVE ONLY COLLECTED MONEY FROM PHILANTROPHIC WHITE PEOPLE TO SELL OUT THE RACE AND TO FEED THEMSELVES WITHOUT ANY SACRIFICE. THE VILLAINS DO NOT MEAN WHAT THEY SAY. SHOW THEM A DOLLAR AND IN FIVE MINUTES IT DISAPPEARS.

THE LAZY GOOD FOR NOTHING NEGRO AGITATORS AND PARASITES HAVE BROUGHT THEIR FIGHT TO HARLEM TO ANTAGOINIZE THE UNIVERSAL NEGRO IMPROVEMENT ASSOCIATION FOR AUGUST.

THE CHALLENGE IS ACCEPTED

IF THE PARASITES HAVE ANY MANHOOD AS GARVEY HAS ALWAYS DONE TO SHOW UP THEIR INSINCERITY, HE INVITES THEM TO MEET HIM ON A PUBLIC PLATFORM AND LET THE PUBLIC DECIDE BETWEEN THEM.

ASK SOME OF THE GAS BAGS ABOUT THE ELEVATOR MEN AND SWITCH BOARD UNION

LONG LIVE AFRICA! **LONG LIVE THE NEGRO RACE!**

Schomburg Collection, New York Public Library

trust. I feel that I have been denied justice because of prejudice. . . .

The temporary ruin of the Black Star Line has in no way affected the larger work of the Universal Negro Improvement Association, which now has 900 branches with an approximate membership of 6,000,000. This organization has succeeded in organizing the Negroes all over the world and we now look forward to a renaissance that will create a new people and bring about the restoration of Ethiopia's ancient glory.

Being black, I have committed an unpardonable offense against the very light colored Negroes in America and the West Indies by making myself famous as a Negro leader of millions. In their view, no black man must rise above them, but I still forge ahead determined to give to the world the truth about the new Negro who is determined to make and hold for himself a place in the affairs of men. The Universal Negro Improvement Association has been misrepresented by my enemies. They have tried to make it appear that we are hostile to other races. This is absolutely false. We love all humanity. We are working for the peace of the world which we believe can only come about when all races are given their due.

We feel that there is absolutely no reason why there should be any differences between the black and white races, if each stop to adjust and steady itself. We believe in the purity of both races. We do not believe the black man should be encouraged in the idea that his highest purpose in life is to marry a white woman, but we do believe that the white man should be taught to respect the black woman in the same way as he wants the black man to respect the white woman. It is a vicious and dangerous doctrine of social equality to urge, as certain colored leaders do, that black and white should get together, for that would destroy the racial purity of both.

We believe that the black people should have a country of their own where they should be given the fullest opportunity to develop politically, socially and industrially. . . . It is because of this belief no doubt that my Negro enemies, so as to prejudice me further in the opinion of the public, wickedly state that I am a member of the Ku Klux Klan, even though I am a black man.

I have been deprived of the opportunity of properly explaining my work to the white people of America through the prejudice worked up against me by jealous and wicked members of my own race. My success as an organizer was much more than rival Negro leaders could tolerate. They, regardless of consequences, either to me or to the race, had to destroy me by fair means or foul.

. . . Booker Washington aptly described the race in one of his lectures by stating that we were like crabs in a barrel, that none would allow the other to climb over, but on any such attempt all would continue to pull back into the barrel the one crab that would make the effort to climb out. Yet, those of us with vision cannot desert the race, leaving it to suffer and die. . . .

Gumby Collection, Columbia University Library.

Negro Migration to the North after World War I

The migration of blacks from South to North during and after World War I was one of tremendous magnitude. It generated enthusiasm among thousands by promising a utopian land of jobs and opportunity. While many Negroes found their lives improved by the change, others were disillusioned when they reached the crowded ghetto areas; they had left the poverty of the farm for the privation of the slum. The following documents illustrate the desire of many to emigrate, some of the problems they encountered in the North and their concern for those left behind in the South.

Editor of the Chicago defender, please permit me space in your paper to say a few wards about our Country, . . . Well this little town is 107 Miles from Savannah and 85 miles from Macon. this is a splendid farm section for Coin [corn] and Cotton. it in the county of Jefferson. some of the farmers rease a nuff to do them in this section i am glad to say that the white and Collard gets along very well to gather; there haven been eny lynching in this section. but the Collord people are not sadesfied at ther treetment. Duren the month of April and may when the Tax Collector who dutie it was to have the Regester Book in ever district so the collrd could regester he fail to do so. then when we ast him to do so he head them to Read Certain things and if they Miss a ward he would turn them down. therefore our people Could not Vote in this Last Election.

Mr. Editor Since Cotton has advance up to such a good price the Lan Lords in some section cut out renting Land and farmers who owen ther stock will have to work on shers. the Lan Lord furnesh the Land and the fudlizer. and the Labour furnish the Labour and the stock. they usuley give 30 and 35 acres to the plow. and the renter usuley pay a thousand lbs of Lent Cotton to the plow. . . .

Mr. Editor since this Migration question awaken up in this Country it has put this county in a wark [*sic*] as never be for. you cannot hir [hear] northing but the north in this country, while our people down here are a fread of the cold, but they are leaving every day in croud for the north. they are tired of the tretment they have been getting hear in the south and since the opeturnety has open up in the north some of them are leaving regardless to weather, and after the Cold weather is over i am a fread ther will not be room for the negros from the south.

Mr. Editor some time ago we read in the Alabama paper of the advice from the Bishop of the wilberforce uneversity to his Conference in Alabama. Advisen them to stay in the south and buy homes and farms and larg track of Lan. and that the south was the best place for them.

i wander did the Bishop read of Lynching of that good citizens of Abbiville, s.c. who was worth $20.00 and hundard of outher good men who has been hung up by thes Midnight Mobes [mobs]. and yeat the bishop Advise them to stay in a country like that. it seem to me that all the bishop wants is for his church to Live and the rest may die. dear freinds, when thes Mobes get After you you Must go, home or land. so Mr. Editor our people are Leaving the south in Large Numbers, for we want to be in a country wher ther is peace and happiness and wher our wifes and doughters will be respected.

Yours truley, W. A. McCloud,
wadley, GA 12/28/16

* * * * *

Shreveport, La.
Jan 16-1923

Mr. John T. Clark

Dear Sir:

This comes to inform you that I would like to come to Pittsburgh, Pa. if I could get there and get a good job for my self and 3 boys. I saw your remarks about southern labor in Pittsburgh plants. Mr. Clark, I have a wife and nine children. I have been on the plantations all my life on the big farms. For the last few years I have been coming out in debt. Short crops and boll weevils and the high cost of living has been bringing me out behind in debt on the share crop system, and conditions don't look any better yet.

If there was some way I could get up there with my family, I will come. I would like a good job, a paying job, for my self and 3 boys. I believe we could get use to the cold weather up there. I am a colored man with plenty ambition and no money and can't get any.

I remain yours truly,

W. B. Mitchell
Shreveport, La.
Rt. 3 Box 35

* * * * *

December 19, 1916

The Rev. Richard Carroll
Columbia, S.C.

My Dear Co-Worker:

Your letter to hand this very hour, and as to the great exodus of our people I am ready to answer you in definite words relative to its benefits:

I am positive that it's not the best thing for our people to do, especially this season of the year. We have here now, hundreds who are suffering intensely, many of whom have money but cannot get accommodations. The good ones from the South are being made to suffer with the bad because of many unreasonable things committed by the thoughtless. I know this will eventually work against all of us in the North, thus I am sparing no time in trying to meet the issue. I appreciate your voice being lifted openly against this exodus unless the people know where they are going before they leave there.

Yours for every good work

Rev. J. C. Austin, B.D., D.D
Ebenezer Baptist Church
Corner Wylie and Devillers streets
Pittsburgh, Pa.

* * * * *

[Letter to the *Chicago Defender*]

Atlanta, Ga.
April 11, 1917

Dear Sir

I am a reader of your paper and we are all crazy about it and take it every Saturday and we raise a great howl when we dont get it. Now since I see and feel that you are for the race and are willing to assist any one so I will ask you to please assist me in getting imployment and some place to [live]. . . like all great race transitions, when a whole people by one unchecked impulse acting as one man inaugurates a crusade of change, seeking new surroundings and conditions in distant spots and lands, there is sure to be more or less suffering and hardship; not anticipated, or if so, not guarded against or prepared for. Thousands upon thousands of the "best folks" of the South, the best families, have trudged and are preparing to migrate northward; and in the main, are taking with them, or have temporarily provided for the women folks of their households that they shall not be left behind to become the defenseless prey and victims of the white ruffians of the South. But, while this is true, it is also true, that there are many others gone or preparing to go who have, or will leave behind them a daughter here, a sister, wife or mother there, helpless and unprotected from this modern Sodom and Gomorrah, as far as the honor and virtue of colored women is concerned. This is a cruel and disturbing fact, and it is high time to sound the alarm, to be followed, let us hope, by a concerted movement upon the part of the thoughtful and Christian leaders of the Race, North and South, to allay and minimize its dangers. Bureaus for the purpose of obtaining information and extending "first aid" and advice should be established in those sections of the South where the migrating movement is of larger volume, that the helpless left behind may be advised and shielded in the absence of their natural protectors. Is it not a matter worthy of the immediate consideration of the colored branches, male and female, of the Y.M.C.A.s scattered throughout the North and South, including the press, pulpit and club? Could these forces, which mean so much in the general uplift of the Race, engage in a more worthy and needed movement?

C.V.B. Algiers, La.

Carter G. Woodson Papers, Library of Congress.

A Black Man's Reactions to the Post-World War I Race Riots

In 1919, race riots occurred, in no definite pattern, all over the country. In Chicago, on July 27, 1919, a riot erupted that lasted five days. During those days, Negroes were assaulted by whites who entered the ghetto and destroyed life and property. In one instance, whites drove through the area shooting at Negro pedestrians. In retaliation, Negroes looted stores owned by whites.

In an effort to prevent further violence, the Governor of Illinois appointed a commission of six Negroes and six whites to investigate the riot. One member of the commission, Victor F. Lawson, editor of the Chicago Daily News, *received the following letter from a Negro war veteran stating the attitudes of Negroes and possible causes of the conflict between the races.*

My dear Mr. Lawson:—

As the cause of the Negro in America is one that is nearer and dearer to my heart than any other, it has become an obsession with me, and for that reason I am taking the liberty of inflicting upon you this unsolicited treatise on the subject. . . .

I take it that the object of this commission is to obtain by investigation and by conference the cause or causes of the friction between the two races that started the molecules of race hatred into such violent motion as to cause the heterogenous mixture to boil over in the recent race riots.

Few white men know the cause, for the simple reason that few white men know the Negro as an entity. On the other hand, I daresay that almost any Negro that you might meet on the street could tell you the cause, if he would, for it is doubtful—aye, very doubtful—if he would tell you, because Negroes have become highly suspicious of white men, even such white men as they deem their friends ordinarily. The Negro has always been and is now largely a menial dependent upon the white man's generosity and charity for his livelihood, and for this reason he has become an expert cajoler of the white man and a veritable artist at appearing to be that which he is not. . . .

Unfortunately it is always by the larger class—the menial, servitor and flunkey class—that the race is judged. Even at that, we would not object to being judged by this class of our race, if those who did the judging had a thorough knowledge of the individuals who make up this class. Unfortunately they have not this knowledge nor can they get it except through the instrumentality of just such a commission as that to which you gentlemen have been assigned. The white man of America knows just about as much about the mental and moral calibre, the home life and social activities of this class of colored citizens as he does about the same things concerning the inhabitants of the thus far unexplored planet of Mars. If any white man were to be asked what he thought of George the porter on the Golden State Limited; or of James the waiter on the Twentieth Century diner; or of Shorty who gives him his billiard cue at Mussey's; or of Snowball who polishes his boots at the Palmer House; or of that old gray-haired relic of by-gone days . . . who withholds his hat and menaces him with a long-handled whisk broom until he capitulates with a nickel; I say were you to ask any white man concerning these dusky servitors he would tell you that he was either honest or dishonest, that he was either industrious or lazy, that he was smart or stupid as the case might be. He will discuss him in a general superficial sort of way and if you press him further you will be surprised to know that in spite of his years of acquaintance with the subject he knows absolutely nothing about intellect, ability, ambitions[,] the home life and environment of one with whom he has come into daily contact for years. He is just a "nigger" and he takes him for granted, as a matter of course. . . .

I can . . . be surveyed by the most critical of Sherlock Holmes's [*sic*] and I will wager that none of them can accurately deduce what

I am or what I represent. They cannot tell whether I am well off or hard up; whether I am educated or illiterate; whether I am a northerner or a southerner; whether I am a native born Negro or a foreigner; whether I live among beautiful surroundings or in the squalor of the "black belt." I defy the shrewdest of your pseudo detectives to know whether I am a reputable citizen or whether I am a newly arrived crook. They cannot tell by looking at me what my income is. . . . The point is that I am only an ordinary, average Negro and that the white man is constantly making the mistake of discounting us and rating us too cheaply. He should wake up to the fact that brain is not peculiar to any race or nationality but is merely a matter of development.

This in a measure explains how the American white man knows less about the American Negro than the latter does about the former. . . .

The further causes of the apparent increased friction between the two races, in my opinion, is due to the gradual and inevitable evolution—metamorphosis, if you please—of the Negro. The Negro has also progressed in knowledge by his study of the white man, while the white man blinded by either his prejudice or by his indifference has failed to study the Negro judiciously, and as a consequence, he knows no more about him than he did fifty years ago and still continues to judge him and to formulate opinions about him by his erstwhile standards. Today we have with us a new Negro. A brand new Negro, if you please. . . .

Take the late war for example, and consider the effect that it has had upon the Negro, by and large. I believe that the mental attitude of the Negro that went to war is comparable in a certain degree to the mental attitude of most of the Negroes throughout the country; so far as the awakenings are concerned. The Negro of this country has gone through the same evolution that the white man has, in his own way; and in a large percentage of the total, that way is not far removed from the way the white man's mind thought out the matter or is thinking it out, especially the soldier mind. The Negro of our country . . . the Negro of the mass I mean, is comparable in his awakening and in his manner of thought after that awakening, to these white boys who went to war. The white soldiers—being young—had but little thought of anything but their immediate concerns, and the Negro, until lately, had but little thought of anything but his immediate concerns—being segregated. How I loathe that word. . . .

When the Negro ponders the situation—and now he is beginning to seriously do that—it is with a feeling of poignant resentment that he sees his alleged inferiority constantly and blatantly advertised at every hand, by the press, the pulpit, the stage and by the glaring and hideous sign-boards of segregation. Try to imagine, if you can, the feelings of a Negro army officer, who clothed in the full panoply of his profession and wearing the decorations for valor of three governments, is forced to the indignity of a jim-crow car and who is refused a seat in a theatre and a bed in a hotel. Think of the feelings of a colored officer, who after having been graduated from West Point and having worked up step by step to the rank of colonel to be retired on account of blood pressure—and other pressure—in order that he might not automatically succeed to the rank of general officer. Try to imagine the smouldering hatred within the breast of an overseas veteran who is set upon and mercilessly beaten by a gang of young hoodlums simply because he is colored. Think of the feelings in the hearts of boys and girls of my race who are clean, intelligent and industrious who apply for positions only to meet with the polite reply that, "We don't hire niggers." Think how it must feel to pass at the top of the list and get notice of appointment to some nice civil service position that is paid for out of the taxes of the commonwealth, and upon reporting to assume the duties thereof, to be told that there has been a mistake made in the appointment. . . .

We ask not charity but justice. We no longer want perquisites but wages, salary and commissions. Much has been said anent the white man's burden. We admit to having been a burden, just as an infant that cannot walk is at one time a burden. But in the natural order of things the infant soon ceases to be a burden and eventually grows up to be a crutch for the arm that once carried him. We feel that now we are able to take our first, feeble diffident steps, and we implore the white man to set his burden down and let us try to walk. Put us in your counting rooms, your factories and in your banks. The young people who went to school with us and who learned the three R's from the same black-board as ourselves will surely not object to working with us after we have graduated. If they do, it will only be because they are not yet accustomed to the new conditions. That is nothing. People soon become accustomed to new things and things that seem at first preposterous soon become commonplace. We have surely proven by years of unrequited toil and by constant and unfaltering loyalty and fealty that we are worthy of the justice that we ask. For God's sake give it to us!

Stanley B. Norvell

William M. Tuttle, Jr., "Views of a Negro during 'the Red Summer' of 1919: A Document," *Journal of Negro History*, LI (July 1966).

Herbert J. Seligmann on Lynching

The lynching of Negroes, particularly in the South, is one of the worst blots on the history of twentieth-century America. Herbert J. Seligmann, a member of the Committee of 100 of the NAACP, went south in 1919 to investigate lynchings. A portion of his report of two incidents is included here.

Investigation covering Jackson, Vicksburg, Miss., and Memphis, Tenn., May 18 to 25, 1919.

Itinerary: Left New York City Friday May 16. Arrived Memphis Sunday May 18, departing the same day for Jackson, arriving morning of Monday May 19. Pickens, Miss., May 20 to investigate reported lynching of discharged soldier and woman, and same night to Vicksburg to investigate killing of Lloyd Clay. Departed for New Orleans night of May 21, returning to Memphis May 23. Memphis to New York night of May 24.

Interviews: R. R. Church in Memphis. Mr. Church believed the antagonism between white and colored races in the South was becoming more intense. Federal action seemed his only hope of averting serious conflict. Negroes were arming, he said, and on my second visit to Memphis, I overheard Mr. Church talk over the telephone with the Mayor of the city and tell him that the Negroes would not make trouble unless they were attacked but in that event they were prepared to defend themselves.

Perry Howard in Jackson. Mr. Howard, the leading colored attorney of Jackson, said the Negroes there were armed and prepared to defend themselves from mob violence. He recited an incident of November, 1918, when two white United States soldiers insulted a colored girl and slapped the face of her escort. He resented their actions and showed fight. The streets filled when the police attempted to arrest the colored man who was surrounded by men of his own race, all armed. Upon advice of Mr. Howard the police desisted from their attempt to make the unjustified arrest. Mr. Howard said bloody conflicts impended in a number of southern cities. There would be a great labor exodus from the South, said Mr. Howard, if there were labor opportunities in the North and the colored men had means to get away. The best colored people, he said, were in dread of what might at any moment break about them. Mr. Howard attributed the

LYNCHINGS BY STATES AND COUNTIES IN THE UNITED STATES 1900 TO 1931

(DATA FROM RESEARCH DEPARTMENT, TUSKEGEE INSTITUTE)

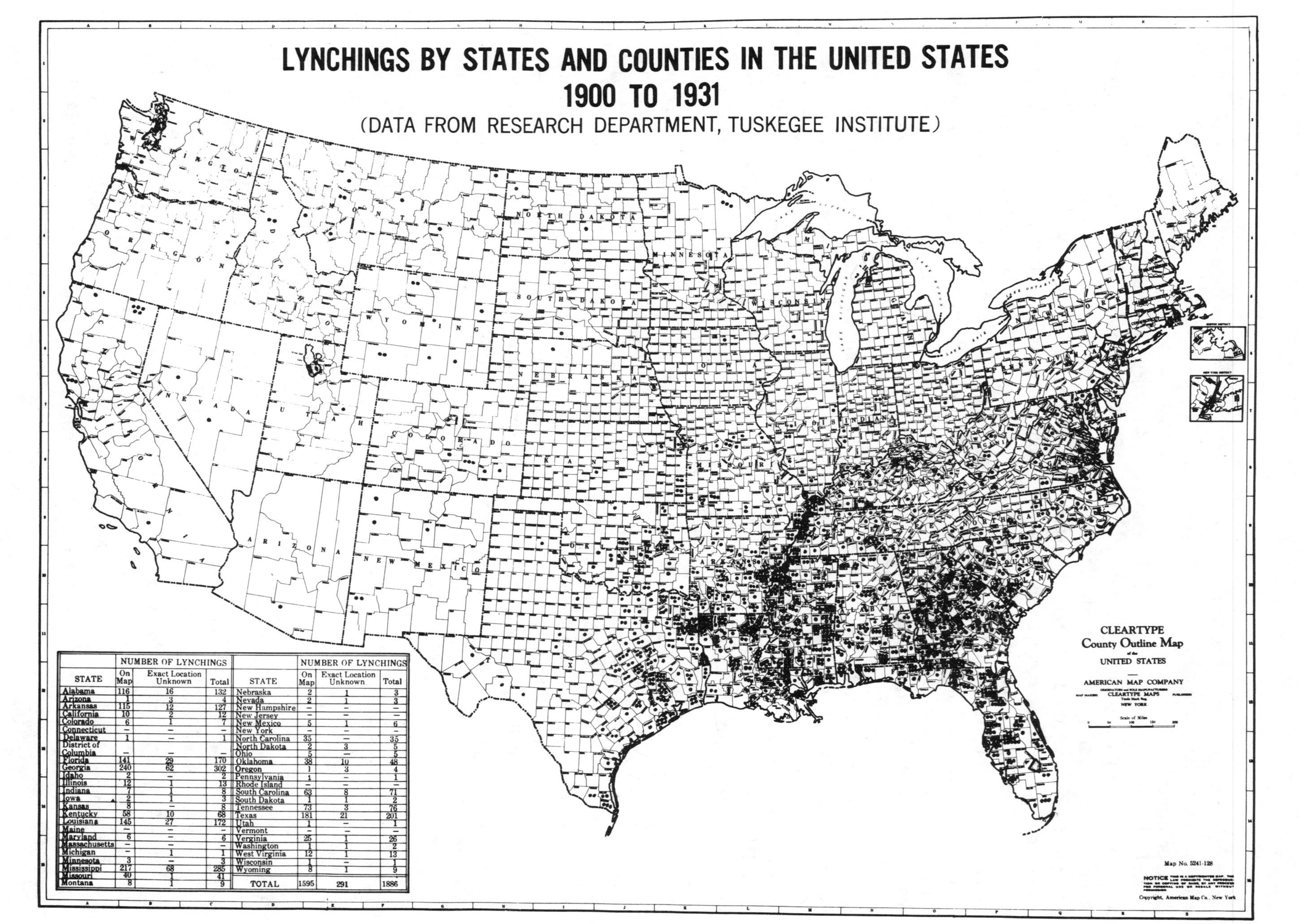

STATE	NUMBER OF LYNCHINGS On Map	Exact Location Unknown	Total	STATE	NUMBER OF LYNCHINGS On Map	Exact Location Unknown	Total
Alabama	116	16	132	Nebraska	2	1	3
Arizona	1	3	4	Nevada	2	1	3
Arkansas	115	12	127	New Hampshire	–	–	–
California	10	2	12	New Jersey	–	–	–
Colorado	6	1	7	New Mexico	5	1	6
Connecticut	–	–	–	New York	–	–	–
Delaware	1	–	1	North Carolina	35	–	35
District of Columbia	–	–	–	North Dakota	2	3	5
				Ohio	5	–	5
Florida	141	29	170	Oklahoma	38	10	48
Georgia	240	62	302	Oregon	1	3	4
Idaho	2	–	2	Pennsylvania	1	–	1
Illinois	12	1	13	Rhode Island	–	–	–
Indiana	7	1	8	South Carolina	63	8	71
Iowa	2	1	3	South Dakota	1	1	2
Kansas	8	–	8	Tennessee	73	3	76
Kentucky	58	10	68	Texas	181	21	201
Louisiana	145	27	172	Utah	1	–	1
Maine	–	–	–	Vermont	–	–	–
Maryland	6	–	6	Verginia	25	1	26
Massachusetts	–	–	–	Washington	1	1	2
Michigan	–	1	1	West Virginia	12	1	13
Minnesota	3	–	3	Wisconsin	1	–	1
Mississippi	217	68	285	Wyoming	8	1	9
Missouri	40	1	41				
Montana	8	1	9	TOTAL	1595	291	1886

present intensity to (1) Politicians and publications like Vardaman and his weekly, (2) Campaign for equal rights for Negroes, (3) Prejudice against Negro induction into the army.

Dr. A. R. Quinn in Vicksburg. He believed "the government was responsible" for inducting Negroes into the army, thus putting them on an equality with white men. Negroes, he said, should not have served in the war. He condemned the agitation for equal rights for Negroes. To meet the lynching evil Dr. Quinn predicted the resurrection of the Ku Klux Klan among "the best people" of the South. Dr. Quinn did not know he was talking to an investigator.

Marshall Ballard, editor of the *Item,* New Orleans. He did not believe there was any solution of the race problem. The present situation, he believed, was a heritage of carpet baggerism, a product of cheap politicians and the press who pushed race hatred in default of other issues, and the "exasperating" ignorance and inefficiency of the colored workman. He concurred in the often expressed view that the Negro race was inferior and left the problem at that point.

Rene Clair, wine merchant of New Orleans. Mr. Clair deplored lynching, though only in half hearted fashion. He represented a point of view typical of certain cultured Southerners, in that he insisted the Negro race was inferior to the white and would never in the South be admitted to political, economic or social equality. The Negro's part in the war, and especially the belief, widely held throughout the South, that Negro soldiers had been received on equal terms by white women in France, contributed to the tensity of the race antagonism.

Rudolf Giefers, candidate for election to the Louisiana state legislature, held that lynching was necessary, that the Negro race should never be enfranchised, that "educating Negroes only makes confidence men of the males and prostitutes of the females." Mr. Giefers gets along with individuals of the race by knocking them down when he considers it necessary.

Practically all intelligent Southerners agree that federal action is the only way to stop lynching, though extremists, like Dr. Quinn of Vicksburg, with living memories of the Civil War, says they will execute summary vengeance on offenders against Southern womanhood regardless of consequences.

Herbert J. Seligmann, investigator

* * * * *

The Lynching of Eugene Green. From reports and papers in possession of Judge Teat of Jackson, Miss.

On February 1, 1919, Eugene Green, Negro, became intoxicated and, while resisting arrest, shot William Hagan, town marshal of Belzoni, Miss., the bullets penetrating the lungs and intestines. Hagan was confined to his bed for three weeks.

Green fled to relatives on the farm of Fred Westfall, five miles west of Jackson. Mr. Westfall surrendered Green to the sheriff of Hinds County, receiving $500 reward offered for the capture of Green by O. J. Turner, sheriff of Humphreys County in which the shooting had taken place. Turner arrived in Jackson on February 28 to take the prisoner. A writ of habeas corpus was served on Turner returnable before Circuit Judge W. H. Potter on March 15. The writ was taken to insure that Green would be kept safely and brought back at that time.

Sheriff Turner was warned of the danger that Green would be lynched if he was taken to Belzoni. He persisted in carrying his prisoner there on March 1. No guard was stationed at the jail. That night the lights in Belzoni were turned off and a mob sawed off two padlocks on the calaboose in which Turner kept the prisoner. Green repeatedly screamed, arousing the people in the vicinity and one lady telephoned to Sheriff Turner saying that a mob was breaking into the jail. Turner failed to arrive at the jail in time to intercept the mob although they took from 30 to 40 minutes to break open the jail doors and get Green. A jailor who slept 50 feet away from the scene of commotion "did not awake." The prisoner was never again seen.

Sheriff Turner replied to the writ of habeas corpus directing him to produce the prisoner before Judge Potter on March 15 by saying that the prisoner had been removed by unknown parties.

Green was believed to have been killed and his body sunk in the Yazoo River from a bridge a quarter of a mile distant from the calaboose. Sheriff Turner, who lives four blocks from the calaboose, was said to have been at home during the attack on the jail. Warning of the lynching was given Turner in the feeling shown by a crowd which met the train on which he brought Green to Belzoni.

The names of those in the mob are locally known. Two men living nine miles from Belzoni were in town the next day, one of them heavily intoxicated. The lights of the town were turned off shortly after midnight. The manager and superintendent of the municipal lighting plant was J. J. Sisloff. William Cummings was jailor and deputy sheriff.

Judge Teat of Jackson, Mississippi, characterized the proceedings as an insult in the face of law, in that contempt had been shown of the writ of habeas corpus. The court had commanded an officer to return his prisoner, surrendered to him by law-abiding citizens. The sheriff, according to Judge Teat, offered no protection, no guard and there was no investigation following the lynching. A motion by Judge Teat to have the sheriff declared in contempt of court was denied. . . . Citizens of Belzoni remarked to an investigator that the people of the Mississippi Delta sometimes had to do things not strictly in accord with law.

Herbert J. Seligmann, investigator

NAACP Papers, Library of Congress.

Walter White Reflects on President-Elect Warren G. Harding

The election of Warren G. Harding to the Presidency brought new hope to Afro-Americans after the restrictive actions of the previous Wilson administration. Walter White, Executive Secretary of the NAACP, made a trip to Marion, Ohio, to confer with the President-elect on matters relating to blacks. The following report of White's visit candidly reflects the attitude of Mr. Harding.

REPORT OF THE SECRETARY'S VISIT TO SENATOR HARDING

The Secretary visited Senator Warren G. Harding on Saturday, January 15 [1921], at Marion, Ohio. Mr. Harding was cordial, stating that he had been obliged to refuse hundreds of persons who wished to talk with him but that he granted the Secretary an interview feeling that he spoke for an organization which represented the Negro race.

The Secretary took up with Mr. Harding various points as expressed in our program for 1921.

INTER-RACIAL COMMISION: The Senator appeared to be most interested in the point regarding the appointment of a national inter-racial commission for the purpose of making a study of race conditions and race relations in the United States. He remarked that that was really an idea worth consideration. The Secretary gained the impression that Mr. Harding will take some action on this point.

COLORED ASSISTANTS IN DEPARTMENTS: Mr. Harding also listened in a receptive manner to the suggestion of the appointment of colored assistant secretaries in the Departments of Labor and Agriculture.

TWENTY-FOURTH INFANTRY: As to the point relative to the exercise of executive clemency in the case of the members of the Twenty-fourth Infantry imprisoned at Leavenworth, Mr. Harding expressed a willingness to review the whole question of the Houston affair and give it consideration. It came out in his conversation, however, that during his vacation at Brownsville, Texas, he had the whole story of the "Brownsville riot" told to him from the point of view of the local white people. The Secretary endeavored to impress upon him the fact that Brownsville was an entirely closed incident and that, at any rate, Houston was to be viewed at a different angle. Mr. Harding remarked that he was quite sure the colored soldiers shot up Brownsville and that they did so because they were not allowed to drink in white saloons. The Secretary informed him that a mammoth petition would be presented to him in behalf of the soldiers of the Twenty-fourth Infantry imprisoned at Leavenworth. Mr. Harding asked that he not be rushed in the matter and that he be given several months after going into office before being asked to do anything.

NEGRO VOTE: Regarding the Negro vote in the South, Mr. Harding revealed that he felt the whole matter should be adjusted through time. This evidently comes from a desire on his part to break the solid South or, at any rate, to set up a functioning Republican Party in the Southern states. He said that he had an idea how the whole question could be solved politically. The gist of his solution was that colored people in the South should willingly accept white leadership until such time as prejudice was worn down. The Secretary called his attention to the fact that under existing conditions colored men were not even allowed to accept white leadership. He remarked that that was a condition which would have to be met.

N.A.A.C.P.: The Secretary spoke to Mr. Harding at some length regarding the work of the Association and its anti-lynching fight, also the anti-Ku Klux Klan fight. Mr. Harding condemned the Ku Klux Klan movement. The Secretary asked if he would not make a statement to that effect. Mr. Harding said that at this time he was making no public statements, cautioning the Secretary that he did not consider this conversation an interview.

In speaking of the Inter-Racial Commission, the Secretary called Senator Harding's attention to the fight which the Association had made and is still making in the Arkansas riots cases.

HAITI: Mr. Harding showed his first signs of enthusiasm when the Haitian question was brought up by the Secretary. He chuckled over the fact that it had been a very telling campaign issue. The Secretary asked him if he had seen a copy of the Haitian pamphlet. He replied that he had seen it, had read it, and had it in his files. The Secretary called the Senator's attention to the fact that he had tried to have the pamphlet published by the Republican National Committee but that they did not seem to have money enough to do it, so the N.A.A.C.P. did it at its own expense, sending copies to all newspapers and other mediums of publicity. That seemed to please Mr. Harding very much. He said that as soon as he took charge of the government he would call for an inquiry from the State Department on the Haitian question.

SUMMARY: On the whole, the interview with Mr. Harding was perhaps as satisfactory as could be expected. The trouble with Senator Harding is, first of all, that he is a man of very little imagination and seemingly of very little human sympathy. He is an average, decent American citizen but also a hard, practical and perhaps rather timid politician. More serious still, from our point of view, is the fact that he knows absolutely nothing about the race question. All that he seems to know about Negroes is what he has gathered from the rather sorry specimens in and about Marion. Also, he has undoubtedly been influenced by southern men during his trip South, and he is going South again next week.

Nevertheless, the Secretary feels that Senator Harding intends to be just and fair. In fact, he stated that in very definite terms. The Secretary suggested to him that the colored people were entitled to justice and fairness, but that they expected just a little more, and that is an interest which would be sympathetic because their case is a special one. The Secretary referred to such statements as were frequently given out by Theodore Roosevelt in which he specifically referred to the colored people of the United States and their just rights as such, citing that these statements not only influenced the Nation at large but greatly heartened the colored people themselves.

Mr. Harding will need to be educated on the race question. Perhaps he can be. The Secretary regards it as hopeful, at any rate.

At the conclusion of the Secretary's visit, Mr. Harding extended to him a very cordial invitation to come to Washington and talk over all the matters regarding the race situation.

In beginning the interview and closing it the Secretary impressed upon Mr. Harding that the colored people of the United States would not be satisfied merely with the appointment of individuals to office—that they were more interested in measures than they were in political appointments, and that they were entitled to some share in the administration of the government.

NAACP Papers, Library of Congress.

James Weldon Johnson and the Anti-Lynching Bill

James Weldon Johnson, Executive Secretary of the NAACP, was active in seeking federal legislation prohibiting lynching. In the period from 1920 to 1929, there were 309 people lynched in the United States, the majority of whom were Negroes. Congressman L. C. Dyer of Missouri introduced an anti-lynching bill that was passed by the House of Representatives in 1922 but failed to pass in the Senate. Johnson recorded the incidents that occurred in the House at the time the bill was passed.

. . . I was back in Washington on January 10. The Anti-Lynching Bill was taken up on that day, but side-tracked for a week for the Post Office Appropriation Bill. On the seventeenth, debate was resumed; then consideration was postponed another week for another appropriation bill. I began to suffer qualms of anxiety. I wondered if the men with whom I had been dealing were merely giving me and the Association and the Negroes of the country a little "run-around." In the morning on the twenty-fourth, I went to see Mr. Mondell. He told me that the Dyer bill would not be taken up because there was another appropriation bill to be disposed of. He said that some of the leaders wanted more time, and that it might be best to leave it until the thirtieth, then keep it up until it was passed. He added that he had called a meeting of Republican leaders in the Speaker's room, to discuss the matter, and was on his way there. We came out of his office together; he went to the Speaker's room, and I went to my accustomed place in the gallery to sit and read the morning papers, while waiting for the opening hour. While the roll was being droned out, I saw Mr. Mondell beckoning me from the floor to meet him in the lobby. When I reached him, he told me rather excitedly that the Dyer bill would be taken up the next day, whether the appropriation bill was out of the way or not, and pushed through to a finish.

Debate opened on the next day and grew more bitter as it went along. Speeches of the most truculent character were made by Representatives Sisson, of Mississippi, and Blanton, of Texas, both of whom spoke not only in favor of mob rule, but in utter defiance of anything the federal government might propose to do about it. Most of the Southern opponents of the bill argued that rape was the cause of lynching, and that, in such cases, the white community simply went mad and was not accountable for its acts which, after all, were in fulfillment of a "higher law." . . .

. . . It had been part of my work to keep the sponsors of the bill supplied with facts and figures. They had the figures from me showing that less than seventeen per cent of the victims of lynching in thirty-three years had even been charged by the mob with rape. But the piece of data that completely swept away the "usual crime" argument, was a list of dates and places, and of the names of sixty-four Negro women who had been lynched. The supporters of the bill made some good speeches and used the statistics that had been furnished to them with telling effect. The most eloquent of these speeches was made by Burke Cochran, a Democrat.

The news that the Anti-Lynching Bill was being debated jammed the galleries on the following day; the majority of the crowd being Negroes. There was intense excitement. At a point in one of the speeches, the Negroes in the galleries broke the rules and rose and cheered. A voice from the floor shouted, "Sit down, you N———!" And a voice from the galleries shouted back, "You're a liar! We're not N———." The Speaker announced that he would have the galleries closed if there was any further applause. At three o'clock the bill went to a vote, and at three-thirty the Speaker declared it passed by a vote of 230 to 119.

James Weldon Johnson, *Along This Way* (New York, 1933).

Congressman L. C. Dyer on the Anti-Lynching Bill

In subsequent sessions of Congress, Dyer and others attempted to place pressure on members of the Senate Judiciary Committee to get the anti-lynching legislation brought before the Senate. In a speech before the NAACP in Chicago in 1922, Dyer told of the internal conflict in Congress regarding the bill.

A sincere and earnest effort has been made by the House of Representatives in the past several Congresses to pass this measure. . . . In the 67th Congress, this legislation passed by a very large majority. The United States Senate failed in that Congress to pass it. The House of Representatives has been ready, and still is, to pass this legislation at any time. It has been considered useless, however, to do so, in view of the action of the Senate when this legislation went before them in the 67th Congress. They allowed a small number of Senators to put on a filibuster and stop its passage there. We all know that the Senate could then, and could now, if it wanted to, adopt a cloture rule which would limit debate and enable its members to vote. With the House in favor of it, it could have become a law signed by the President who has stated many times that he favors it.

A hearing was held by the Judiciary Committee of the Senate upon the Bill introduced by Senator McKinley, in the Senate, the same one that I introduced in the House. At the hearing on February 16, a number of friends of this legislation appeared in favor of it. Among them was Mr. James Weldon Johnson, Secretary of the National Association for the Advancement of Colored People. He made a very splendid address and furnished very complete data and reasons for the enactment of the legislation into law. In addition to that, he furnished an able legal brief showing the constitutionality of the legislation. No one appeared at the hearing in opposition to the Bill. Notwithstanding this, the Judiciary Committee of the Senate not only has failed, but it has refused by a vote of its members to favorably report this Bill to the Senate.

Since the Judiciary Committee of the Senate has had this legislation directly before them, as stated above, and as they have had a hearing upon it and then refused to report it to the Senate, it is apparent to everyone that the fault lies entirely with the Senate, and that it would not only be foolish from a legislative standpoint, but that it would be insulting to those who are especially urging this legislation to keep repeatedly passing it in the House. . . .

NAACP Papers, Library of Congress.

Walter White Investigates Lynchings

Walter White of the National Association for the Advancement of Colored People traveled freely in the South for many years as a result of his blue eyes and light complexion. He often investigated lynchings and other problems in race relations while "passing" for white. The following excerpt is from a most unusual firsthand account of his experiences.

Nothing contributes so much to the continued life of an investigator of lynchings and his tranquil possession of all his limbs as the obtuseness of the lynchers themselves. Like most boastful people who practice direct action when it involves no personal risk, they just can't help talk about their deeds to any person who manifests even the slightest interest in them.

Most lynchings take place in small towns and rural regions where the natives know practically nothing of what is going on outside their own immediate neighborhoods. Newspapers, books, magazines, theatres, visitors and other vehicles for the transmission of information and ideas are usually as strange among them as dry-point etchings. But those who live in so sterile an atmosphere usually esteem their own perspicacity in about the same degree as they are isolated from the world of ideas. They gabble on *ad infinitum,* apparently unable to keep from talking.

In any American village, North or South, East or West, there is no problem which cannot be solved in half an hour by the morons who lounge about the village store. World peace, or the lack of it, the tariff, sex, religion, the settlement of the war debts, short skirts, Prohibition, the carryings-on of the younger generation, the superior moral rectitude of country people over city dwellers (with a wistful eye on urban sins)—all these controversial subjects are disposed of quickly and finally by the bucolic wise men. When to their isolation is added an emotional fixation such as the rural South has on the Negro, one can sense the atmosphere from which spring the Heflins, the Ku Kluxers, the two-gun Bible-beaters, the lynchers and the anti-evolutionists. And one can see why no great amount of cleverness or courage is needed to acquire information in such a forlorn place about the latest lynching.

Professor Earle Fiske Young of the University of Southern California recently analyzed the lynching returns from fourteen Southern States for thirty years. He found that in counties of less than 10,000 people there was a lynching rate of 3.2 per 100,000 of population; that in those of from 10,000 to 20,000 the rate dropped to 2.4; that in those of from 20,000 to 30,000, it was 2.1 per cent; that in those of from 30,000 to 40,000, it was 1.7; and that thereafter it kept on going down until in counties with from 300,000 to 800,000 population it was only 0.05.

Of the forty-one lynchings and eight race riots I have investigated for the National Association for the Advancement of Colored People during the past ten years all of the lynchings and seven of the riots occurred in rural or semi-rural communities. The towns ranged in population from around one hundred to ten thousand or so. The lynchings were not difficult to inquire into because of the fact already noted that those who perpetrated them were in nearly every instance simple-minded and easily fooled individuals. On but three occasions were suspicions aroused by my too definite questions or by informers who had seen me in other places. These three times I found it rather desirable to disappear slightly in advance of reception committees imbued with the desire to make an addition to the lynching record. One other time the possession of a light skin and blue eyes (though I consider myself a colored man) almost cost me my life when (it was during the Chicago race riots in 1919) a Negro shot at me thinking me to be a white man.

In 1918 a Negro woman, about to give birth to a child, was lynched with almost unmentionable brutality along with ten men in Georgia. I reached the scene shortly after the butchery and while excitement yet ran high. It was a prosperous community. Forests of pine trees gave rich returns in turpentine, tar and pitch. The small towns where the farmers and turpentine hands traded were fat and rich. The main streets of the largest of these towns were well paved and lighted. The stores were well stocked. The white inhabitants belonged to the class of Georgia crackers—lanky, slow of movement and of speech, long-necked, with small eyes set close together, and skin tanned by the hot sun to a reddish-yellow hue.

As I was born in Georgia and spent twenty years of my life there, my accent is sufficiently Southern to enable me to talk with Southerners and not arouse their suspicion that I am an outsider. (In the rural South hatred of Yankees is not much less than hatred of Negroes.) On the morning of my arrival in the town I casually dropped into the store of one of the general merchants who, I had been informed, had been one of the leaders of the mob. After making a small purchase I engaged the merchant in conversation. There was, at the time, no other customer in the store. We spoke of the weather, the possibility of good crops in the Fall, the political situation, the latest news from the war in Europe. As his manner became more and more friendly I ventured to mention guardedly the recent lynchings.

Instantly he became cautious—until I hinted that I had great admiration for the manly spirit the men of the town had exhibited. I mentioned the newspaper accounts I had read and confessed that I had never been so fortunate as to see a lynching. My words or tone seemed to disarm his suspicions. He offered me a box on which to sit, drew up another one for himself, and gave me a bottle of Coca-Cola.

"You'll pardon me, Mister," he began, "for seeming suspicious but we have to be careful. In ordinary times we wouldn't have anything to worry about, but with the war there's been some talk of the Federal government looking into lynchings. It seems there's some sort of law during wartime making it treason to lower the man power of the country."

"In that case I don't blame you for being careful," I assured him. "But couldn't the Federal government do something if it wanted to when a lynching takes place, even if no war is going on at the moment?"

"Naw," he said, confidently, obviously proud of the opportunity of displaying his store of information to one whom he assumed knew nothing whatever about the subject. "There's no such law, in spite of all the agitation by a lot of fools who don't know the niggers as we do. States' rights won't permit Congress to meddle in lynching in peace time."

"But what about your State government—your Governor, your sheriff, your police officers?"

"Humph! Them? We elected them to office, didn't we? And the niggers, we've got them disfranchised, ain't we? Sheriffs and police and Governors and prosecuting attorneys have got too much sense to mix in lynching-bees. If they do they know they might as well give up all idea of running for office any more—if something worse don't happen to them—" This last with a tightening of the lips and a hard look in the eyes.

I sought to lead the conversation into less dangerous channels. "Who was the white man who was killed—whose killing caused the lynchings?" I asked.

"Oh, he was a hard one, all right. Never paid his debts to white men or niggers and wasn't liked much around here. He was a mean 'un, all right, all right."

"Why, then, did you lynch the niggers for killing such a man?"

"It's a matter of safety—we gotta show niggers that they mustn't touch a white man, no matter how low-down and ornery he is."

Little by little he revealed the whole story. When he told me of the manner in which the pregnant woman had been killed he chuckled and slapped his thigh and declared it to be "the best show, Mister, I ever did see. You ought to have heard the wench howl when we strung her up."

. . . In 1926 I went to a Southern State for a New York newspaper to inquire into the lynching of two colored boys and a colored woman. Shortly after reaching the town I learned that a certain lawyer knew something about the lynchers. He proved to be the only specimen I have ever encountered in much travelling in the South of the Southern gentleman so beloved by fiction writers of the older school. He had heard of the lynching before it occurred and, fruitlessly, had warned the judge and the prosecutor. He talked frankly about the affair and gave me the names of certain men who knew more about it than he did. Several of them lived in a small town nearby . . .. When I asked him if he would go with me to call on these people he peered out the window at the descending sun and said, somewhat anxiously, I thought, "I will go with you if you will promise to get back to town before sundown."

I asked why there was need of such haste. "No one would harm a respectable and well-known person like yourself, would they?" I asked him.

"Those mill hands out there would harm anybody," he answered.

I promised him we would be back before sundown—a promise that was not hard to make, for if they would harm this man I could imagine what they would do to a stranger!

When we reached the little mill town we passed through it and, ascending a steep hill, our car stopped in front of a house perched perilously on the side of the hill. In the yard stood a man with iron gray hair and eyes which seemed strong enough to bore through concrete. The old lawyer introduced me and we were invited into the house. As it was a cold afternoon in late Autumn the gray-haired man called a boy to build a fire.

I told him frankly I was seeking information about the lynching. He said nothing but left the room. Perhaps two minutes later, hearing a sound at the door through which he had gone, I looked up and there stood a figure clad in the full regalia of the Ku Klux Klan. I looked at the figure and the figure looked at me. The hood was then removed and, as I suspected, it was the owner of the house.

"I show you this," he told me, "so you will know that what I tell you is true."

This man, I learned, had been the organizer and kleagle of the local Klan. He had been quite honest in his activities as a Kluxer, for corrupt officials and widespread criminal activities had caused him and other local men to believe that the only cure rested in a secret extra-legal organization. But he had not long been engaged in promoting the plan before he had the experience of other believers in Klan methods. The very people whose misdeeds the organization was designed to correct gained control of it. This man then resigned and ever since had been living in fear of his life. He took me into an adjoining room after removing his Klan robe and there showed me a considerable collection of revolvers, shot guns, rifles and ammunition.

We then sat down and I listened to as hair-raising a tale of Nordic moral endeavor as it has ever been my lot to hear. Among the choice bits were stories such as this: The sheriff of an adjoining county the year before had been a candidate for reëlection. A certain man of considerable wealth had contributed largely to his campaign fund, providing the margin by which he was reëlected. Shortly afterwards a married woman with whom the sheriff's supporter had been intimate quarreled one night with her husband. When the cuckold charged his wife with infidelity, the gentle creature waited until he was asleep, got a large butcher knife, and then artistically carved him up. Bleeding more profusely than a pig in the stock yards, the man dragged himself to the home of a neighbor several hundred yards distant and there died on the door-step. The facts were notorious, but the sheriff effectively blocked even interrogation of the widow!

I spent some days in the region and found that the three Negroes who had been lynched were about as guilty of the murder of which they were charged as I was. Convicted in a court thronged with armed Klansmen and sentenced to death, their case had been appealed to the State Supreme Court, which promptly reversed the conviction, remanded the appellants for new trials, and severely criticized the judge before whom they had been tried. At the new trial the evidence against one of the defendants so clearly showed his innocence that the judge granted a motion to dismiss, and the other two defendants were obviously as little guilty as he. But as soon as the motion to dismiss was granted the defendant was rearrested on a trivial charge and once again lodged in jail. That night the mob took the prisoners to the outskirts of the town, told them to run, and as they set out pumped bullets into their backs. The two boys died instantly. The woman was shot in several places, but was not immediately killed. One of the lynchers afterwards laughingly told me that "we had to waste fifty bullets on the wench before one of them stopped her howling."

Evidence in affidavit form indicated rather clearly that various law enforcement officials, including the sheriff, his deputies, various jailers and policemen, three relatives of the then Governor of the State, a member of the State Legislature and sundry individuals prominent in business, political and social life of the vicinity, were members of the mob.

The revelation of these findings after I had returned to New York did not add to my popularity in the lynching region. Public sentiment in the State itself, stirred up by several courageous newspapers, began to make it uncomfortable for the lynchers. When the sheriff found things getting a bit too unpleasant he announced that he was going to ask the grand jury to indict me for "bribery and passing for white." It developed that the person I was supposed to have paid money to for execution of an affidavit was a man I had never seen in the flesh, the affidavit having been secured by the reporter of a New York newspaper.

A narrower escape came during an investigation of an alleged plot by Negroes in Arkansas to "massacre" all the white people of the State. It later developed that the Negroes had simply organized a cooperative society to combat their economic exploitation by landlords, merchants, and bankers, many of whom openly practiced peonage. I went as a representative of a Chicago newspaper to get the facts. Going first to the capital of the State, Little Rock, I interviewed the Governor and other officials and then proceeded to the scene of the trouble, Phillips county, in the heart of the cotton-raising area close to the Mississippi.

As I stepped from the train at Elaine, the county seat, I was closely watched by a crowd of men. Within half an hour of my arrival I had been asked by two shopkeepers, a restaurant waiter, and a ticket agent why I had come to Elaine, what my business was, and what I thought of the recent riot. The tension relaxed somewhat when I implied I was in sympathy with the mob. Little by little suspicion was lessened and then, the people being eager to have a metropolitan newspaper give their side of the story, I was shown "evidence" that the story of the massacre plot was well-founded, and not very clever attempts were made to guide me away from the truth.

Suspicion was given new birth when I pressed my inquiries too insistently concerning the share-cropping and tenant-farming system, which works somewhat as follows: Negro farmers enter into agreements to till specified plots of land, they to receive usually half of the crop for their labor. Should they be too poor to buy food, seed, clothing and other supplies, they are supplied these commodities by their landlords at designated stores. When the crop is gathered the landowner takes it and sells it. By declaring that he has sold it at a figure far below the market price and by refusing to give itemized accounts of the supplies purchased during the year by the tenant, a landlord can (and in that region almost always does) so arrange it that the bill for supplies always exceeds the tenant's share of the crop. Individual Negroes who had protested against such thievery had been lynched. The new organization was simply a union to secure relief through the courts, which relief those who profited from the system meant to prevent. Thus the story of a "massacre" plot.

Suspicion of me took definite form when word was sent to Phillips county from Little Rock that it had been discovered that I was a Negro, though I knew nothing about the message at the time. I walked down West Cherry street, the main thoroughfare of Elaine, one day on my way to the jail, where I had an appointment with the sheriff, who was going to permit me to interview some of the Negro prisoners who were charged with being implicated in the alleged plot. A tall, heavy-set Negro passed me and, *sotto voce,* told me as he passed that he had something important to tell me, and that I should turn to the right at the next corner and follow him. Some inner sense bade me obey. When we had got out of sight of other persons the Negro told me not to go to the jail, that there was great hostility in the town against me and that they planned harming me. In the man's manner there was something which made me certain he was telling the truth. Making my way to the railroad station, since my interview with the prisoners (the sheriff and jailer being present) was unlikely to add anything to my story, I was able to board one of the two trains a day out of Elaine. When I explained to the conductor—he looked at me so inquiringly—that I had no ticket because delays in Elaine had given me no time to purchase one, he exclaimed, "Why, Mister, you're leaving just when the fun is going to start! There's a damned yaller nigger down here passing for white and the boys are going to have some fun with him."

I asked him the nature of the fun.

"Wal, when they get through with him," he explained grimly, "he won't pass for white no more."

Walter White, "I Investigate Lynchings," *American Mercury,* XVI (January 1929).

Clarence Darrow on Religion and Race

Clarence Darrow, noted defense attorney who often worked for equal rights for Negroes, was regarded by his contemporaries as unconventional in attitude and behavior. The following letter to James Weldon Johnson illustrates Darrow's willingness to speak out for the Negroes' rights, as well as his attitude toward religious activities.

April 17, 1928

Mr. James Weldon Johnson,
c/o N.A.A.C.P.,
69—5th Avenue,
New York City

My dear Johnson:

When I was in Florida someone sent me a newspaper report from Washington which contained a resolution of the colored preachers that I was not to speak at any of their churches when I came there. Somehow, I do not find fault with it. I do not blame them for feeling that my talks, which always slam the preachers, generally do not exactly fit a temple of god. The only excuse I could see for their having me in a church is that you have often told me that a large part of the money for paying for churches was given on the theory that they really did use their places for halls, at least you said something like this, and something like this is probably true. If they take the money for that purpose, it seems to me they ought to admit a fellow like me whom they know is speaking for the Negroes, and if they feel they cannot, why it ought to be understood when they raise money.

However, I had no feeling about the matter. I have promised to go to Washington and am also going to Springfield. I have heard from Washington since but no information as to where I am to speak. I have been embarrassed several times in speaking in halls for the Negroes by having some damn fool preacher start the thing off with a prayer and close with a benediction. I don't have this even among white christians, who are bad enough, if I am speaking in their churches. I can see some point in conforming and would not raise the question, but I wish you would tell them that when I speak in a hall I don't want them to do it. I am not interested in God, and he is not interested in the colored people. I don't think they ought to impose it on me.

Mind, this does not go as to the churches but tell them that if a meeting is held in a hall that I resent it. I don't believe in their forcing themselves on a fellow like me and shall be apt to say something about it in my remarks if it is done.

I expect to be in New York in the forenoon of the 23rd and also a part of the time at least on the 24th and 25th. With all good wishes, to yourself and wife, I am as ever

Your friend,

Clarence Darrow

NAACP Papers, Library of Congress.

Father Divine Explains His Mission

By the early 1920's, a self-proclaimed Messiah had come to the aid of his people. By the 1930's, his fame was widespread. The Reverend M. J. Divine, better known as Father Divine, appealed directly to the masses, establishing "heavens" for his followers. Below is an excerpt from one of his speeches.

. . . PEACE EVERYONE! Now you are HAPPY, and I am GLAD! It is indeed Wonderful! I can Say once again, here you are and there I am, —there I sit and here you stand. That is one Eternal mystery, One in all, and all in One. That is the way Christ was to Come, that is the Way He Came,—It is indeed Wonderful, —to be living in an Age where we are conscious of the actual materialization of every real, profitable, and desirable Spiritual unfoldment. It is indeed Wonderful! Your fore-ancestors and thousands of the relatives today are still in the darkness of misunderstanding, believing GOD to be merely Something in the mystical and Spiritual Realm that has no business down here on the material plane. It is indeed Wonderful!

GOD would not be Omnipotent, GOD would not be Omniscient, GOD would not be Omnipresent if He were bound to the Spiritual plane alone. It is indeed Wonderful! I have just as much right in politics as in anything else! I am Spiritualizing material things and materializing Spiritual things and I have brought the Heaven to the Earth, and I have made the Earth the Heaven. That is what I have done! And I shall universally establish it and all mankind shall realize, GOD is not a GOD afar off, but GOD is a GOD at hand.

GOD shall Rule in the affairs of men, for He Condescended to make Himself flesh when He was SPIRIT, that mankind might realize, GOD is tangible, and natural, and real, and practical. I am not seeking any political office, I WOULD NOT HAVE A POLITICAL OFFICE. I HAVE TWENTY MILLION FOLLOWERS SO SAY MY REPRESENTATIVES. It is indeed Wonderful! But I am here to emphasize the great significance of the recognition of the actual materialization of Righteousness, Justice and Truth. It is no longer something mystical or imaginary, as your fore-ancestors have taught you. GOD has made Real, the Spiritual things, for they were only an imagination in your mystical conception. This Life, this Love, this Spirit, this Work, and this Fundamental, being the Christ of Whom you say I Am, as a Principle has come, and you have declared both He and It have been Personified, that all mankind might realize GOD Deals and Rules in the affairs of men.

I will make everyone sit up and take notice! I will let them see, GOD had Dominion on the material plane as well as on the mental and Spiritual planes. It is indeed Wonderful! Not an Official that will be elected,—if he does not deal justly and righteously among the people, shall remain in office. It is indeed Wonderful! I will prove to the world conclusively, GOD has something to do with the material things of life. That is why I Came in a Bodily Form. At this recognition, "Every knee must bend and every tongue must confess." You may try to ignore Me, but I WILL MAKE YOU BOW YOUR KNEES.

Think it not strange because I am in such a Meeting as this. I have a RIGHT to any meeting where living people are. It is indeed Wonderful! I mean to bring into actual materialization, your fondest imaginations for which you have been praying. It is indeed Wonderful; There is not enough power on the face of the Earth to hinder Me in accomplishing that for which I Came. It is indeed Wonderful!

I will call your attentions to the fact that after the "Jim Crow Law" came out in the South, I Said,—"I will go South as a Person, and I will break down the wall of partition between the races, creeds and colors, and I will present My Body as a Living Sacrifice, and I will accomplish My Mission, if I have to throw off this Body." ("Thank you Father,"—came from the immense Audience.) It is indeed Wonderful! Personally, I have gone through all parts of the South, presenting My Body as a Living Sacrifice to bring about a general moral betterment and bring about a universal Brotherhood of Man, that they might recognize GOD as their Father. It is indeed Wonderful!

For this cause I came, and for this purpose I stand, and I will have it, the Universe over, even as I have it on My immediate Staff. There shall be no division among My People, and MY People are of EVERY NATION, LANGUAGE, RACE, CREED, and COLOR. That is who I am Representing, and that is why I have All Power. That is why I am limitless, financially, socially, intellectually, and in every imaginable way. . . .

I further wish to say we have some Mottoes that I have Composed for the Statute Book of the different Governments of our present Civilization,—not only this Government, but it must be recognized by all. It is indeed Wonderful! We will read just a Motto for your consideration. Peace everybody! This little motto, I have been giving out for quite some time. It reads as follows—

"We the Inter-racial, International, Inter-denominational and Inter-religious co-workers, As Representatives of the Christ Consciousness and Ever-Presence of GOD, As being called Father Divine's Peace Mission Workers, Do demand the release thru commutation of the life-sentence of the Scottsboro boy, and other legal means of releasing the nine boys; And also we demand the Freedom and extermination of the mistreatment of the Jews in Germany and all other countries; And we demand the equal rights and Religious Liberty according to Our Constitution. I Thank you. . . ."

New York *News* (New York), November 10, 1934.

In Praise of World War I Black Troops

The thread of racial discrimination is woven into every aspect of the history of this nation. In all the wars Americans have fought, Negroes have served with honor and distinction; but inevitably criticism has followed each of their endeavors.

World War I found Negroes serving in France with the American Expeditionary Forces. Seven years after the war drew to a close, discussion was still being conducted on their abilities as soldiers. In the following letter, written in 1925 to the New York Herald Tribune, *Captain L. Edward Shaw of the 369th Infantry stated his views of the colored troops with whom he served.*

I have read with much interest and appreciation General Bullard's Memoirs [dealing with Negro troops]. His comments on the colored soldier, and Major Hamilton Fish's letter in *The Herald Tribune* of June 12 in reply, stir me to add my humble comment to this most interesting controversy.

I was one of the original officers in Colonel Hayward's 15th N.Y. Infantry—369th U.S. Infantry—and served continuously with that regiment during the war. I have since the war been constantly engaged in welfare work among the veterans of the regiment and the colored people of Harlem generally. I believe that I understand the American Negro, and my experience with him under the most trying conditions had made me a stanch supporter of his race.

Since the war I have been answering constantly one question: "What do you really think of the colored soldier?" My answer has always been, and still is, "If there were another war to-morrow I should try to go with the colored troops."

The 369th Infantry, the writer's regiment, could and did hold under the worst shellfire. Contrary to Major Hamilton Fish's statement in his letter in *The Herald Tribune,* this was not always true of the French Negro troops. Often after severe shelling on several occasions our French General Le Bue and his staff of the 161st French Division, 4th French Army, were astounded at this quality in our regiment and repeatedly stated that they dared not risk their colored soldiers as holding troops under bombardment. We saw this to be true in relieving one of the famous Moroccan regiments in the Champagne in July under heavy shellings. They "had the wind up" so much that they literally knocked our men down in their haste to get out of their positions when our reliefs appeared.

Major Fish fails to note that General Bullard did not say that the colored soldier lacks courage. In fact, he states that in his military experience prior to the World War the conduct of colored troops was excellent.

The history of the Civil and Spanish American wars confirms this statement. General Bullard confines his criticism of the colored soldier to the 92nd Division, whose war record apparently substantiates it. The fault, however, is not with the colored soldier in this division, but with his leaders and the administration that sent him into battle untrained.

In closing I wish to call . . . attention to the dedication in Harlem on Sunday, June 14, at 3 o'clock, on Edgecombe Avenue and 136th Street, of a Square to Private Dorrance Brooks, New York colored boy, born on 130th Street, educated in the New York public schools, killed in action in the Argonne-Meuse leading forward a remnant of a section of the Third Machine Gun Company, 369th Infantry, after his four white officers, two colored sergeants and two colored corporals had been killed or wounded. As the grave of the Unknown Soldier at Washington honors all soldier dead of the nation, let this Square, dedicated to a humble colored soldier from New York City honor the valor of the American colored soldier and stand as a permanent answer to all uninformed or prejudiced critics of the colored soldier.

New York Herald Tribune, June 14, 1925.

Negro Farm Problems

After World War I, there were large shifts in the Negro population. Blacks were moving from the South to the North, from rural to urban centers. Many who attended the National Agricul-

tural Conference of 1922 were concerned about the increasing discontent among Negro farmers, particularly the sharecroppers and tenant farmers. The following report was submitted by the sub-committee on Negro farm problems.

January 27, 1922

REPORT OF SUB-COMMITTEE 5j
OF COMMITTEE ON COSTS, PRICES,
AND READJUSTMENTS, OF NATIONAL
AGRICULTURAL CONFERENCE

NEGRO FARM PROBLEMS

We, the Committee on Negro Farm Problems, after careful consideration of the conditions that confront Negro farmers throughout the United States, respectfully submit the following report:

We first of all call your attention to the fact that there is a greater percentage of the Negro population who are farm operators than of any other racial group in this country, and that out of a total of 925,708 Negro farmers, 218,612 are owners. The Negro farmers operated, in 1920, a total of 41,432,182 acres. The value of the land and buildings owned and in the care of these Negro farmers amounts to $2,257,645,325, according to the Census of 1920, which represents an increase of $1,334,927,622 during the last ten years.

In view of the splendid progress shown above we feel that every effort should be made to encourage Negro farmers to buy and own their own farms, as ownership has generally proved to be a potent factor in the higher development of all classes of citizenship.

Due to the fact that slightly more than 75 per cent of the Negro farmers are in the tenant class, we feel that an intensive and sympathetic study should be made of all conditions peculiar to this form of land tenure, to the end that we may be able to offer recommendations for the social and economic betterment of this class of our farming population.

As there is great suffering throughout the country among Negro farmers on account of the lack of ready money, and as there are large quantities of farm products on hand for which they have not been able to find a market, we urge that special attention be given to the formation of cooperative marketing associations among this group, and wherever possible these farmers be accorded the same advantages in existing organizations in their respective communities as other subscribing members.

There is a special need for a more favorable application of the Federal Farm Loan Act in its relation to colored farmers so that they may be able to obtain all of the assistance that may be had through this helpful source and be relieved from the too frequent pressure of local money loaners.

There is much dissatisfaction among the rural districts on account of poor school facilities which, in many cases, have been the cause for a general migration from the farms to the cities. Because of this we urge a more liberal support from the state and local governments.

We need a more generous Federal and State support of our Negro agricultural colleges and a closer supervision of their activities, as they constitute the principal sources for intelligent agricultural leadership.

There should be a more adequate distribution of Federal funds that are allocated to the different states under the Smith-Lever and the Smith-Hughes Acts so that Negro farmers may receive a greater benefit, to the end that we may have a larger number of well-trained men and women to advise and to work in the rural districts. This is especially necessary because of the fact that this class of our farming population has had less advantage than most of the other farming groups.

Since the Negro farmer has made such splendid progress in farm ownership and has contributed so largely to the wealth of the Nation, it is essential, if he is to remain on the farms, that every effort should be made to protect him in the enjoyment of his life and property.

Respectfully submitted,

The Committee on Negro Farm Problems

Chairman:	Benj. F. Hubert	Alabama
Secretary:	Charles E. Hall	Illinois
	W. S. Scarborough	Ohio
	R. W. Westberry	South Carolina

W. S. Scarborough Papers, Wilberforce University.

A Historian Surveys the Negro Churches

In 1928, Dr. Carter G. Woodson of the Association for the Study of Negro Life and History employed Lorenzo J. Greene, a graduate student at Columbia University, to participate in a survey of Negro churches. Greene and others compiled a series of statistics which Woodson later incorporated into a volume dealing with Negro churches. In the process of carrying out his assigned duties, Greene kept a diary of his experiences. Below is an excerpt from this diary relating an experience in Baltimore.

Rev. S. came in—tall, searching eyes, with an affable and almost obsequious expression. Yes, he had been a Methodist preacher. Had been humiliated at the convention. Lacked $10.00 of the $110.00 which his parish was to bring to the General Conference. Ridiculed by Bishop. Told he was too small for charge. Resigned, but kept the $100.00.

Asked how he had conceived the idea of a mission, he responded that one night while on his way home he stumbled across a man lying in the snow. Helping him to his feet, he sobered him enough to ask where he lived. The fellow had answered he had no home. A few moments after leaving him he heard a crash and turning saw an officer running toward the man. The latter had thrown a stone through the plate glass window of a jewelry store. Naturally, the man was arrested. The next day S. went down to the court to inquire into the disposition of the man. He had been sentenced to six months in jail. Upon S.'s plea for clemency, the sentence was commuted to 90 days.

Later S. informed his wife that since nothing was being done to feed and house colored vagrants, he himself would start a mission. This in his own church. Having done so, he went to a bakery, and asked the proprietor for any stale bread he might have daily, citing his purpose for doing so. The baker cheerfully assented. A butcher gave him meat scraps and bones from which he made hash and soup. Charitable-minded people gave him clothing. Cards were distributed to police stations and other public places stating that homeless men would be housed at S.'s mission, and also fed till they could find either employment or a means to leave the city. S. occupies a position here equivalent to that of Urban Ledoux of New York City, called Mr. Zero, whose famous bread line is an institution in New York.

Rev. S. is astute. He exploits, but hides his exploitation under the garb of charitable and unselfish ministrations. His is a subtle sort of self-seeking. Certainly, a less innocuous sort than that of many orthodox preachers. S. has a restaurant which yields a nice income, runs a farm which he works with vagrants in summer for room and board, and also a wood yard where wood is sawed by the same kind of labor. To the world at large, the wood constitutes a legitimate means by the sale of which the mission can be carried on. But Rev. S. is receiving a handsome profit himself.

Last year he attempted to buy a steamboat, paid $2,000.00 on it, then found out that the whites with whom he had purchased the steamer had defrauded him out of his portion. On its first excursion the boat leaked so that it barely made part of the return trip. S. then was declared the owner by the whites. He was haled to court, but through the aid of influential white friends, managed to squirm out of the clutches of the law.

Anything that he desires in reason, S. informs me, he can get from the whites. He displayed letters from police chiefs, desk sergeants and other whites directing men—floaters, vagrants and drunkards—to go to S.'s mission. His is the only colored organization which is permitted to beg on the streets like the Salvation Army. At Christmas time he pays men $2.50 a day to stand on street corners, garbed as Santa Claus, and solicit funds. They are equipped with a bell, and an iron pot. . . .

He pays $11.00 per week for his mission. Informed me how he was opposed by the orthodox churches. Preaches on the streets at times, says Dr. H. Raises $15.00 after ten minutes preaching. Is only such mission in Maryland. Whatever the virtues of the individual, the mission is rendering a distinct service. Were S. as solicitous for the upbuilding of the mission as he is for the fattening of his own purse, he could have developed an institution that would not only render a larger service to the community but also constitute a source of pride and satisfaction to the owner. But self-preservation, I suppose, is the first law of him who gets it.

Courtesy of Dr. Lorenzo J. Greene, Lincoln University, Jefferson City, Mo.

The Findings of a Black Conference Held during the Depression

Negro Americans were more cruelly affected by the Depression than their white counterparts, a fact that was reflected in the phrase "last hired, first fired," which referred to Negro labor of all kinds. In an effort to unify the Negro people and thus gain greater political power, a nonpartisan conference of Negroes was held in Washington, D.C., in 1931. Below are some of the conclusions reached by the conference.

FINDINGS OF THE NON-PARTISAN CONFERENCE ASSEMBLED IN WASHINGTON, D.C. DECEMBER 2, 3, AND 4, 1931

The Non-Partisan Conference, composed of representative delegates from both political parties from all sections of the country as well as religious, civic, fraternal and benevolent organizations, assembled in the city of Washington, District of Columbia, December 2, 3, and 4, 1931, to present the following declaration of principles and purposes to the Negro race and to the American people.

This declaration does not engage to include a complete bill of grievances, nor yet a catalog of common place virtues and values upon which all good citizens must agree, but a practical agenda, with constructive purpose.

OUR AMERICANISM

We wish to reaffirm our undeviating devotion to the principles of American institutions, as set forth in the Declaration of Independence and the Constitution of the United States, believing that no other foundation can be laid than that which has been laid.

COMMUNISM

We warn members of the race against the specious pleas of Communism, whose basic principles are vitally at variance with our received ideals of free institutions. While no underprivileged minority may be expected to be incurious to the experiments of aggrieved groups in other parts of the world, struggling to throw off the shackles of oppression, yet the American Negro must rely for relief upon the American ideal. In the modified language of Frederick Douglas [*sic*], 'The Constitution is the ship, all else is the sea. . . .'

COLORED WOMEN

Women have been given equal political power with men. In the Northern States, where the franchise is unrestricted, Negro females are more numerous than the males, and consequently have greater political potentiality.

We call upon our women voters everywhere to arouse from their political lethargy and qualify and vote according to their convictions to promote the best interest of their sex, section, race and nation. We especially urge the women delegates to this conference to go back to their several communities and make themselves evangels of this doctrine.

DISFRANCHISEMENT IN SOUTHERN STATES

The Negro in the South is the only element of our population that labors under the disability of disfranchisement. This does not apply equally in all Southern States. In Delaware, Maryland, West Virginia, Kentucky and Missouri, there is no race distinction or discrimination in the franchise. In Florida, Arkansas, Texas, Tennessee, the only restriction placed upon the suffrage is the imposition of the poll tax which applies to white and black alike. In eight Southern States there are constitutional limitations upon the ballot calculated to shut out the Negro and which effectively accomplish that purpose. In all the Southern States, with the exceptions just mentioned, the whites rely upon the traditional shyness and timidity of the Negro to frighten him from the polls. The two million unhindered Negro voters in the North are deeply concerned about the four million disfranchised ones in the South.

ELIGIBLE NEGRO VOTERS IN THE SOUTH

There are thousands of eligible Negro voters in every Southern State under existing limitations. They should be encouraged to qualify and vote under these restrictions until such time that they can be removed. They should not permit themselves to be too easily intimidated. No man is worthy of his rights, unless he has the courage to stand up and manfully contend for them. It ought not require any extraordinary courage for an eligible Negro in Mississippi or Georgia to demand of local authorities that they live up to the law, which they themselves have made. . . .

LYNCHING

Lynching is the climax of lawlessness. America is the wealthiest and wickedest nation on the face of the globe according to the showing of its own list of recorded crime. It is the only nation which indulges in the pastime of lynching and burning its own citizens. While it may be rejoined that the nation itself, as such, does not indulge in such gruesome practices, yet from a broader point of view what the nation permits, the nation commits. This stigma stains the honor of the national escutcheon and constitutes the crowning disgrace of democracy. In the words of Woodrow Wilson, "every case of lynching has been a blow at the heart of orderly law and human justice."

We are not willing to allow the impression to go unchallenged that lynching is a peculiar form of iniquity visited only upon the Negro race or that it is confined to any particular group of States. Every State in the Union, except the six New England States, bears blood stains of victims of mob violence. Fourteen hundred white men and women have been lynched and burned at the stake during the past 40 years. But the Negro is made to bear the chief brunt of this iniquity. He becomes a ready victim, because he is more easily handled by the cowardly mob. "The people who are lynched easiest, will be lynched oftenest." But recital of gruesome happenings and idle wailings are impotent without a remedy.

THE REMEDY

A. We are more than pleased to learn of the good work recently undertaken by the Southern Commission on Lynching to study the cause, extent and cure of this crime.

B. We urge Negroes everywhere, not only to observe the law, but to be circumspect in their conduct so as to avoid even the appearance of evil and to give no pretext or color of excuse for mob violence.

C. We urge the States where the outbreak of mob violence occurs most frequently to enact laws punishing participants in the mob, intent on inflicting punishment on an uncondemned citizen.

D. We urge the President to send a message to Congress and to the Country as Woodrow Wilson did during the time of War, to arouse the conscience of the nation to the enormity of this iniquity.

E. We call upon Congress to utilize its

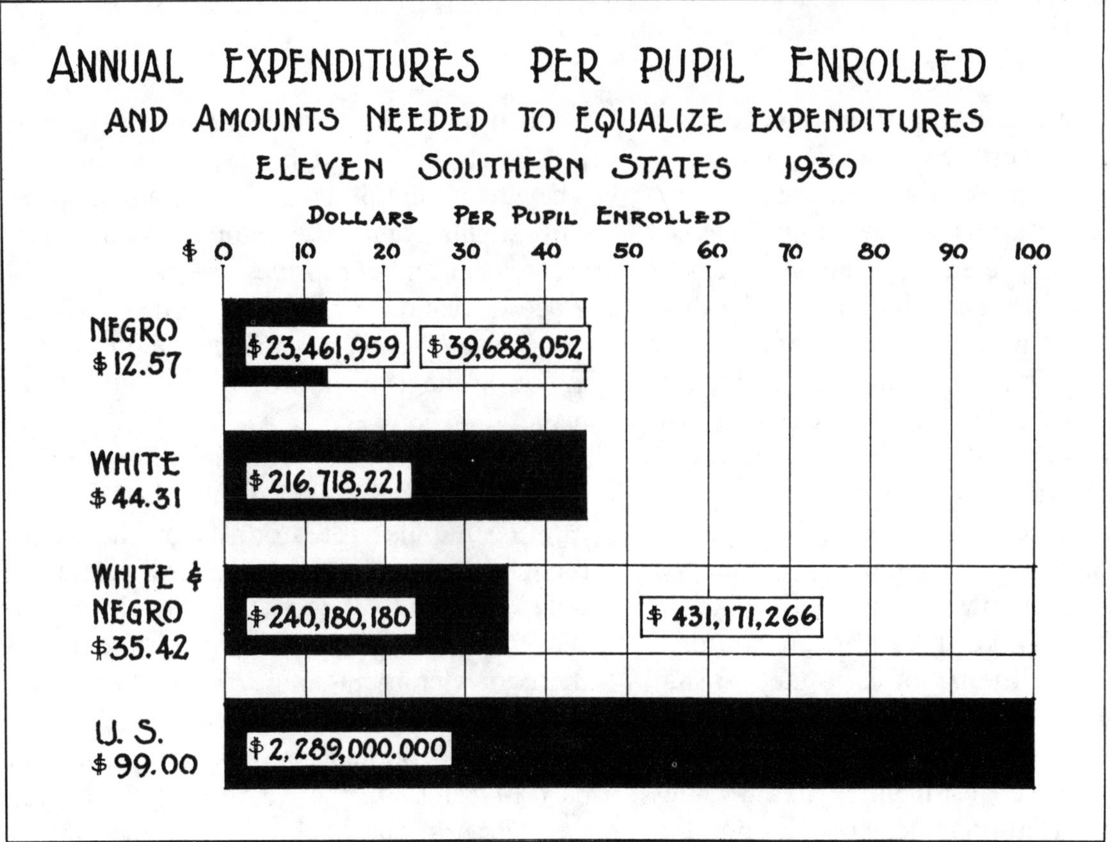
ANNUAL EXPENDITURES PER PUPIL ENROLLED
AND AMOUNTS NEEDED TO EQUALIZE EXPENDITURES
ELEVEN SOUTHERN STATES 1930
DOLLARS PER PUPIL ENROLLED
$ 0 10 20 30 40 50 60 70 80 90 100
NEGRO $12.57
$23,461,959
$39,688,052
WHITE $44.31
$216,718,221
WHITE & NEGRO $35.42
$240,180,180
$431,171,266
U. S. $99.00
$2,289,000.000

Julius Rosenwald Fund

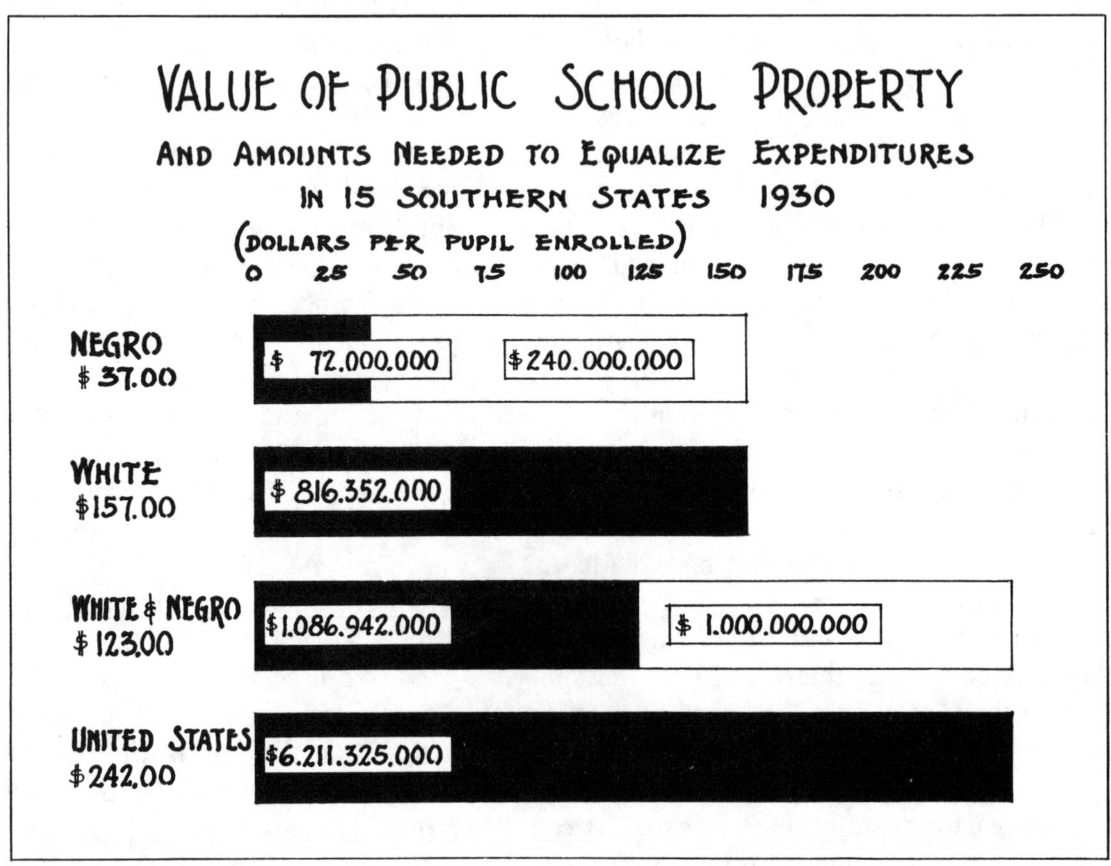
VALUE OF PUBLIC SCHOOL PROPERTY
AND AMOUNTS NEEDED TO EQUALIZE EXPENDITURES
IN 15 SOUTHERN STATES 1930
(DOLLARS PER PUPIL ENROLLED)
0 25 50 75 100 125 150 175 200 225 250
NEGRO $37.00
$ 72.000.000
$240.000.000
WHITE $157.00
$ 816.352.000
WHITE & NEGRO $123.00
$1.086.942.000
$ 1.000.000.000
UNITED STATES $242.00
$6.211.325.000

Julius Rosenwald Fund

keenest legal talent to devise an effective law which will put an end to the most malignant evil that afflicts the American nation.

NATIONAL AID TO NEGRO EDUCATION

We wish to adopt the minority report of the National Advisory Committee on Education, signed by John W. Davis, President, State College of West Virginia, Mordecai W. Johnson, President, Howard University, and R. R. Moton, President, Tuskegee Institute, which reads as follows:

1. That for a limited number of years the Federal Government shall make to any State or States such special grants in aid of the development of Negro education therein, and in addition to any and all prevailing grants in aid of education in general, as shall be determined to be wise, after a careful study of factors involved in the educational finances of the said State or States, and as may be recommended by a joint committee in each State created for that purpose and representing the Federal and State Governments and the Negro citizens of that State.

2. That the division of Negro Education in the Office of Education, or in lieu thereof, a specially appointed National Advisory Commission on Negro Education, shall make such studies in the field of Negro Education, in addition to the studies provided for in the recommendations of the majority report, as may be needed to determine how the helpful purposes of the Federal government, provided for above, may be most constructively carried through. . . .

ECONOMICS AND INDUSTRY

A. In this day of deep depression and unemployment, of which the Negro sustains the heaviest brunt, we urge our people everywhere to be thrifty, frugal, and industrious, reliable and dutiful in the performance of any task which their hands may find to do.

B. We urge the white labor world, feeling the effect of the common depression, to lay aside their customary intolerance against their Negro laborers and fellow-workers, and to evince a willingness to share with him the limited opportunities, rather than strive to exclude him on the ungenerous plea, "lest there be not enough for you and us."

C. We urge the capitalists and masters of industry to apportion fairly among black and white workers alike, both work and pay in this dark day of industrial uncertainty.

THE OUTLOOK

Finally, we would encourage the race to face the future, with optimism and hope. It is a far cry from the starting point of a human chattel to the fullness of the statue of American citizenship; although, we have not yet reached the mark of the high calling, yet our progress has been marvelous. We may gain encouragement and hope by looking back upon the path already trod as well as by regarding the uncompleted journey which lies before us. In the accomplishment of this goal, we must rely upon ourselves, upon the innate sense of justice and fair play of the American people and upon the gracious favor of almighty God.

Kelly Miller, Washington, D.C., Chairman.
Judge W. C. Hueston, Gary, Indiana.
Bishop E. D. W. Jones, Washington, D.C.
Miss Nannie H. Burroughs, Washington, D.C.
Rev. Dr. J. C. Austin, Chicago, Illinois.
Robert L. Vann, Pittsburgh, Pa.

FINDINGS COMMITTEE

Hon. Oscar De Priest, Chairman.
James E. Kelley, Secretary.
Mrs. Blanche A. Washington, Corresponding Secretary.
Morris Lewis, Treasurer.

CONFERENCE OFFICERS

Schomburg Collection, New York Public Library.

Carter G. Woodson on Negro Self-Help

In the 1930's, Carter G. Woodson envisioned a better life for his people. He stressed the necessity of self-help among the great majority of Ne-

groes, who were educationally and financially deprived, and the need for middle-class Negroes to involve themselves in the struggles of their less fortunate brothers.

Yesterday I saw two Negro boys peddling vegetables from door to door. Having failed to find employment as waiters, they had to take up this sort of work. I asked them how they were getting along with the task.

"It's a hard job," said one of them, "but it is better than begging. We are a little tired at night after doing this all day, but I have the satisfaction that I am making my living honestly."

"I get something else out of it," said the other boy.

"Every day I succeed in coming out all right, I feel more confident that I can do something to make an opportunity for myself. I am looking forward to doing this work on a larger scale."

I found in town the other day also a Negro who connects with farmers in Maryland and Virginia and enables them to dispose of their fresh produce at a fair price to families preferring this to that which has lost its life by long exposure in passing through so many hands. The man finds his task more desirable than holding a job by precarious tenure, when he has to wonder whether the next appropriation will be cut or whether he will be dismissed from the service to make provision for someone else.

In a small city I found a Negro with an up-to-date dyeing establishment with every equipment that a modern plant needs. Prepared to do the work thoroughly, he is making money while rendering satisfactory service by showing Negroes of diminished income how they can dye their cast off clothing and remake it in the fashion of today for just a fraction of what less valuable garments of the sort would cost new.

An enterprising fellow in an eastern city is planning to open a small factory to produce handkerchiefs, neckties, aprons, and house dresses which do not require as much outlay as more expensive garments, and he is working out a sales agency force to peddle these from door to door just as other oppressed elements have done when excluded from the established commercial channels.

Another Negro, still more ambitious, is already making a living by selling desirable ladies' apparel. He is fortunate in knowing not only the art of making such garments, but he has also some knowledge of how to market his products. With proper encouragement and patronage he will succeed. He does not handle costly clothing; but he is selling useful garments at a fair price, and he is thus making it possible for other Negroes to earn a living without begging someone else for an opportunity.

While these enterprising people are thus making efforts to get Negroes out of the bread line, there are others who are apparently doing everything possible to hold them in it. Such are the Negroes drawing high salaries and spending their money foolishly for the gewgaws and toys of life. These persons, moreover, are not the Negroes who have never had the chance to learn better, but too often they are the so-called highly educated Negroes who, in school, never learned anything else. Although they have some book learning, they are still in the playful, childlike stage.

The Negroes' point of view, therefore, must be changed before we can set up a leadership which will bring us out of the wilderness.

I feel equally discouraged when I see a minister driving up to his church on Sunday morning in a Cadillac. He does not come to feed the multitude spiritually. He comes to fleece the flock. The appeal he makes is usually emotional. While the people are feeling happy the expensive machine is granted, and the prolonged vacation to use it is easily financed. Thus the thoughtless drift backward toward slavery.

When I see a physician drive to one's door in his Pierce-Arrow, I do not get the impression he has come to treat the patient for a complaint. He has come to treat him for a dollar. With leeches of this type feeding upon an all but impoverished people and giving them nothing back, there can be no hope for advancement.

No people can go forward when the majority of those who should know better have chosen to go backward, but this is exactly what most of our leaders do. Not being learned in the history and background of the race, they figure out that there is no hope for the masses; and they decide, then, that the best thing they can do is to exploit these people for all they can and use the accumulations selfishly. Such persons have no vision and therefore perish at their own hands.

The Negro race will never move forward until the man who has a few thousand dollars learns to feel dissatisfied until he has helped some other member of the race to earn as much; until the man who has been enlightened dedicates himself to the task of leading others out of darkness; until the man who sees a needy cause will learn to die for it . . . such men will not be strewn with roses. They have this consolation, however, in remembering that "For me to live is Christ, and to die is gain."

Carter G. Woodson Papers, Library of Congress.

A Black Man Writes for Help

The quality of "separate but equal" schools in the South is illustrated in the following letter. A man with a seventh-grade education requests help in finding employment and further schooling.

Tyler Texas
Agost 1, 1934

Dear sir

I have Been reading in the papers how you have helped people of our race for instance the scottsBor case. [For me] it is almost as Bad although i have my freedom to a certain extent an no more. beyond a reasonable doubt you [k]now how negroes are treted down here. i have tried in every town close to me to enlist in the army or any Branch of it with no luck or the foures [Forestry] Camps. ethier i am trying to sopport my sister an mother an canot get wor[k] of any kind i know you can get one in some kind of school or let me have the address of some recuting officer that will help me i want to make a living an get an edecation. i am texas Born, 19 yers of age 5 ft 7 in tall weigh 154 pounds 7 grade. talented for music christian athleth [athlete] sound meantly an physicaly. Write let me [k]now wud you can do for me. I am Begging for that kind of help or information.

Cordily yours

J D Reed

Carter G. Woodson Papers, Library of Congress.

The Plight of Missouri Sharecroppers

In the late 1930's, in southeast Missouri, an effort was made to organize the Sharecroppers and Tenant Farmers Union to secure better wages and working conditions for poor white and Negro agricultural workers. These letters were sent to Dr. Lorenzo J. Greene, of Lincoln University, Jefferson City, Missouri, after he had visited the area and showed a willingness to aid the sharecroppers.

Prof. Green — Wyatt Mo.
Lincoln University — 5/17/1939

Dear Prof.

I am Writing you in regards Of My eviction from the Farm. I Was on Mr. O. A. Reeves Farm about 1½ Miles south West of Deventer, Mo. Mr. O. A. Reeves sent Me a Written Notice to Me At Night About 9 oclock by A deputy Constable of Wyatt Mo. Mississippi Co. The notice telling Me To quit Procession [possession] . . . Written Jan. 3 1939 [and] to give [up] Prossession by the 15th day of January 1939. I felt it to be unlegal and I carry The Notice to the State Atorney and ask him About it and he told Me That he, Mr. Reeves, did Not Need to gave Me but 10 days and said That Mr. Reeves had give me plenty of time and That he Would Advise Me to Move, That I have got 12 days and I should give Mr. Reeves his house and not have no trouble, for a share Cropper did Not hafter have but 10 days, so I begain to Walk looking for a place and I could Not fine no place and I had no Money for Mr. Reeves had Not settle with Me and a deal of others. . . . he also put our Cotton in The government loan and Ask none of us anything bout it . . . I begain to Protest to Mr. Reeves about my Cotton. I Made 9 bails of Cotton and Mr. Reeves Would not allow Me to put my part of cotton in The government loan so I Could be entitle to father [further] Payment should Cotton go up on the Market. And also Mr. Reeves in 1938 tryed to get Me to sign Over My 1937 government Payment and because I Would Not do it he was Very hard to get alonge With. now I made 2 crops of Cotton on Mr. O. A. Reeves Farm, one doring [during] 1937–1938. I work 15 acerage of cotton in 1937. and When I received My government Payment Mr. Reeves Just turn in For Me 5½ acerage [acres] of cotton When he should have turn in 15 acerage for Me. I tryed to get Consideration from Washington D.C. from the Department of Agriculture; they defored [referred] My letter to Jefferson City Mo. and Jefferson City defored it To Columbia, Mo. and they Just Continure To hold for The landlored and I just Could not get but $11.52. . . . I pick and gin 15 bails Of Cotton and My 1937 payment Just come to $11.52 when they got Throu. . . . now I has Not yet got My 1938 Payments. Now it is more harder To get what You Make in This County after making [it] than it is To Work and Make it. Now Mr. O. A. also Charge Me $2.50 for gardin after The Crops Was laid by, and he also Charge 75 cent per bail for To hall it to the gin and he should Not have Charge anything. The many landlords had come to an agreement they Was gonіng [going] to Work the farms On a ⅝ Bases . . . that Mean That the share croppers Would not get but 3 bails of Cotton out of 8 Bails, so all of the farmers begain to give they labor notice To Move, and you could not go To No other place and get no sheair Crop other than on a ⅝ Bases. . . . Then mooven [moving] taken place On about Jan. 9–10–11–12 And . . . Highway 62 and 61 begain to get busy and I and My group Came To This Church (sweet home) . . . And have been here ever sent [since] That time. We Came To This Church and it begain to snow and sleat and rain. . . . We stayed here at This Church, sweet home, and it has been the Only home for us up until Now . . . We have been threaten by The White peoples of This County and We also have been treated Verry Cool by our Own County laws. And Now We are faceing A lawsuit. 3 of this group have allready got summons to Court The first Monday in June. They are Trying To get us out of this Church. I am unable . . . to no whate Will be The result. . . . I guss [guess] This is Where We Will be untill they sue us Off this ground. so I shall close . . . Tractors and preduction [production] have put a Many farmers out of work and off the farm; so they want we Poor peoples to work for .75 cent and $1.00 per day and We just Cant live at Those prices . . . this bein all From sweet home Church Camp

Walter Johnson Wyatt Mo.

* * * * *

My name is Gladys Fields. I am 17th Years old and Me and My Mother and Father move out on the Hi Way The 10th of January and We have suffered . . . from the Tiem [time] we come out until Now. we have had a hard time every since We Been out on The hiWay. Some Time . . . half necket [naked] and Treated like a Dog from White Focks [folks]. We was Drove from The hiway and The state Petrolems [patrols] Move us in The Jail house Yard and They made us Move in a old Colored Man gardin Spot and The Women the [they were] renting from Made us Move from Their and We Move Down to The School house, and looking To hafter Move from Their pretty soon. We is hungry Now and no Way To get nothing to Eate. In [I'm] closing May letter But Not My heart and Still leaving Me hunyry [hungry] and out Dorse [out-of-doors].

Originals in the possession of Dr. Lorenzo J. Greene, Jefferson City, Missouri.

The Scottsboro Case

On March 25, 1931, nine Negro youths were arrested near Scottsboro, Alabama, and were subsequently charged with criminal assault. They had boarded a freight train and found themselves with a handful of white youths and two white girls. A fight started, and some of the white boys left the train and summoned the local law authorities. The law officers stopped the train, found the nine Negroes and took them into custody. The girls, who were of questionable reputation, related a horrendous tale of their encounter with the Negroes on the train. Within three weeks, all nine youths had been convicted, and all but one had been sentenced to die. The lone reprieve was granted the youngest, a thirteen-year-old, while another boy of fifteen was among those to receive the death penalty.

The NAACP and the International Labor Defense Committee interceded on behalf of those sentenced, and eventually the case was heard by the United States Supreme Court. On November 7, 1932, the Supreme Court reversed the decisions of the Alabama courts, and the case was brought back for retrial in Alabama. The second indictment and subsequent conviction again went before the Supreme Court, this time with the charge that Negroes had been excluded from the jury. In April 1935, the Court ruled that the case must be retried once again since Negroes had indeed been excluded from jury duty.

In all, there were four trials for one of the Scottsboro boys, Haywood Patterson, with two Negroes serving on the grand jury during the fourth indictment but none serving on the jury that actually brought in a verdict of guilty and a sentence of seventy-five years. During the course of legal proceedings, one of the girls admitted that she had lied. The other maintained that criminal assault had been committed.

The following articles dealing with Alabama justice for the Scottsboro boys were written during the five-year legal dispute. The first article, printed after the first trial, illustrates the local attitude; the second, written after the first Supreme Court decision was handed down, is indicative of opinions held by better-informed Americans.

To those anxious friends of justice who are sincerely exercised about the possible fate of the nine Alabama Negroes now under sentence of death on a charge of criminal assault, let this be said: From the moment of their apprehension till now the Negroes have been under the protection of the laws of Alabama, they have been in the hands of the courts, and they will continue in the hands of the courts until their fate is finally determined. They have appealed to the Supreme Court and it will be January before we shall know whether the men are to have a new trial or whether the original sentence shall be enforced.

In the meantime the situation presents its difficulties. Ordinarily there is no popular debate over the merits of a case pending before the Supreme Court. It is hardly proper, especially in criminal cases, for partisans to argue on the stump and in the press the merits of the issue presented to the court. Under ordinary circumstances there would have been no discussion of the "Scottsboro case," but there is nothing ordinary about the present circumstances. The Supreme Court of Alabama is receiving instructions, none too politely worded, as to what it shall do with reference to these nine Negroes. At least that is the effect of all of the speeches, editorials and telegrams that have been written "protesting against the legal lynching" of these men, even though most of these have been aimed at Governor Miller, due to the fact that the agitators have looked upon the Governor as a sort of court of last resort. Alabama newspapers have thought it necessary to reply to criticisms of their State which they believed to be unjust.

Now the Supreme Court of Alabama is and has always been a conservative, honorable body of men. No tradition of cruelty and callousness tarnishes its name. There has never been a scandal which involved the name of the court.

The Supreme Court of Alabama as it stands is morally and intellectually capable of deciding the appeal of the nine Negroes without prejudice or indifference to elementary human rights. We believe these nine Negroes can trust the Supreme Court to be as fair to them as it would be to nine white men. We believe they can trust Governor Miller, when and if their case comes finally under his official notice, to be as fair to them as to nine white men.

We do not believe that these Negroes have been the victims of injustice at any point since their arrest. We do not believe that any of their rights will be jeopardized between now and the end of their sordid story.

The *Advertiser* satisfied itself at the time of the trial that Alabama had deported itself with dignity, self-restraint and as a State having a sense of justice and love of law and order, that the men were guilty as charged and that there was no occasion for popular agitation about miscarriage of justice, etc. If it had been in any doubt about the matter it would have gladly led the pack in demanding a new deal for the condemned men.

If, however, the Supreme Court, after a careful painstaking review of all the facts and circumstances, concludes that the men are entitled to a new trial, the *Advertiser* will be satisfied with the decision. In saying this we believe we speak for other newspapers and the leaders of opinion generally in Alabama.

The point we wish to enforce is that nine supposedly friendless Negroes—they are so pictured by their noisy champions—have friends not only on the Supreme bench, not only in the Governor's office, but among the thoughtful, responsible citizens of Alabama generally.

Jay Jackson in *The Chicago Defender.*

"Just for the love of torture."

We do not believe that these men have been wronged, but if it turns out that we are in error, we believe the wrong will be righted by the honorable gentlemen on whom rests the responsibility of making the final decision.

This editorial is directed at the Dreisers, the Steffanses, the Einsteins, the New York *World-Telegrams, The Nation* and other sensitive "liberals" who have questioned whether Alabama is capable of acting justly in this instance. We should like for them to feel reassured and to act a little more sensibly than they have acted to date. Let them cease attacking a State on the ground that it is about to "lynch" nine men, and remember that Alabamians passed up a real opportunity to lynch them at the time of their capture preferring to have them tried in an orderly, decent manner as befits a civilized people.

The Montgomery Advertiser, July 24, 1931.

When the Scottsboro case was appealed to the United States Supreme Court in November, three points were raised: (1) there was not a fair, impartial, and deliberate trial; (2) the boys were denied the right of counsel; and (3) qualified Negroes were systematically excluded from the jury. The court chose to put aside as "without merit" the first and third points, although, as Morris L. Ernst pointed out in our issue of December 7, they were socially much more significant than the second. A new trial was ordered on the ground that the defendants were denied the right of adequate counsel. In the trial which has just ended at Decatur, Alabama, Haywood Patterson had the right of counsel. The defense of Samuel Leibowitz was a brilliant example of legal art. He succeeded in dramatizing the utter helplessness of nine Negro boys, innocent or guilty, once they were caught in the destroying passion of race hatred.

Judge James E. Horton was scrupulous in his conduct of the case, and his charge to the jury indicated his own awareness of the violent forces at work in his court. The most casual reading of newspaper accounts of the testimony—and the press is to be highly commended for its covering of the Decatur trial—indicates reasonable doubt of the guilt of Haywood Patterson. The girls involved were common prostitutes. Their testimony was flatly contradictory and one of them repudiated her previous testimony. Yet the jury not only brought in a verdict of guilty, but imposed the savage sentence of death, although Alabama law provides an alternative sentence for rape of ten years to life imprisonment.

In so doing the jury expressed the will of a community which hates and fears the Negro because it has wronged him so deeply through so many generations. Mr. Leibowitz obviously foresaw this all-too-probable conclusion. By his insistence on bringing out convincing evidence that Negroes have been systematically excluded from jury service in Alabama, he established that issue so firmly that the Supreme Court will find it difficult to dismiss it as "without merit" when the case again goes to Washington—as it will unless the Alabama Supreme Court should reverse the Decatur decision. Furthermore, in the course of his defense Mr. Leibowitz was careful to hold up to the public view the race prejudice of more than one variety that showed itself on every hand. Aside from the continuous threats of mob action, two remarks by the prosecution in the course of the trial should be sufficient for any person of sound mind outside of Alabama. "Show them that Alabama justice cannot be bought and sold with Jew money from New York," shouted Solicitor Wade Wright. "I don't care what her [Victoria Price's] previous convictions or actions may have been," said Attorney-General Knight, "but she never lived with niggers." Surely no human being, though he might be guilty of the worst crime, should be forced to submit his right to live to the passions that were flaunted inside and outside the courtroom at Decatur.

The Scottsboro boys still have a chance for liberty, but it may be a matter of years—and years pass slowly in the cells that the South reserves for its Negro "citizens." Meanwhile, we urge our readers to contribute as generously as they can to the Scottsboro defense fund.

"Alabama Justice," *Nation* (April 19, 1933).

A Negro Execution in Kentucky

While the Scottsboro boys escaped the death penalty, Rainey Bethea of Owensboro, Kentucky, was less fortunate. Convicted of criminally assaulting a white woman, he was sentenced to be hanged for his crime. The following newspaper article tells of the hanging.

Owensboro, Ky., Aug. 14 [1936]—As the first flush of dawn bathed Kentucky's Blue Grass country in a radiance of soft color, Rainey Bethea, a hulking Negro boy of 22, spun to his death at the end of a rope today.

Sheriff Florence Thompson, official executioner, did not spring the trap. Gray-faced, she stood by while a Louisville ex-policeman snapped the lever which sent Bethea plunging to his doom.

While the Negro's body still quivered in the throes of death agony, a mob of blood-hungry spectators swarmed over the gallows and tore at his body for souvenirs.

Bethea's frightened face bobbed crazily on his broken neck as the crowd tore the death hood from his head and ripped it to shreds. The doctors had just pronounced him dead. It took 16 minutes to ascertain that his heart had stopped.

Sheriff Thompson, who gave indications that she might spring the trap throughout the night, lost her nerve at the last minute.

Weakly she waved Arthur "Dare Devil Dick" Hasch to the gallows and he sprang eagerly to the task.

A shudder shook the woman sheriff as the Negro boy's body fell through the trap.

More than 20,000 spectators, who split the night air with bloodthirsty screams before the execution, witnessed Daviess County's first hanging in 31 years.

They booed as Father Lammans of the Cathedral of the Assumption, Louisville, ministered the last rites of the church to the quivering victim who walked bravely to the noose with his chin up.

In the moment of suspense preceding the springing of the trap, women shrilled their pleas for action with:

"Tip it off there, tip it off."

Bethea stood facing the crowd, the whites of his eyes rolling horribly as he heard the crowd yell for his blood. Then G. Phil Hanna, wealthy stock breeder, who hangs for a hobby, slipped the hood over Bethea's face and adjusted the hemp around his neck.

Then he motioned to Hasch and a second later Bethea's body plummeted through the trap. It swayed slowly as the Negro kicked his legs in the last struggle.

Several doctors marched to the platform, stethoscopes in hand. A hush fell over the crowd. But as Bethea was officially pronounced dead, a savage roar burst forth and the spectators surged forward to the gallows.

Sheriff Thompson and her deputies were helpless to prevent the ghoulish souvenir hunters from reaching their prey. In a moment the boy's body was stripped of every bit of clothing.

The crowd was in a gay holiday mood as the stars lit the sky promising an early dawn. They came by auto and mule team from the surrounding hills.

They imbibed freely in corn liquor but no one got out of hand until it was all over.

Tolerant hill-billy wise-cracks kept the crowd in good humor, but as the night wore on they began thirsting for blood and just before dawn they set up a ferocious patter of yells:

"Bring that boy on."

"Let's hang him."

"Boy, would I like to spring that trap!"

"Oh, lady sheriff, where's our victim?"

Bethea, who had been brought furtively from his cell in the State prison at Louisville, quaked in the small wooden jail as he heard the cries.

Tears streamed down his gray-black face as he pleaded with his jailers:

"Take me outa here. I ain't a-scared. Take me before dat mob does."

A lane was cleared through the jeering mob as Bethea, now eager for death, almost danced through it. A shot-gun squad tramped at his heels.

Bethea halted before he mounted the steps to the scaffold. He bowed his head and prayed brokenly. The spectators hooted and cheered. The Negro began to break.

Little boys and girls in the crowd clapped their hands vigorously at the macabre scene.

A hearse stood beside the gallows. Youngsters scrambled to its top to get a better view. They shook their fingers derisively at the victim.

The Chicago Defender *"How about a New Deal on this?"*

Sheriff Thompson, who is the widowed mother of four children, led the death march. She kept wringing her hands nervously and gazing apprehensively at the silhouette of the gallows. She did not intimate until the last minute that she was not going to spring the trap. But she must have had it fixed with Hasch as he jumped readily to the job as Sheriff Thompson motioned him to step forward.

Hasch wore a white linen suit. As is Hanna's custom when he loops the noose around the neck of a victim, he kept whispering words of cheer to Bethea, who nodded his head in response.

The din was terrific at the moment.

A 16-year-old mother carrying a babe in arms screamed at the top of her lungs:

"Hang it on him! Hang it on him."

The scene of the execution was the yard of the county garage, a plot of about one and a half acres, fenced off from a larger vacant area.

Kentucky's criminal law provided the open air spectacle by stipulating that in cases of criminal assault, the execution shall be held in public.

Mrs. Bess Schacklett, who lives across the street, ran about the crowd inviting friends to a "necktie breakfast" when it was over.

Walter Scholz, 19, bragged that he and five other lads who accompanied him from Jacksonville, Fla., were the farthest travelling spectators for no better reason than a great urge to see that Bethea got "what he deserved."

Spectators who expected to see a pleading, cringing figure on the gallows, were disappointed by Bethea's bravado.

Gumby Papers, Columbia University Library.

A Redcap Illustrates the Need for Negro Laborers to Organize

Before unionization of the redcaps, in every railroad terminal in the country men were earning their living from tips alone and, in many cases, were finding it necessary to pay the head porter in order to secure and hold their jobs. Surprisingly, many of the black elite who emerged in the 1940's and later, had worked their way through college as redcaps. Their incentive to achieve was no doubt increased by the circumstances under which they were forced to work. This description of life in the terminal was written by an unknown redcap in the 1930's.

I had decided to become a red-cap, and on a day off from my eighteen-dollar-a-week job I went to one of the big railway terminals in an Eastern city. It was two days before the Fourth of July, and the great station was in turmoil. Thousands of footsteps echoed and reechoed through the spacious waiting-rooms, and departing vacationists jammed the outer concourse. Sweaty, baggage-laden red-caps elbowed their way through the crowds. Some of them were familiar figures—limping, bunion-footed old men, treading gingerly, straining at heavy leather. One very old man—he must have been eighty—dazed and slow-moving, appeared to have lost entirely his sense of direction and was buffeted around by the crowd. Younger and sprightlier men were weaving their way to parcel room and taxi stand. Others, perhaps the lazy ones, lounged indifferently on the outskirts of the crowd.

A panting six-footer, lathered in sweat, loomed alongside. Crystallized particles of salt glistening in irregular traces on his uniform showed where the perspiration had dried. I asked him where to go to see about getting a job as a red-cap and he directed me, between heavy puffs, to the station-master's office. I spoke to a clerk there who frowned and told me brusquely that I would have to wait. I sat looking through a window at the teeming crowd on the concourse, thickly dotted with red-caps, and tried to figure out just what my takings at a dime or quarter per bag would amount to. Certainly it would be more than the eighteen dollars I was getting.

A rotund, red-faced official, the station-master, waddled into the room, and the clerk told him what I wanted. With a smirk he sent me to the Negro red-cap chief in an office on the lower concourse. The chief was sitting at a desk, sphinx-like and sweating. He eyed me indifferently, but when he learned my business he told me affably enough to "kuntak Potah 449," who would fix me up.

When I found Porter 449 our interview was brief. I was instructed to produce $25 and keep my mouth shut. The idea of buying the job was revolting, but after thinking it over I felt that the price might be reasonable after all, and early next morning, weighted down with half my rent money, which I was sure I could replace by the end of the week, I contacted Porter 449 again, this time in a phone booth. He grinned as I turned over the money to him and helped me find a second-hand uniform and cap. He took my address and gave me a numbered badge, with the warning: "Membah, fellah, on dis heah job 'de passingah's allus right.' " Then he led me to the locker-room.

The locker-room, a stench-ridden, windowless cavern on the lower level, accommodated four hundred Negroes. It was crowded with men. Some were sleeping soundly, others jabbering loudly; some were naked, about to put on uniforms or street clothes. High-smelling socks stiff with dirt, sweaty shirts draped over the backs of benches, cockroaches cavorting on the littered floor. In the reeking germ-laden air I was actually afraid to breathe. Yet no one seemed to mind, and soon I too got used to the awful place.

Adjoining a stinking lavatory where two toilet bowls served four hundred red-caps stood a "Hole in the Wall" cook-shop, and it was here that Porter 449 advised me to eat and to guzzle corn liquor, as the place was under the supervision of the clique he represented.

I had become a red-cap, and soon I was escorting passengers to trains from the cab-stand, picking up jobs in the waiting-rooms, in the concourse, everywhere. My pockets bulged with dimes and quarters. Passengers "Georged" and "Samboed" me, as I had heard them "George" and "Sambo" others. As the day wore on business increased. Late into the night we were held on duty. I shall never know how many passengers I put on wrong trains that first day, but that was their hard luck. Many complaints were lodged, but since passengers almost always neglected to note their porter's number nothing happened.

At ten o'clock that night the day watch was relieved after sixteen hours. This was one of the "get-away" days for red-caps—the eve of a national holiday. On such days money was there for the taking. Down in the locker-room men with dislocated and swollen arches swore at the Creator for making them black. Men with murmuring hearts gasped faintly and inhaled air that was poison to the lungs. Others, racked with pain, nursing abdominal ruptures and wrenched backs, slumped in misery on the hard benches. Here and there the iron men among us were dolling up for a big night at the uptown dance halls. But all of them would have to report at six-thirty next morning or face suspension. Working a double shift on one day was no excuse for tardiness the next.

My wife had grown nervous over my absence—like other red-cap wives she soon learned that at holiday time she should look for me only when she saw me—but when at last I crawled home and spread my silver pile on the table, she counted $14. I told her to wake me at five o'clock, and without even taking a bath crept into bed with every joint afire. I never again earned $14 in any one day, but I was satisfied that my $25 had not been badly invested.

The Negro officers, the only paid men in the set-up, saw to it that the black hundreds under them toed the mark; and they lived up to the traditions of their overseer ancestors. Old and young alike hustled to meet their obligations. Uniforms had to be paid for, and the prices fluctuated with the needs of the cabal of grafters who, under the protection of the station-master, ruled over us. The monthly dues of a dollar for insurance against death and sickness had to be met, and in addition we were forced each week to sacrifice a day to the system. On his "street-duty" day a red-cap stationed at transit exits, where public porters solicited, could earn practically nothing. Negroes from all the black areas of the globe carried bags. Doctors, lawyers, and preachers herded with crooks, confidence men, and convicts to serve the traveling public.

For seven years I carried on, serving a public for whom red-caps always grinned. I saw youths, buoyant with hope, working alongside their fathers, soon converted into liquor-heads. I saw porters made to pay a second time for uniforms for which they held receipts. I saw red-caps lose a day's pickings for being five minutes late, and the same men held over at other times for hours, to satisfy the whim of some job-nursing official. I saw company doctors issuing the same pills for hernia as for heart trouble. I saw station detectives receiving protection money from Porter 449, czar of the racket, and I saw porters dismissed for possessing "number slips."

Then suddenly the black mantle of the depression covered the land. The unsalaried red-caps were hardest hit, though there were salary and staff reductions all around. The cabal tightened up, and to balance its budget worked out a new plan: Fire fifty. Then hire fifty others at $25 each. Net profit $1,250. Among the first fifty were counted the honest, the indifferent, the infirm, and next to my name on the list of those headed for the street appeared that of the old man.

Cornelius Johnson in *Bags and Baggage*.

The fifty on the list left for home and the bread lines—all but the old man, to whom the depot had become existence itself. His fingers, curved and semi-rigid from half a century of bag gripping, could adjust themselves to nothing else. His insurance premiums forfeited through dismissal, homeless and penniless, the old man haunted the scene of his labors for several days. Snatching at bags to which he was now no longer entitled, waving at taxis as they roared into the terminal, shuffling aimlessly across the path of hurrying passengers, the veteran was finally barred from the depot. In despair he wandered along the street aimlessly and finally threw himself under the wheels of a car rather than face the uncertainties of a bread line. As for me, I discovered that relief rations were more appetizing than the hash poked out to me from "The Hole in the Wall."

Courtesy of the United Transport Service Employees Union Archives, Chicago, Illinois.

A Black Man's Attitudes toward Red Russia

America has been looked upon by the downtrodden and oppressed peoples of the world as the haven of freedom. At the same time, Negroes living within the United States have frequently found it necessary to go elsewhere in the world in search of freedom and equality. The irony of this situation is illustrated in the following autobiographical account by journalist Homer Smith. The brief selections excerpted here tell first of his emigration to Russia in 1932 and then of his efforts to get his Russian wife out of the Soviet Union years later.

What had started me, *a twenty-two year old American* Negro, on the long road from Minneapolis to Moscow?

To be free, to walk in dignity—for these precious privileges some men will go anywhere, sacrifice anything. In quest of these rights immigrants have come from all over the world to America. I yearned to stand taller than I had ever stood, to breathe total freedom in great exhilarating gulps, to avoid all the hurts that were increasingly becoming the lot of men (and women) of color in the United States. The solution seemed simple to me: Russia was the only place where I could go and escape color discrimination entirely. Moscow seemed the answer.

As a student at the University of Minnesota in the School of Journalism (then called Department of Journalism), I knew that the best I could ever hope for was to work, as I had been doing since my junior year, in the post office—the safe, secure job for a Negro in the thirties. Newspapers weren't hiring Negroes in those days and though I might have gotten a job on one of the Negro papers elsewhere represented on campus, it was something less than I aspired to. I read avidly the reports of the Soviet experiment, the Five Year Plan, and the classless Society that was abuilding in Russia. The *Daily Worker* wrote glowingly that Soviet Russia was the one political state which stood for social justice for all oppressed peoples.

Who, I thought, was more oppressed than the Negro? Who else was being lynched with hideous regularity? Twenty Negroes in 1930 alone. Then in 1931 the Scottsboro Case hit the front pages. Nine Negro boys were sentenced to death, for allegedly raping two white girls who were riding the same freight train with them. One day, after some heated words in a restaurant about not getting waited on, I made my decision.

Naturally, my father and mother were aghast at the idea. My staunchly Christian mother was particularly upset and tried hard to dissuade me. "Of all places, that atheistic country," she said. "France, almost any place else, but Russia—" But I was of age, earning my own money and there was nothing they could do to stop my wanderlust. I had to see for myself.

I began getting my dollars and clothes together. Being somewhat conservative, though toying with radical ideas, I had no desire to starve in the streets of Moscow. So I sent off a letter to the Moscow Post Office, stating my qualifications, and was thrilled to receive a reply almost immediately offering me a position as consultant to the Moscow Post Office at a higher salary than I was then receiving.

The Negro Press had no correspondent in Russia and the editors of the several papers I approached were agreeable that I represent them under my pen-name of Chatwood Hall, which actually was a pen-name I had coined while a university student.

I had my first contact with Russian officialdom at the border station of Byeloostrov. The customs officials were very courteous and correct, but they examined my baggage most carefully. Upon finding several American newspapers and magazines in one valise, they requested me to leave them at the customs station, assuring me that they would be sent on later to my Moscow address. They never arrived.

. . . .

When I arrived in Russia, the state frontiers were static and embraced about 8,170,000 square miles, with a population of approximately 160 million. Now, as my residence was coming to an end, expansionism had swallowed up 13,000 square miles of eastern Finnish territory, 72,000 square miles of eastern Poland and the three Baltic states of Latvia, Lithuania and Estonia, and Bessarabia and northern Bukovina had been forcibly detached from Roumania. The country had expanded to 8,348,000 square miles and had increased its population to 190,000,000.

In the summer of 1946, my decision was reached. I accepted a position working in the Editorial Department of the English section of the Ethiopian Government's Press and Information office. I could continue to write for AP and the Negro Press from Ethiopia and most important of all, as a foreign correspondent, the Russians could not very well place any obstacles in the way of my leaving the country to take up a new assignment. Marie Petrovna was another matter. She was Russian and exit visas just were not given Russians to go abroad, not even the wives of American correspondents. The assumption was (and is) that the people belong to the STATE.

Something happened—I don't know what—but one day I received a telegram in Addis Ababa from my wife telling me she had been granted an exit visa and was on her way. She would take the earliest plane out of the country for Teheran.

But then oil and politics, a highly explosive mixture intervened. Russia had been negotiating for an oil concession in northern Persia. But Persia had refused to grant it. Relations became strained between the two countries. Aeroflot, the Russian civil airline abruptly stopped flying to Teheran, and no other airline flew into or out of Russia in those days.

Nevertheless, my wife got started and flew to Baku, Aeroflot's southern terminus inside Russia, near the Persian border. From there she booked passage on a small boat across the Caspian Sea to the northern Persian port of Pehlevi.

At Baku, before boarding ship, the Russian customs officials would not permit her to take out her gold jewelry or diamonds. She had to surrender these, with the promise that they would be sent to her relatives in Moscow. That was in 1947, the gold jewelry and diamonds had not reached the relatives in Moscow by the summer of 1963.

Marie Petrovna reached Ethiopia from Teheran and joined me for a residence in Africa that was to last until 1962, when I returned to my native land and brought Marie Petrovna and our two children to what is for her the Promised Land.

Homer Smith, *Black Man in Red Russia* (Chicago, 1964).

Oscar De Priest Discusses the House of Representatives' Restaurant

Oscar De Priest, first Negro to serve in the United States Congress since 1901, sponsored a House resolution that would make it illegal to deny service to Negroes in the House dining room. His action followed a protest movement that began in 1933, when several prominent Negroes were refused service because of their color. Dr. Charles H. Wesley of Howard University, in an effort to test the discriminatory policy of the establishment, went to the dining room with three white friends for lunch. When Wesley approached, he was asked if he was of foreign descent. He replied that he was an American Negro, and service was denied him but offered to the whites in his party. The attendant publicity about this incident and others like it, combined with the De Priest resolution, eventually brought about a change in the regulations.

MR. DE PRIEST. Mr. Chairman and members of the Committee, I came to Washington as a Representative in Congress on the 15th of April 1929. Up until the 23d day of last

January I never heard this question raised which has now been raised by the Chairman of the Committee on Accounts this year. On that day when my secretary went into the grillroom downstairs he was told by Mr. Johnson that by the orders of the Chairman of the Committee on Accounts he could not be served in that restaurant.

I read in the newspapers an interview where the Chairman of the Committee on Accounts said that no Negro had been served there and would not while he was here. I hope he was not quoted correctly.

I want to say that if the chairman was quoted correctly in that article "that Negroes had not been served there before" he was mistaken. I have seen them there in the grillroom several times. In the last 5 years I think I have seen them there 50 times.

I want to say further, after talking with some Members of the Committee on Accounts, that this question has never been raised in the committee before, and never was raised officially in the committee, if I am correctly informed.

It seems to be an arbitrary ruling on that question.

The restaurant of the Capitol is run for the benefit of the American people, and every American, whether he be black or white, Jew or Gentile, Protestant or Catholic, under our constitutional form of Government, is entitled to equal opportunities.

I introduced a resolution on the 24th of January, asking for an investigation of this ruling by the chairman of the committee. That resolution went to the Committee on Rules. The Committee on Rules has not acted as yet. I waited 30 legislative days, and then I filed a petition with the Clerk of this House to discharge the Committee on Rules and to bring the resolution to the floor of the House.

That resolution calls for an investigation only. If the Chairman of the Committee on Accounts has that power, I would like to know it. If the Chairman of the Committee on Accounts has that power, the American people are entitled to know it.

I am going to ask every justice-loving Member in this House to sign that petition, as that seems to be the only way it can be threshed out on the floor of the House.

I come from a group of people—and I am proud of it and make no apology for being a Negro—who have demonstrated their loyalty to the American Government in every respect, making no exception. They have always proved to be good American citizens and have supported the Constitution. I challenge any man to contradict that assertion. If you are going to keep them good American citizens, like I pray they shall always be, it must be done by defending their rights as American citizens.

If we allow segregation and the denial of constitutional rights under the dome of the Capitol, where in God's name will we get them?

I appreciate the conditions that pertain in the territory where the gentleman comes from, and nobody knows that better than I do.

But North Carolina is not the United States of America; it is but a part of it, a one forty-eighth part. Then I expect, too, as long as I am a Member of this House, to contend for every right and every privilege every other American citizen enjoys; and if I did not, I would not be worthy of the trust reposed in me by my constituents who have sent me here. [Applause.]

This is not a political problem. Someone said that I was trying to play politics. I did not instigate this; I did not start it; but, so help me God, I am going to stay to see the finish of it.

MR. BLANTON. Mr. Chairman, will our colleague yield to me for a question?

MR. DE PRIEST. Not now, MR. BLANTON; and I consider you one of the best friends I have on the Democratic side.

MR. BLANTON. I thought therefore you would yield for a question.

MR. DE PRIEST. I shall later on, but not now.

THE CHAIRMAN. The gentleman declines to yield.

MR. DE PRIEST. I say to the Members of this House—and I have no feeling in the matter—this is the most dangerous precedent that could be established in the American Government. If we allow this challenge to go without correcting it, it will set an example where people will say Congress itself approves of segregation; Congress itself approves of denying one tenth of our population equal rights and opportunity; why should not the rest of the American people do likewise? I have been informed that if I insisted on pressing this question it might hurt my usefulness down here. If I did not press it, I would not stay here very long. The people who sent me here would retire me next November, and they would rightly retire me because I should not be here if I did not stand up for a group of people who have always been on the square with this Government. I did not come here from a group of people who have committed treason against the Government; I did not come here from a group of people who are Communists or Socialists; I come here from the most loyal American citizens that we have.

During the World War when emissaries of the enemy were scattering pamphlets over the battlefields of Europe asking the colored people to desert the colors because they received inhuman treatment in America, no colored man deserted, and no man can say and history does not record when a Negro deserted the colors—not one. How do you expect them to go on giving loyal service to America, at a time when there is unrest over the whole world, when the Reds are trying to make inroads amongst my group because they are the lowest in the scale of society, from an economic standpoint, unless we give them something like a square deal in this country? I appreciate all that has been done so far, but the work has not been completed yet. And I say further, ladies and gentlemen of the Congress, that America never will be what it was intended to be until every citizen in America has his just rights under the Constitution. [Applause.] I would not have filed this petition if I could have gotten a hearing before the Committee on Rules. I asked for it. I was not even given the courtesy of a hearing before that committee.

MR. LUNDEEN. Mr. Chairman, will the gentleman yield?

MR. DE PRIEST. Yes.

MR. LUNDEEN. Will the gentleman tell us how many names are on that petition now?

MR. DE PRIEST. There were 93 names on it an hour ago.

MR. BLANTON. Mr. Chairman, will our colleague yield to me now?

MR. DE PRIEST. Yes; I yield with pleasure to the gentleman from Texas.

MR. BLANTON. The restaurant is for the benefit of the Members of the Congress because we have to be here at meal time.

MR. DE PRIEST. I agree with the gentleman.

MR. BLANTON. Has not our colleague been allowed to go in there every time he wanted to? He can go in there right now and take anybody with him that he wishes to take.

MR. DE PRIEST. That is all true.

MR. BLANTON. What more do you ask? You go there at will and are allowed to take your friends with you at will. Is not that equal justice and right to you, the same as to the rest of us?

MR. DE PRIEST. I am asking for the same rights for my constituents that the gentleman from Texas wants for his, and that is all.

MR. BLANTON. But our colleague from Illinois does go in that restaurant whenever he wishes, and he takes his colored friends with him whenever he wishes to do so.

MR. DE PRIEST. I am not asking privileges for OSCAR DE PRIEST or proper treatment for him down there, because I will take care of that, but I am asking for those people who have no voice in this Congress, just like you, MR. BLANTON, would do if some of your constituents came here from Texas and were refused to be served in that restaurant. You would raise more hell than anybody I know of about it. [Laughter and applause.] I have been here long enough to know just what you would do, and I would vote with you on raising that hell. I would say that you were right, and that your constituents had a right to have the same treatment that I want for mine.

THE CHAIRMAN. The time of the gentleman from Illinois has expired.

MR. MCLEOD. Mr. Chairman, I yield the gentleman 10 minutes more.

MR. BLANTON. We have stood with you generously in helping to build up Howard University.

MR. DE PRIEST. Yes; and I expect you to stay with me.

MR. BLANTON. We have given it more than any white university in the United States.

MR. DE PRIEST. Do you want me to tell you why?

MR. BLANTON. Because the colored race sadly needs good teachers, and good nurses, and good dentists, and good doctors, and good preachers.

MR. DE PRIEST. All that is true, and I expect you to keep on doing it, you, especially to help. And while we are talking about Howard University, I might say that personally I am very sorry that those boys came down here from that university the other day as they did. If they had consulted me I would have told them to stay away from here. Another thing—I have investigated and I have found that the boy who has been locked up was not a student at Howard University. I do not know anything about the rest of them, but if they were from Howard University, they are just like the uncontrolled youth of any college or school. There are very few colleges which do not have some radicals in them.

I do not claim the Negro race is any better than anybody else. I know we have our criminal element, just like you have your criminal element. None of us is perfect, but it behooves all of us to do the best we can and respect the rights of the other fellow in America. Whether they be large or small, rich or poor, it makes no difference. Somebody said this was a peanut affair. Well, I agree with you. It ought to have been so small that no man in this House could have been small enough to bring it up. There was no occasion for it whatever.

The secretary who works for me I have known for 40 years. He is a Christian gentleman, a great deal better Christian than I ever thought of being or ever expect to be. There certainly can be no fault found with his personal conduct. He has been in that restaurant dozens of times. Perhaps he needs it worse than any other man down here. You know the condition in Washington and I know it. The public restaurants outside do not serve Negroes, and you know it. It is necessary for him to have some place to eat here, or else bring his lunch with him.

I appreciate the fact, as the gentleman said, that we have a restaurant for Members only, and that restaurant for Members only you cannot get into half the time on account of outsiders. Is that not true? I would like to see the Committee on Accounts bar everybody from the restaurant for Members only except Members and their friends who accompany them.

I was there with my wife and Professor Johnson's wife, and we had to wait 10 minutes to get a table because outsiders had crowded the restaurant. Every Member knows that is true.

To show you the subterfuge practiced; in the last 4 or 5 days they have taken down the sign which read "public restaurant", and placed a sign "For Members only." I asked Mr. Johnson, the manager, personally, why it was done. He said, "I had orders to do it from the Chairman of the committee." I said, "Is it a subterfuge"? He said, "You understand what is going on." I certainly do. That sign was put there to keep only Negroes out. One man was asked if he was a foreigner. If he had said "Yes" he would have been served. Has the time come when American citizens cannot be served and aliens can? Of course, every alien has every right that he is entitled to, so long as he is law-abiding, but at least we are entitled to the same treatment as every other American citizen, and we will be satisfied with nothing less than that.

MR. GAVAGAN. Will the gentleman yield?

MR. DE PRIEST. I yield.

MR. GAVAGAN. I am sorry to break into the gentleman's remarks, but I would like to take this opportunity to express my entire accord with the statements expressed and enunciated by you, and to say to you openly that I am trying to get sufficient signatures to your petition now on the Speaker's desk, so that we may discuss this question fully and openly on the floor. [Applause.]

MR. DE PRIEST. I thank the gentleman.

I want to say that all of my friends are not on the Republican side of the aisle, and all of my enemies are not on the Democratic side either. Since I have been in Congress I have tried to so conduct myself that I would command the respect of every Member of Congress. I have not imposed my society on any Member on either side of the House. I think every man has the right to select his own society. I would not say that, except that I received a letter from a Member of this Congress, which I am going to read into the RECORD. . . .

> HON. OSCAR DE PRIEST,
> *House Office Building, Washington, D.C.*
> DEAR SIR: I have your letter of the 7th instant enclosing House Resolution 236. I presume you desire a reply to this letter.

Which I did.

> I note the contents of the resolution and desire to state that I was raised among Negroes in the South and they have always been my personal friends. I work with them on my farm and pay them the same price that I pay white men for the same work. I treat them well and enjoy their confidence.
>
> I am willing to allow them every right to which they are entitled under the Constitution and laws, but I am not in favor of social equality between the races.

And I do not give a damn about it, brother. It does not mean anything to me at all.

> If there are enough Negroes around the Capitol to justify a restaurant for them to patronize, I would have no objection to establishing a restaurant for their use.

That we do not want and we will not accept.

> I neither eat nor sleep with the Negroes, and no law can make me do so.
>
> I think this explains my position clearly.
>
> GEORGE B. TERRELL, *of Texas.*

[Applause from the southern Members.]

I expected that applause. I expected certain gentlemen here to applaud that statement. I know what your feelings are and I understand them thoroughly. You did not disappoint me by applauding. I would have been surprised if you had not applauded.

Nobody asked the gentleman to sleep with him. That was not in my mind at all. I do not know why he thought of it. [Laughter.] I am very careful about whom I sleep with. [Laughter.] I am also careful about whom I eat with; and I want to say to you gentlemen that the restaurant down here is a place where one pays for what one gets. If I go in there, sit down to a table, I pay for what I get, and I am not courting social equality with you. That does not mean anything in America. Social equality is something that comes about by an exchange of visits from home to home and not appearing in the same public dining room. You might as well say I was seeking social equality if I rode in the same Pullman car with you. It would not be any special credit to me to be in there.

Congressional Record, 73rd Congress, 2nd session (Washington, 1934). *Copy courtesy of Dr. Charles H. Wesley, Washington, D.C.*

A. Philip Randolph Discusses the Proposed 1941 March on Washington

A. Philip Randolph, President of the Brotherhood of Sleeping Car Porters, conceived the original plan of a march on Washington by tens of thousands of Negroes in 1941. It was, as he describes it below, an attempt to get the federal government to put pressure on business to hire Negro workers in defense industries. So successful was his projected plan for bringing thousands into the hallowed sanctuary of government, that his demands were met and the march was cancelled.

WHY AND HOW THE MARCH WAS POSTPONED

Briefly, why the March? The March-on-Washington was the last resort of a desperate people who had failed to get decisive results in the form of jobs in National Defense through conferences, petitions and appeals to leaders of government and private industry.

Conferences had been held with the President, Secretary of the Army, Henry L. Stimson, Secretary of the Navy, Frank Knox, Co-Director of the Office of Production Management, Sidney Hillman, National Director of National Youth Administration, Aubrey Williams, Mayor LaGuardia and many others by Walter White, Mary McLeod Bethune, Dr. Channing H. Tobias, Lester Granger, Dr. F. D. Patterson, Dr. Rayford H. Logan, T. Arnold Hill, George Goodman, Will Alexander, Judge William H. Hastie, Dr. Robert C. Weaver and others. In these conferences, government leaders were genial, gracious and reassuring of their opposition to discrimination on account of race, color, creed or national origin. But Negroes got no jobs.

As a result of the failure of these conferences by honest, able and courageous Negro leaders, the idea of the March-on-Washington was conceived by the writer. Articles on the proposed march were written and sent to the Negro press. Happily the press, that is the Negro press, I add this emphasis because the white press maintained a dreadful conspiracy of silence on the March idea, received the plan for Negroes to March-on-Washington for jobs and justice in National Defense with an open mind and gave it general support, with the exception of the Pittsburgh *Courier* which opposed the March editorially although carrying news releases on it.

Here is one exception with the white daily press. It is "P. M." This paper promptly championed the March idea.

While the March-on-Washington was being discussed in the Negro press, "P. M." had waged a vigorous fight in page after page for the right of Negroes to jobs in National Defense.

Soon the movement to March-on-Washington captured the imagination of the Negroes all over the country and spread like a prairie fire.

No section of the Negro people refused to respond to the "Call" to Negro America to mobilize 100,000 strong to March-on-Washington for jobs in National Defense. Negro preachers, doctors, lawyers, teachers, students, youth, laborers, trade unionists, women, children, business men, editors, reporters, artists, soldiers, yes, Negro America of every stratum, calling and endeavor, rallied to the new adventure in Negro mass action for jobs and dignity.

Never, verily, had Negroes of hand and brain been so deeply stirred before to struggle for their rights. And they struggled together.

But white America was unaware of these stirrings of the Negro for new economic opportunities. The press and radio were silent.

Meanwhile, an avalanche of Negro discontent and resentment to discriminations was rolling up and gathering a telling and threatening force and the March-on-Washington was rapidly taking on the character of a crusade.

It is significant of racial solidarity that the National Negro Women's Council had been called to meet in Washington, D.C., by its leader, Mrs. Mary McLeod Bethune one day before the March. And the NAACP, one of the leading exponents of the March, cut short its National Conference one day to permit its delegates to participate in the March. The New England Convention of Negro Baptists Preachers endorsed the March and demonstrated its spirit by singing "Onward Christian Soldiers, Marching as to War," following a talk by the National Director of the March. Mount Olivet Baptist Church of New York upon an appeal by the National Director and Rev. O. Clay Maxwell, its able pastor, collected one hundred fourteen dollars and forty cents ($114.40) and contributed it to the March.

But no apparent concern had been manifested about the March by Government leaders, until the National Director addressed a letter to President Roosevelt, requesting him to speak to the Marchers at the Monument of Abraham Lincoln following the March, July 1st. Letters were also addressed to . . . Mayor LaGuardia and Mrs. Roosevelt, requesting them to speak to the Negro Marchers.

Shortly following the sending of these letters, the National Director and Walter White were called for conferences with Mrs. Roosevelt and Mayor LaGuardia. They were urged to call off the March, expressing fears that the March would harm the Negro. Their requests were refused.

Later a conference was called at the White House by the President in which sat Walter White, Frank R. Crosswaith, Chairman of the Negro Labor Committee of Harlem, Layle Lane, Vice-President of the American Federation of Teachers and the Writer.

The whole question of the March on Washington was discussed by the President, Secretary of War Stimson, Secretary of the Navy Knox, Mayor LaGuardia, Hillman and Knudsen, Anna Rosenberg of the Social Security Board and Aubrey Williams of N.Y.A. Following the conference with the President, he ordered these heads of the departments of the Government to find a remedy for this problem of discrimination on account of race, color, creed or national origin in National Defense. This White House Conference was held on June 18th and the President issued the famous Executive Order, June 25th, despite strenuous opposition from some powerful department heads.

When the Executive Order was issued, the National Director called up Walter White of the NAACP, in Houston, Texas, and placed the matter before him and he expressed his agreement to postponement. He then called Henry K. Craft of the Harlem YMCA in New York City and he indicated his agreement to postponement. Mr. Craft was also requested to contact other members of the National Negro March-on-Washington Committee to get their decision on the question of postponing the March in view of the issuance of the Executive Order, the main objective of the March-on-Washington. All of the Members reached agreed to postponement. Two of the members of the Committee, Rev. A. Clayton Powell, Jr., and Richard Parrish, Chairman of the Youth Division, have opposed postponement.

Simply stated, the March was postponed because its main objective, namely, the issuance of an Executive Order banning discrimination in National Defense, was secured in conference with the President.

What about discrimination in the departments of the Federal Government? This was one of our objectives. While it was one of our objectives, it was not our main objective. We consider that it is much more important to get jobs for Negroes in National Defense, than to get them in the Army or Navy or air corps, although we shall continue to fight to abolish discriminations on account of race, color, creed or national origin in all departments of the government and the armed forces of the nation.

The National Negro March-on-Washington Committee would have been placed in an untenable, absurd, and ridiculous position had it rejected its chief objective when offered by the President on the grounds that we didn't get everything we wanted as a pretex[t] for Marching-on-Washington anyhow. . . .

In the face of this significant achievement, the March could not with reason and sanity be carried on unless the main purpose of the movement was to *March for the sake of the march and not to get jobs for the Negro Masses*. . . .

Therefore, I want to make it clear, that the purpose of the March-on-Washington movement was not to serve as an agency to create a continuing state of sullen unrest and blind resentment among Negroes against discriminations. There is sufficient of this. Its purpose was and is to achieve a specific and definite thing, namely, elimination of barriers to jobs for Negroes. It would have constituted a definite betrayal of the interests of the Negro masses if the National Negro March-on-Washington Committee after receiving from the President the main object of its struggle, the Executive Order, had defiantly waived it aside and marched on Washington. Such strategy would have promptly and rightly been branded as a lamentable specie of infantile leftism and an appeal to sheer prima donna dramatics and heroics.

While the March-on-Washington had positive and practical aims, it was and is fundamentally spiritual and moral in content and implication. It is the first demonstration on a national scale of the faith of the Negro people in themselves, in their own capacity to win their rights against opposition. Those of us who had the privilege to play some part in it have a solemn responsibility, obligation and duty to remain true to that faith of the Negro masses. This means that those who are guiding it must subordinate their own interests and future to the interests and future of the Negro people.

Schomburg Collection, New York Public Library.

Discrimination in the Armed Forces during World War II

The thread of racism is woven into the cloth of United States history. With the advent of World War II, Negro soldiers were drafted along with whites. There was discrimination in the draft system, however, which resulted in a case reaching the United States Supreme Court on appeal. In Winfred William Lynn *v.* Colonel John Downer, Commanding Officer, Camp Upton, New York, *the plea was made that Negroes were being illegally drafted under a "Jim Crow" system that set their names apart from the white potential inductees and selected them on a quota basis. According to the Selective Service Act, no one was to be discriminated against "because of his race, creed or color," therefore, Lynn initiated a case in the courts to test this system of drafting Negroes.*

By the time the case reached the Supreme Court, Lynn was fighting in the Pacific, and the Court refused to hear it. The inequity in the draft system prevailed throughout the war; and it was not until 1948, when President Truman issued a proclamation desegregating the armed forces, that the dual system was abandoned.

Lynn Committee to Abolish Segregation
in the Armed Forces
360 West 125 Street
N.Y. 27, N.Y.

The Supreme Court's Great Moot Suit

June 1, New York City: Last Monday the U.S. Supreme Court refused to review the Winfred Lynn case, involving racial discrimination in selection for the American Army. The Court's refusal even to hear the case was unexpected since one of the three judges in the lower court had ruled in Lynn's favor. The Supreme Court evidently regarded the Lynn Case as "too hot to handle."

Today, the Lynn Committee to Abolish Segregation in the Armed Forces revealed the U.S. Supreme Court's reason for refusing to review the case. The Clerk of the Court informed Arthur Garfield Hays, Lynn's attorney, by telephone: "The petition for a writ of certiorari is denied on the ground that the case is moot, it appearing that petitioner is no longer in respondent's custody."

In less technical language, the Court holds that the Lynn Case is "moot"—that is, it cannot now be decided one way or the other—because the "petitioner" (Winfred Lynn) is no longer in the "custody" of the "respondent" (Colonel Downer, commandant at Camp Upton, N.Y. at the time Lynn originally brought his suit). This amazing pronouncement of the Supreme Court, which bids fair to make legal history, ignores the *reason* Lynn is no longer in Colonel Downer's custody, which is, of course, that he is a soldier in the Army and was ordered overseas to the Pacific area several months ago. The Government's right hand, the Supreme Court, apparently takes no responsibility for what the Government's left hand, the Army, is doing.

Thus was born the Supreme Court's great Moot Suit. This issue, of course, has been pulled out of a hat at the last moment. The question of "mootness" was not even raised in the lower courts. . . .

Schomburg Collection, New York Public Library.

A Black Soldier Writes to Langston Hughes

After being drafted into the armed forces on a discriminatory basis, Negro soldiers found their fortunes did not improve with donning the uniform. In a letter to writer Langston Hughes, who had published an article on the conditions of Negroes in the armed services, a young soldier from South Camp, Florida, related the following incident.

Dear Mr. Hughes:

Hardly had the printer's ink dried on your article in regard to how a Negro Soldier must express himself before more evidence had sprung up to support your argument.

Early this week a Negro soldier was sent to Section 8 and charged with insanity because he stood in pain on sick call and told the Captain just what any real sick man would have said. The private had been discharged from the Base Hospital, but not fit for duty. He went to the Camp Dispensary for further treatment, the attending physician used abusive language after the private had expressed himself. So the Captain sent for the Major to come over and the private was sent to the psychotherapy. I learned the private is now up for a discharge.

A few Sundays ago General Arnold from Washington, D.C. visited this area. Well, troops were instructed to hide outside of the latrine and the barracks. But somehow there were three privates just wasn't all hid and as provident would have it. Just as the noted Visitor and General's party stopped in front of the Mess Hall, the three privates came to attention and handsomely saluted the General. Pausing after saluting, the General began questioning them softly. All eyes and peeping ears were turned in this direction then. The General proceeded with his inspection. The privates held their places. In a few minutes, General Arnold was gone. These privates were surrounded by fellow soldiers anxious to know what the General inquired of them.

For the first week things went on well. But at this writing, two of these three privates are in the guard house now. The charge against them is! Insubordination.

South Camp Commanding Officer is a Mississippian, Charles Munnis.

There have been several Eastern and Midwestern Officers but Headquarters will not let them nice officers stay over the 1800 Negro troops in South Camp

P.F.C. Andrew Banks.

Schomburg Collection, New York Public Library.

A Negro Battalion in World War II

In spite of segregation and discrimination, Negro soldiers served creditably in the armed forces. The following is a brief account of the first Negro tank unit to see action in Europe.

Early in November, 1943, the 761st Tank Bn. commanded by Lt. Col. Paul Bates, of Boonton, N.J., was committed as attached armor in the 26th Infantry Div. in the 3rd U.S. Army under Gen. Geo. Patton, becoming the first Negro Tank unit to go into action in American history. The entire enlisted personnel was Negro.

At St. Nicholas Du Port, France on 2 Nov. 1944 Gen. Patton addressed us as follows: "Men, you are the first Negro Tankers ever to fight in the American Army. I would have never asked for you if you weren't good. I have nothing but the best in my army. I don't care what color you are, so long as you go up there and kill those Kraut. Everyone has their eyes on you and are expecting great things from you. Most of all your race is looking forward to you. Don't let them down, and, don't let me down."

Well, we didn't let our race down; we didn't let Gen. Patton down, and we certainly didn't let the United States down. We remained in combat for 183 long, hard days.

The 761st Tnk Bn. fought in six European countries: France, Holland, Belgium, Luxembourg, Austria and Germany. It was at various times attached to the 3rd, 7th, and 9th U.S. Armies. During these campaigns the battalion furnished tank support for the 26th, 71st, 79th, 87th, 95th and 103 Infantry Divisions; and also the 17th Airborne Div. in the "Battle of the Bulge."

The 761st Tank Bn. was engaged in five major campaigns: 1) The Battle for the Saar Basin, 2) The Battle of Moreville, France, 3) The Battle of the Bulge, 4) The breakthrough in the Siegfried Line to get to the Rhine River, 5) "Task Force Rhine" in Germany.

Eight enlisted men in the battalion won battlefield commissions. Decorations included: 69 Bronze Stars, 4 with clusters, 11 Silver Stars, three of them posthumously awarded, 3 Certificates of Merit, 296 Purple Hearts, 8 with clusters, making a grand total of 391 battle awards. The 761st Tank Battalion itself received four Battle Stars.

Normal battalion strength was 750 men and 54 medium Sherman Tanks. These 32-ton

DAMAGE TO THE ENEMY—Task Force Rhine

31 Pill boxes
29 88MM anti-tank guns
1 170MM Artillery gun
833 enemy killed
49 Machine gun nests
4 Self-propelled guns
12 Kitchen vehicles
100 Enemy injured
20 75MM Anti-Tank guns
12 37MM guns
200 horses killed or captured
3,206 enemy captured

TOTAL DAMAGE TO THE ENEMY IN THE WAR

58 Pillboxes
64 88MM anti-tank guns
34 Tanks
51 Panzerfausten (bazookas)
3 Armored cars
3 Ammunition dumps
1 Battery of 88MM Artillery
4 Airfields, 3 in Germany, 1 in Austria
650 enemy injured
331 Machine gun nests
8 self-propelled guns
4 German tanks (destroyed by Germans)
461 All-type wheeled vehicles
17 Mortar positions
12 Kitchen vehicles
2 Transport Aircraft destroyed
1 Radio station captured at Salz, Germany
23 75MM anti-tank guns
6 20MM anti-aircraft guns
24 bazooka teams
9 Nebelwefern (smoke screen throwers)
12 Ammunition trucks
1 20MM Mortar and 40-rounds-ammo
2 Armed supply dumps
7 towns captured and 3 destroyed
6,246 enemy killed
15,818 enemy prisoners

vehicles mounted a 76mm cannon, 2 Cal. 30 Browning machine guns with 4,000 rounds of ammunition, 1 Cal. 50 anti-aircraft (Browning) gun with 350 rounds of ammunition, 12 hand grenades and 144 76mm shells.

The 761st spearheaded the famous "Task Force Rhine" attack which crashed through the rugged mountain defenses in the Siegfried Line in the Neider Schlettenbach-Reisdorf-Klingmunster area. "Task Force Rhine" included the 2nd Bn. of the 103rd Inf. Div. 409 Regt. A detachment of combat engineers, a platoon from the 614th Tank Destroyer Bn., another famous Negro unit, and the 761st Tank Battalion.

In three days the task force opened up a big hole in the Siegfried defenses through which the entire 14th Armored Div., 263 tanks and 10,937 men passed. This occurred on 24 March, 1944. We continued on to ultimate victory over the enemy.

Total casualties credited to the 761st directly and indirectly—129,540.

Above figures compiled by the units with which the 761st fought and are recorded in the files of the Dept. of the Army. Office of the Chief of Military History, Washington 25, D.C.

The coat of arms of the 761st is a black panther with the slogan "Come Out Fighting" inscribed beneath it, and it is worn on both shoulder straps of the uniform and on the overseas cap.

31 enlisted men and three officers were killed in action. . . .

On May 6th, 1945 the 761st Tank Battalion made contact with the Russian First Ukrainian Army commanded by Marshall Ivan S. Koniev at Steyr, Austria. On May 8, 1945, the war ended.

Compiled by Walter Lewis,
National Historian, 761st Tank Battailon

Walter Lewis, "A Brief History of the 761st Tank Battalion in World War II," *Negro History Bulletin,* XXIX (November 1965).

The Detroit Race Riot

On June 20, 1943, a race riot occurred in Detroit that was the most violent of its kind up until that time. The riot lasted more than twenty-four hours and resulted in the loss of thirty-four lives and the destruction of more than two million dollars worth of property. The underlying causes of the riot, which was sparked by an incident between white sailors and Negro civilians, were disillusionment on the part of southern blacks coming North for wartime jobs and the violent animosity of the local white laboring class.

A crowd of white men, mostly youths, with a sprinkling of soldiers and sailors, ranged up and down the six-block stretch on Woodward north of Peterboro, attacking every colored man they could catch.

A northbound Woodward street car was stopped at Mack when the rioters pulled the trolley from the wire. Mobs poured in the front and side doors after two colored persons. Screaming women in the rear of the car jumped or were carried out the open back window while the mob dragged its two victims out the doors.

The two men were beaten down to the iron-grilled floor of the car stop and pounded with fist and feet into semi-consciousness before police arrived and took them to Receiving Hospital.

At least 25 cars driven by colored persons were turned over and burned on Woodward and adjoining streets and alleys.

One of the first—a large black Lincoln Zephyr—was turned over just east of Woodward on Stimson after a crowd of 50 men had captured the driver and dragged him behind a billboard. The colored man escaped with blood running from cuts on the face and shoulders where the clothing had been torn away.

The crowd then turned its attention to the car and was about to tip it over when two mounted police charged up, swinging long nightsticks and driving the crowd back.

Jay Jackson in *The Chicago Defender*

"Hitler's little helper."

Hardly had the police turned their backs when the crowd charged on the car again, pushing it over on its side. One of the men then rushed forward, wrenched off the gasoline tank cover, permitting the gasoline to flow onto the pavement.

Another man threw a match in the gasoline and the car was wrapped in flames 30 feet high in a matter of seconds. The Fire Department was called but arrived after the fire had been extinguished by an attendant at a nearby gasoline station.

Rioters ranged through the alleys looking for stones and pieces of metal which they threw at colored persons' cars that were going too fast to be stopped.

Such an attack was made on a colored soldier, who had a colored girl with him. A rioter standing less than 10 feet from the car hurled a large stone through the open front window.

The car sped away, however, with members of the mob on foot in hot pursuit until several began shouting, "He's a soldier, let him go."

A youth who appeared to be only 16 or 17 years old threw a rock the size of a fist at the window of a southbound suburban bus in which a colored person was riding.

A police cruiser containing four officers arrived on the scene as the rock was thrown.

The youth was seized by police and put into the car, but the mob surrounded the car, shouting, "Let him go." The police released him when the crowd packed so tightly around the car that it couldn't be moved.

Trucks with colored drivers were stoned on sight.

Colored on foot were beaten.

As soon as one appeared on Woodward, the shout "There's one, go get him!" went up along the street and running men converged from all sides. Usually the colored man was caught, beaten and allowed to limp away before police reached the scene.

Other times officers arrived after the victim had been knocked to the pavement, and stood protectingly over him until he could be bundled into a squad car and taken away.

Many of the rioters bore wounds they had collected in fighting during the night or early morning and the sight of men still fighting despite bandaged heads or arms in slings was not uncommon.

One man, wearing a once-white shirt that was nearly in ribbons, walked up and down the street with the mob, openly boasting that "I killed one of them at 2:30 this morning."

The tide of battle swept up and down Woodward with clocklike regularity as the mobs chased colored north and south. Proprietors of some stores on the street locked their doors. Hundreds of women congregated on the sidewalks, mostly as spectators, although some took an active part as self-appointed lookouts to shout "There comes one," to the men when a colored man appeared.

Here and there in the crowd were some who did not share in the spirit of the occasion. This element was dealt with in various ways.

An elderly Catholic priest who attempted to aid a colored family halted by the mob at Cass and Stimson was shouldered, respectfully but firmly out of the way.

"You'd better get out of here," one man said. "I'm a religious man myself, but we're up against a situation here that religion can't solve. You've no business here."

The priest attempted to reason with the man, and with the other bystanders, but suddenly there was a cry, "There goes one—let's get him!" and the mob set off after new quarry, leaving the priest without an audience.

A tall, slim youth on the northeast corner of Woodward and Mack tried to make a speech from an automobile bumper.

"This is no way to act when our country is at war," he pleaded.

That was as far as he got.

"Ah, shut up," yelled one of his hearers.

"Let's get him, too," suggested another. The youth got down from the bumper and stood on the corner, shaking his head but keeping quiet.

In front of a florist's shop on Woodward, an old lady, speaking in a trembling European accent, said:

"Oh, this is terrible. It's just like back in the old country. I didn't think America was like this."

"Listen," a large lady responded, "you better be careful how you're talking."

"But," the old woman said, "this is supposed to be a democracy. This is supposed to be a land of freedom."

"Listen," said the other, "I believe in democracy just as much as you do. I'm a native-born American and I've got menfolks on the battlefield. But you better not stick up for that race or you're going to get yourself into trouble!"

The cry of "Hitlerism" was raised frequently during the day—not by the victims, but by the members of the mob.

Whenever policemen rescued a colored person from the crowd, the rioters jeered the police.

When officers attempted to drive them back to the curb by means of tear-gas bombs, a mighty roar of indignation arose.

"Just like Germany!" the mob yelled. "Just like Hitler!"

A surly white youth, briefly in the clutches of the law, muttered: "Yah—you damn Gestapo!"

Newcomers to the scene were quickly inflamed with excitedly told reports from the colored sector.

"They just killed fifteen white men over on Hastings," someone shouted. Again, "They just killed a 12-year-old white girl over on Hastings!"

Youthful bands of white trouble-makers circulated through the downtown area, some with the knuckles of their right hands bound with tape so that they might be more effective in combat.

Tear-gas was resorted to on one occasion by police to break up their forays but in the Cadillac Square-City Hall area they persisted most of the day.

Between 1 and 2:30 p.m., four riots occurred within a stone's throw of the City Hall, with only three policemen available to break them up.

About 1:30 a group of 50 or 60 white disturbers, bearing an American Flag apparently seized from a sidewalk standard, marched two abreast through Monroe to Randolph molesting every youthful colored person in sight. Older colored men and women were ignored.

At Woodward and Monroe police used a tear-gas bomb to disperse a gang which had pushed and jostled several colored youths.

Three policemen stationed at Majestic Building, City Hall and on Woodward below Fort had a busy time.

In front of the Family Theatre on Cadillac Square a colored youth with white-rimmed sun glasses was rescued by a scout car after being struck several blows.

Policemen rushed another colored youth into the City Hall after he had been assaulted by a white group.

Another melee found a colored youth pummelled by several whites in the middle of Michigan, at the City Hall crossing, until police rescued the victim.

On E. Grand River, near Woodward, police dispersed a group of fourteen or fifteen white boys attired in white sailor hats, who had been beating a colored lad.

In front of the City Hall, small gangs of white youths began to surround a colored man at the bus stop. Three sailors, none of them more than 20, stepped in and broke it up.

"He isn't doing you guys any harm," said one of the sailors. "Let him alone !"

"What's it to ya?" growled one of the hoodlums.

"Plenty!" snapped the sailor. "There was a colored guy in our outfit, and he saved a couple of lives. Besides you guys are stirring up something that we're fighting to stop."

Believing for a few minutes Monday afternoon that a colored mob was about to attack Police Headquarters, officers there formed a riot squad of the whole as they watched the group of 200 marching down Beaubien toward the station.

Riot guns and tear gas were hastily given the officers, who prepared to turn the throng back. It was not until they saw that the members of the group were wearing official arm bands that the police realized they were colored OCD workers and air-raid wardens, mobilized to aid in quelling the riot.

Detroit Free Press, June 30, 1943.

Claude McKay Writes to Max Eastman on Racism

Claude McKay, poet and author, was a member of the Harlem Renaissance in the 1920's. Of West Indian descent, he was one of the more radical Negro intellectuals and had been called a Communist because of his militant stand on the racial issue. The letter which follows, written by McKay to columnist Max Eastman, repudiated this label while confirming his dissatisfaction with all who permit discrimination.

St. Joseph's Hospital, Albuquerque, N.M.
Sept. 16, 1946

Dear Max:

. . . You know that intellectually I do my thinking for myself and I don't know if you remember when you were living in Marcel

Cachin's house at Antibes and had written the book "Science and Revolution" in which you declared to the world that you were a Marxist and I read the manuscript and told you that I did not believe that Marxism was a science. And I believed that John Stuart Mill was a greater social economist than Marx whose first and second books on socialism I had seriously read in London back in 1920.

Therefore I am not mouthing any Stalin propaganda slogans. I am not a Marxist or Communist and never was one, but if Communists sometimes say the truth in spite of all their lies I am not going to say that the truth is not the truth. . . .

Whatever the Soviet nation has done is not worse than what the British Empire has done in its 300 years more or less of world domination. Have you forgotten the revolt at Lucknow when Indians were shot like balls through the mouths of British cannon? Have you forgotten the degrading conditions at Amritsar at the end of the last world war, when the Governor had Indian natives crawl on their bellies before white troops?

I have always thought that every Englishman and American is a dyed in the wool hypocrite when it comes to seeing and facing other people's problems. In all my life I have never been a reactionary and I won't be one now mouthing occasional pieces for the capitalist press, because I know one thing, the capitalists do not want me and I don't want anything of them; whatever the Soviets are bringing into the world it is something new just as the Mohammedan regime which swept through Asia and Africa and Spain in the Seventh Century. It wasn't that Mohammedanism was better than Christianity but it happened that Christianity then was rotten to the core. I am a Catholic because I believe that the Catholic Church has a spiritual message for mankind's spiritual nature which we can get from no heads of states.

I subscribe wholeheartedly to Sec. [Henry] Wallace's speech of Sept. 12. I would prefer that my name in history should stand beside his instead of the neo-reactionaries of the New Leader. In my opinion no state is perfect because mankind is far from perfection. I do not fear that the Russian system will ever conquer America but I do not care if it conquers the people of Asia and Africa. I do not think that, mouthing goodwill, the democracies have anything to offer such people. I should say to the so-called democracies of the United States and Great Britain: set your own house in order and do not try to scare up a war against Soviet Russia.

I am not a partisan of Communism, nevertheless I have nothing but contempt for people who accepted Lenin's dictum about the bourgeoisie and now are opposed to the Russian Government for trying to bring it about in devious ways. I joined the Catholic Church because structurally, traditionally and fundamentally it is the foe of Communism, and please remember that there is a formidable left wing within the Catholic Church because it can accommodate all, even you.

Claude McKay

Schomburg Collection, New York Public Library.

Black Troops in the Korean Conflict

Racial bars within the United States Armed Forces were officially banned in 1948, when President Truman issued his Executive Order for this purpose. Nevertheless, separate Negro units still existed when the United States entered the Korean War in June 1950. This news account reveals the bravery of a Negro unit within the U.S. 3rd Division at Hungnam.

A gallant Negro infantry platoon fought off the most threatening approach yet to a Communist break-through into the Hungnam beachhead.

The United States unit was led by Lieut. Harry E. Sutton of 1100 Franklin Avenue, the Bronx, New York, when the North Koreans made their wild charge.

The Red assault disintegrated when each United States soldier was down to his last ammunition clip of eight bullets. That's how close the Communists came to penetrating at least the outer United Nations defense ring. . . .

A famous Third Division regiment was holding part of the hilly eastern flank of the beachhead. Lieutenant Sutton's platoon was assigned to a long, three-humped ridge.

Lieutenant Sutton has been a soldier a long time and an infantry lieutenant five years. He spotted his men in strong points on the three ridge nipples and along the World War I type trenches that civilian workers had gouged in the frozen earth.

He was worried. Fresh North Korean soldiers—reorganized, re-equipped and fanatic—were on the next ridge line over. On his right flank they had strongpointed a hill that surrounding crags masked from United States artillery.

At 7:45 A.M. Monday the Communists struck. Crawling up the bare windswept ridge came three groups of twenty men—one group on each flank, one dead center. Just a small attack, but made by ferocious men who would not stop even when wounded.

The United States soldiers moved back and forth in their old-fashioned trench, picking off the Reds.

"But they kept coming and coming," Lieutenant Sutton said. "All day small groups of them kept coming. We would wipe out this bunch and before we knew it the Reds were back again."

The Communists from the ridgeline opposite tried to pin down Lieutenant Sutton's men with fire so the assault groups could reach the trench line. The Reds were firing captured United States Browning automatic rifles, machine guns and Garrand rifles.

M/Sgt. Tyler Collins of Malone, Fla., stood bolt upright and picked off seven Communists. A bazooka man killed ten with a single shell. But the Reds kept coming for more than eleven hours. Finally at 7 P.M. there was a break.

"We have licked them," the G.I.'s told each other jubilantly. Small arms began again from the opposite ridge. There was no assault this time, just the continual bark of snipers' rifles through the long, frigid night.

At 6 A.M. Tuesday the Reds assaulted "Sutton Ridge." From the ridge opposite the center of the line came a fierce wall of fire.

A suicide enemy force struck up the slope against the left flank.

Lieutenant Sutton was not too worried about these two fronts—the massed firepower of United States artillery could hit there.

But from the hill on the right—masked from the guns by the other hills—the main force of the enemy was assaulting in the darkness. The Reds were coming down a precipitous slope, tying short fiber ropes on scrub pines and lowering themselves. . . .

Once inside the trenches the Reds turned the United States soldiers' own machine gun down the ridgeline.

Pfc. Elijah Whitley of Toledo, Ark., replied with his Browning automatic rifle, silencing the machine gun. Along the ridgeline, Lieutenant Sutton and his men rolled hand grenades down the slope. In the breaking dawn they could see the Communists crumple and tumble down the slope and then see new men replace them. Bodies were strewn crazily on the slopes.

"We gave them everything we had," Lieutenant Sutton said.

That was enough. The last fanatic charge disintegrated.

Reinforcements reached the United States line. United States mortars thumped down on the enemy-held right-hand ridge nipple. Lieutenant Sutton led a counter-attack. The enemy was driven off it and Lieutenant Sutton's men again held all of the ridge.

The New York Times, December 22, 1950.

Willard S. Townsend on the Labor Movement

The annals of labor history in the United States include no Negro who achieved more for black workers than Willard Townsend. Organizer and long-term president of the United Transport Service Employees, he was also the first Negro to sit on the governing board of an international union, the CIO. When the AF of L and the CIO merged in 1955, Townsend was joined in the labor hierarchy by A. Philip Randolph, who had organized the pullman porters' union under the jurisdiction of the AF of L.

Townsend served the labor union movement not only in this country but abroad: on several occasions he was designated by CIO and United States government officials as a representative to foreign labor conferences. This excerpt from his writings explains his attitude toward the labor movement.

I am in the labor movement today for two reasons: (1) There are a few basic needs essential to the well-being of every man and woman in our modern civilization. I, and millions of working men and women—as well as the coupon-cutters—want these needs satisfied. (2) The labor movement, in my judgment, offers the best means of attaining our goals. Here is what we want:

Job opportunity based on ability
Job security
Decent hours of work
Decent working conditions
Adequate pay
Adequate housing
Adequate health protection
Adequate education
Opportunity to enjoy some recreation and hobbies
Equal voting rights
Protection of civil rights
Old-Age security.

Since I am a man who has always worked for a living, I discovered early that achievement of these ends would take some "doings." About the same time I also discovered that my wants were not unique. They are entertained by millions the world over. In fact, they are universal. They may not be crystallized in these exact terms, but they are present in substance.

Experience on my first job convinced me that progress cannot be made alone. Who would help me? Who was concerned for my welfare? Logically, the answer was, men in a similar situation. On that job we organized a union. Help and encouragement came from many quarters. As we worked, sacrificed, and struggled together, my conviction grew stronger that only through the labor movement would working people anywhere in the world realize their objectives.

In the railroad industry, for example, opportunity for advancement on the basis of ability is denied Negroes. Under this policy intelligent men and women capable of serving as information clerks, office employees, ticket sellers, stewards, or engineers, are not even considered for the jobs. Discrimination is not directed exclusively against Negroes and other minority groups. A man's religious or political faith, his family connections may be the determining factor rather than his training and experience in securing a job, or being considered for promotion.

But, having been hired, job security is another matter. Thousands of factors, remote and immediate, enter the picture. With exception of a few boom periods, wage earners have endured a never-ending struggle to make ends meet. Add to this the ever-present possibility of indiscriminate firing or furloughing, and you can see the degree of assurance and peace of mind enjoyed by the majority of workers. Union contracts have done more to stabilize job tenure than any other single element in the industrial picture.

Reasonable hours of work and decent working conditions are the due of every laboring man and woman. . . . During wartime, production quotas spurred employers to recognize the fact and act upon it. Time studies proved what the man in the streets has long known; namely, beyond a given limit, efficiency decreases.

It is not our claim that there are no employers who consider these factors in the conduct of their business, but there are certainly too few. Labor unions are more interested in the health and welfare of the worker than many companies' safety engineers. From experience, its members know the physical hazards. From experience they are also aware of the psychological hazards. The overbearing straw boss, the stool pigeon, attrition in the industry, are risks as real as defective machinery.

And now we come to that complex variable, adequate pay—currently "take home pay." To me, adequate pay roughly is sufficient money on which to live comfortably, not exist. If I am helping to produce the wealth of the world, I want to enjoy some of the good things of life here and now. I want my child to have as much education as his talents and inclination would lead him to acquire. If a member of my family is ill, or suffers an accident, I want to provide the best medical care available. I want to be able to afford a vacation when circumstances other than monetary permit. These are things for which I want a salary large enough to decide personally how they shall be handled. I don't want to look to charity for them, or do without.

I've heard men say, "The company gave us a raise." Rarely has this happened. Primarily, wages have increased because of union pressure, and, even after negotiated, are sometime nullified by legal loopholes and intricate dodges. A very good example is the case of dining-car employees in the railroad industry. Before passage of the Fair Labor Standards Act, waiters' uniforms, meals, and lodging, when on duty, were furnished by the carrier. After payment of the minimum wage became mandatory, railroads began deducting the cost of the above-mentioned items from waiters' salaries. This is only one of many similar cases being pressed by organized labor to correct evasion of the law.

For many years a number of individuals and organizations have worked to make old-age security in America a reality. Labor unions are playing a major role in the struggle, for the homes of children and in-laws. County, state and municipal institutions are unfortunately filled with the indigent aged from the ranks of wage earners.

Working jointly with men and women in the labor movement to achieve these goals has been an education to me.

To have a small part, to be able to make a little contribution to this phase of human progress is the reason I am in the labor movement.

Willard S. Townsend, "Goals Attained through Unionism," in *7th Biennial Convention of the United Transport Service Employees* (Chicago, 1950).

An Attempt at Open Housing in Cicero, Illinois

In 1951, a young Negro couple from Chicago tried to move to the suburban village of Cicero. They were attacked by members of the white community, their apartment was damaged and a small race riot occurred. This account of the event was chronicled by Walter White of the NAACP.

"That mob at Cicero Thursday night was made up of insane people," Cook County Sheriff John A. Babb told me, and there is ample evidence of the truth of his statement. . . . their violence against Harvey Clark Jr., World War II veteran and graduate of Fisk University, was greater than that of many mobs in the deep South. Two days after the worst of the rioting, the atmosphere of bitterness and potential renewal of almost insane determination to bomb or to destroy brick by brick the attractive twenty-family apartment house at 6132-42 W. 19th St., in Cicero, was such that it was almost tangible. Such fury has its roots in maladies which exist in other Mid-Western cities and towns as well as in other parts of the country and it is important to look at the causes rather than at the rioting itself. The mobbists are not the most important actors in the grim tragedy. They are the dupes of powerful forces, some of them highly respectable and others exceedingly sinister.

As part of the background, let's look at the plight of Harvey Clark and his wife Johnetta, also a college graduate, and their two children aged eight and six. The Clarks moved to Chicago from Nashville, Tenn., in 1949. At first he worked as an insurance salesman and later as a bus driver for the Chicago Transit Authority. Because as a Negro he was restricted in finding a home, the best accommodation he could secure was one-half of a small two-room apartment on Chicago's South Side for which he paid $12.50 a week, or approximately $56 a month. The Clarks occupied a tiny bedroom while another family of five occupied the equally small living room. The apartment was located in a vermin-infested building which can most charitably be described as a fire trap. The shy and cultured Mrs. Clark fought a desperate battle against vermin and dirt. Each day Mr. Clark was forced to travel twenty-four miles to and from the bus terminal from which he started and ended his daily run. When the Cicero apartment house was bought by a group of Negroes and a five-room apartment in a clean, modern building was made available to them at $60 a month, the joy of the Clarks knew no limit.

Being recent newcomers to Chicago, they were unaware that no Negroes had ever been permitted to live in Cicero, Berwyn or several other villages to the west of Chicago. All he knew was that the new and attractive apartment in which he and Mrs. Clark could bring up their children in decent surroundings was only a mile and half from his place of employment. When Cicero policemen barred him from moving his furniture into the home and held him in custody for more than two hours until Cicero residents could return from work to form the mob which later burned the Clark furniture and made a shambles of the twenty-apartment building, Mr. Clark became aware of the maelstrom of hate and racial prejudice into which he had been thrown. . . . Of the 70,000 inhabitants of Cicero, half are registered on the rolls of the church. Only three of the twenty churchmen of Cicero dared comment on the riot the Sunday following the outbreak. One of them told of appealing to the police to stop the disorder and of being told, "We don't want the blankety-blanks in here anyway, and this is our way of getting them out."

At the root of the trouble is the confinement of Negroes to the perilously overcrowded ghetto of Chicago on the South Side. Unscrupulous landlords, both white and Negro, have exploited this situation mercilessly. Efforts of Negroes to find decent homes outside the restricted area have been thwarted by real estate associations, mortgage companies and banks, which have refused to sell, rent or grant loans to Negroes outside the ghetto. . . .

Troubled days lie ahead because such prejudices are not easily eradicated. Mr. Clark has announced his determination as a matter of principle to return to Cicero to live. He is backed in that determination by powerful minorities, church, labor and veterans' groups. The Chicago newspapers, with one exception, have been unequivocal in denunciation of the riot and in affirmation of Mr. Clark's right to live wherever he is able to live. . . .

NAACP Papers, Library of Congress.

Mary McLeod Bethune's "Last Will and Testament" to Her People

Mary McLeod Bethune was born into a large, poverty-stricken southern family. An unusually talented woman, she secured an education, later founded a college, organized the National Council of Negro Women and became one of the most eloquent and admired voices in the Negro protest movement. During the New Deal, she served as a member of President Roosevelt's "Black Cabinet." To chart her many achievements would be monumental: she literally lived for her people. In 1955, she wrote her "Last Will and Testament," which was published posthumously in Ebony *magazine.*

Sometimes as I sit communing in my study I feel that death is not far off. I am aware that it will overtake me before the greatest of my dreams—full equality for the Negro in our time—is realized. Yet, I face that reality without tears or regrets. I am resigned to death as all humans must be at the proper time. Death neither alarms nor frightens one who has had a long career of fruitful toil. The knowledge that my work has been helpful to many fills me with joy and great satisfaction.

Since my retirement from an active role in educational work and from the affairs of the National Council of Negro Women, I have been living quietly and working at my desk at my home here in Florida. The years have directed a change of pace for me. I am now 78 years old and my activities are no longer so strenuous as they once were. I feel that I must conserve my strength to finish the work at hand.

Already I have begun working on my autobiography which will record my life-journey in detail, together with the innumerable side trips which have carried me abroad, into every corner of our country, into homes both lowly and luxurious, and even into the White House to confer with Presidents. I have also deeded my home and its contents to the Mary McLeod Bethune Foundation, organized in March, 1953, for research, interracial activity and the sponsorship of wider educational opportunities.

Sometimes I ask myself if I have any other legacy to leave. Truly, my worldly possessions are few. Yet, my experiences have been rich. From them, I have distilled principles and policies in which I believe firmly, for they represent the meaning of my life's work. They are the product of much sweat and sorrow. Perhaps in them there is something of value. So, as my life draws to a close, I will pass them on to Negroes everywhere in the hope that an old woman's philosophy may give them inspiration. Here, then, is my legacy.

I leave you love. Love builds. It is positive and helpful. It is more beneficial than hate. Injuries quickly forgotten quickly pass away. Personally and racially, our enemies must be forgiven. Our aim must be to create a world of fellowship and justice where no man's skin, color or religion, is held against him. "Love thy neighbor" is a precept which could transform the world if it were universally practiced. It connotes brotherhood and, to me, brotherhood of man is the noblest concept in all human relations. Loving your neighbor means being interracial, interreligious and international.

I leave you hope. The Negro's growth will be great in the years to come. Yesterday, our ancestors endured the degradation of slavery, yet they retained their dignity. Today, we direct our economic and political strength toward winning a more abundant and secure life. Tomorrow, a new Negro, unhindered by race taboos and shackles, will benefit from more than 330 years of ceaseless striving and struggle. Theirs will be a better world. This I believe with all my heart.

I leave you the challenge of developing confidence in one another. As long as Negroes are hemmed into racial blocs by prejudice and pressure, it will be necessary for them to band together for economic betterment. Negro banks, insurance companies and other businesses are examples of successful, racial economic enterprises. These institutions were made possible by vision and mutual aid. Confidence was vital in getting them started and keeping them going. Negroes have got to demonstrate still more confidence in each other in business. This kind of confidence will aid the economic rise of the race by bringing together the pennies and dollars of our people and ploughing them into useful channels. Economic separatism cannot be tolerated in this enlightened age, and it is not practicable. We must spread out as far and as fast as we can, but we must also help each other as we go.

I leave you a thirst for education. Knowledge is the prime need of the hour. More and more, Negroes are taking full advantage of hard-won opportunities for learning, and the educational level of the Negro population is at its highest point in history. We are making greater use of the privileges inherent in living in a democracy. If we continue in this trend, we will be able to rear increasing numbers of strong, purposeful men and women, equipped with vision, mental clarity, health and education.

I leave you a respect for the uses of power. We live in a world which respects power above all things. Power, intelligently directed, can lead to more freedom. Unwisely directed, it can be a dreadful, destructive force. During my lifetime I have seen the power of the Negro grow enormously. It has always been my first concern that this power should be placed on the side of human justice.

Now that the barriers are crumbling everywhere, the Negro in America must be ever vigilant less his forces be marshalled behind wrong causes and undemocratic movements. He must not lend his support to any group that seeks to subvert democracy. That is why we must select leaders who are wise, courageous, and of great moral stature and ability. We have great leaders among us today: Ralph Bunche, Channing Tobias, Mordecai Johnson, Walter White, and Mary Church Terrell. (The latter two are now deceased.) We have had other great men and women in the past: Frederick Douglass, Booker T. Washington, Harriet Tubman, Sojourner Truth. We must produce more qualified people like them, who will work not for themselves, but for others.

I leave you faith. Faith is the first factor in a life devoted to service. Without faith, nothing is possible. With it, nothing is impossible. Faith in God is the greatest power, but great, too, is faith in oneself. In 50 years the faith of the American Negro in himself has grown immensely and is still increasing. The measure of our progress as a race is in precise relation to the depth of the faith in our people held by our leaders. Frederick Douglass, genius though he was, was spurred by a deep conviction that his people would heed his counsel and follow him to freedom. Our greatest Negro figures have been imbued with faith. Our forefathers struggled for liberty in conditions far more onerous than those we now face, but they never lost the faith. Their perseverance paid rich dividends. We must never forget their sufferings and their sacrifices, for they were the foundations of the progress of our people.

I leave you racial dignity. I want Negroes to maintain their human dignity at all costs. We, as Negroes, must recognize that we are the custodians as well as the heirs of a great civilization. We have given something to the world as a race and for this we are proud and fully conscious of our place in the total picture of mankind's development. We must learn also to share and mix with all men. We must make an effort to be less race conscious and more conscious of individual and human values. I have never been sensitive about my complexion. My color has never destroyed my self respect nor has it ever caused me to conduct myself in such a manner as to merit the disrespect of any person. I have not let my color handicap me. Despite many crushing burdens and handicaps, I have risen from the cotton fields of South Carolina to found a college, administer it during its years of growth, become a public servant in the government of our country and a leader of women. I would not exchange my color for all the wealth in the world, for had I been born white I might not have been able to do all that I have done or yet hope to do.

I leave you a desire to live harmoniously with your fellow men. The problem of color is world-wide. It is found in Africa and Asia, Europe and South America. I appeal to American Negroes—North, South, East and West—to recognize their common problems and unite to solve them.

I pray that we will learn to live harmoniously with the white race. So often, our difficulties have made us hyper-sensitive and truculent. I want to see my people conduct themselves naturally in all relationships—fully conscious of their manly responsibilities and deeply aware of their heritage. I want them to learn to understand whites and influence them for good, for it is advisable and sensible for us to do so. We are a minority of 15 million living side by side with a white majority. We must learn to deal with these people positively and on an individual basis.

I leave you finally a responsibility to our young people. The world around us really belongs to youth for youth will take over its future management. Our children must never lose their zeal for building a better world. They must not be discouraged from aspiring toward greatness, for they are to be the leaders of tomorrow. Nor must they forget that the masses of our people are still underprivileged, ill-housed, impoverished and victimized by discrimination. We have a powerful potential in our youth, and we must have the courage to change old ideas and practices so that we may direct their power toward good ends.

Faith, courage, brotherhood, dignity, ambition, responsibility—these are needed today as never before. We must cultivate them and use them as tools for our task of completing the establishment of equality for the Negro. We must sharpen these tools in the struggle that faces us and find new ways of using them. The Freedom Gates are half a-jar. We must pry them fully open.

If I have a legacy to leave my people, it is my philosophy of living and serving. As I face tomorrow, I am content, for I think I have spent my life well. I pray now that my philosophy may be helpful to those who share my vision of a world of Peace, Progress, Brotherhood and Love.

Mary McLeod Bethune, "My Last Will and Testament," *Ebony,* X (August 1955).

Brown v. *Board of Education*

Fifty-eight years after the Supreme Court of the United States promulgated the doctrine of "separate but equal" facilities for black citizens, it moved to reverse itself in the education cases that came before the Court in 1954. Argued effectively by the NAACP legal counsel, Thurgood Marshall, the defense was able to show the devastating effects of segregated education on Negro children. In a unanimous decision, written by Chief Justice Earl Warren, the Court drew heavily on psychological studies showing the wholly unequal results of this type of education. The 1954 decision granted a one-year delay for the purpose of further argument. Thus, May 17, 1955 became the landmark date on which the Court ordered desegregation of schools "with all deliberate speed."

These cases come to us from the States of Kansas, South Carolina, Virginia, and Delaware. They are premised on different facts and different local conditions, but a common legal question justifies their consideration together in this consolidated opinion.

In each of the cases, minors of the Negro race, through their legal representatives, seek the aid of the courts in obtaining admission to the public schools of their community on a nonsegregated basis. In each instance, they had been denied admission to schools attended by white children under laws requiring or permitting segregation according to race. This segregation was alleged to deprive the plaintiffs of the equal protection of the laws under the Fourteenth Amendment. In each of the cases other than the Delaware case, a three-judge federal district court denied relief to the plaintiffs on the so-called "separate but equal" doctrine announced by this Court in *Plessy* v. *Ferguson,* 163 U.S. 537. Under that doctrine, equality of treatment is accorded when the races are provided substantially equal facilities, even though these facilities be separate. In the Delaware case, the Supreme Court of Delaware adhered to that doctrine, but ordered that the plaintiffs be admitted to the white schools because of their superiority to the Negro schools.

The plaintiffs contend that segregated public schools are not "equal" and cannot be made "equal," and that hence they are deprived of the equal protection of the laws. . . .

An additional reason for the inconclusive nature of the [14th] Amendment's history, with respect to segregated schools, is the status of public education at that time [1868]. In the South, the movement toward free common schools, supported by general taxation, had not yet taken hold. Education of white children was largely in the hands of private groups. Education of Negroes was almost nonexistent, and practically all of the race were illiterate. In fact, any education of Negroes was forbidden by law in some states. Today, in contrast, many Negroes have achieved outstanding success in the arts and sciences as well as in the business and professional world. It is true that public school education at the time of the Amendment had advanced further in the North, but the effect of the Amendment on Northern States was generally ignored in the congressional debates. Even in the North, the conditions of public education did not approximate those existing today. The curriculum was usually rudimentary; ungraded schools were common in rural areas; the school term was but three months a year in many states; and compulsory school attendance was virtually unknown. As a consequence, it is not surprising that there should be so little in the history of the Fourteenth Amendment relating to its intended effect on public education.

In the first cases in this Court construing the Fourteenth Amendment, decided shortly after its adoption, the Court interpreted it as proscribing all state-imposed discriminations against the Negro race. The doctrine of "separate but equal" did not make its appearance in this Court until 1896 in the case of *Plessy* v. *Ferguson, supra,* involving not education but transportation. . . . Our decision, therefore, cannot turn on merely a comparison of these tangible factors in the Negro and white schools involved in each of the cases. We must look instead to the effect of segregation itself on public education.

In approaching this problem, we cannot turn the clock back to 1868 when the Amendment was adopted, or even to 1896 when *Plessy* v. *Ferguson* was written. We must consider public education in the light of its full development and its present place in American life throughout the Nation. Only in this way can it be determined if segregation in public schools deprives these plaintiffs of the equal protection of the laws.

Today, education is perhaps the most important function of state and local governments. Compulsory school attendance laws and the great expenditures for education both demonstrate our recognition of the importance of education to our democratic society. It is required in the performance of our most basic public responsibilities, even service in the armed forces. It is the very foundation of good citizenship. Today it is a principal instrument in awakening the child to cultural values, in preparing him for later professional training, and in helping him to adjust normally to his environment. In these days, it is doubtful that any child may reasonably be expected to succeed in life if he is denied the opportunity of an education. Such an opportunity, where the state has undertaken to provide it, is a right which must be made available to all on equal terms.

We come then to the question presented: Does segregation of children in public schools solely on the basis of race, even though the physical facilities and other "tangible" factors may be equal, deprive the children of the minority group of equal educational opportunities? We believe that it does. . . . To separate them from others of similar age and qualifications solely because of their race generates a feeling of inferiority as to their status in the community that may affect their hearts and minds in a way unlikely ever to be undone. The effect of this separation on their educational opportunities was well stated by a finding in the Kansas case by a court which nevertheless felt compelled to rule against the Negro plaintiffs:

> Segregation of white and colored children in public schools has a detrimental effect upon the colored children. The impact is greater when it has the sanction of the law; for the policy of separating the races is usually interpreted as denoting the inferiority of the negro group. A sense of inferiority affects the motivation of a child to learn. Segregation with the sanction of law, therefore, has a tendency to [retard] the educational and mental development of negro children and to deprive them of some of the benefits they would receive in a racial[ly] integrated school system.

Whatever may have been the extent of psychological knowledge at the time of *Plessy* v. *Ferguson,* this finding is amply supported by modern authority. Any language in *Plessy* v. *Ferguson* contrary to this finding is rejected.

We conclude that in the field of public education the doctrine of "separate but equal" has no place. Separate educational facilities are inherently unequal. Therefore, we hold that the plaintiffs and others similarly situated for whom the actions have been brought are, by reason of the segregation complained of, deprived of the equal protection of the laws guaranteed by the Fourteenth Amendment. This disposition makes unnecessary any discussion whether such segregation also violates the Due Process Clause of the Fourteenth Amendment.

Because these are class actions, because of the wide applicability of this decision, and because of the great variety of local conditions, the formulation of decrees in these cases presents problems of considerable complexity. On reargument, the consideration of appropriate relief was necessarily subordinated to the primary question—the constitutionality of segregation in public education. We have now announced that such segregation is a denial of the equal protection of the laws. In order that we may have the full assistance of the parties in formulating decrees, the cases will be restored to the docket, and the parties are requested to present further argument on Questions 4 and 5 previously propounded by the Court for the reargument this Term. The Attorney General of the United States is again invited to participate. The Attorneys General of the states requiring or permitting segregation in public education will also be permitted to appear as *amici curiae* upon request to do so by September 15, 1954, and submission of briefs by October 1, 1954.

It is so ordered.

Brown v. *Board of Education,* 347 U.S. 483 (1954).

Daisy Bates and the Little Rock Children

In 1957, three years after the initial school desegregation order was handed down by the United States Supreme Court, one of the most disgraceful racial encounters in American history occurred in Little Rock, Arkansas. Daisy Bates, state president of the NAACP and wife of the editor of the local Negro newspaper, helped a group of black children integrate Central High School. Nine students were scheduled to meet and travel together to enroll in the school on opening day in September 1957. At the last minute, the plans for meeting were changed, and one of the young girls, Elizabeth Eckford, was not notified. As a result, she arrived alone at the school, where she was met by a mob of hostile whites.

Eventually, President Eisenhower was forced to send in federal troops to escort the young stu-

dents to school and preserve the peace. In this excerpt from her book, Daisy Bates recalls the story of Elizabeth Eckford's shocking experience on that September day in Little Rock.

Elizabeth, whose dignity and control in the face of jeering mobsters had been filmed by television cameras and recorded in pictures flashed to newspapers over the world, had overnight become a national heroine. During the next few days newspaper reporters besieged her home, wanting to talk to her. The first day that her parents agreed she might come out of seclusion, she came to my house where the reporters awaited her. Elizabeth was very quiet, speaking only when spoken to. I took her to my bedroom to talk before I let the reporters see her. I asked how she felt now. Suddenly all her pent-up emotion flared.

"Why am I here?" she said, turning blazing eyes on me. "Why are you so interested in my welfare now? You didn't care enough to notify me of the change of plans—"

I walked over and reached out to her. Before she turned her back on me, I saw tears gathering in her eyes. My heart was breaking for this young girl who stood there trying to stifle her sobs. How could I explain that frantic early morning when at three o'clock my mind had gone on strike?

In the ensuing weeks Elizabeth took part in all the activities of the nine—press conferences, attendance at court, studying with professors at nearby Philander Smith College. She was present, that is, but never really a part of things. The hurt had been too deep.

On the two nights she stayed at my home I was awakened by the screams in her sleep, as she relived in her dreams the terrifying mob scenes at Central. The only times Elizabeth showed real excitement were when Thurgood Marshall met the children and explained the meaning of what had happened in court. As he talked, she would listen raptly, a faint smile on her face. It was obvious he was her hero.

Little by little Elizabeth came out of her shell. Up to now she had never talked about what happened to her at Central. Once when we were alone in the downstairs recreation room of my house, I asked her simply, "Elizabeth, do you think you can talk about it now?"

She remained quiet for a long time. Then she began to speak.

"You remember the day before we were to go in, we met Superintendent Blossom at the school board office. He told us what the mob might say and do but he never told us we wouldn't have any protection. He told our parents not to come because he wouldn't be able to protect the children if they did.

"That night I was so excited I couldn't sleep. The next morning I was about the first one up. While I was pressing my black and white dress—I had made it to wear on the first day of school—my little brother turned on the TV set. They started telling about a large crowd gathered at the school. The man on TV said he wondered if we were going to show up that morning. Mother called from the kitchen, where she was fixing breakfast, 'Turn that TV off!' She was so upset and worried. I wanted to comfort her, so I said, 'Mother, don't worry.'

"Dad was walking back and forth, from room to room, with a sad expression. He was chewing on his pipe and he had a cigar in his hand, but he didn't light either one. It would have been funny, only he was so nervous.

"Before I left home Mother called us into the living-room. She said we should have a word of prayer. Then I caught the bus and got off a block from the school. I saw a large crowd of people standing across the street from the soldiers guarding Central. As I walked on, the crowd suddenly got very quiet. Superintendent Blossom had told us to enter by the front door. I looked at all the people and thought, 'Maybe I will be safer if I walk down the block to the front entrance behind the guards.'

"At the corner I tried to pass through the long line of guards around the school so as to enter the grounds behind them. One of the guards pointed across the street. So I pointed in the same direction and asked whether he meant for me to cross the street and walk down. He nodded 'yes.' So, I walked across the street conscious of the crowd that stood there, but they moved away from me.

"For a moment all I could hear was the shuffling of their feet. Then someone shouted, 'Here she comes, get ready!' I moved away from the crowd on the sidewalk and into the street. If the mob came at me I could then cross back over so the guards could protect me.

"The crowd moved in closer and then began to follow me, calling me names. I still wasn't afraid. Just a little bit nervous. Then my knees started to shake all of a sudden and I wondered whether I could make it to the center entrance a block away. It was the longest block I ever walked in my whole life.

"Even so, I still wasn't too scared because all the time I kept thinking that the guards would protect me.

"When I got right in front of the school, I went up to a guard again. But this time he just looked straight ahead and didn't move to let me pass him. I didn't know what to do. Then I looked and saw that the path leading to the front entrance was a little further ahead. So I walked until I was right in front of the path to the front door.

"I stood looking at the school—it looked so big! Just then the guards let some white students go through.

"The crowd was quiet. I guess they were waiting to see what was going to happen. When I was able to steady my knees, I walked up to the guard who had let the white students in. He too didn't move. When I tried to squeeze past him, he raised his bayonet and then the other guards closed in and they raised their bayonets.

"They glared at me with a mean look and I was very frightened and didn't know what to do. I turned around and the crowd came toward me.

"They moved closer and closer. Somebody started yelling, 'Lynch her! Lynch her!'

"I tried to see a friendly face somewhere in the mob—someone who maybe would help. I looked into the face of an old woman and it seemed a kind face, but when I looked at her again, she spat on me.

"They came closer, shouting, 'No nigger bitch is going to get in our school. Get out of here!'

"I turned back to the guards but their faces told me I wouldn't get help from them. Then I looked down the block and saw a bench at the bus stop. I thought, 'If I can only get there I will be safe.' I don't know why the bench seemed a safe place to me, but I started walking toward it. I tried to close my mind to what they were shouting, and kept saying to myself, 'If I can only make it to the bench I will be safe.'

"When I finally got there, I don't think I could have gone another step. I sat down and the mob crowded up and began shouting all over again. Someone hollered, 'Drag her over to this tree! Let's take care of the nigger.' Just then a white man sat down beside me, put his arm around me and patted my shoulder. He raised my chin and said, 'Don't let them see you cry.'

"Then, a white lady—she was very nice—she came over to me on the bench. She spoke to me but I don't remember now what she said. She put me on the bus and sat next to me. She asked me my name and tried to talk to me but I don't think I answered. I can't remember much about the bus ride, but the next thing I remember I was standing in front of the School for the Blind, where Mother works.

"I thought, 'Maybe she isn't here. But she has to be here!' So I ran upstairs, and I think some teachers tried to talk to me, but I kept running until I reached Mother's classroom.

"Mother was standing at the window with

her head bowed, but she must have sensed I was there because she turned around. She looked as if she had been crying, and I wanted to tell her I was all right. But I couldn't speak. She put her arms around me and I cried."

Daisy Bates, *The Long Shadow of Little Rock* (New York, 1962).

Ministers Sign a Petition in North Carolina

The first incident in the "sit-in movement" occurred before World War II. In 1960, however, a sit-in was held in Greensboro, North Carolina, that became the catalyst of the civil rights movement that has swept the United States in the 1960's. Soon after Negro students at North Carolina A & T College attempted to integrate restaurants in their area, they were joined by faculty members and local whites; their accomplishment was the end of segregated eating facilities. In Chapel Hill, a group of local ministers lent their support to the movement by publicizing the following petition.

STATEMENT OF CONVICTIONS

We, the undersigned ministers, living in Chapel Hill, feel that we would be remiss in our responsibility if we did not express publicly certain convictions that we hold in regard to the current crisis in human relations within this community. We, therefore, desire to bear our witness in the following statements:

(1) We encourage all of our fellow-citizens to endeavor to understand the real basis of these protests against some particular practices. We know of no better way to convey this than by quoting the following statements adopted by the group that is making these protests locally:

We do NOT picket just because we want to eat. We can eat at home or walking down the street.

We do NOT picket to express our anger or resentment at anyone.

We do NOT picket to humiliate anyone or put anyone out of business.

We DO picket to protest the lack of dignity and respect shown us as human beings.

We DO picket to enlist the support of all (whatever their color) in getting the services in business places that will grant us dignity and respect.

We DO picket to help the businessman make changes that will bring us closer to the Christian and Democratic practices.

(2) We affirm our own conviction that what these "protestors" are seeking is only that to which they are justly and rightfully entitled as citizens.

(3) We deplore the fact that any group of our citizens is placed in the position of having to *ask* to be treated with dignity and respect. We confess our own responsibility for the existence and toleration of such attitudes and practices as make this request necessary.

(4) We commend the leaders of these current protests for their dedication to the principles of NON-VIOLENCE. We believe that the right to protest in this fashion is a right generally recognized in our society—both by our laws and our "sense of fair play." Those who exercise this right peaceably deserve the full protection of our law enforcement agencies.

(5) We express our concern for those businessmen who may find themselves caught between their sense of right and their fear of economic suffering should they follow a course of serving all patrons on an equal basis.

(6) We pledge our support to any and all business concerns which will follow the policy of "equal treatment for all," and we call upon all persons who are willing to support such business concerns to encourage them by giving them open assurance of such support.

[This petition was signed by 27 individuals.]

Courtesy of Professor Wilhelmena S. Robinson, Yellow Springs, Ohio.

Students Stage a Sit-In in the North

Southerners were not alone in their distaste for allowing the races to break bread together. In the abolition state of Ohio, students at Central State University in Wilberforce, joined by students from neighboring colleges, picketed for the same rights sought by students throughout the South. This news report details the final capitulation of the restaurant owners to the students' demands.

Picketing of Geyer's Restaurant, closed since Saturday when a group of Negro students staged a sitdown demonstration there, ended yesterday with the conclusion of an agreement between representatives of the students and the restaurant.

At a meeting held last night in the office of Xenia Police Chief Robert D. Killeen, details of an agreement were outlined, under which the restaurant agreed to serve all persons. In return, the students have agreed not to overcrowd the restaurant.

Present at the settlement meeting were Killeen, City Solicitor Philip Aultman, Robert R. Williams, executive vice president of the National Food Service Association, and Dr. David Hazel of Central State College.

The demonstration began Saturday morning when a group of Central State and Wilberforce University students began entering the restaurant for service. They were served, but they claimed the service was hostile. And when more students began to enter the place, George D. Geyer Jr., co-owner with his brother, Robert W. Geyer, said the place was closed, and had all of the lights turned out.

After the conference in Killeen's office, Williams announced the agreement to a rally of 500 students at Central State College.

Yesterday, Gov. Michael V. DiSalle had urged the students to use Ohio law to achieve settlement of the problem. But the Civil Rights Commission's executive director then referred to the law as inadequate and outmoded.

Frank W. Baldau, the director, gave this evaluation, although he joined with the governor in condemning the picketing.

DiSalle said the law was a good one which should be tested before it is disregarded.

Baldau said that as far as he could learn the law had never been successfully used in a criminal suit.

The law was adopted in 1884. It provides that a person who feels he has been discriminated against in a restaurant, hotel, amusement park or other public accommodation may file a civil suit. Evidence must be presented to convince a jury that discrimination actually occurred.

As an alternative, a county prosecutor or city solicitor or other legal agents can bring a criminal suit, again before a jury.

The law provides fines of $50 to $500 and, in criminal prosecutions, prison terms up to six months.

Baldau pointed out that persons driving through Ohio who were denied lodgings because of their race would have to return to the state or stay in Ohio for months if they wanted to sue the innkeeper.

He said the law has been successfully applied in civil actions a number of times in Northern Ohio, but rarely in Southern Ohio. He said he understands only two civil suits and no criminal suits have ended in convictions in Hamilton county in the law's 76-year history.

James T. Henry Sr., Negro vice president of Xenia City Commission, told the students on Central State campus to "be there" when the restaurant reopens today, but to "take it easy."

Henry said he had argued with Geyer and his brother, Robert, for seven years.

"One last thing before I die," he said today. "I will ask forgiveness for the things I have said to the Geyers which were not calculated to improve things." . . .

Xenia Daily Gazette (Xenia, Ohio), March 8, 1960.

C. Eric Lincoln and the Black Muslims

As the battle for civil rights became more intense, various groups which previously had received little attention gained increasing notice. One such group, the Black Muslims, was led by convert Elijah Poole, who had changed his named to Elijah Muhammad. Originally a religious group that followed the traditions of Islam, the Muslims became increasingly concerned with racial problems in this country. Professor C. Eric Lincoln of Atlanta University wrote a comprehensive and thoughtful volume on this movement. The following letters to Professor Lincoln illustrate two very different reactions to his book, The Black Muslims in America.

Chicago, Illinois
[March 30, 1961]

Dr. C. Eric Lincoln

Dear Sir,

I read what you had to say in regards to the Black Muslims in America as being anti-American, I AM ONE OF THEM. I am so glad sir that God almighty sent the man representing Black Muslims to save me and my beautiful black daughter from people like you and your Jew educator bent on killing black people I would give my life for him if it was necessary but he does not require this of us. In your American religion, a black woman and a black man are compelled to give their only life that they will ever have to save lives of white people and I am not that big-hearted.

You sir, with this kind of ignorance and a college prefessor teaching Negroes to kill them selves for white people it is no wonder our children are in such a mess and white people will never allow you niggers to teach their children in school and I don't blame them.

It is no wonder that we who did attend America's colleges end up scrubbing floors, killing each other for the white man, stealing, lieing, dope heads, Christians, drunkards, jail birds, haters of everything Godly and lovers of everything Devil. You are a perfect example of Slavery teachings from your white boss and your Jew educator. The American way of life is founded on destroying black people and saving white people and Negroes live it to the letter. Those of us who love our lives and our children and want to live just as strongly as whites are running to Elijah Muhammad and when the day comes for us to meet face to face with people like you trying to force us to lay down our lives to save a white race of whores whom you love I am affraid we will have to take your lives to save our children. When it is done this way how do you like it. You must be a dammed fool to expext black women to give birth to our little babies and then put them out to be killed to save a white baby.

White people themselves are so afraid of educated Negroes who Hate Black Muslims, yet you say you have been studying us for over six years and came up with an answer like this. Also you seem to resent our clean way of life so much so you would rather say that we are KKK's in reverse than to say that God must be with the Muslims they never give the government one ounce of trouble. Black Muslims don't practice your filth and evil way of life so you mean to tell the world you hate us for this and call your self a follower of Christ; what kind of Christ are you following Mr. Fool?

White people are beginning to realize that they are in hell because of who hate these black Muslims the way you do and in the very near future for them to get ease from their troubles they are going to beat you nigger Christians like dogs and make you run to Muhammad or get off the planet and the black Muslims will not come to your aid, you ask for it.

Herein is something for you to study about the Muslims and we will send you as many as you like [for] your students.

Miss Thelma X

* * * * *

Brooklyn, N. Y.
31 July 1961

Dear Dr. Lincoln,

It was with great interest that I read your book "The Black Muslims in America". It was an extremely thorough-going analysis of not only the Black Muslim movement, but their interrelationship with Orthodox Islam, the Muslim world and America.

At the risk of boring you, let me introduce myself.

I am an *Orthodox* Negro Muslim and come from a solid middle-class background. My sociological situation is rather awkward as a result.

As a youngster, I received the usual middle-class Negro "catechism" of what to do and not to do, what attitudes I must assume as a reaction to the "Negro problem" etc., which I tried to learn and fulfill. Moving along in life, I soon discovered that it made no sense. Life was and is too short for such posturing, and for all my education and family background—superior to that of many whites—I found myself liable to as much insult as though I amounted to nothing. Furthermore, I felt that what lay at the bottom of the "problem" was something Negroes could do nothing about, namely, that they had no "culture" or roots of their own. Certainly, the American way of life is all they know, but since they are not wholly accepted they become a people in a culture but not of that culture, a somewhat unique position. Therefore, if it is not the "Black Muslims", it will be some other group purporting to give the Negro some history or eponymous ancestors to which they may refer with some pride.

The average Middle Class Negro has managed to attain some material advantages and he can feel some sense of well-being because of them. The masses have not even this opiate and come up sharply against the question: "Who am I?, where am I going?"

In my particular case, I had a nice home, my parents were property-owning, solid middle class professional people, but I still felt the need to belong to something or somewhere. This was one of the reasons for my conversion—from High-Church Episcopalianism, incidentally.

While I can understand the feelings of the "Black Muslims", they do not provide an answer for me, knowing from sad experience that education or lack of it tends to raise barriers to understanding among people. Secondly, Islam is a well established religion with stated rituals to be observed and adhered to and not to be altered and adjusted to someone's whim. Trafficking with God, the Qur'an and the Hadith is highly offensive. Thirdly, I find it difficult to believe the myths propagated by Elijah Muhammad and his ministers, fairy tales are the forte of the Brothers Grimm. On the other hand, the educated Eastern Muslims are, in many cases are rather reticent about consorting with Negroes.

I do wish you had said more about the reaction of Orthodox Negro Muslims. I had expected that, in addition to mentioning Talib Dawud Ahmed, you might have mentioned the Islamic Mission of America on State Street in Brooklyn, which has a charter from New York State and is the most efficient and reliable Islamic Organization among Negroes.

I would also like to ask you if you could provide me with the address of the Headquarters of the African-Asian Drums, headed by Abdul Basit Naeem. It was he that converted me and over the years I have lost contact with him.

Again, let me congratulate you on a job well done. The book was a marvel of scholarship.

Very truly yours,

(Mrs.) J—— C——

C. Eric Lincoln Papers, Atlanta University Library.

"There Is a Time for Anger"—Malcolm X

After several years as a Black Muslim, Malcolm X became disenchanted with the tenets of Elijah Muhammad. Although they did not renounce the religious aspects of the movement, Malcolm and his followers became increasingly concerned with the creation of a separate nation, or state, for blacks. Murdered in 1965 by one of his own race, during a lecture, Malcolm became more of a Messiah after his death, especially to young Negroes, than he had been during his life. These excerpts from his autobiography illustrate his militant philosophy.

They called me "the angriest Negro in America." I wouldn't deny that charge. I spoke exactly as I felt. "I *believe* in anger. The Bible says there is a *time* for anger." They called me "a teacher, a fomentor of violence." I would say point blank, "That is a lie. I'm not for wanton violence, I'm for justice. I feel that if white people were attacked by Negroes—if the forces of law prove unable, or inadequate, or reluctant to protect those whites from those Negroes—then those white people should protect and defend themselves from those Negroes, using arms if necessary. And I feel that when the law fails to protect Negroes from whites' attack, then those Negroes should use arms, if necessary, to defend themselves."

"Malcolm X Advocates Armed Negroes!"

What was wrong with that? I'll tell you what was wrong. I was a black man talking about physical defense against the white man. The white man can lynch and burn and bomb and beat Negroes—that's all right: "Have patience" . . . "The customs are entrenched" . . . "Things are getting better."

Well, I believe it's a crime for anyone who is being brutalized to continue to accept that brutality without doing something to defend himself. If that's how "Christian" philosophy is interpreted, if that's what Gandhian philosophy teaches, well, then, I will call them criminal philosophies.

I tried in every speech I made to clarify my new position regarding white people—"I don't speak against the sincere, well-meaning, good white people. I have learned that there *are* some. I have learned that not all white people are racists. I am speaking against and my fight is against the white *racists.* I firmly believe that Negroes have the right to fight against these racists, by any means that are necessary."

But the white reporters kept wanting me linked with that word "violence." I doubt if I had one interview without having to deal with that accusation.

I *am* for violence if non-violence means we continue postponing a solution to the American black man's problem—just to *avoid* violence. I don't go for non-violence if it also means a delayed solution. To me a delayed solution is a non-solution. Or I'll say it another way. If it must take violence to get the black man his human rights in this country, I'm *for* violence exactly as you know the Irish, the Poles, or Jews would be if they were flagrantly discriminated against. I am just as they would be in that case, and they would be for violence—no matter what the consequences, no matter who was hurt by the violence.

White society *hates* to hear anybody, especially a black man, talk about the crime the white man has perpetrated on the black man. I have always understood that's why I have been so frequently called "a revolutionist." It sounds as if *I* have done some crime! Well, it may be the American black man does need to become involved in a *real* revolution. . . .

So how does anybody sound talking about the Negro in America waging some "revolution"? Yes, he is condemning a system—but he's not trying to overturn the system, or to destroy it. The Negro's so-called "revolt" is merely an asking to be *accepted* into the existing system! A *true* Negro revolt might entail, for instance, fighting for separate black states within this country—which several groups and individuals have advocated, long before Elijah Muhammad came along. . . .

I am in agreement one hundred per cent with those racists who say that no government laws ever can *force* brotherhood. The only true solution today is governments guided by true religion—of the spirit. . . .

Malcolm X, *The Autobiography of Malcolm X* (New York, 1964).

The Mississippi Summer Project of 1963

The following letters were written by students who went to the South in 1963 to take part in the massive voter-registration project and to teach in the "freedom schools" under the auspices of the Mississippi Summer Project. Their descriptions of the black poor differ little from those written by observers more than a century ago, shortly after the Civil War.

Ruleville

There are people here without food and clothing. Kids that eat a bit of bread for breakfast, chicken necks for dinner. Kids that don't have clothes to go to school in. Old old people, and young people chop cotton from sun up till sun down for $3 a day. They come home exhausted, its not enough to feed their family on. It's gone before they can earn it. . . . Some people down here get welfare. It amounts to about $45 a month. Pay the average $15 rent and you have a family "living" on $30 for four weeks. . . .

In Sunflower County alone there are 4,270 Negro families and 720 white families living in poverty. At the same time there are just over 100 families who own and control most of the county. Negro people are being kicked out of jobs, off share-cropping etc. to remove them from Mississippi. Mechanization of farms (plantations), usage of agricultural sprays, etc. provide the excuse and the agency to force the Negro to leave Mississippi. By no means is this the only means used, though . . . Mississippi might be described as a state where people are harassed and intimidated—once because they were black and the means of production; now because they are black and a challenge to the status quo.

The other day a shipment of food and clothing arrived for the Negroes. Man, you don't know the "trouble" that something like this makes. The needs down here have to be measured by the truck loads or train loads. The shipment does not bring enough to go around. . . .

* * * * *

Hattiesburg, July 4

Every time I talk to people, I hear about things which bring tears to my eyes. I have begun, finally, to feel deep inside me this horrible double existence Negroes have to lead in both North and South . . . the strategies they must learn to survive without either going crazy or being physically maimed—or destroyed. Mr. Reese describes how a Negro must learn to walk through a crowd: weaving, slightly hunched—shuffling helps—in order to be as humbly inconspicuous as possible. . . . Then I hear from men who served in Korea or elsewhere, that they alone had no flag to fight for . . . I talked with a fellow whose closest buddy [in the Army] had been a white man from Mississippi; when they were homeward bound on the train and they crossed the Mason-Dixon line, the white man left his seat beside the Negro to change seats with another Negro.

I could go on and on about all the people I've met . . . it takes coming down here to grasp all this, no matter how many books we've read.

Elizabeth Sutherland (ed.), *Letters from Mississippi* (New York, 1965).

The Birmingham Manifesto

On April 3, 1963, members of the Southern Christian Leadership Conference joined with the Rev. Fred Shuttlesworth and the Alabama Christian Movement for Human Rights for an assault on racism in Birmingham. The violence of the resulting struggle flashed across television screens throughout the world; women and children beaten by police officers, bullied with cattle prods, mowed down by fire hoses and brutally pursued by dogs. The name "Bull" Connor, Birmingham's Chief of Police, became synonymous with racial hate, and the American people received a glimpse of their society that they had long chosen not to see. The tragedy of four little children killed in a church basement when members of the Ku Klux Klan bombed that sanctuary on September 15, 1963, represented the low point in the black quest for equality. However, through all the horror and violence of that long summer, many Negroes in Birmingham remained committed to the Manifesto which decreed that "The Beloved Community can come to Birmingham."

The patience of an oppressed people cannot endure forever. The Negro citizens of Birmingham for the last several years have hoped in vain for some evidence of good faith resolution of our just grievances.

Birmingham is part of the United States and we are *bona fide* citizens. Yet the history of Birmingham reveals that very little of the democratic process touches the life of the Negro in Birmingham. We have been segregated racially, exploited economically, and dominated politically. Under the leadership of the Alabama Christian Movement for Human Rights, we sought relief by petition for the repeal of city ordinances requiring segregation and the institution of a merit hiring policy in city employment. We were rebuffed. We then turned to the system of the courts. We weathered set-back after set-back, with all of its costliness, finally winning the terminal, bus, parks and airport cases. The bus decision has been implemented begrudgingly and the parks decision prompted the closing of all municipally-owned recreational facilities with the exception of the zoo and Legion Field. The airport case has been a slightly better experience with the experience of hotel accommodations and the subtle discrimination that continues in the limousine service.

We have always been a peaceful people, bearing our oppression with super-human effort. Yet we have been the victims of repeated violence, not only that inflicted by the hoodlum element but also that inflicted by the blatant misuse of police power. Our memories are seared with painful mob experience of Mother's Day 1961 during the Freedom Rides. For years, while our homes and churches were being bombed, we heard nothing but the rantings and ravings of racist city officials.

The Negro protest for equality and justice has been a voice crying in the wilderness. Most of Birmingham has remained silent, probably out of fear. In the meanwhile, our city has acquired the dubious reputation of being the worst big city in race relations in the United States. Last fall, for a flickering moment, it appeared that sincere community leaders from religion, business and industry discerned the inevitable confrontation in race relations approaching. Their concern for the city's image and commonweal of all its citizens did not run deep enough. Solemn promises were made, pending a postponement of direct action, that we would be joined in a suit seeking the relief of segregation ordinances. Some merchants agreed to desegregate their rest-rooms as a good-faith start, some actually complying, only to retreat shortly thereafter. We hold in our hands now, broken faith and broken promises.

We believe in the American Dream of democracy, in the Jeffersonian doctrine that "all men are created equal and are endowed by their Creator with certain inalienable rights, among these being life, liberty and the pursuit of happiness."

Twice since September we have deferred

our direct action thrust in order that a change in city government would not be made in the hysteria of community crisis. We act today in full concert with our Hebraic-Christian tradition, the law of morality and the Constitution of our nation. The absence of justice and progress in Birmingham demands that we make a moral witness to give our community a chance to survive. We demonstrate our faith that we believe that The Beloved Community can come to Birmingham.

We appeal to the citizenry of Birmingham, Negro and white, to join us in this witness for decency, morality, self-respect and human dignity. Your individual and corporate support can hasten the day of "liberty and justice for all." This is Birmingham's moment of truth in which every citizen can play his part in her larger destiny.

The Alabama Christian Movement for Human Rights, in behalf of the Negro community of Birmingham.

F. L. Shuttlesworth, President
N. H. Smith, Secretary

Courtesy of the Association for the Study of Negro Life and History.

The Letter of Martin Luther King, Jr., from a Birmingham Jail

The Southern Christian Leadership Conference, led by Dr. Martin Luther King, Jr., evolved from the Montgomery Improvement Association, which he founded during the successful boycott of the Montgomery, Alabama, transit system. Mrs. Rosa Parks had refused to sit in the rear of a bus, in the "Colored" section, and her courageous action had inspired the Negroes of Montgomery, under the leadership of King, to demand an end to segregated public transportation in the city.

When their goal had been reached, Dr. King returned to his home in Atlanta and became assistant pastor of his father's church. Immediately, he began to put his nonviolent-protest philosophy to work in a wider sphere. During the next eight years, he was jailed more than thirty times in the cause of peaceful demonstrations for civil rights for Negroes. This excerpt is from a letter written in 1963 from the Birmingham city jail in response to a statement issued by a group of white clergymen who criticized Dr. King's actions. The letter was written on scraps of paper and toilet tissue and smuggled out of the jail.

We have waited for more than 340 years for our constitutional and God-given rights. The nations of Asia and Africa are moving with jetlike speed toward the goal of political independence, and we still creep at horse-and-buggy pace toward the gaining of a cup of coffee at a lunch counter. I guess it is easy for those who have never felt the stinging darts of segregation to say "wait."

But when you have seen vicious mobs lynch your mothers and fathers at will and drown your sisters and brothers at whim; when you have seen hate-filled policemen curse, kick, brutalize and even kill your black brothers and sisters; when you suddenly find your tongue twisted and your speech stammering as you seek to explain to your six-year-old daughter why she can't go to the public amusement park that has just been advertised on television, and see tears welling up in her little eyes when she is told that "Funtown" is closed to colored children, and see the depressing clouds of inferiority begin to form in her little mental sky, and see her begin to distort her little personality by unconsciously developing a bitterness toward white people; when you are humiliated day in and day out by nagging signs reading "white" and "colored," when your first name becomes "nigger" and your middle name becomes "boy" (however old you are) and your last name becomes "John," and when your wife and mother are never given the respected title "Mrs."; when you are harried by day and haunted by night by the fact that you are a Negro, living constantly at tiptoe stance, never quite knowing what to expect next, and

Liederman in *The Long Island Daily Press.*

"Women and children first."

plagued with inner fears and outer resentments; when you are forever fighting a degenerating sense of "nobodyness"—then you will understand why we find it difficult to wait. . . .

In your statement you asserted that our actions, even though peaceful, must be condemned because they precipitate violence. Isn't this like condemning the robbed man because his possession of money precipitated the evil act of robbery? Isn't this like condemning Socrates because his unswerving commitment to truth and his philosophical delvings precipitated the misguided popular mind to make him drink the hemlock? Isn't this like condemning Jesus because his unique God-consciousness and never-ceasing devotion to God's will precipitated the evil act of the Crucifixion? . . .

The question is not whether we will be extremist but what kind of extremist will we be. Will we be extremists for hate or will we be extremists for love? Will we be extremists for the preservation of injustice—or will we be extremists for the cause of justice? In that dramatic scene on Calvary's hill, three men were crucified for the same crime—the crime of extremism. Two were extremists for immorality, and thus fell below their environment. The other, Jesus Christ, was an extremist for love, truth and goodness, and thereby rose above his environment. So, after all, maybe the South, the nation and the world are in dire need of creative extremists. . . .

Before the Pilgrims landed at Plymouth, we were here. Before the pen of Jefferson etched across the pages of history the majestic words of the Declaration of Independence, we were here. For more than two centuries, our foreparents labored in this country without wages; they made cotton "king," and they built the homes of their masters in the midst of brutal injustice and shameful humiliation—and yet out of a bottomless vitality, they continued to thrive and develop. If the inexpressible cruelities of slavery could not stop us, the opposition we now face will surely fail. We will win our freedom because the sacred heritage of our nation and the eternal will of God are embodied in our echoing demands.

Negro History Bulletin, XXXI (May 1968).

The Nobel Peace Prize Speech of Martin Luther King, Jr.

In 1964, for the second time in history, an American Negro was awarded the Nobel Peace Prize. Dr. Ralph Bunche had been the first to receive this award in 1950 for supervising the truce and armistice agreements between Israel and the Arab states. Dr. Martin Luther King, Jr., the second Afro-American to receive the prize, delivered a moving acceptance speech in Oslo, Norway. Excerpts of his speech are included here.

Your Majesty, your Royal Highness, Mr. President, excellencies, ladies and gentlemen:

I accept the Nobel prize for peace at a moment when 22 million Negroes of the United

States of America are engaged in a creative battle to end the long night of racial injustice. I accept this award in behalf of a civil rights movement which is moving with determination and a majestic scorn for risk and danger to establish a reign of freedom and a rule of justice.

I am mindful that only yesterday in Birmingham, Alabama, our children, crying out for brotherhood, were answered with fire hoses, snarling dogs and even death. I am mindful that only yesterday in Philadelphia, Mississippi, young people seeking to secure the right to vote were brutalized and murdered.

I am mindful that debilitating and grinding poverty afflicts my people and chains them to the lowest rung of the economic ladder.

Therefore, I must ask why this prize is awarded to a movement which is beleaguered and committed to unrelenting struggle: to a movement which has not won the very peace and brotherhood which is the essence of the Nobel prize.

After contemplation, I conclude that this award which I received on behalf of that movement is profound recognition that nonviolence is the answer to the crucial political and moral question of our time—the need for man to overcome oppression and violence without resorting to violence and oppression.

Civilization and violence are antithetical concepts. Negroes of the United States, following the people of India, have demonstrated that nonviolence is not sterile passivity, but a powerful moral force which makes for social transformation. Sooner or later, all the people of the world will have to discover a way to live together in peace, and thereby transform this pending cosmic elegy into a creative psalm of brotherhood.

If this is to be achieved, man must evolve for all human conflict a method which rejects revenge, aggression and retaliation. The foundation of such a method is love.

From the depths of my heart I am aware that this prize is much more than an honor to me personally.

Every time I take a flight I am always mindful of the many people who make a successful journey possible, the known pilots and the unknown ground crew.

So you honor the dedicated pilots of our struggle who have sat at the controls as the freedom movement soared into orbit. You honor, once again, Chief [Albert] Luthuli of South Africa, whose struggles with and for his people, are still met with the most brutal expression of man's inhumanity to man.

You honor the ground crew without whose labor and sacrifices the jetflights to freedom could never have left the earth.

Most of these people will never make the headlines and their names will not appear in *Who's Who*. Yet the years have rolled past and when the blazing light of truth is focused on this marvelous age in which we live—men and women will know and children will be taught that we have a finer land, a better people, a more noble civilization—because these humble children of God were willing to suffer for righteousness' sake.

I think Alfred Nobel would know what I mean when I say that I accept this award in the spirit of a curator of some precious heirloom which he holds in trust for its true owners—all those to whom beauty is truth and truth beauty—and in whose eyes the beauty of genuine brotherhood and peace is more precious than diamonds or silver or gold.

The tortuous road which has led from Montgomery, Alabama, to Oslo bears witness to this truth. This is a road over which millions of Negroes are travelling to find a new sense of dignity. This same road has opened for all Americans a new era of progress and hope. It has led to a new civil rights bill, and it will, I am convinced, be widened and lengthened into a superhighway of justice as Negro and white men in increasing number create alliances to overcome their common problems.

I accept this award today with an abiding faith in America and an audacious faith in the future of mankind. I refuse to accept the idea that the "isness" of man's present nature makes him morally incapable of reaching up for the eternal "oughtness" that forever confronts him.

I refuse to accept the idea that man is mere flotsam and jetsam in the river of life which surrounds him. I refuse to accept the view that mankind is so tragically bound to the starless midnight of racism and war that the bright daybreak of peace and brotherhood can never become a reality.

I refuse to accept the cynical notion that nation after nation must spiral down a militaristic stairway into the hell of thermonuclear destruction. I believe that unarmed truth and unconditional love will have the final word in reality. This is why right temporarily defeated is stronger than evil triumphant.

I believe that even amid today's mortar bursts and whining bullets, there is still hope for a brighter tomorrow. I believe that wounded justice, lying prostrate on the blood-flowing streets of our nations, can be lifted from this dust of shame to reign supreme among the children of men.

I have the audacity to believe that peoples everywhere can have three meals a day for their bodies, education and culture for their minds, and dignity, equality and freedom for their spirits. I believe that what self-centered men have torn down men other-centered can build up. I still believe that one day mankind will bow before the altars of God and be crowned triumphant over war and bloodshed, and nonviolent redemptive goodwill will proclaim the rule of the land. "And the lion and the lamb shall lie down together and every man shall sit under his own vine and fig tree and none shall be afraid." I still believe that we shall overcome.

This faith can give us courage to face the uncertainties of the future. It will give our tired feet new strength as we continue our forward stride toward the city of freedom. When our days become dreary with low-hovering clouds and our nights become darker than a thousand midnights, we will know that we are living in the creative turmoil of a genuine civilization struggling to be born.

Today I come to Oslo as a trustee, inspired and with renewed dedication to humanity. I accept this prize on behalf of all men who love peace and brotherhood.

Martin Luther King, Jr., "The Nobel Peace Prize Speech," *Negro History Bulletin*, XXXI (May 1968).

© 1963 Mauldin.

"What do you mean, 'not so fast'?"

From the beginning of the so-called Negro Revolution and the insane antics identified with it, I had taken the same position editorially and in my column that I had throughout the years. I had opposed all of the Marches on Washington and other mob demonstrations, recognizing them as part of the Red techniques of agitation, infiltration, and subversion. This was indicated by the fact that invariably they were proposed, incited, managed, and led by professional collectivist agitators, whose only interest in the workers was to exploit them; backed by the proliferation of "liberals" of position and influence who always run interference for them by "explaining" and defending their course.

I had consistently warned Negroes for forty years that their miseries could not be alleviated in any way by mob action, nuisance provocations, and civil disobedience. The waving of empty pistols, accompanied by insults, imprecations, and denunciations of white people, generally and specifically, was quite futile, and would simply create what Negroes could not afford: that is to say, more enemies. Week after week I pressed the point (as I had since 1923). But under the influence of their white (or Red) mentors, a contaminated Negro leadership snapped at the Communist bait, received the support of white "liberals" charting a course of disaster, and like pied pipers led the lunatic fringe astray.

During that hectic period when traffic was being disrupted and stalled, public works interrupted, city officials picketed and insulted, garbage tossed on streets and lawns, and when supposedly intelligent young Negroes were sprawling on court house steps yammering spirituals and the slogan, "We Shall Overcome," first popularized by the Castro forces, and people of worth were being obscenely traduced, I held to my position. Of course this made me an "Uncle Tom" to those people who had no answers to what I was writing and saying. It was ever thus.

What was especially galling to me was that practically all of the communications media—newspapers, magazines, radio, and television—not only surrendered to this hysteria religiously and monotonously repeating all of the self-serving fictions of the civil rights agitators, but virtually excluded contrary comment. Negroes who had lived in various communities for a lifetime and were intelligent and informed were almost never asked to write or comment on this manufactured phenomenon. Only on two occasions did any of the swarm of reporters ever ask me anything. Nor did they bother to interview hundreds of outstanding Negroes about the merits of the tactics and strategies being used. Many of these, of course, might have feared to be frank and thus risk the resultant epithets and characterizations by which the mob sought to silence objections. Some of the most obscene and scurrilous letters I have ever received (all anonymous, of course) came during that period, and my wife and daughter were not spared. . . .

There is not a Negro community in the country today that does not have more areas of good, often new, housing than of bad. This is not due to any street demonstrations but to a sustained effort through the years by public and private interests to improve housing. Moreover, it is only the result of poor Negro leadership that many unsightly and unsanitary blocks of houses have not been razed and replaced. A few enlightened colored leaders have achieved this in several parts of the country, notably some preachers who eschewed soapboxes and demonstrations. After all, the welfare of Negroes is primarily the responsibility of Negroes. Unfortunately, this responsibility has been too often avoided or ignored as men who should have known better "idealistically" chased butterflies. . . .

This is all deplorable but is not to be solved by name-calling, the shouting of obscenities, and raising the racist bogey. It calls for statesmanship which, unfortunately, has been sadly lacking among Negroes, and also among

Black Ministers on Racism and the Elections of 1966

The role of the church must be considered in any evaluation of the Negroes' struggle for equal rights. The road to success for many of the early black leaders was by way of the ministry. Frequently, the ministers and bishops of the various churches have been the local spokesmen for their entire group. Having the dual capacity of ministering to their own parishioners as well as serving as the link with the white community, many of the "Lord's ordained" have sought to mitigate the struggle for civil rights rather than lead it. The exceptions are numerous; but, on the whole, only in the second half of the twentieth century has there been a trend toward involvement in civil rights activities by the black clergy.

In November 1966, more than 170 members of the National Committee of Negro Churchmen issued, at the Statue of Liberty, a statement on racism and the approaching elections. Among this number, the absence of southern clergymen was noticeable. Fear of retaliation against themselves, their churches and their parishioners undoubtedly was an influential factor for many southern ministers. However, the traditional concept of the Negro minister as placater of the white community is being reversed, even in the South, by the younger, newly emerging clergy.

RACISM AND THE ELECTIONS
The American Dilemma: 1966
Issued November 3, 1966
at the Statue of Liberty
by the
National Committee of Negro Churchmen

A few days ago the 80th anniversary of the Statue of Liberty was celebrated here on Liberty Island. . . . We, an informal group of Negro churchmen, assembled from the four corners of this land, gather here today in order to highlight the critical moral issues which confront the American people in those elections—issues symbolized here in the Statue of Liberty.

Our purpose here is neither to beg nor to borrow, but to state the determination of black men in America to exact from this nation not one whit less than our full manhood rights. We will not be cowed nor intimidated in the land of our birth. We intend that the truth of this country, as experienced by black men, will be heard. We shall state this truth from the perspective of the Christian faith and in the light of our experience with the Lord of us all, in the bleakness of this racially idolatrous land.

The inscription inside the Statue of Liberty, entitled "The New Colossus," refers to America as the "Mother of Exiles." It concludes with these moving words:

> "Keep ancient land, your storied pomp!"
> Cries she
> With silent lips. "Give me your tired, your
> poor,
> Your huddled masses yearning to breathe free.
> The wretched refuse of your teeming shore.
> Send these, the homeless, tempest-tost to me
> I lift my lamp beside the Golden Door!"

This poem focuses on the linked problems of identity and power which have been so tragically played out on the stage of this nation's history. "Mother of Exiles" and "The New Colossus"—these symbols capture both the variety of groups and experience out of which this nation has been hammered and the fervent hope of many early Americans that in this land the world would see a new and more human use of power, dedicated to the proposition that all men are created equal.

We remind Americans that in our beginnings we were all exiles, strangers sojourning in an unfamiliar land. Even the first black men who set foot on these shores came, as did most white men, in the role of pilgrims, not as slaves. Sharing common aspirations and hopes for a land where freedom could take root and live, for the briefest of moments black men and white men found each other in a community of trust and mutual acceptance.

However, if America became a "Mother of Exiles" for white men she became at the same time a cruel system of bondage and inhumanity to black men. Far from finding here a maternal acceptance, her black sons were thrust into the depth of despair, at times so hopeless that it wrung from their lips the sorrow song: "Sometimes I feel like a motherless child." What anguish is keener, what rejection more complete, or what alienation more poignant than this experience which called forth the metaphor, "motherless child"?

But that is only part of our story. For somewhere in the depth of their experience within this great land, those same black men and women found a ground of faith and hope on which to stand. Never accepting on the inside the identity forced upon them by a brutalizing white power, they also sang—even prior to emancipation—"Before I'll be a slave, I'll be buried in my grave and go home to my Lord and be free." A faith of this quality and integrity remains alive today.

There is, to be sure, a continuing dilemma of "crisis and commitment" in our country. But, it is not the quarrels among the civil rights leaders, nor is it the debate about Black Power, nor is it the controversy surrounding the riots in our cities. The crisis is what it has always been since shortly after the first black Americans set foot upon these shores. It is not a crisis rooted in the Negro community. It is a "crisis of commitment" among white Americans who have consistently taken two steps forward toward becoming mature men on race and one and a half steps backward at the same time. The power of "The New Colossus" has never been fully committed to eliminating this monstrous racism from the life of the American people.

Look at the record of fitful and mincing steps forward and of cowardly steps away from the goal of racial justice. The slaves were freed in 1863, but the nation refused to give them land to make that emancipation meaningful. Simultaneously, the nation was giving away millions of acres in the midwest and west—a gift marked "for whites only." Thus an economic floor was placed under the new peasants from Europe but America's oldest peasantry was provided only an abstract freedom. In the words of Frederick Douglass, emancipation made the slaves "free to hunger; free to the winter and rains of heaven . . . free without roofs to cover them or bread to eat or land to cultivate. . . . We gave them freedom and famine at the same time. The marvel is that they still live."

We should, therefore, be neither shocked nor surprised that our slums today confront us with the bitter fruits of that ancient theft. Is it conceivable that the shrill cry "Burn, Baby, Burn" in Watts, Los Angeles, and across this country, could ever be invented by men with reasonable chances to make a living, to live in a decent neighborhood, to get an adequate education for their children? Is it conceivable that men with reasonable prospects for life, liberty and the pursuit of happiness for themselves and for their children could ever put the torch to their own main streets? The answer is obvious. These are the anguished, desperate acts of men, women and children who have been taught to hate themselves and who have been herded and confined like cattle in rat-infested slums.

Frederick Douglass is indeed correct when he suggests that "the marvel is that Negroes are still alive" not to mention sane. Look at the record. We submit that to pass a Civil Rights Bill as this nation did in 1875 and then refuse to enforce it; to pass another Civil Rights Bill (weaker this time) in 1964 and then refuse to enforce it; to begin an antipoverty program with insufficient funds in the first place and then to put the lion's share of this miniscule budget into Head Start programs when unemployment among Negro men continues to sky-rocket; to declare segregation in our schools unconstitutional as the Supreme Court did in 1954, and then refuse to end it forthwith; to set up guidelines for desegregating hospitals and then refuse to appropriate moneys for the enforcement of these guidelines; to insist on civil rights legislation aimed at the south and then to defeat the first piece of such legislation relevant to areas outside the south; to preach "law and order" into the anguish of Negro slums in full view of the contributions of policemen to that anguish and then to insist that policemen be their own judges; to hear suburban politicians declaim against open occupancy in one breath and in the very next breath insist that they are not racists: these are the ironies which stare us in the face and make it all but impossible to talk about how much "progress" has been made. The fact of the matter is if black Americans are not accorded basic human and constitutional rights which white Americans gain immediately upon their entry into citizenship, then there really are no substantive gains of which to speak.

Therefore, we will not be intimidated by the so-called "white backlash," for white America has been "backlashing" on the fundamental human and constitutional rights of Negro Americans since the 18th century. . . .

But: Let us try to be very clear about one thing, America. Black Americans are determined to have all of their full human and constitutional rights. We will not cease to agitate this issue with every means available to men of faith and dignity until justice is done.

We are dealing at bottom with a question of relationship between black and white, between rich and poor, ultimately between believers in different gods. We support all of our civil rights leaders for we believe that they all have important insights to share with us on this critical question. For our part, we submit that our basic goal in this struggle is to make it possible for all persons and groups to participate with power at all levels of our society. Integration is not an aesthetic goal designed to add token bits of color to institutions controlled entirely by whites. Integration is a political goal with the objective of making it possible for Negroes and other Americans to express the vitality of their person
life in institutions which funda
long to all Americans.

If the tremendous power of t
this "New Colossus"—begins to
conquering limbs astride from la
then we are bound to forget tl
poor, the "huddled masses yea
free." America is rich and pc
America is neither infinitely ricl
otent. Even America must make

We submit that the resolution
which is upon us requires a chan
tion's priorities. The welfare and
Americans is more important th
ties being given to military exp
exploration or the production c
jet airliners.

To this end, we of the Negro c
a massive mobilization of the res
Negro community in order to gi
in the fulfillment not only of ou
but in order to help produce a mc
America.

We further call upon white c
join us by endeavoring to mo
sources of the white community
with us the task at hand.

Finally, we say to the Ame
white and black, there is no tu
the clock of time. . . .

Again we say: America is at t
Either we become the democrac
come, or we tread the path to se

Original in the possession of Bishop G
Washington, D.C.

A Negro Conservative Writes a
the Contemporary Scene

While most of the black com
agreement with the protest movem
a few exceptions. This excerpt is f
Conservative, *by George S. Schu*
the Pittsburgh Courier.

whites. Thus we have had this craven acceptance and condoning of anti-social agitations and demonstrations which have too often led to arson, vandalism, and killings. My position was and is that none of these deplorable situations has been improved by attacks on "whitey," the "white power structure" (which often merely means the Government) and the suddenly obnoxious "white liberals." In defending(?) their position, the self-styled Negro spokesmen have done more to increase racial antagonism than has the Ku Klux Klan. I have frequently commented on their vested interest in disaster.

Not having any illusions about white people per se, I have long been fearful that this increasing racial animosity, exacerbated by the Communist-influenced policies of Negro racial agitation, might lead to actual civil war which would certainly lead to genocide. Nobody who knows history can discount this. Like the colored people, whites also have their callous and craven politicians, their professional agitators, and their swarms of the mentally deficient, and their number and influence is not decreased by calling them dirty names and figuratively tramping on their corns. . . .

To elicit more sympathy for their cause, the radical Negro agitators operating on the white collar front have been engaging in a veritable campaign of Negro mass disparagement. They write theses on the "failure" of the Negro family, dwell on the "helplessness" of the colored community, emphasize the high incidence of crime, disease, narcotics addiction, and other social evils. The white sociologists and welfarists vie with them with a suspicious relish reminiscent of the Negrophobic propaganda of a half century before, when such hatemongers as Thomas Dixon held literary sway. The picture of Negro life that emerges is pessimistic and frightening, tending to make insistence on integration ridiculous. Thus, the proclaimed aims are defeated in advance. The prestige given to public nuisance and civil disobedience hurt rather than help the Negro future. Racial adjustment is delicate and difficult enough without the efforts of all the sorcerer's apprentices who for the past half decade have devoted themselves to performing miracles that became shambles. . . .

George S. Schuyler, *Black and Conservative* (New Rochelle, N.Y., 1966).

"To Fulfill These Rights"

Associate Justice of the United States Supreme Court Thurgood Marshall gave the following address at the 1966 White House Conference on Civil Rights. At that time, Marshall was serving as Solicitor General of the United States. Previously, as director of the NAACP legal staff, he had been instrumental in winning many legal decisions involving the Negro, including the important Brown v. Board of Education *school desegregation cases of 1954 and 1955. In this speech, Marshall traces the legal and social position of the Negro people in this country, stressing his faith in the law as the ultimate solution for the black American dilemma.*

My immediate task in this conference "To Fulfill These Rights" is to place the present in proper perspective. In order to do this I have been requested to review the historical background of the struggle for racial equality in this country. I am indebted to our well-known historian John Hope Franklin for the materials covering the period up to 1900.

If we are to fulfill these rights, if we are promptly and effectively to bridge the gap between theory and practice, we must first realize fully the depth of the problem of racial prejudice and discrimination in this country. There are today two groups of Americans sincerely interested in the problems. One group believes we have made tremendous progress in the last two decades and thinks little more is needed—that, given time, the problem will solve itself. The other group recognizes the progress that has been made, yet views the present achievement as no more than a firm base from which to launch the final attack on the causes of racial and religious prejudice. Both groups need to pause for a consideration of the background history of this problem.

Recalling the dark past and contrasting it with the dramatic accomplishments of the last decade might comfort those who believe the struggle is now over. To that group I say, try to sell that to a Negro in Watts or Mississippi. But to those of us who know the struggle is far from over history has another lesson: it tells us how deeply rooted habits of prejudice are, dominating the minds of men and all our institutions for three centuries; and it cautions us to continue to move forward lest we fall back.

Long before Thomas Jefferson talked about certain inalienable rights in the Declaration of Independence, Americans faced experiences that assisted them in defining for themselves what those rights were. At one time it was the right to worship God as they saw fit. At another time it was the right to protection of their government—the government of the Mother Country or the government in the colonies. At still another time it was the right to a fair administration of justice. The tenuous status of the Negro, even in the seventeenth century, helped Americans think through one of the most important rights of all, the right to liberty.

The existence of slavery in the colonies at the time that they were fighting for their political independence proved to be a serious embarrassment. It was scarcely possible to limit the great principles of freedom, stated so eloquently by Jefferson, to the white people of the emerging United States. It was an iniquitous scheme, Mrs. John Adams said, to fight for what they were daily robbing and plundering from those who had as good a right to freedom as the patriots had. Negroes heartily agreed. In Massachusetts Negroes insisted that they had "in common with all other men a natural and inalienable right to that freedom which the great parent of the universe hath bestowed equally on all mankind and which they have never forfeited by any compact or agreement whatever." Thus, Negroes early saw the intellectual inconsistency of a country's seeking for some of its citizens what it would deny to others. For the next two centuries, Negroes would continue to strive to eliminate this patent inconsistency. Once the colonies gained their independence and became the United States of America, hardly a year passed that did not witness some new abuses of Negro slaves and some new denials of the rights even of those who had gained their freedom.

As early as 1782 Thomas Jefferson, in his *Notes on Virginia*, took cognizance of the unfortunate influences of slavery on the master as well as the bondsman. It did not create a condition, he argued, in which the rights of human beings could be effectively protected. But when he was Secretary of State a decade later, Jefferson received a letter from the Negro astronomer and mathematician, Benjamin Banneker, that stated much more cogently than Jefferson had expressed the importance of extending to all persons, regardless of race, the rights to which they were entitled. "I hope you cannot but acknowledge," Banneker told Jefferson, "that it is the indispensable duty of those, who maintain for themselves the rights of human nature, and who possess the obligations of Christianity, to extend their power and influence to the relief of every part of the human race, from whatever burden or oppression they may unjustly labor under; and this, I apprehend, a full conviction of the truth and obligation of these principles should lead all to."

As slavery became more deeply entrenched and as the prospect for relief appeared more and more remote, Negroes—and a few white friends—stepped up their campaign for the extension to all peoples the rights enjoyed by whites. In 1829 Robert Young, a New York free Negro, published his *Ethiopian Manifesto, Issued in Defence of the Blackman's Rights, in the Scale of Universal Freedom.* Later in the same year David Walker, a Boston free Negro, published his *Appeal in Four Articles* in which he demanded that Negroes be given the same rights as whites. Both Young and Walker wrote before William Lloyd Garrison began to publish his abolitionist newspaper, *The Liberator.* And it is not without significance that Negroes supported Garrison long before he was able to secure the support of a sufficient number of whites to keep his enterprise going.

If slavery persisted in the Southern states, it was the Northern states that did much to deny free Negroes their rights in the dark days before the Civil War. In 1830 a mob drove eight Negroes out of Portsmouth, Ohio. For three days, in 1829, bands of whites in Cincinnati took the law in their own hands and ran out of the city those Negroes who did not have the bonds required by law. In New York state, there were riots in Utica, Palmyra, and New York City in 1834 and 1839. In 1834 a mob of whites marched down into the Negro section of Philadelphia and committed numerous acts of violence. They wrecked the African Presbyterian Church, burned homes, and mercilessly beat up several Negroes. Similar uprisings occurred in subsequent years. American antislavery organizations and Negro conventions were unable to generate sufficient public opinion to put down the wholesale denial of the rights of the darker peoples of the United States. It was this state of affairs that caused the Negro minister, Henry Highland Garnet, to say to his Negro brethren, "The diabolical injustices by which your liberties are cloven down, neither God nor angels, or just men, command you to suffer for a single moment. Therefore, it is your solemn and imperative duty to use every means, both moral, intellectual, and physical that promises success."

One might have thought that the Civil War, in which scores of thousands of white Americans gave their lives and in which 186,000 Negroes fought, would have settled once and for all the question of equal rights for Americans. But this was not the case. Even the most elementary rights were denied the freed men at the end of the Civil War. It mattered not how many sacrifies Negroes had made to save the Union, how many were men of education and property, how loyal they were to the finest traditions of American democracy, they had few rights that anyone was bound to respect. In no Southern state, for example, were they given the vote until more than two years following the war.

In 1867 some Negroes got the vote, but not all. Some got a few other rights, but not all. And whenever and wherever they secured some of their rights, it took extraordinary courage—even gallantry—to exercise them. For they had little or no protection, either at the local level or from the federal government. Schools were segregated, even where Negroes had some political power. (They never had much.) People laughed when Negroes sat down in a restaurant to have a cup of coffee or when they tried to get accommodations in a hotel. The Civil Rights Act of 1875, before the Congress for five years before it was finally passed, was not effectively enforced anywhere. When the Supreme Court declared it unconstitutional in 1883, few Americans took notice of it; for the Act was already a dead letter in Atlanta, San Francisco, Chicago, Washington, and New York. Responsible citizens boasted of this fact.

The Fourteenth Amendment, never an effective shield for human rights, became the mechanism by which corporate businesses took on human traits and enjoyed protection that few black human beings ever enjoyed. One Southern state after another amended its constitution to disfranchise as many Negroes as possible without disfranchising, as one leader put it, a single white man. And no strong voice was raised against this blasphemy of American democratic practices. In these years, when white America was anxious to settle down to the relatively quiet task of exploiting the nation's human and physical resources, there was no time to consider basic human rights, no interest in securing to all Americans the rights that were celebrated in the centennial of the nation's birth.

When the 145 Negroes assembled in Chicago in 1890 to organize the Afro-American League of the United States, they knew that they had few if any friends in high places, few if any white Americans who would stand with them in the fight for their rights. One thing they knew, however, and it was that they had become the custodians of America's ideals, the conservators of America's professions of equal rights. They could well have been proud of their own role as they pledged themselves "to protect against taxation; to secure a more equitable distribution of school funds; to insist upon a fair and impartial trial by a judge and jury; to resist by all legal and reasonable means mob and lynch law; and to insist upon the arrest and punishment of all such offenders against our legal rights."

Their protests did not prevent the effective disfranchisement of Negroes in every Southern state. They did not prevent the enactment of highly imaginative segregation statutes that would reveal a remarkable resourcefulness of Americans in their efforts to degrade an entire race of people. They did not prevent the increase of lynchings or the emergence of the new urban phenomenon, the race riot. These Negroes were consoled, however, by their sure knowledge that their footing was firm and their case was sound. But they knew that W. E. B. Du Bois was also correct when he said that "the problem of the twentieth century would be the problem of the color line."

1900–1929

The dawn of the Twentieth Century, whatever other promises it held out, offered no basis for hope to the Negro. He was disfranchised throughout the South, increasingly segregated, relegated to menial jobs, and forgotten by all. In 1894, to "close the wounds" between North and South Congress had repealed much of the Reconstruction legislation—effectively withdrawing the Negro from the protection of law. The courts, too, had abandoned him. Even the Supreme Court of the United States wanted to hear no more of Negro rights. It had just invalidated most of the Civil Rights Acts of 1870, 1871 and 1875, legitimized compulsory segregation, blocked transfer to the federal court of discriminatory State prosecutions against the Negro, and closed its own doors to claims of jury discrimination and political disfranchisement. In short, white supremacy was now the law of the land.

Perhaps there were some who philosophized that, since things could not get worse, they would get better. But they were wrong. This was a dark hour, indeed; yet, a blacker night would come, and the sun would not come out for a very long time.

The first three decades of the Twentieth Century brought no concrete relief to the Negro. To be sure, there was an occasional pious declaration by the President or another high federal official. But nothing was done by any government, federal, State or local, to improve prevailing conditions. On the contrary, during this period disenfranchising laws were multiplied, enforced segregation—once confined to a few activities and a few States—now reached farther and deeper, literally separating the races from cradle to grave. And the federal government, under President Wilson—otherwise a liberal—officially adopted the policy, segregating government offices and the military services.

There were, it is true, a few majestic declarations by the Supreme Court in support of Negro rights. In 1915 the "grandfather clause" was struck down. Two years later racial zoning ordinances were held unconstitutional. In one case, the Court voided the conviction of Negroes whose mock trial was dominated by a hostile mob. And, at the end of the period, State rules barring Negroes from Democratic primaries were invalidated. But these decisions were a long time bearing fruit. They were easily circumvented. Substitutes for the grandfather clause were quickly found in the familiar "constitutional interpretation" test and comparable devices, which would not be struck until 40 years later. "Voluntary" exclusion of Negroes from primaries was soon approved, and only fell in 1944. The private restrictive covenant replaced the racial zoning ordinances and it was held legal; the Supreme Court did not ban State enforcement of these arrangements until 1948. And, by only slightly less flagrant methods, Negroes continued to be denied judicial due process. In short, however praiseworthy its decisions (and since these were the NAACP's first victories, I would be the last to understate them), the Supreme Court had not significantly changed the Negro's condition. He had still not obtained the right to vote; nor was he freed from residential segregation or assured a fair trial. And, even more important, the Negro and a few white friends were fighting alone.

Nor were the advocates of white supremacy content to have all the wealth and all the votes and all the law on their side. The Klan was revived, lynchings increased to extraordinary numbers, and race riots erupted.

These were, indeed, the darkest days. But, at least, in a small way, the Negro began to protest and to organize. The NAACP and the Urban League were formed. Du Bois and others rejected the acquiescent philosophy of Booker T. Washington. They found a very few friends in the white community. It would be a long time before their call would be heard, even among Negroes. Yet, they kindled a flame that, much later, would finally awaken the Nation.

1929–1948

There was to be very little concrete change in the next two decades, between 1929 and 1948. The Depression hit most people hard, but the poor hardest of all. And of course Negroes were poor. Nor did the New Deal bring dramatic relief to the Negro. Indeed, the Negro could not easily appreciate that he was being dealt a new hand in the supposed reapportionment of the Nation's riches. Again, he seemed to have been left out of the deal.

Segregation by law persisted and intensified. The new federal agencies adopted the policy; the old ones, like the military establishments, continued their own exclusionary practices. In the Thirties and early Forties the FHA gave an important push to residential segregation by restricting their insurance on loans to racially "homogeneous" neighborhoods. Though in decreasing numbers, lynchings persisted, as did race riots.

Yet, there were signs of change. Nothing actually changed for the average Negro during the period, but, at least, it now seemed clear that a new direction was beginning and that, eventually, things would improve. However ineffective they then were, it is significant that a Civil Rights Section in the Department of Justice and an FEPC Committee were created. Indicative, also, was the appointment of Negroes—including William Hastie and Robert Weaver—to relatively high government positions. Most important, perhaps, was the growing national concern with the problem of equality—evidenced in the organizational efforts to promote the cause of civil rights and the outspoken statements of prominent figures, both in and out of government. But, again, there would be a while to wait before practical benefits would come.

1948 to the Present

The real march forward for the American Negro begins in 1948, first by very small steps, later by much bigger ones.

In that year, the Executive Branch of the federal government officially revoked its discriminatory policies and began a slow effort to undo what it had done. The desegregation of the armed forces was undertaken. Discrimination in government hiring was ordered stopped. And FHA reversed its stand on the insurability of homes in mixed neighborhoods. So, also, in 1948—urged to do so by the first *amicus curiae* brief ever filed by the United States in private civil rights litigation—the Supreme Court held unconstitutional judicial enforcement of racially restrictive covenants.

Now, at last, the movement toward equality was under way. Two years later—again at the urging of the Solicitor General, who took issue with the I.C.C.—the Supreme Court outlawed segregation in railroad dining cars. And, at the same Term, the Court in effect barred segregation in State graduate schools. By 1953 the Court had declared illegal discrimination by places of public accommodation in the Nation's Capitol—the Department of Justice having once more intervened on the side of Negro rights against the local authorities, as it would do henceforth with increasing frequency. And, the next year, the landmark School Segregation Cases would be decided.

These decisions and those which were to follow were not always self-executing. The District of Columbia promptly implemented the rule against discrimination in places of public accommodation and the ban on school segregation. A few border States accepted the *Brown* decision with good faith. But, in much of the South, there was to be "massive resistance" for a decade and more. Nevertheless, the tide had turned irrevocably and the tactics of delay and evasion could only postpone, not defeat, the victory won.

Equally important is the role of the legislative branch of the federal government. For the first time, the Court was not to remain alone in translating the constitutional promise of equality. At last, the Congress intervened with positive civil rights legislation—the first since 1875. I need not elaborate here the familiar Civil Rights Acts of 1957, 1960 and 1964 and the Voting Rights Act of 1965.

Nor can we underestimate the significance of the changed role of the Executive Branch in this new era. I have already noted that my predecessors intervened in most of these cases on the side of Negro rights. Also, the civil rights legislation enacted is largely the product of Administration proposals. Perhaps most important, the Executive Branch has undertaken as never before to enforce and implement the court decisions and the new laws. Little Rock and Oxford, Mississippi, are the most dramatic examples. But, there are countless other daily occasions when the President, the Attorney General, and the Civil Rights Division of the Department of Justice act to "execute" the law of the land.

Conclusion

I will attempt no assessment of how far we have come and what is left to be done. Clearly, there remains a great deal of work in translating into concrete reality the rights already won, and new tools must still be forged. That is the goal of the proposed Civil Rights Act of 1966. There are, however, some lessons for the future in the history of the struggle for Negro rights.

What is striking to me is the importance of law in determining the condition of the Negro. He was effectively enslaved, not by brute force, but by a law which declared him a chattel of his master, who was given a legal right to recapture him, even in free territory. He was emancipated by law, and then disfranchised and segregated by law. And, finally, he is winning equality by law.

Of course, law—whether embodied in acts of Congress or judicial decisions—is, in some measure, a response to national opinion, and, of course, non-legal, even illegal events, can significantly affect the development of the law. But I submit that the history of the Negro demonstrates the importance of getting rid of hostile laws and seeking the security of new friendly laws. Provided there is a determination to enforce it, law *can* change things for the better. There is very little truth in the old refrain that one cannot legislate equality. Laws not only provide concrete benefits; they can even change the hearts of men—some men, anyway—for good or evil. Certainly, I think the history I have just traced makes it clear that the hearts of men do not change of themselves.

Of course, I don't mean to exaggerate the force of law. Evasion, intimidation, violence, may sometimes defeat the best of laws. But, to an important degree, they, too, can effectively be legislated against. The simple fact is that most people will obey the law. And some at least will be converted by it. What is more, the Negro himself will more readily acquiesce in his lot unless he has a legally recognized claim to a better life. I think the Segregation decision of 1954 probably did more than anything else to awaken the Negro from his apathy to demanding his right to equality.

It seems to me that the experience under the recent public accommodations law and the Voting Rights Act of 1965 proves the point. Of course there have been resistance and evasion and intimidation in both cases. But it must have surprised the cynics that so many restaurants in fact desegregated in obedience to the law and, more so, that so many Negroes in Alabama and elsewhere are actually voting less than a year after the Voting Act was passed.

I do not suggest a complacent reliance on the self-executing force of existing laws. On the contrary, I advocate more laws and stronger laws. And the passage of such laws requires untiring efforts.

Just as Supreme Court decisions on the "White Primary," "Restrictive Covenants," and school segregation provided the impetus for the stepped-up protests of Negroes, we must use the present tools—not as an end, but, rather as additional incentive to restudy and renew our drive toward ending the gap between theory and practice.

Moreover, laws have only limited effect if they are not vigorously enforced. What I do say is that I have faith in the efficacy of law. Perhaps that is because I am a lawyer and not a missionary. But I think history—which proves so many things—proves me right.

Courtesy of Associate Justice Thurgood Marshall.

Negroes Riot in Newark

In 1964 in Harlem, a neighborhood in New York, a race riot took place that was one of the most violent the nation had ever experienced. The smoldering despair and resentment of the Negro community, underscored by the feeling among the younger, more militant black leaders who had become increasingly influential during the 1960's, was triggered by an arrest. This was the first of a series of riots that were to scar the major cities of America. By the summer of 1967, more race riots were occurring than at any other time in the history of the country. After scores of riots had been started by whites, black people in the ghettoes were expressing their dissatisfactions in a similar manner. This description of the onset of violence in Newark, New Jersey, was given by a young black eyewitness.

What made the people really mad was that the state troopers caught a man about 20 to 29 (he drinks a lot, you know, a wine-head) walking through this restaurant. These state troopers drove by at full speed, at 50 miles per hour, and shot him in the back of the head and just kept going straight up the street. After that some of these man gangs, not boy gangs, raided Sears and Roebuck's [*sic*].

The main thing is that nobody was looting stores at first. But when the cops started banging people on the head, they started throwing bottles and stuff and some went and busted out store windows. At first nobody did anything.

It started with the younger crowd, ten year

olds, going to their favorite stores. They went in, and then everybody else got the idea to go. But looting was not what started the whole thing.

We got bed springs and as the cop cars came around the street the bedsprings were thrown out in the street and the cop cars could not ride over them. When they tried to back up, we threw springs behind them.

Then we started throwing rocks because we had no ammunition to shoot back. The cops were shooting people down as fast as they could.

Courtesy of the Student Nonviolent Coordinating Committee, Atlanta, Georgia.

A Black Power Conference

As the civil rights movement gained momentum in the 1960's, new groups were formed within the Negro community. All were seeking freedom, but each stressed different methods for reaching its goal. The roots of the NAACP, the Urban League and even the Congress of Racial Equality went back too far into an accommodating past to satisfy most of the young, more militant Negroes, who advocated the concept of Black Power. Among the proponents of Black Power, who have been the least understood of the participants in the civil rights movement, are those who advocate using violence if it is necessary to gain their rights; those who press in peaceful ways for political and economic power; and those who seek a separate, autonomous political state for the Negro people as the final solution to the struggle for freedom. This excerpt from statements made after a Black Power Conference in Newark, New Jersey, in 1967 presents one attitude toward the racial problems in America.

The Black Power Conference in Newark is another example of how the leadership looks at the masses of black people. It was held in the rich business district of Newark, in the Episcopal Diocese house and two of the richest hotels there. Also, it cost $25 to attend, which put it out of the reach of the poor working class black man.

At first they didn't even want to let Newark people in without paying. Then it came to light that it was just to let people blow off steam, but to keep the old leadership in the spotlight, that all the projects afterward would be decided on by leaders who would then tell those who attended what to do. We changed some of that, but not everything.

Ever since the rebellions in Harlem and Watts in 1964 and 1965 there has been a movement among the black masses of America toward either total freedom or death. Harlem and Watts manifested the fact that the civil rights movement was dead; that the black man in this country wanted more than just civil rights.

The black people want Freedom and Self-Determination which, in itself, means the total overthrow of this society—in other words, revolution. And that is just what it's called by the youth as well as by the old—the Revolution.

Herblock © 1966 in *The Washington Post.*

The name of Black Power caught on. We have pride in being black. We see both young and old (but mainly the youth) taking an interest in black art and culture. The fact that they are now supporting the black artists and writers and studying their own history to find out about themselves points this out. They are calling each other brother and sister and literally meaning it.

But though the Black Power slogan is popular, it is not the name that the masses give to what they are doing. They have another name for it. It is Revolution.

Courtesy of the Student Nonviolent Coordinating Committee, Atlanta, Georgia.

The Report of the 1968 National Advisory Commission on Civil Disorders

Following the race riots that occurred in cities across the nation in the summer of 1967, President Lyndon B. Johnson appointed a commission to investigate the underlying causes of these riots and the dissatisfactions which precipitated them. The following excerpts from the "Summary" of the report of the commission are repetitive of similar findings in the past but are more striking in their truthful analysis that white racism was the basic cause for rioting.

The summer of 1967 again brought racial disorders to American cities, and with them shock, fear, and bewilderment to the Nation.

The worst came during a 2-week period in July, first in Newark and then in Detroit. Each set off a chain reaction in neighboring communities.

On July 28, 1967, the President of the United States established this Commission and directed us to answer three basic questions:

What happened?

Why did it happen?

What can be done to prevent it from happening again?

To respond to these questions, we have undertaken a broad range of studies and investigations. We have visited the riot cities; we have heard many witnesses; we have sought the counsel of experts across the country.

This is our basic conclusion: Our Nation is moving toward two societies, one black, one white—separate and unequal.

Reaction to last summer's disorders has quickened the movement and deepened the division. Discrimination and segregation have long permeated much of American life; they now threaten the future of every American.

This deepening racial division is not inevitable. The movement apart can be reversed. Choice is still possible. Our principal task is to define that choice and to press for a national resolution.

To pursue our present course will involve the continuing polarization of the American community and, ultimately, the destruction of basic democratic values.

The alternative is not blind repression or capitulation to lawlessness. It is the realization of common opportunities for all within a single society.

This alternative will require a commitment to national action—compassionate, massive, and sustained, backed by the resources of the most powerful and the richest nation on this earth. From every American it will require new attitudes, new understanding, and, above all, new will.

The vital needs of the Nation must be met; hard choices must be made, and, if necessary, new taxes enacted.

Violence cannot build a better society. Disruption and disorder nourish repression, not justice. They strike at the freedom of every citizen. The community cannot—it will not—tolerate coercion and mob rule.

Violence and destruction must be ended—in the streets of the ghetto and in the lives of people.

Segregation and poverty have created in the racial ghetto a destructive environment totally unknown to most white Americans.

What white Americans have never fully understood—but what the Negro can never forget—is that white society is deeply implicated in the ghetto. White institutions created it, white institutions maintain it, and white society condones it.

It is time now to turn with all the purpose at our command to the major unfinished business of this Nation. It is time to adopt strategies for action that will produce quick and visible progress. It is time to make good the promises of American democracy to all citizens—urban and rural, white and black, Spanish-surname, American Indian, and every minority group.

Our recommendations embrace three basic principles:

> To mount programs on a scale equal to the dimension of the problems;
>
> To aim these programs for high impact in the immediate future in order to close the gap between promise and performance;
>
> To undertake new initiatives and experiments that can change the system of failure and frustration that now dominates the ghetto and weakens our society.

These programs will require unprecedented levels of funding and performance, but they neither probe deeper nor demand more than the problems which called them forth. There can be no higher priority for national action and no higher claim on the Nation's conscience.

We issue this report now, 5 months before the date called for by the President. Much remains that can be learned. Continued study is essential.

As Commissioners we have worked together with a sense of the greatest urgency and have sought to compose whatever differences exist among us. Some differences remain. But the gravity of the problem and the pressing need for action are too clear to allow further delay in the issuance of this report. . . .

The "typical" riot did not take place. The disorders of 1967 were unusual, irregular, complex, and unpredictable social processes. Like most human events, they did not unfold in an orderly sequence. . . .

The President directed the Commission to investigate "to what extent, if any, there has been planning or organization in any of the riots." . . .

On the basis of all the information collected, the Commission concludes that:

> The urban disorders of the summer of 1967 were not caused by, nor were they the consequence of, any organized plan or "conspiracy." . . .

In addressing the question "Why did it happen?" we shift our focus from the local to the national scene, from the particular events of the summer of 1967 to the factors within the society at large that created a mood of violence among many urban Negroes.

These factors are complex and interacting; they vary significantly in their effect from city to city and from year to year; and the consequences of one disorder, generating new grievances and new demands, become the causes of the next. Thus was created the "thicket of tension, conflicting evidence, and extreme opinions" cited by the President.

Despite these complexities, certain fundamental matters are clear. Of these, the most fundamental is the racial attitude and behavior of white Americans toward black Americans.

Race prejudice has shaped our history decisively; it now threatens to affect our future.

White racism is essentially responsible for the explosive mixture which has been accumulating in our cities since the end of World War II. . . .

The causes of recent racial disorders are embedded in a tangle of issues and circumstances—social, economic, political, and psychological—which arise out of the historic pattern of Negro-white relations in America. . . .

We describe the Negro's experience in America and the development of slavery as an institution. We show his persistent striving for equality in the face of rigidly maintained social, economic, and educational barriers, and repeated mob violence. We portray the ebb and flow of the doctrinal tides—accommodation, separatism, and self-help—and their relationship to the current theme of Black Power. We conclude:

> The Black Power advocates of today consciously feel that they are the most militant group in the Negro protest movement. Yet they have retreated from a direct confrontation with American society on the issue of integration and, by preaching separatism, unconsciously function as an accommodation to white racism. Much of their economic program, as well as their interest in Negro history, self-help, racial solidarity and separation, is reminiscent of Booker T. Washington. The rhetoric is different, but the ideas are remarkably similar. . . .

Although there have been gains in Negro income nationally, and a decline in the number of Negroes below the "poverty level," the condition of Negroes in the central city remains in a state of crisis. Between 2 and 2.5 million Negroes—16 to 20 percent of the total Negro population of all central cities—live in squalor and deprivation in ghetto neighborhoods.

Employment is a key problem. It not only controls the present for the Negro American but, in a most profound way, it is creating the future as well. Yet, despite continuing economic growth and declining national unemployment rates, the unemployment rate for Negroes in 1967 was more than double that for whites. . . .

A striking difference in environment from that of white, middle-class Americans profoundly influences the lives of residents of the ghetto. . . .

Today, whites tend to exaggerate how well and quickly they escaped from poverty. The fact is that immigrants who came from rural backgrounds, as many Negroes do, are only now, after three generations, finally beginning to move into the middle class.

By contrast, Negroes began concentrating in the city less than two generations ago, and under much less favorable conditions. Although some Negroes have escaped poverty, few have been able to escape the urban ghetto. . . .

One of the first witnesses to be invited to appear before this Commission was Dr. Kenneth B. Clark, a distinguished and perceptive scholar. Referring to the reports of earlier riot commissions, he said:

> I read that report . . . of the 1919 riot in Chicago, and it is as if I were reading the report of the investigating committee on the Harlem riot of '35, the report of the investigating committee on the Harlem riot of '43, the report of the McCone Commission on the Watts riot.
>
> I must again in candor say to you members of this Commission—it is a kind of Alice in Wonderland—with the same moving picture reshown over and over again, the same analysis, the same recommendations, and the same inaction.

These words come to our minds as we conclude this report.

We have provided an honest beginning. We have learned much. But we have uncovered no startling truths, no unique insights, no simple solutions. The destruction and the bitterness of racial disorder, the harsh polemics of black revolt and white repression have been seen and heard before in this country.

It is time now to end the destruction and the violence, not only in the streets of the ghetto but in the lives of people.

Report of the 1968 National Advisory Commission on Civil Disorders, March 1, 1968.

Whitney M. Young, Jr., Recounts Some Early Life Experiences

Whitney M. Young, Jr., became executive director of the Urban League in 1961. Since that time, he has gained recognition as one of America's most capable Negro leaders. In the statement below, Young tells of his own early experiences that motivated him to devote his life to working for improvement in race relations.

After a century of progress and change, racism is still a feature of American life, and the person and property of Negro citizens are still less respected and less secure than those of white citizens. This is a lesson I learned quite early in life.

By all standards, my parents occupied positions which made them respected community leaders. But I can remember incidents . . . which made it quite clear to me as I was growing up that, solely because of their color, they had fewer options and prerogatives than white families of lower social standing.

My father was president of Lincoln Ridge School, near Louisville, Kentucky, and my mother was the first Negro postmistress in the United States, so I was fortunate in that I escaped the brutal poverty which most Negroes were subjected to. I was fortunate too, in that my parents placed great emphasis on excellence and the importance of education.

My father strongly believed in preparing oneself, in the expectation that people must be prepared to take advantage of the opportunities which he felt sure would come. He placed great emphasis on personal responsibility and achievement, often saying that "a man good for excuses is good for nothing." I was surrounded by books and a love of learning, and I was given a motivation and an accelerated education denied most children.

My mother was totally devoted to people, and had a genuine concern for the welfare of others that is all too rare. I would like to think that I have derived from my parents both this respect for excellence and concern for people.

As an educator, my father had to contend with forces in the South which objected to Negroes getting an education or otherwise putting themselves in a position to escape the lot of the field hand, good for what labor could be extracted from him and for little else. For the Negro was seen not as a man, but as a resource for economic exploitation. . . .

Each semester my father would go out to the rural plantations to recruit Negro youth for his school. The plantation owners did not like to see a potential farmhand become a literate, self-sufficient citizen, so the first thing Father did when he rode into town in his old buggy was to find the local Negro, and each town had one, who was oblivious to intimidation. It was, of course, all the better if this man was big and strong. Together they would travel around the countryside recruiting young people.

He needed such protection and had to resort to this and other devious means, because of the limits placed on the Negro male. The Southern ethos was to keep the male down and the Negro family as consciously disorganized after slavery as it was deliberately destroyed during slavery.

I can recall another incident which illustrates this. My father took me to a local store to buy a suit and when we arrived home my mother didn't like it because the alterations were badly done. She took the suit back to the store, where she argued the manager into taking it back.

But she was the one who had to go. By the unwritten law of the South my father was forbidden to dispute with a white man. Even though he held a position of prominence in the community, he was still subject to the restrictions placed on Negro men, restrictions which prevented them from assuming all the duties and responsibilities of the male in our society.

These were the ways in which I was made aware of the pervasive atmosphere of racism. Because the small towns surrounding the school were so dependent upon it economically, there were few overt racial incidents. In fact, there were some white teachers at the school, but looking back I can see now that they were there to assume "the white man's burden" as missionaries, and not as committed liberals. . . .

It was . . . educational opportunity that led me to enlist in the Army in 1942. I still had

Yardley in *The Baltimore Sun.*

"Me? . . . I'm only on my way to save democracy in Vietnam!"

hopes of becoming a doctor, and since I couldn't afford to finance my education, I planned on being sent to medical school by the Army. But places in the only two Negro medical schools in the South were filled for the next four years, and so I was assigned to MIT [Massachusetts Institute of Technology] to take an accelerated engineering course as preparation for assignment to a combat engineering outfit.

The Army I entered was quite different from the Army of today. Last summer I went to Vietnam and I could see the tremendous changes that have taken place since my days as a soldier in a segregated Army. In Vietnam I saw total integration on all levels. Negro officers and sergeants were in positions of battle command, and color played no apparent factor in determining a man's authority or responsibility. It is important to point to this change in the military, for it has occurred in a very few years, and it offers a model for the rest of society, for it shows that racism can be rooted out in every other area of our national life in which it has become a fixture.

What I saw and heard in Vietnam was a far cry from my experiences in World War II. The outfit I was assigned to was called a combat engineering outfit, but that really meant a service road-building company. It was then general practice to relegate the segregated Negro units to rear-guard action and not trust them with responsibility in the difficult front-line operations. This policy was breached in my unit only once—for the Battle of the Bulge, when the dire need for manpower overcame color prejudice.

All the men in my unit were Negroes, most of them from the South. All of the officers were white Southerners. Neither group had much of an educational background. I can recall the day I reported for duty. I could see that my commanding officer was pleased—I was over six feet tall and weighed 190, perfect for service in a work battalion. But then he looked at my record and his face fell. He could accept the fact that I was a Negro, but not that I was a Negro with a college degree and 2½ years at Massachusetts Institute of Technology.

While we were stationed in the United States, the officers ruled by fear. They had the authority and the means to enforce their will, so they were able to dominate the men, but they never won their respect. This was due partly to the natural animosity of the men toward white Southerners who were little different from the racists in their home towns, and partly to the knowledge that these officers were their superiors only because they were white. There were a few Negroes in the company who had a college education and who were capable of wearing brass or silver bars, and the men were aware that color determined who their officers would be.

When we reached overseas the situation changed drastically. The officers could no longer rule on the basis of fear, for now the camp was bristling with loaded guns and racial tension. They would get orders from headquarters to do certain things and the men would refuse to carry them out. The officers got to the point where they were terrified of the men, afraid to speak to them, even afraid to come out of their tents at night.

As first sergeant, it was my duty to attempt to bridge this fear-gap between men and officers. Over a period of time, I spent long hours with the officers, trying to convince them that they had to treat the men with respect for their feelings and their manhood. Slowly, I could see them change their attitudes as they came to respect the men they got to know. And with the change in attitudes came a change in the fear and tension that had dominated the camp.

This experience decided me on a career in race relations. I thought that I might be able to help change the similar situation which existed on a much larger scale back home. I was convinced that this was a problem which called for education on both sides: education for the Negro in skills to make up for centuries of slavery and discrimination; and education for white people in exposure in human relations and to teach them appreciation and respect for the Negro as an individual.

I had seen how people could modify their attitudes when it became necessary for them to do so, and I had seen how simple contact with Negroes had wrought deep changes in individuals who had never before questioned the myths about race they were brought up to believe.

An experience I had at MIT illustrates this last point. I arrived there with three other Negroes, the first to take part in that Army program. At first they didn't know what to do with us, so they put us off in a room while they had a meeting. We figured out what they must be talking about and decided we wouldn't segregate ourselves, so when they came to us and said: "Of course, you fellows want to stay together," we said: "No, not unless it was a rule of the Army or MIT, and if so, we want to know more about it." They had to admit that there was no such rule, and the captain in charge finally ended the discussion by saying that vacancies would have to be filled as they occurred, and I was sent up to a room to join two whites who were rooming together.

When I announced I was to be their new roommate, one of them, from Mississippi, walked out of the room. He came back when he was told he had to, but he didn't speak to me for three weeks. Then we spoke occasionally, then studied together, and finally we were double-dating and became the best of friends. At the end of six months I was best man at his wedding. In fact, he once paid me the greatest compliment I suppose a white Southern gentleman can make—he told me that he would be flattered if I were to marry his sister. . . .

I naturally gravitated toward the Urban League and to a career with this interracial agency which is devoting its efforts to making available badly needed services to the Negro community while at the same time influencing, through education and example, the people who have the jobs to give and the leadership standing or status to bring about lasting change.

Courtesy of the late Whitney M. Young, Jr., Urban League, New York, N.Y.

Senator Edward W. Brooke on the Poor People's Campaign

Edward W. Brooke of Massachusetts was the third Negro to be sent to the United States Senate and the first to be popularly elected. His election was a great tribute to his ability since Negroes comprised less than four per cent of the population that sent him to Congress. Brooke's arrival in 1967 as the lone member of his race in the Senate placed him in the singular position of primary defender of the rights of the Negro people. Although he specifically stated that he was elected not as a Negro but on his qualifications, it was difficult for Brooke to escape the role in which he was cast. Shortly after the assassination of Martin Luther King, Jr., in 1968, Brooke arose in the

Senate to eloquently plead the cause of the poor people whom Dr. King had planned to lead in a mass march on the nation's capital.

MR. BROOKE. Mr. President, I have listened most attentively to the discussion today. I know that the Nation is apprehensive; I know that the Senate is apprehensive. We are all concerned about the march on Washington and the form that that march will take. . . .

When Martin Luther King led his peaceful demonstration in Washington it was called by many persons a magnificent demonstration. Many persons have given credit to that march for the passage of the Civil Rights Act of 1964 and the Voting Rights Act of 1965.

It has been said on the floor of the Senate today that when people come to Washington in small numbers to protest they will be listened to and their grievances acted upon. But, Mr. President, our law guarantees the right of peaceful protest. Protest has always been a manner in which the people of this country have brought their grievances to Government. Nowhere in the law is it said that number shall be 1, 100, 1,000, 10,000, or 100,000 people. If a million people want to march to Washington, I know of no law that would prohibit them from peacefully coming to the seat of their Government to voice their protest and to voice their grievances.

I certainly have always been, I am, and I pray I always will be an advocate of nonviolence. Martin Luther King was an advocate of nonviolence. The Reverend Ralph Abernathy, his successor, has stated he is an advocate of nonviolence.

Mr. President, I think that we should presume that the march on Washington is going to be a peaceful, nonviolent demonstration. Under the law there is a presumption of right and not a presumption of wrong. There is no basis for a presumption that this march on Washington will be violent.

Oh, I know there have been some regrettable statements made. There have been some regrettable statements made by the leaders of the march. There have been some regrettable statements made on the floor of the Senate. However, Mr. President, we need to look at what men do rather than what men say. It is not a time for us to push the panic button.

If ever there was a time in this country for saneness, caution, calm thinking, and reasoning, it is now. Our country has never known such problems of this magnitude before in its history.

We do know there have been wrongs in this country. A significant minority of people in this country have been discriminated against and segregated for centuries. A significant number of black and white people in this country are poor. We know it is our responsibility to remove all vestiges of discrimination and segregation. We also know it is our responsibility to help the poor help themselves to have a better standard of living, quality education, and decent housing for them and for their children.

Mr. President, I presume that this march on Washington is what it is said to be and no more. I have faith and confidence that Dr. Abernathy and those leaders of the march are coming to Washington for the purposes they have stated and no more. I do believe and I hope I am right that they are coming because they want to protest to their Government and that they want to bring grievances to their Government affecting the poor people of this country, and no more.

What is our responsibility, Mr. President? No. 1, we have laws to protect us. There is no lack of law in this country to protect us against violence. We have police in the city of Washington who did a very credible job recently and who have been working for several months now with the leaders of the march on Washington so that it will be a peaceful and nonviolent march.

They have been training so they can protect life, limb, and property in this city. I heard the chief of that Police Department say to the public that he thought this might be a magnificent demonstration and that he had confidence it would be peaceful and nonviolent.

In addition thereto we have Federal troops to protect life, limb, and property. There need be no great fear that Government is going to grind to a halt. I, for one, and I think every Member of this Congress and I think every member of the Government intends to come to work as usual and conduct work as usual during the march on Washington.

There are those who have grievances and who wish to present those grievances in a lawful manner. Those grievances will be listened to and to the extent that we are able to do so, hopefully, we will act upon those grievances, and favorably.

Inflammatory talk, either by those who are leaders of the march, or those on the outside, in government, can only bring about the dire effects which we hope and pray we can avoid.

This is not the time for name-calling, or intemperate talk. This is the time for all men of good will to act responsibly and do their job as they see it.

We cannot be compared with the newly independent States in Africa, or any other country. The problems which we are confronting in our country today are unique to the United States of America. Our system of government itself is unique. We have, since our beginnings, declared to the world that "all men are created equal," that all men who have grievances can come to their government and say, "These are my grievances. Hear me." This I presume to be what the people who are marching on Washington intend to do.

Oh, Mr. President, I may be wrong. I am mindful of that. I know very well that when 10 or more persons are gathered together, with tensions as high as they are today in this country, and certainly will be in the cities, there is always the possibility that one intemperate act on the part of one individual even, could ignite an already flammable situation, and there could be disorder.

Our Government understood that when it first gave its citizens the right of protest. They had lived with it for generations. I believe that we will be able to cope with it successfully now. We have the institutions. We know our jobs. We must have the courage to do our jobs.

Thus, I hope that Senators, as I have said, apprehensive as they may be—and I share their apprehension—will recognize that the people who come to Washington come with a right, a right guaranteed to them by the law of the land.

I know of no way in which we can stop that march. I do not think that if we could, we should stop the march. I think that we should welcome the marchers to Washington.

I certainly think, in addition thereto, that the marchers must recognize they have a responsibility: One, they have a responsibility to confine their activities to the purpose of their march; namely, to present their grievances to their Government. Two, they have the responsibility to clearly define what those grievances are—and I do not mean in vague or ambiguous terms, because I have heard them say that they intend to stay here until such time as their requests or demands are adhered to.

Our Government cannot act responsibly unless there are responsible goals established, set forth, and clearly defined by those who march.

The marchers also have a responsibility to police themselves, to see that they do not violate the law in any respect.

Mr. President, we have good precedent for that in the march led by the Reverend Martin Luther King, Jr., to which I have referred, and in which there was no violence.

Let me just say on this subject that I hope we will take this opportunity to turn what many fear to be a possibly disastrous and devastating situation in our Nation's Capital into a magnificent demonstration of the guaranteed right of protest and the Government's favorable action upon the grievances contained in that protest.

Mr. President, I think that now is the time for faith, confidence, and courage.

Congressional Record, 90th Congress, 2nd session (Washington, 1968).

Charles Evers on the Southern White Press

Charles Evers, brother of slain civil rights worker Medgar Evers and Director of the Mississippi NAACP, writes of the negative view toward the Negro that is displayed by the southern white press.

WE MISSISSIPPIANS are between the river and the deep blue sea, and I'm going to talk about what the press has done for us there. But in doing this, there is the risk that we may all wind up walking out saying "the hell with the press."

The press has been and is one of the worst enemies, along with the police, that the Negro has in Mississippi. I can only speak for Mississippi, not Los Angeles or Chicago, because Mississippi is the only place I really know about.

Every newspaper in Mississippi—with one exception—has damned the Negro. That one exception is the Greenville *Delta Democrat-Times.* Hodding Carter and his parents down through the years have tried to do what was fair. But the rest of the papers have picked out all the things that the Negro may have done wrong and blown them into the biggest balloon you can imagine. The editors down there always come out with racist statements and have caused more unrest and humiliation for Mississippi Negroes than any other single institution I can think of.

The paper there in Jackson is the worst in the nation. The editor himself writes inflammatory statements like these: "The way to keep the nigger down is to visit him the night before the election." If a Negro who is down and out and hungry makes the mistake of stealing a chicken, they write it to sound like he stole the First National Bank. The things that you would read in the newspapers, hear over our radio and TV stations are almost unbelievable.

When Sidney Poitier won an Oscar, the newscaster on a Jackson station said "Although he won it, well, you know, we don't approve of it." Can you imagine that, a newscaster saying "he won it, but we know he doesn't deserve it and we don't approve of it."

The newscasters call us "niggers" openly. This wasn't yesterday, it was today, and the FCC hasn't done anything about it. We have filed a complaint with the FCC against WLBT in Jackson because of their unfair reporting. But many of the television station reporters go around, trying to find the wrong and evil and the worst part of the Negro, and that's how they show us on the six o'clock news.

As Hodding can tell you, my brother Medgar and I were struggling for a long time, but it wasn't until the national and international press began to come into Mississippi that we were able to get people to start seeing what was happening in Mississippi.

I remember very clearly a speech I gave in Nashville in 1964. I said "If the whites don't stop beating and mistreating and burning our churches and killing our brothers and our sisters, we're going to shoot back." What did the headlines say the next day? "Evers Says Negroes Will Shoot Whites." This type of thing goes on all the time

Now I don't agree with a lot of the things that Stokely Carmichael says, but the press doesn't print what Stokely really says. They don't print it all; they print just enough to mislead. And they don't ask why he says these things. Like all the rest of us, he's a victim of the press.

All we ask the press to do is to be fair, to point out the evils that the whites bring on us and point out the good we are trying to do.

When Stokely or I say things, just print what we say and why we say it; don't cut it up and make it sound different.

Let me make it clear: I am not a Black Nationalist. I am not an extremist one way or the other. I just believe that every American should be treated equally. I could never go around preaching against the whites what they have preached against us. But America is falling apart today because of the hatred and bigotry and racism. What is destroying us is the way you treat us. Medgar and I always believed in democracy and I don't care what anybody says, I still believe in it, and I'll always believe in it. But I don't believe we can make it work with us Negroes on the outside.

The only way we're going to destroy the evils that exist in America is for all of us to get in there and knock the hell out of them. Hate is so destructive, it destroys everything—and it has no color lines. It destroys black and white, Indians, Japanese, and Chinese.

My brother Medgar was shot down for no reason other than that he wanted to be an American. That's the kind of thing hate produces. I can't teach hate; I want no part of hate because I personally have suffered too much from hate and I know what hate will do.

The press can eliminate a lot of hate by printing the truth, by telling white America what it is really like to be a Negro and that this type of thing cannot exist. White Americans are sick and their minds are twisted. We've got to straighten them out and heal them; we've got to save America because it is our home as well as the white's. It's not a white man's country; it belongs to all of us. For example, the press doesn't show the contribution we Negroes are making in Vietnam.

Instead, the press destroys everything that we try to do. For instance, you never show the times we go in and try to reason and negotiate with the whites in Mississippi. You only show us marching and cussing and picketing; it's only news when we are calling whites a bunch of racists and bigots, hunkies or what not. You don't explain that we're doing that because we are frustrated as a result of the whites not listening to us.

You jump on Stokely and ride him right down, but you follow George Wallace around like he was something good to eat. Dr. King spoke once or twice against the Vietnam war and you play it up continually, but then there's old Senator Eastland who has disavowed and disobeyed every law in the book and you never mention it.

Since my brother was killed, 45 Negroes have been murdered in Mississippi. But you don't report that; it's not important.

No, gentlemen of the press, you've done a great injustice to the Negro cause. Now, since you have done that injustice, I beg you to change and give us an equal chance.

Jack Lyle (ed.), *The Black American and the Press* (Los Angeles, 1968).

Tomorrow's Leadership Sets the Stage

In the following discourse, a black student leader at Howard University states the desires and frustration of today's young militant who will be tomorrow's leader. This document includes many of the aims that blacks have been striving for through the years and projects the growing crisis for America if the present deterioration of race relations continues.

Black Power to my mind means a social and economic and political type of power. Now Black Power was first advocated or espoused by Stokely Carmichael, whose concern is with Black Power here in the United States. I think that there are three ways to solve the racial dilemma in this country: by the dissolution of the black people within the United States (going back to Africa); through separatism; or by complete revolution. I think a revolution here—a bloody revolution—may be necessary. I think this is the way the civil rights revolution is going to turn.

When you talk about a political sense, I think you are talking about the United States political situation, a democracy. Now I'm not interested in integrating or amalgamating myself into the system because this country is a hypocrite, it is completely hypocritical. I can give you examples of that. Freedom here is a drag; it's espoused by the Constitution; this is the land of the free and the home of the brave; George Washington never told a lie. All these things are stupid stories that white America puts forth, they're completely fictitious tales. What I would like to have here is a true democracy—a democracy of the people, not a democracy of the dollar. Therefore, my concern at this point is with the social and economic problems of the Negro, not with his political situation, because politically the Negro has no power.

It is my feeling that there is quite a bit of forcefulness in words. Now the word black has always had a negative connotation because the majority of the American people are white. If you look up black in the dictionary, you will find 100 definitions for it. If you look up white, you will find 130 definitions for it. Under white you find "purity and innocence." Under black you find "death and damnation." So the word black has quite a bit of force in the white community—a definite negative connotation.

The word power in the United States has always been linked with violence and the use of weapons. When you put two negative words like that together (black and power), Whitey is scared. He has got to be scared, because he thinks in terms of his own use of the language.

I feel that for too long black people have been trying to amalgamate themselves into a society that is completely foreign to them. The white community's whole basis for survival is status. My hatred for the white system is based on its complacency, the white man's opportunistic tactics. The United States is capitalistic; to me that means it is vulturistic, it consumes other people to survive. White Americans are parasitic, and they have been preying on black people for 400 years as a means for their economic salvation. They are still doing it.

I believe the civil rights movement, as typified by the tactics of Martin Luther King, has been dead for eight years now—since about 1960. When King died, he was already going out of power, he had had his show. He had made his contribution to the black community, and his main failing, as I see it, was his not taking into consideration the amount of change that had taken place since his first efforts.

There have been too many black people die for the United States, too many fighting and dying in our wars only to come home and not be able to get home rule, not be able to eat and drink in the same places white people can, not be able to assimilate into what they believe is the white Christian way. Black people get tired of seeing Amos and Andy on TV; get tired of seeing black people shuffling around; get tired of seeing black people pray-in, sit-in; beg-in. It's time for a new day, it's time for a change. Because of the black dilemma, black people tend to be pessimistic about the system. It is necessary to move away from the system. I see separation as the answer. I see dissolution as an answer—that is, going back to Africa without 200, 400 or 600 more years of struggle. When you go from elevator boy to cook to Chase Manhattan clerk or postal clerk that may be a substantial change in pay, but American society is going along at a faster pace than black people are. That is why black leaders are advocating anarchy.

Stokely Carmichael has been grossly misunderstood by white society because of his Black Power slogan. Both he and H. Rap Brown tend toward anarchy, toward complete dissolution of the United States. They feel there is no need to shuffle along anymore, no need to beg the white man to let us into society. If the United States does not believe in what it has embodied in the Constitution—that is Human Rights—then it has to be destroyed. And I am all for destroying it!

Regarding the Kerner Riot Commission Report, I think their concept of a polarization developing in the society between the races is valid. I think black people are beginning to reconcile themselves with their African heritage. I think this is a good trait. They are trying to develop a racially and culturally independent sphere in which they can revolve. Now black people are starting to see their blackness as something not to abhor because it is not white. The phrase Black is Beautiful has meaning and relevance.

I think in the past I wasn't racially concerned. I was naive enough to think that blackness or whiteness was of no consequence, that every man could be seen by his own intellectual capabilities and cultural tastes; and this isn't real life, this is fantasy. I see the recent demonstrations as a part of the black awareness, and I think this is a necessary thing. I feel that the slogan "I ain't gonna shuffle no more" is what black people need.

I don't think there is any need for black people to be so defensive at this point, to be so immature as to think they have to go by white standards. I think black people are moral people. I think they are humans and they can define their own standards.

The thing that needs to be done is far less talk and much more action; and if the country isn't ready to give black people freedom, justice and equality *now,* and by now I don't mean the day after tomorrow, I mean today—in my lifetime—we will *replace* American society. I am not just talking about helter-skelter confusion killing, I am talking about a systematic killing, if that's what it takes. I'm talking about replacing hypocrisy with democracy. If I have to kill every Whitey I see on the streets I'll do this, if I can achieve my ends. I can't see any end in sight for the killing, rioting and looting because this has become a new means of protest for black people in our society.

Clifton Brown, of Howard University, Washington, D.C., recorded the remarks of Gilbert Mayers of New York, a third-year student in the Howard University School of Engineering and Architecture and a militant leader in the 1968 student revolt on the Howard University campus.

Index

Page numbers in *italic type* refer to illustrations.

Black Ministers on Racism and the Elections of 1966

The role of the church must be considered in any evaluation of the Negroes' struggle for equal rights. The road to success for many of the early black leaders was by way of the ministry. Frequently, the ministers and bishops of the various churches have been the local spokesmen for their entire group. Having the dual capacity of ministering to their own parishioners as well as serving as the link with the white community, many of the "Lord's ordained" have sought to mitigate the struggle for civil rights rather than lead it. The exceptions are numerous; but, on the whole, only in the second half of the twentieth century has there been a trend toward involvement in civil rights activities by the black clergy.

In November 1966, more than 170 members of the National Committee of Negro Churchmen issued, at the Statue of Liberty, a statement on racism and the approaching elections. Among this number, the absence of southern clergymen was noticeable. Fear of retaliation against themselves, their churches and their parishioners undoubtedly was an influential factor for many southern ministers. However, the traditional concept of the Negro minister as placater of the white community is being reversed, even in the South, by the younger, newly emerging clergy.

RACISM AND THE ELECTIONS

The American Dilemma: 1966

Issued November 3, 1966
at the Statue of Liberty
by the
National Committee of Negro Churchmen

A few days ago the 80th anniversary of the Statue of Liberty was celebrated here on Liberty Island. . . . We, an informal group of Negro churchmen, assembled from the four corners of this land, gather here today in order to highlight the critical moral issues which confront the American people in those elections—issues symbolized here in the Statue of Liberty.

Our purpose here is neither to beg nor to borrow, but to state the determination of black men in America to exact from this nation not one whit less than our full manhood rights. We will not be cowed nor intimidated in the land of our birth. We intend that the truth of this country, as experienced by black men, will be heard. We shall state this truth from the perspective of the Christian faith and in the light of our experience with the Lord of us all, in the bleakness of this racially idolatrous land.

The inscription inside the Statue of Liberty, entitled "The New Colossus," refers to America as the "Mother of Exiles." It concludes with these moving words:

> "Keep ancient land, your storied pomp!"
> Cries she
> With silent lips. "Give me your tired, your poor,
> Your huddled masses yearning to breathe free.
> The wretched refuse of your teeming shore.
> Send these, the homeless, tempest-tost to me
> I lift my lamp beside the Golden Door!"

This poem focuses on the linked problems of identity and power which have been so tragically played out on the stage of this nation's history. "Mother of Exiles" and "The New Colossus"—these symbols capture both the variety of groups and experience out of which this nation has been hammered and the fervent hope of many early Americans that in this land the world would see a new and more human use of power, dedicated to the proposition that all men are created equal.

We remind Americans that in our beginnings we were all exiles, strangers sojourning in an unfamiliar land. Even the first black men who set foot on these shores came, as did most white men, in the role of pilgrims, not as slaves. Sharing common aspirations and hopes for a land where freedom could take root and live, for the briefest of moments black men and white men found each other in a community of trust and mutual acceptance.

However, if America became a "Mother of Exiles" for white men she became at the same time a cruel system of bondage and inhumanity to black men. Far from finding here a maternal acceptance, her black sons were thrust into the depth of despair, at times so hopeless that it wrung from their lips the sorrow song: "Sometimes I feel like a motherless child." What anguish is keener, what rejection more complete, or what alienation more poignant than this experience which called forth the metaphor, "motherless child"?

But that is only part of our story. For somewhere in the depth of their experience within this great land, those same black men and women found a ground of faith and hope on which to stand. Never accepting on the inside the identity forced upon them by a brutalizing white power, they also sang—even prior to emancipation—"Before I'll be a slave, I'll be buried in my grave and go home to my Lord and be free." A faith of this quality and integrity remains alive today.

There is, to be sure, a continuing dilemma of "crisis and commitment" in our country. But, it is not the quarrels among the civil rights leaders, nor is it the debate about Black Power, nor is it the controversy surrounding the riots in our cities. The crisis is what it has always been since shortly after the first black Americans set foot upon these shores. It is not a crisis rooted in the Negro community. It is a "crisis of commitment" among white Americans who have consistently taken two steps forward toward becoming mature men on race and one and a half steps backward at the same time. The power of "The New Colossus" has never been fully committed to eliminating this monstrous racism from the life of the American people.

Look at the record of fitful and mincing steps forward and of cowardly steps away from the goal of racial justice. The slaves were freed in 1863, but the nation refused to give them land to make that emancipation meaningful. Simultaneously, the nation was giving away millions of acres in the midwest and west—a gift marked "for whites only." Thus an economic floor was placed under the new peasants from Europe but America's oldest peasantry was provided only an abstract freedom. In the words of Frederick Douglass, emancipation made the slaves "free to hunger; free to the winter and rains of heaven . . . free without roofs to cover them or bread to eat or land to cultivate. . . . We gave them freedom and famine at the same time. The marvel is that they still live."

We should, therefore, be neither shocked nor surprised that our slums today confront us with the bitter fruits of that ancient theft. Is it conceivable that the shrill cry "Burn, Baby, Burn" in Watts, Los Angeles, and across this country, could ever be invented by men with reasonable chances to make a living, to live in a decent neighborhood, to get an adequate education for their children? Is it conceivable that men with reasonable prospects for life, liberty and the pursuit of happiness for themselves and for their children could ever put the torch to their own main streets? The answer is obvious. These are the anguished, desperate acts of men, women and children who have been taught to hate themselves and who have been herded and confined like cattle in rat-infested slums.

Frederick Douglass is indeed correct when he suggests that "the marvel is that Negroes are still alive" not to mention sane. Look at the record. We submit that to pass a Civil Rights Bill as this nation did in 1875 and then refuse to enforce it; to pass another Civil Rights Bill (weaker this time) in 1964 and then refuse to enforce it; to begin an anti-poverty program with insufficient funds in the first place and then to put the lion's share of this miniscule budget into Head Start programs when unemployment among Negro men continues to sky-rocket; to declare segregation in our schools unconstitutional as the Supreme Court did in 1954, and then refuse to end it forthwith; to set up guidelines for desegregating hospitals and then refuse to appropriate moneys for the enforcement of these guidelines; to insist on civil rights legislation aimed at the south and then to defeat the first piece of such legislation relevant to areas outside the south; to preach "law and order" into the anguish of Negro slums in full view of the contributions of policemen to that anguish and then to insist that policemen be their own judges; to hear suburban politicians declaim against open occupancy in one breath and in the very next breath insist that they are not racists: these are the ironies which stare us in the face and make it all but impossible to talk about how much "progress" has been made. The fact of the matter is if black Americans are not accorded basic human and constitutional rights which white Americans gain immediately upon their entry into citizenship, then there really are no substantive gains of which to speak.

Therefore, we will not be intimidated by the so-called "white backlash," for white America has been "backlashing" on the fundamental human and constitutional rights of Negro Americans since the 18th century. . . .

But: Let us try to be very clear about one thing, America. Black Americans are determined to have all of their full human and constitutional rights. We will not cease to agitate this issue with every means available to men of faith and dignity until justice is done.

We are dealing at bottom with a question of relationship between black and white, between rich and poor, ultimately between believers in different gods. We support all of our civil rights leaders for we believe that they all have important insights to share with us on this critical question. For our part, we submit that our basic goal in this struggle is to make it possible for all persons and groups to participate with power at all levels of our society. Integration is not an aesthetic goal designed to add token bits of color to institutions controlled entirely by whites. Integration is a political goal with the objective of making it possible for Negroes and other Americans to express the vitality of their personal and group life in institutions which fundamentally belong to all Americans.

If the tremendous power of this nation—this "New Colossus"—begins to move "with conquering limbs astride from land to land," then we are bound to forget the tired, the poor, the "huddled masses yearning to be free." America is rich and powerful. But America is neither infinitely rich nor omnipotent. Even America must make choices.

We submit that the resolution of the crisis which is upon us requires a change in the nation's priorities. The welfare and dignity of all Americans is more important than the priorities being given to military expansion, space exploration or the production of supersonic jet airliners.

To this end, we of the Negro church call for a massive mobilization of the resources in the Negro community in order to give leadership in the fulfillment not only of our own destiny but in order to help produce a more sane white America.

We further call upon white churchmen to join us by endeavoring to mobilize the resources of the white community in completing with us the task at hand.

Finally, we say to the American people, white and black, there is no turning back of the clock of time. . . .

Again we say: America is at the crossroad. Either we become the democracy we can become, or we tread the path to self-destruction.

Original in the possession of Bishop George W. Baber, Washington, D.C.

A Negro Conservative Writes about the Contemporary Scene

While most of the black community was in agreement with the protest movement, there were a few exceptions. This excerpt is from Black and Conservative, *by George S. Schuyler, editor of the Pittsburgh* Courier.

From the beginning of the so-called Negro Revolution and the insane antics identified with it, I had taken the same position editorially and in my column that I had throughout the years. I had opposed all of the Marches on Washington and other mob demonstrations, recognizing them as part of the Red techniques of agitation, infiltration, and subversion. This was indicated by the fact that invariably they were proposed, incited, managed, and led by professional collectivist agitators, whose only interest in the workers was to exploit them; backed by the proliferation of "liberals" of position and influence who always run interference for them by "explaining" and defending their course.

I had consistently warned Negroes for forty years that their miseries could not be alleviated in any way by mob action, nuisance provocations, and civil disobedience. The waving of empty pistols, accompanied by insults, imprecations, and denunciations of white people, generally and specifically, was quite futile, and would simply create what Negroes could not afford: that is to say, more enemies. Week after week I pressed the point (as I had since 1923). But under the influence of their white (or Red) mentors, a contaminated Negro leadership snapped at the Communist bait, received the support of white "liberals" charting a course of disaster, and like pied pipers led the lunatic fringe astray.

During that hectic period when traffic was being disrupted and stalled, public works interrupted, city officials picketed and insulted, garbage tossed on streets and lawns, and when supposedly intelligent young Negroes were sprawling on court house steps yammering spirituals and the slogan, "We Shall Overcome," first popularized by the Castro forces, and people of worth were being obscenely traduced, I held to my position. Of course this made me an "Uncle Tom" to those people who had no answers to what I was writing and saying. It was ever thus.

What was especially galling to me was that practically all of the communications media —newspapers, magazines, radio, and television—not only surrendered to this hysteria, religiously and monotonously repeating all of the self-serving fictions of the civil rights agitators, but virtually excluded contrary comment. Negroes who had lived in various communities for a lifetime and were intelligent and informed were almost never asked to write or comment on this manufactured phenomenon. Only on two occasions did any of the swarm of reporters ever ask me anything. Nor did they bother to interview hundreds of outstanding Negroes about the merits of the tactics and strategies being used. Many of these, of course, might have feared to be frank and thus risk the resultant epithets and characterizations by which the mob sought to silence objections. Some of the most obscene and scurrilous letters I have ever received (all anonymous, of course) came during that period, and my wife and daughter were not spared. . . .

There is not a Negro community in the country today that does not have more areas of good, often new, housing than of bad. This is not due to any street demonstrations but to a sustained effort through the years by public and private interests to improve housing. Moreover, it is only the result of poor Negro leadership that many unsightly and unsanitary blocks of houses have not been razed and replaced. A few enlightened colored leaders have achieved this in several parts of the country, notably some preachers who eschewed soapboxes and demonstrations. After all, the welfare of Negroes is primarily the responsibility of Negroes. Unfortunately, this responsibility has been too often avoided or ignored as men who should have known better "idealistically" chased butterflies. . . .

This is all deplorable but is not to be solved by name-calling, the shouting of obscenities, and raising the racist bogey. It calls for statesmanship which, unfortunately, has been sadly lacking among Negroes, and also among